REAGAN'S GUN-TOTING NUNS

REAGAN'S GUN-TOTING NUNS

THE CATHOLIC CONFLICT OVER COLD WAR HUMAN RIGHTS POLICY IN CENTRAL AMERICA

THERESA KEELEY

CORNELL UNIVERSITY PRESS

Ithaca and London

First published 2020 by Cornell University Press
Printed in the United States of America

Library of Congress Cataloging-in-Publication Data

Names: Keeley, Theresa, 1976–author.
Title: Reagan's gun-toting nuns : the Catholic conflict over
    Cold War human rights policy in Central America /
    Theresa Keeley.
Description: Ithaca [New York] : Cornell University Press,
    2020. | Includes bibliographical references and index.
Identifiers: LCCN 2019048999 (print) |
    LCCN 2019049000 (ebook) | ISBN 9781501750755
    (hardcover) | ISBN 9781501750762 (pdf) |
    ISBN 9781501750779 (epub)
Subjects: LCSH: Maryknoll Sisters—Political activity—
    Central America—History—20th century. |
    Catholics—Political activity—United States—History—
    20th century. | Catholics—Political activity—Central
    America—History—20th century. | Religion and
    politics—United States. | Catholic Church and world
    politics—History—20th century. | Christianity and
    international relations—History—20th century. |
    United States—Foreign relations—Central America. |
    Central America—Foreign relations—United States. |
    United States—Foreign relations—1981–1989. | United
    States—Politics and government—1981–1989. |
    Central America—Politics and government—1979–
Classification: LCC BX1407.P63 K44 2020 (print) |
    LCC BX1407.P63 (ebook) | DDC 261.8/708828273—dc23
LC record available at https://lccn.loc.gov/2019048999
LC ebook record available at https://lccn.loc.gov
    /2019049000

To Elli and Maura

CONTENTS

Acknowledgments   ix

Introduction: Catholic Divisions,
U.S.–Central America Policy,
and the Cold War   1

1. From Senator McCarthy's Darlings
   to Marxist Maryknollers   14

2. Religious or Political Activists
   for Nicaragua?   41

3. Subversives in El Salvador   69

4. U.S. Guns Kill U.S. Nuns   101

5. Reagan and the White House's
   Maryknoll Nun   131

6. Real Catholics versus Maryknollers   161

7. Maryknoll and Iran-Contra   188

8. Déjà Vu: Jesuits and Maryknollers   211

Epilogue: Women, the Catholic Church,
and U.S.–Central America Relations
after the Cold War   240

Notes on Research Methods   251

Notes   253

Primary Sources   317

Index   325

ACKNOWLEDGMENTS

Although my name is listed as author, this work would not have been possible without the overwhelming support of others. No matter what I say, I cannot adequately express my gratitude to them.

Michael Sherry encouraged me to write what I found interesting and exciting. He supported me and challenged me when I needed to be. Mike patiently listened as I talked through issues, and always found a way to ask the most penetrating questions, especially when I felt my project was headed in ten different directions. He read countless drafts and generously gave his time. His ability to be an exemplary teacher and scholar while never seeming to let the pressure of the academy bother him always put me at ease.

Andrew Rotter let me into his oversubscribed Vietnam class in 1997, and it is because of him that I applied to graduate school. His example in the classroom made me want to be a historian. Andy's constructive criticism of my work and his insights into professional life (and life in general) were invaluable. He patiently responded to every one of my questions.

I also benefited from the contributions of many others. Brodwyn Fischer helped me develop this book from its earliest stages. Her demanding but fair questions led me to examine U.S. influence in Latin America without losing sight of Latin Americans who both vehemently opposed and welcomed that intervention with open arms. Robert Orsi pushed me to examine the personal faith of my actors and theology's role. Time and again, he encouraged me to think about how Catholicism may have played a different role in my story than Protestantism. Like others, Michael Allen offered suggestions, but what I most appreciated were his written critiques. He often encapsulated what I was trying to say better than I could. He also thoughtfully passed along archival materials he thought would be of interest. Alex Owen piqued my interest in the relationship between power, discourse, and gender. Josef Barton identified key Spanish-language sources. T. H. Breen urged me to consider how my work spoke to those outside of my field.

Many others at Northwestern deserve my thanks. My amazing writing group—Rebecca Marchiel and Celeste McNamara—offered constructive criticism and made writing a more enjoyable process. I also owe a debt of gratitude to Anastasia Polda, Alex Gourse, Alex Hobson, Laila Ballout, Wen-Qing Ngoei, Andrew Warne, Stefanie Bator, Charlotte Cahill, Meghan Roberts, Susan Hall, and members of the North American Religious Workshop, especially Matthew Cressler, Brian Clites, and Monica Mercado.

At Georgetown, Carole Sargent and the meetings she organized through the Office of Scholarly Publications helped me to better understand the publishing process and how to tackle writing projects while teaching. My colleagues in the History Department pushed me to be a better teacher and scholar. I especially thank Carol A. Benedict, Tommaso Astarita, Joseph McCartin, Katie Benton-Cohen, and David Painter.

Colleagues at the University of Louisville have always made themselves available to answer my questions or just to talk. I have valued their guidance throughout this process. Robin Carroll and Lee Keeling helped me navigate university bureaucracy, including the byzantine funding procedures.

Over the years, I have benefited from hearing others' insights on my work, including at the 2011 Society of Historians of American Foreign Relations (SHAFR) Summer Institute led by Carol Anderson and Tom Zeiler, the Global America Workshop, SHAFR conferences, and conferences hosted by the Cushwa Center and the Conference of History of Women Religious. I am especially indebted to women religious who shared their perspectives as missionaries and as protesters of U.S.–Central America policy.

Others graciously shared their experiences. I am grateful to the Maryknoll Sisters, who invited me to share meals, meetings, and stories with them. Teresa Leung hosted me at the Maryknoll Motherhouse. I would not have been able to make these connections without my aunt, Barbara Delaney, who left Maryknoll after a brief time but still maintained friendships with some of the sisters. It was a coincidence that I chose to study Maryknoll; I had no idea of her connection when I began this book.

In Central America, too, I received help. In El Salvador, I thank the Centro de Intercambio y Solidaridad and my host family. In Nicaragua, I benefited from the New Haven / León Sister City Project's connections and expertise.

Katherine Massoth offered insightful critiques on every chapter and kept me on schedule. Catherine Osborne read the entire manuscript and shared her Catholic theological expertise. She also helped with images, as did Peter Ringenberg. Sara Bornemann brought a fresh set of eyes to the manuscript. I thank Michael McGandy and Kate Gibson for their guidance throughout the publishing process and the reviewers who pushed me to refine my argument.

My research and writing would not have been possible without financial and research support. I received a Charlotte W. Newcombe Foundation Fellowship, a SHAFR Myrna F. Bernath Fellowship, and travel grants from the Center for the United States and the Cold War, the Cushwa Center for the Study of American Catholicism at the University of Notre Dame, and the Rockefeller Archive Center. Northwestern University provided a yearlong writing fellowship, research grant, and summer language travel grant. A fellowship from the Nicholas D. Chabraja Center for Historical Studies introduced me to broader ways of thinking about history. Elzbieta Foeller-Pituch was particularly helpful and supportive in my endeavors. My revisions were supported by grants from Georgetown University's School of Foreign Service and a Richard and Constance Lewis Fellowship in Latin American & Iberian Studies from the University of Louisville. The Commonwealth Center for the Humanities and Society as well as the History Department at the University of Louisville also provided financial support.

Countless archivists, especially Ellen Pierce and Stephanie Conning at the Maryknoll Mission Archives, offered helpful suggestions and assistance. Maryknoll Sister Betty Ann Maheu allowed me to view papers not yet part of the archives. At the Museo de la Palabra y la Imagen, Carlos Henríquez Consalvi gave me access to his personal collection of *La Crónica del Pueblo*.

I thank the editors of *Diplomatic History* for allowing me to reproduce parts of "Reagan's Real Catholics vs. Tip O'Neill's Maryknoll Nuns: Gender, Intra-Catholic Conflict, and the Contras," 40, no. 3 (2016): 530–558 and the editors of *Catholic Historical Review* for granting me permission to adapt portions of "Medellín is 'Fantastic': Drafts of the 1969 Rockefeller Report on the Catholic Church," 101, no. 4 (2015): 809–834. Parts of chapters 2 and 5 were first published in "Not Above the Fray: Religious and Political Divides' Impact on U.S. Missionary Sisters in Nicaragua," *U.S. Catholic Historian* 37, no. 1 (2019): 147–166, copyright © [2019] The Catholic University of America Press.

My family was with me throughout every step of this process and, perhaps unknowingly, served as models for the competing Catholicisms I study. My siblings, Jen Keeley Di Liberto, Chris Keeley, Beth McDermott, and Rose Vanella, and my aunts, Anna Mae and Miriam Keeley, all helped. They, my grandparents Frank and Dorothy Slavin and the Miami crew, never rolled their eyes as I talked about my work, and even asked about it. My parents, Jim and Pat Keeley, have been amazing. They read countless drafts over a decade and asked clarifying questions that pushed me. I now see the seeds of this book in my trips to the Irish Center with my dad to hear about the hunger strikers and my Catholic Ukrainian kindergarten days where I learned the dangers of communism (from a large nun wielding a paddle while yelling in Ukrainian). I thank them for those unique experiences. Most of all, I thank them for believing in me, especially when I doubted myself.

Mike Fine supported my decision to leave public interest law and move half-way across the country. After suffering through another bar exam, he endured endless conversations about liberation theology, U.S. foreign policy, and nuns and received a crash course in Catholicism in the process. This book would not have been possible without his love and encouragement, especially at the end when he found creative ways to keep the girls occupied. There were days when Elli enthusiastically placed her "puter" next to mine and did "work" while we tried to prevent Maura from spitting up on my keyboard. Now they are old enough to ask if I "really *have* to write a nonfiction book"; *Harry Potter* would be much more fun. For all of this and more, I thank Mike.

REAGAN'S GUN-TOTING NUNS

Introduction
Catholic Divisions, U.S.–Central America Policy, and the Cold War

In early 1987, William A. Wilson, the first U.S. ambassador to the Vatican, wrote to his close friend Ronald Reagan in anticipation of the president's trip to Europe. Wilson relayed Cardinal William Wakefield Baum's belief that Western Europeans were "beginning to experience a spiritual fatigue leading to a moral fatigue," which Pope John Paul II concluded required "re-evangelization." Baum saw the United States as the "only source of secular leadership" for this effort.[1]

Instead of dismissing the idea of his involvement—as a Protestant or as U.S. president—in Catholic Church matters, Reagan sympathized. He noted how wayward Catholics posed a problem for his administration. Reagan referred to "a faction within the clergy that is out of step with basic moral tenets." As he recalled, "When I spoke a few years ago at the Notre Dame commencement, a group of Maryknoll nuns came down from Chicago and picketed the campus in protest against my being there. A sizeable number of that Order are today supportive of the Communist government of Nicaragua."[2]

Reagan's May 1981 speech at Notre Dame was nearly six years earlier, yet Maryknollers' involvement stayed with him. The women were not the only protesters. The president also mentioned Maryknoll without any prompting from Wilson, a self-identified "conservative, even sometimes called a reactionary" Catholic who believed that "many" of the changes of Vatican II—the worldwide conference of Catholic bishops from 1962 to 1965—"came rather rapidly."[3] Instead, Reagan revealed his absorption of conservative Catholic views. Even in the midst of the Iran-Contra investigations, the president remembered the sisters. For nearly his entire presidency, the Maryknoll Sisters hung like an albatross around Reagan's neck.

Following conservative Catholics' lead, Reagan and his White House regarded the Maryknoll Sisters as synonymous with wayward Catholicism and the protest movement against U.S. policy toward El Salvador and Nicaragua. This public association began in December 1980, when Salvadoran National Guardsmen raped and murdered two of the community's members, along with another nun and a lay missionary. Collectively known as the "four American churchwomen," they were Maryknoll nuns Ita Ford and Maura Clarke, Ursuline nun Dorothy Kazel, and Maryknoll lay missioner Jean Donovan. News coverage of their exhumation introduced many in the United States to El Salvador and sparked a widespread protest movement against U.S. policy. In the following six months, the White House received *ten times* more protest letters about their deaths than about the 444-day Iran hostage crisis.[4] A special panel, appointed by the secretary of state to assess the U.S. government's handling of human rights in El Salvador, concluded that "this particular act of barbarism and attempts by the Salvadoran military to cover it up did more to inflame the debate over El Salvador in the United States than any other single incident."[5]

In response to the murders, the lame-duck Jimmy Carter administration cut U.S. aid to El Salvador, while Reagan officials characterized the women as political activists and gunrunners who died in a shoot-out, contrary to the evidence. Their response prompted the original query for this project: Why would officials repeatedly make comments that were likely to be a public relations disaster? Why, especially, would Secretary of State Alexander Haig, a Catholic whose brother was a Jesuit priest, do so when he knew how upsetting such remarks about nuns could be to Catholics? The answer, I discovered, was that officials' remarks about Maryknollers tapped into conservative Catholic concerns about the congregation's move away from anticommunism.

To conservative Catholics, the women's deaths were the unsurprising result of Maryknoll's misguided activities. During the 1950s, the congregation cooperated with Central Intelligence Agency (CIA) and State Department anticommunist efforts, yet by the 1970s Maryknoll challenged CIA interventions in Latin America and the agency's use of missionaries for intelligence purposes. Most controversially, Maryknollers opposed U.S.-backed Nicaraguan president Anastasio Somoza in the late 1970s. Consequently, even before the churchwomen's murders, many conservative Catholics associated Maryknoll with an errant view of Catholicism.

On the other hand, for many liberal Catholics, the churchwomen's deaths prompted an interest in U.S.–Central America policy and served as an activist gateway. They described the churchwomen, who worked to combat structural inequality, as human rights advocates living out the spirit of the Gospel. They were martyrs whose deaths symbolized an immoral U.S. foreign policy that trained and armed the Salvadoran security forces.

After the murders, Maryknollers continued to be a thorn in the U.S. government's side. Citing their firsthand experience, Maryknoll sisters disputed the Reagan administration's assessment of Central America and encouraged many Catholics to question its policy. As nuns, the women also compromised the U.S. government's self-portrayal as the alternative to godless communism. By analyzing the sisters as religious and political actors, *Reagan's Gun-Toting Nuns* contributes to scholarship that explores the relationship between Catholicism and feminism.[6]

Reagan officials' response to the sisters revealed the administration's perceived loss of control over its Central America agenda and conservative Catholics' concerns about the church's direction. As historian Emily Rosenberg has proposed, "Discourses related to gender may provide deeper understanding of the cultural assumptions from which foreign policies spring."[7] Reagan officials critiqued the sisters as women, rather than as nuns, or they attempted to erase the sisters' religious standing by portraying them as non-nuns who acted inappropriately or, even worse, as communists. Although Maryknoll priests and brothers also served in Central America and opposed U.S. policy, the White House and its Catholic allies focused nearly exclusively on the Maryknoll Sisters. By examining Maryknoll sisters as subjects of gendered discourse, *Reagan's Gun-Toting Nuns* advances U.S. foreign relations scholarship that primarily analyzes how men have evaluated, and often critiqued, each other's behavior in gendered terms.[8]

Maryknoll's questioning of U.S. Cold War policy mattered because of the congregation's place among U.S. Catholics. As the preeminent U.S. missionary congregation, Maryknoll was the prism through which many U.S. Catholics saw themselves as part of a global Catholic community. Before Maryknoll's founding in 1911, all U.S. missionary endeavors were Protestant, while the Vatican considered the United States itself a mission field until 1908, making the notion of U.S. Catholics assisting with the church's evangelization efforts elsewhere unthinkable.[9]

"Maryknoll" refers to two separate entities: the Maryknoll Fathers and Brothers and the Maryknoll Sisters. "Maryknoll" comes from "Mary's Knoll," the name founders Fathers James A. Walsh and Thomas F. Price gave to New York land that became the congregation's headquarters after they prayed for

Mary's assistance with their new endeavor.[10] The Maryknoll Fathers and Brothers, officially the Catholic Foreign Mission Society in America, were founded in 1911.[11] Nine years later, the Vatican recognized the Maryknoll Sisters, officially the Foreign Mission Sisters of St. Dominic and later, the Maryknoll Sisters of St. Dominic. At the time, thirty women belonged to the community, which Mary Josephine "Mollie" Rogers founded in 1912. The sisters traveled to China, their first mission abroad, in 1921.[12]

The Maryknoll Sisters were unique. Unlike other U.S. communities of women religious, Maryknollers were not associated with a European community, enabling them to craft their own outlook and customs. Most significantly, the sisters' missionary focus sent them into the world, allowing them to communicate with other nuns. For other congregations, these restrictions on contact did not change until the 1960s.[13]

Maryknoll's influence far outpaced its numbers, largely due to its media presence. Even at its height, priests, nuns, and brothers never numbered more than three thousand. In 1907 Father Walsh began publishing *A Field Afar*, later *Maryknoll* magazine, to attract support for a U.S.-based missionary endeavor. He wanted U.S. Catholics to see beyond their local communities and envision themselves as "members of a universal Church." The magazine showcased Maryknollers' work (usually the men's), allowing Catholics to share in their undertakings. *Maryknoll* attracted supporters and served as a recruiting tool. Both women and men cited it as a reason they entered. As late as 1978, 20 percent of Maryknoll sisters credited the publication as "one of the most important influences" on their vocations. The magazine, and often visits from Maryknollers, formed an integral part of parochial school for many Catholics during the early Cold War.[14]

Vatican II and Catholic Fractures

White House critiques of murdered Maryknollers and the outraged response echoed the divide among Cold War Catholics that surfaced in the 1960s around the civil rights movement and Vatican II. This council of the world's more than three thousand Catholic bishops dealt with a wide range of issues, including the liturgy, bishops' relationship to the pope, laity's role, nuns' dress, Bible translation, Catholics' stance toward non-Catholics, and seminary curriculum.[15] Vatican II also changed how most Catholics celebrated Mass, as vernacular replaced Latin and the priest turned to face the congregants. These changes were earth-shattering as "Catholics were now asked to do things against which elaborate inhibitions had been built up all their lives."[16] Overall, Vatican II emphasized the church's responsibility to care for people's needs on earth, not just prepare them spiritually for the afterlife. It prompted a world-wide reexamination of the church's role in society and of what it meant to be Catholic.

Some Catholics responded by pushing for more reform, while others lamented the alterations. The Dutch Church issued a new catechism that advocated greater transformation, while France's archbishop Marcel Lefebvre ordained priests who rejected the council's call for ecumenism and the move away from Latin.[17] In the United States, Vatican II accentuated divisions among Catholics. Before the council, Catholics were described as "active" or "lapsed." But afterward, the words "liberal," "conservative," "traditionalist," and "progressive" described people's views on reform.[18] These terms' meanings changed over time, historian John W. O'Malley points out. During the council, a minority opposed reform as inconsistent with the past, while the majority saw continuity. After the 1960s, however, the minority—now known as the conservatives—stressed Vatican II's continuity with the past, whereas liberals highlighted the council's innovation.[19]

After Vatican II, attitudes toward liturgical reform, civil rights, and anticommunism typically went hand in hand.[20] Catholics disagreed over domestic issues, such as abortion, but they also clashed with one another over U.S. foreign policy. Although these Catholic divides deepened around the Vietnam War and resurfaced over Central America, the rupture was pivotal in the 1980s because conservative Catholics formed a close-knit community, well connected to, and often part of, the Reagan administration. It was not merely a case of conservative Catholics sharing Reagan's views or seeing him as a better reflection of their own outlook than U.S. Catholic leadership.[21] The White House sought conservative Catholics' support. For their part, conservative Catholics' access to the Reagan administration allowed them to promote a Central America policy that reflected both their religious and political views. A number of staunchly anticommunist Catholics, such as CIA Director William Casey, Secretary of State Haig, Ambassador at-Large Vernon Walters, and two national security advisors, Richard Allen and William Clark, played instrumental roles in shaping Reagan's Central America policy. Republicans Henry Hyde (IL) and Jeremiah Denton (AL) furthered this agenda in Congress, while political operatives like Paul Weyrich both pushed the White House and furthered its Central America agenda. Significantly, however, conservative Catholics' support for U.S.–Central America policy was the minority view among U.S. Catholics.[22] But as Reagan allies, they had a megaphone to broadcast their views.

Conservative Catholics also had non-Catholics as allies. To gain support for U.S. policy, non-Catholics, including Reagan, interjected themselves into intra-Catholic debates by questioning opponents' patriotism and their authenticity as Catholics. Critics focused on Maryknoll nuns as the epitome of Americans' lack of support for U.S. Cold War foreign policy, of Catholics' abandonment of anticommunism, and of nuns' changing role within the church. At its heart, the controversy asked who could fight the Cold War, shape U.S. foreign policy, and define what it meant to be Catholic.

Religious Restructuring and the Cold War

Existing scholarship prioritizes *inter*religious conflict during the Cold War by contending U.S. policymakers' stereotypes of non-Christian religions shaped foreign policy or by highlighting how the United States contrasted itself with godless communism.[23] Scholars have also examined religion and the Cold War beyond the United States and Soviet Union and an understanding of the conflict between Judeo-Christianity and atheism.[24] On Reagan's Central America policy, historians have stressed conservative religious groups' attempts to influence U.S. policy, examined U.S. government efforts to recruit anticommunist evangelicals to support the Contras (the counterrevolutionaries who sought to overthrow the Nicaraguan government), and analyzed how members of the international anticommunist Right lobbied to finance the Contras and the Salvadoran government as well as aided Salvadoran death squads and sent U.S. citizens to fight for the Contras.[25] On the other hand, scholars have studied how, motivated by their faith, those on the liberal end of the spectrum opposed U.S.–Central America policy both within the United States and through transnational and international connections.[26]

Consequently, the debate over Central America divided religious communities; it was not simply a political divide but revealed developments within the broader U.S. religious landscape, as scholars have begun to acknowledge.[27] In highlighting intrareligious conflict and noting interfaith cooperation, *Reagan's Gun-Toting Nuns* reflects U.S. religion's post–World War II "restructuring" as conservatives felt more in common with conservatives of other denominations than with liberals of their own faith.[28]

I examine how international *intra*religious conflict among Catholics influenced the White House's interpretation of events in Central America and its marketing of U.S. policy, especially during Reagan's first term. The Reagan administration approached Central America as a Catholic problem in responding to its opponents at home and abroad. To counter religious-led protest and to exploit ruptures among Catholics, the White House appealed to U.S., Latin American, and European Catholics using Catholic spokespersons and Catholic language. Reagan officials echoed conservative Catholics' decades-old criticism of Maryknollers by blaming the women for Congress's refusal to fund the Contras. Although prior presidents watched changes in the Latin American Catholic Church with alarm, Reagan's approach was unique. He faced a religious-based protest movement, conservative Catholics played prominent roles in shaping and packaging U.S.–Central America policy, and the White House used Central America to reinvigorate conservatives' support.

By exploring this intra-Catholic debate, I contest scholarly portrayals of religion as separate from a more central Cold War narrative. Historian Andrew Preston has proposed that religion played such a pivotal role that "*the religious Cold War*" is a more accurate description than "religion *and* the Cold War" or "religion *in* the Cold War."[29] But Preston's use of religion as an adjective implies a conflict apart. Though Ronald Reagan saw U.S. intervention in Central America as vital to rolling back communism in the Western Hemisphere, to Nicaraguan, Salvadoran, and U.S. Catholics, U.S. involvement meant much more. With financial support and military aid, the U.S. government bolstered one side in the intra-Catholic battle over the church's direction.

At times, intra-Catholic conflict and U.S. policy were indistinguishable because the White House crafted a foreign policy that reflected conservative Catholics' political views and their vision for the Catholic Church. Catholic beliefs and aesthetics permeated every aspect of the debates about U.S. policy. Protesters dressed as nuns in blood-splattered habits taunted the secretary of state, Congress linked Salvadoran aid to progress in the churchwomen's murder case, Catholic senators sparred over the propriety of hearings on liberation theology's role in revolutionary movements, and Reagan claimed that unlike his 1984 Democratic challenger (who had a Catholic ticketmate), *he* would defend the pope. Understanding how Nicaraguan, Salvadoran, and U.S. Catholics experienced a cold war that overlapped with, and often influenced, the larger battle between the superpowers clarifies why the debate over U.S.–Central America policy was so bitter.

Liberation Theology and Human Rights

Reagan's Gun-Toting Nuns also decenters the United States by showing how U.S. developments were not isolated. Catholics around the world also struggled with the church's direction.[30] In Catholic El Salvador and Nicaragua, these ruptures influenced policy and sparked deadly violence. The movement of religious ideas, political perspectives, and people between Central America and the United States involved an exchange rather than the imposition of U.S.

ideals. This bidirectional influence prompted conservative U.S. Catholics to see Maryknollers—in mission in Central America—as carriers of a corrupt Latin American influence that threatened the United States both religiously and politically.

One of conservative Catholics' biggest concerns about Maryknoll was its support for liberation theology. This style of thought and practice evolved in 1960s Latin America from the ideas of Catholic and Protestant theologians and grassroots activists.[31] Borrowing from Marxist analysis, they promoted action as the starting point for theological reflection and understanding. Liberationists came to understand sin in terms of the oppressive societal structures from which people needed salvation. They stressed the people—the poor in particular—as church, rather than the hierarchy.[32] As one Maryknoller explained, liberation theology is "linking religion and daily struggle, not by providing political formulas but by developing spiritual muscle and perseverance to overcome obstacles, setbacks and persecution in building a world of justice and peace."[33] The doctrine is often associated with one of its founders, Peruvian Catholic theologian Gustavo Gutiérrez, who published *Teología de la liberación* in 1971.[34] Liberation theology became a major source of contention within both Central American and U.S. Catholicism.

Besides the adoption of Marxist analysis, conservative Catholics condemned liberationists' seeming acceptance of guerrilla movements. Liberation theology developed simultaneously with popular armed movements in Nicaragua and El Salvador. Although the two groups did not share the same ideology, as historian Virginia Garrard-Burnett contends, they saw "the roots of injustice and inequality" in similar ways. "Where Marxist guerrillas might blame dependency, exploitation, and capitalism, liberationist Catholics decried 'structural sin' and 'institutionalized violence.'"[35] Critics often did not parse this differing reasoning, concluding that liberationists were either armed guerrillas or, at the very least, their supporters.

Reagan's Gun-Toting Nuns examines religion and human rights activism across political boundaries during the 1970s and 1980s, a subject scholars are increasingly investigating.[36] I use the terms "rights" and "human rights" broadly, as did Maryknollers who did not simply adhere to the conception of the Universal Declaration of Human Rights (UDHR) of the United Nations. Especially in talking to U.S. audiences, Maryknollers spoke of Central Americans having the right to human dignity and self-determination, the right to be free from hunger, illiteracy, sickness, and political and economic domination in their own country as well as globally. Maryknollers, in keeping with liberation theology, prioritized the poor. This conception of human rights mattered because, as Maryknoller Madeline Dorsey explained, the powerful felt threatened when the Salvadoran poor became "more aware of their rights, human rights and equal rights as children of God."[37] In contrast to secular activists faith influenced Maryknollers' understanding of, and push for, human rights.

Terminology

Vatican II, which divided U.S. Catholics into the camps of traditionalists, neo-conservatives, and liberals, dictates my classification of Catholics. Since the first two groups can be broadly classified as conservative Catholics, I use that term to describe them collectively. Conservatives were predominantly "white, middle-class, third- or fourth-generation Americans."[38] They largely supported Reagan's Central America policy, while liberal Catholics formed the opposition.

Traditionalists stressed the need to restore the church to its pre–Vatican II state. With Vatican II, they believed, the church relinquished its unique vision and role in the world. Many saw the council as a result of modernist theologians' manipulation of church leaders and attributed post–Vatican II problems to infiltration by church enemies: modernists and communists. They were particularly worried by the council's decision not to "formally and explicitly . . . condemn communism."[39] To traditionalists, the primary postconciliar problem was a crisis of authority. Like their Latin American counterparts, traditionalists were numerically smaller; yet key representatives—namely, Paul Weyrich, mastermind of conservative grassroots activism and cofounder of the Heritage Foundation and the Moral Majority—had the Reagan White House's ear. The *Wanderer* was the key periodical that aired this group's views.

Catholic neoconservatives, by contrast, generally supported the council but disagreed with how its reforms were implemented. They saw the "spirit of Vatican II" as encouraging Marxist analysis and feminist tendencies in the church, causing a "severe" Catholic identity crisis. They believed the church was becoming politicized and had abandoned its concern with communism and persecution of the church. They emphasized the need for renewal. The neocons saw the church's primary problem as a crisis of faith and viewed the decline of mainline Protestantism as a warning. The Catholic neocons regarded themselves as "more a community of intellectual conversation," not as a "faction" or "camp." They also rejected the charge that they were the "Catholic chaplaincy" of political neocons.[40] A key neocon with ties to the Reagan White House was former liberal Michael Novak, head of the U.S. delegation on the UN Human Rights Commission. These Catholics found that the pages of *Crisis* and, to some extent, the *National Catholic Register* reflected their perspective.

In contrast to these conservatives, liberals saw Vatican II and its reforms as ushering the church into the modern world. They often disparagingly described the preconciliar church as "triumphalist, legalistic, hierarchical, patriarchal, ghetto-like, clericalistic, irrelevant, and obsessive-compulsive." To them, any postconciliar problems resulted from the refusal of an "intransigent minority" to accept change.[41] The *National Catholic Reporter* represented their views. Despite their differences, both liberals and conservatives celebrated American exceptionalism and advocated for its application to the Catholic Church. Liberals cited U.S. democratic principles to promote a more democratic church structure. Conservatives, by contrast, encouraged the application of U.S. principles of free enterprise and, ironically, the Protestant work ethic to Catholic social teaching concerning poverty, wealth, economics, and the state's role.[42]

Similarly, by the late 1970s and early 1980s, Latin American Catholics were fractured into three groups: traditionalist, modernizing, and prophetic. The traditional church historically aligned itself with the politically and economically powerful, guaranteeing a stable social order. A key characteristic of traditionalists was their "visceral, frequently crusading anticommunism." Although Vatican II ended this group's hegemony, a minority of bishops and some older religious still represented this outlook. Conversely, the council strengthened the modernizing church, which originated in the 1930s and 1940s. This group promoted "ecclesiastical reform and the establishment of more democratic church structures." Numerically the largest, modernizers tended to reflect a middle-class viewpoint and often led "the formation of 'Christian' political parties and labor organizations." Rejecting modernizers' piecemeal reform of social and development programs, the prophetic church pushed for radical change. Though the prophetic church was a minority, its influence exceeded its numbers. The prophetic camp pushed for a church that sided with the poor and powerless masses, rather than a church that served as "a privileged guarantor of the existing social order and the values and interests that sustain it." By contrast, modernizers promoted change within the capitalist framework yet were "frequently unaware" of how they supported it.[43] In my research, Salvadoran traditionalists condemned the prophetic church, while after the Nicaraguan revolution, tensions more often involved modernists and prophets.

When considering the relationship between religion and my historical actors, I view religion expansively to include theology, lived faith, and culture. The difference between these lines is not always clear.[44] While the Maryknoll Sisters' theology influenced how they practiced their faith and carried out their missionary work, this was not the case for all Catholics. House Speaker

Thomas P. "Tip" O'Neill, for example, cited his personal ties to Maryknoll rather than specific religious beliefs as the reason he opposed Reagan's Nicaragua policy. For a practicing Catholic "who scheduled the House so he could get ashes on Ash Wednesday" and repeatedly cited nuns' influence on his life, the lines between O'Neill's personal relationships, beliefs, and practices are not easily untangled.[45]

Although "nun" refers to a woman who lives a cloistered or semi-cloistered life of prayer and "sister" describes a woman whose ministry and prayer focus within the world, I use these terms more or less interchangeably because scholarly and popular practice do and because my actors did. The term "women religious" also refers collectively to women who have joined religious orders. When referring to the Roman Catholic Church as an institution, I use the term "church." In examining the church, I focus primarily on sisters, priests, and lay Catholics, rather than prioritize the institutional church.

Maryknollers referred and refer to themselves as "missioners" rather than "missionaries," and during my period of study some non-Maryknollers also used this terminology to talk about the congregation. Neither Catholics nor non-Catholics universally used "missioner" when discussing Maryknoll, however, so I use "missioner" infrequently to avoid confusion. I have retained "missioner" when it is a direct quotation and at times when it is clear I am discussing only Maryknollers or their lay associates.

Scope, Structure, and Title

This project began with the murders of the churchwomen and U.S.–El Salvador relations. It expanded to Nicaragua only when I discovered the Reagan administration's linkage of Nicaragua to El Salvador and its critiques of Maryknollers' influence on Tip O'Neill in the Contra aid debate. Overall, Guatemala played a secondary role in the sources I read.

Maryknollers, however, were in mission in Guatemala and worked to raise U.S. awareness about human rights abuses.[46] It was an uphill battle. The conservative U.S. Catholic press ignored Guatemala; its concern was Nicaragua. The progressive Catholic press covered Guatemala and critiqued the secular media for not giving the country attention. It found the lack of press coverage shocking given that "more priests were murdered in Guatemala than in any other Latin American country."[47] Even the murder of U.S. diocesan priest Stanley Rother in July 1981, eight months after the four churchwomen, did not change the broader U.S. conversation. The U.S. Congress did not repeatedly call for justice, nor did the U.S. embassy prioritize the killing.[48] Overall, the Guatemalan government's counterinsurgency efforts in the 1980s were more "brutal" than those in El Salvador and Nicaragua. From 1980 to 1983 alone, more than 100,000 civilians were killed or were disappeared and over one million displaced.[49]

Reagan's Gun-Toting Nuns consists of eight chapters. "From Senator McCarthy's Darlings to Marxist Maryknollers" explains how Maryknollers' evolving sense of mission and their experiences, particularly in Latin America, transformed them from allies to critics of U.S. Cold War policy and drew the ire of Latin American governments and conservative U.S. Catholics. "Religious or Political Activists for Nicaragua?" shows how Maryknollers' leadership in opposing Nicaraguan president Somoza led conservative U.S. non-Catholics to adopt conservative Catholics' concerns about Maryknoll by the late 1970s. Overlapping chronologically, "Subversives in El Salvador" explains how Maryknollers and other religious, most notably San Salvador's Archbishop Óscar Romero, unsuccessfully tried to persuade Jimmy Carter to accentuate human rights in U.S.–El Salvador policy. By 1980, El Salvador was a major conflict between the White House and the religious community.

The next chapters focus on the Reagan administration. "U.S. Guns Kill U.S. Nuns" examines the murders of the churchwomen and how Reagan officials' critiques revealed that intra-Catholic conflict had become an integral part of U.S.–Central America policy with Reagan's ascension to the White House. "Reagan and the White House's Maryknoll Nun" examines how Reagan's public diplomacy campaign reflected conservative Nicaraguan and U.S. Catholic viewpoints and language. Officials worked with Catholic allies, including a former Maryknoll sister, to critique Maryknoll and liberation theology in the United States, Latin America, and Europe. "Real Catholics vs. Maryknollers" argues that Reagan and his supporters questioned both Tip O'Neill's authenticity as a Catholic and his masculinity because he followed Maryknoll sisters' advice in opposing the Contras. At the same time, the Reagan administration interjected itself into Nicaraguan Catholic debates by promoting Cardinal Miguel Obando y Bravo as a true Catholic in contrast to Nicaragua's foreign minister, Maryknoll priest Miguel d'Escoto. "Maryknoll and Iran-Contra" examines how conservative U.S. Catholics held up Catholic William Casey and former Catholic Oliver North as symbols of true Catholics and patriots, not Maryknollers, whom they blamed for Iran-Contra.

The book concludes with another political turning point, the George H. W. Bush administration, and another Salvadoran massacre. "Déjà Vu: Jesuits and Maryknollers" argues that despite the constant comparisons between the murders of the churchwomen in 1980 and the Jesuits in 1989, intra-Catholic debates no longer held the same political significance for U.S.–Central America relations. Conservative Catholics' imprint on U.S.–Central America policy reached its height with Reagan but began to disintegrate with the Iran-Contra revelations and disappeared under Bush.

The book's title, *Reagan's Gun-Toting Nuns*, brings together the most salacious comments made about the murdered women, especially Alexander Haig's false charge that the women died in a shoot-out. No person uttered the phrase. By juxtaposing "gun-toting" and "nun," the title stresses how entangled Catholic debates about the meaning of Catholic identity were with those about U.S.–Central America policy. The image of a nun as a violent revolutionary not only challenged the murdered churchwomen's status as victims; it also revealed conservative Catholics' objections to nuns' and priests' social activism.

The churchwomen became "Reagan's" in two regards. First, the women as gun-wielding nuns existed only in the imagination of Reagan officials and the president's allies. Second, once the fiction of a violent, powerful Maryknoller was created, the White House and its conservative Catholic supporters perceived the sisters as an omnipresent adversary. Though the murdered churchwomen prompted protests and the sisters were leaders in opposing U.S.–Central America policy, Maryknoll came to represent all resistance to Reagan administration policy.

Chapter 1

From Senator McCarthy's Darlings
to Marxist Maryknollers

In 1975, the Maryknoll Sisters Central Govern-
ing Board wrote to Gerald Ford. The president had denied U.S. involvement
in the overthrow of Chile's democratically elected president Salvador Allende.
Ford also asserted that U.S. covert efforts "to help and assist" Chilean opposition newspapers and political parties were "in the best interest of the people
in Chile and, certainly, in our best interest."[1] But the Maryknoll Sisters disagreed, wondering "by what degree of arrogance do we decide what is in the
best interests of Chile and any other nation?" They continued, "Do we choose
to relate to the world through intimidation, confusion and murder?"[2] The letter was a far cry from the sisters' unwavering support for U.S. Cold War aims
during the 1950s. This chapter explores Maryknollers' evolving sense of mission and their experiences, particularly in Latin America, as they transformed
from well-known government allies in the 1950s to critics in the late 1960s and
1970s. Applying new church teachings, especially from Vatican II and Medellín, seeing the effects of U.S. policy, and living in Right-wing military dictatorships all influenced the shift. Not all Maryknollers lived through these changes
or did so in the same way. But missioners who did, especially those in Guatemala and Chile, found themselves in conflict with Latin American governments
and conservative U.S. Catholics.

Maryknoll's shift challenged the meaning of U.S. Catholic missionary activity. The Cold War U.S. missionaries complemented, if not furthered, U.S.

influence abroad, while Catholics were typically anticommunist. After Vatican II, Maryknoll revisited the model that saw evangelization as missionaries' purpose and communism as the primary adversary. The newer model prioritized social justice and questioned communism as the cause of Third World poverty. In Latin America this divide pitted Catholics against each another, especially as U.S.-backed military governments proliferated. In the United States, anticommunist Catholics charged Maryknollers with importing Latin American Marxism disguised as Catholicism instead of spreading the Gospel abroad.

Maryknoll and the Early Cold War

Maryknoll's core ideals dovetailed with early U.S. Cold War aims. One of the congregation's central tenets was derived from the ancient Christian saying that "the blood of martyrs is the seed of the Church." Founders Fathers James A. Walsh and Thomas F. Price cultivated the "mystique of martyrdom" as the "core of the missionary vocation."[3] Death for the faith was "an ideal, a goal, a grace, the highest of privileges." Maryknoll's magazine *A Field Afar* was filled with biographies, book advertisements, and short stories about martyrs, which Walsh and Price hoped would inspire young U.S. Catholics.[4] Maryknoll Sisters founder and first mother general Mary Joseph Rogers shared this belief.[5]

During and after World War II, Maryknollers were forced to confront the possibility of martyrdom at the hands of communists. After Pearl Harbor, the Japanese interned sisters living in Hong Kong, Manchuria, and the Philippines. From October 1950 to January 1951, communists placed thirty-eight Maryknoll sisters and nearly half the ninety-nine priests and brothers serving in South China under house arrest as U.S. spies. In 1950, communists shot and killed Sister Agnesta Chang in Korea.[6] Mother Mary Joseph characterized this new reality when speaking to senior novices in 1951. As she explained, "This is a very momentous time for you to make your vows . . . as some of our own Maryknollers are being persecuted." Martyrdom was not an abstract concept, but "a possibility for all of us. . . . And it is important that you realize this—as I know you do."[7]

Because Maryknollers assisted the U.S. government during the 1940s and 1950s, China's suspicions were not unfounded. Some Maryknollers flew on U.S. military cargo planes, Maryknoll Bishop Francis X. Ford praised the Chinese Nationalists and invited them to speak at church gatherings, and some churches placed Nationalist flags on their altars.[8] Maryknollers, like other Christian missionaries, worked with the CIA while abroad and received State

Department debriefings upon return.[9] Bishop Ford reported "Communist troop movements, economic conditions, communications, and transport facilities in his area" to the U.S. consulate. After discovering this in Ford's papers, Chinese communists regarded Maryknoll as "the biggest spy ring in China" and sent Ford to a prison camp where he died in 1952. Consistent with other missionaries of the time, Maryknollers were "unconscious" of how or why many Chinese might identify them with Western imperialism. Instead, as a Maryknoll sister recounted, "My thinking was geared to what the U.S. government thought of China. We were not analytical and didn't understand the political situation. We just lived day to day."[10]

Maryknoll sisters in the motherhouse also heard of communism's danger. Maryknoll's second mother general, Mother Columba, chose reading materials and speakers that reflected her anticommunism and support for fellow Catholic Joseph McCarthy.[11] After charging that communists hidden in the State Department were to blame for U.S. foreign policy failures, Wisconsin's junior senator became the public face of the campaign to purge suspected communists from government.[12] As one sister noted of the period, "We were constantly fed McCarthy's ideas." Although some sisters who had been imprisoned in China challenged this black-and-white assessment, Mother Columba rejected their more nuanced view.[13]

On a broader level, the 1950s U.S. Catholic Church "presented a monolithic image,"[14] even though all Catholics did not uniformly support McCarthyism. The church's condemnation of communism long predated the Cold War. In 1846, two years before publication of the *Communist Manifesto*, Pope Pius IX denounced "that infamous doctrine of so-called Communism which is absolutely contrary to the natural law itself, and if once adopted would utterly destroy the rights, property and possessions of all men, and even society itself." Thirty-two years later Leo XIII described communism as "the fatal plague which insinuates itself into the very marrow of human society only to bring about its ruin." In the 1937 encyclical *Atheistic Communism*, Pope Pius XI warned how "bolshevistic and atheistic Communism" sought to shakeup "the social order" and undermine "the very foundations of Christian civilization."[15] Twelve years later, in 1949, the Vatican excommunicated all Catholic Communist Party members.[16]

The 1950s U.S. "religious revival" fostered broader interest in Maryknoll martyrs. Dwight Eisenhower was the first U.S. president baptized while in office, and he often employed religious rhetoric. Congress added "In God We Trust" to coins and "under God" to the Pledge of Allegiance. Catholics, members of the largest religious denomination, were often held up as anticommunist models. Religious-themed books and movies proliferated, including those that positively featured nuns and priests.[17] To Catholics and non-Catholics alike, incarcerated Maryknollers served "as living symbols of the impact of 'godless communism.'" During the decade one of the most popular accounts of missionaries imprisoned in China was *Nun in Red China*, a fictionalized story of Maryknollers by Maryknoller Maria del Rey.[18] The book became the television movie *The Bamboo Cross*, directed by John Ford and starring Jane Wyman, Ronald Reagan's first wife. The sisters also gained attention through features in magazines *Look* and *Cosmopolitan*, and Maria del Rey followed up her success with *Bernie Becomes a Nun* and *Her Name Is Mercy* about a sister working in a refugee clinic during the Korean War.[19]

The pinnacle of media attention came with an April 1955 *Time* story about nuns that focused on Maryknoll and featured Mother Columba on the cover. *Time* characterized the sisters' mission as serving U.S. interests and civilization's. The Maryknoll Sisters were a "worldwide spiritual army" under Mother Columba's "deployment" who served on "all the frontiers of civilization." As *Time* explained, "The missionary sisters of Maryknoll know . . . that the survival of civilization always depends on faith and discipline, often on details." Offering high praise, the article still relied on stereotypes. While *Time* complimented the mother general for her "abilities of a top industrial executive—which she might easily have become," it described the sisters as childlike and naive at times, noting that during "'free periods' the sisters are apt to act as gay and carefree as schoolgirls."[20]

Maryknoll's association with the well-connected Francis Cardinal Spellman also added to the community's high profile. Known as the "American Pope,"[21] Spellman was U.S. Catholicism's public face.[22] Politicians sought his support, given his friendships with U.S. presidents and close connection to Pope Pius XII. Spellman concurrently oversaw Roman Catholics in the U.S. military and, as New York cardinal, served as Maryknoll's official "protector." Consequently, China's expulsion of Maryknollers solidified his anticommunist stance and support for McCarthy.[23]

Though Maryknollers earned their anticommunist credentials in Asia, from 1940 to 1970, the community sent more missionaries to Latin America than any other region. The turn was largely practical. World War II cut off the community's access to its other mission areas.[24] The first Maryknoll priest was sent to Latin America in 1942 and the first sister in 1943.[25] The predominantly Catholic area might have seemed an odd choice, but instead of conversion, Maryknoll Bishop Walsh aimed to "Romanize" the Catholicism Latin Americans practiced.[26]

Maryknoll's move predated both the U.S. government's and the Vatican's growing concern with communism in Latin America. In 1954, the CIA assisted

Guatemalan generals' overthrow of President Jacobo Arbenz, who was portrayed as a communist. The 1959 Cuban Revolution prompted both the U.S. government and the Vatican to unveil plans to counter communism's appeal. In 1961, the first U.S. Catholic president, John F. Kennedy, announced the Alliance for Progress. A Marshall Plan for Latin America, the aid program aimed to counter revolutionary activity and foster development.[27] The same year, Pope John XXIII called for an increased Catholic presence in Latin America, asking U.S. religious congregations and societies to send 10 percent of their members to address the shortage of clergy and religious. By that time, 25 percent of Maryknollers were already in Central and South America.[28]

1960s

During the 1960s, changes in the Catholic Church, U.S. society, and Latin America reshaped Maryknoll. U.S. Catholics splintered as they reconsidered their status as Catholics and Americans. They were especially divided over priests and nuns joining the civil rights movement. Opponents saw religious as engaging in improper political activity, or worse, as supporting communism. As one Cleveland Catholic wrote to her archdiocesan newspaper in 1965, she was "sick at heart" over photos of nuns at the Selma civil rights marches when they "should be down on their knees . . . praying." A man argued that priests should be preaching, not "join[ing] in with Communists and college brats."[29] While the civil rights and antiwar movements caused convulsions in U.S. society, Catholics experienced an overlapping—and separate—"American Catholic Revolution," debating "Roman Catholic belief, worship, ethics, and citizenship,"[30] in light of Vatican II.

Vatican II prompted an exodus from religious orders. The council's promotion of lay life as an alternative "for living out the gospel commitment in the world" erased the laity's inferior status within the church. This reconceptualization led many, both inside and outside the United States, to leave religious life. And Maryknoll felt these pains. Whereas before Vatican II Maryknoll was a primary way for women to serve the church in a missionary capacity, now there were more opportunities, including joining the Peace Corps. From 1940 to 1960, the sisters' community "more than doubled" in size.[31] In 1962, the year Vatican II opened, Maryknoll gained 132 new entrants. In 1970, there were three. Between 1966 and 1974, 379 professed sisters (27.6 percent) left.[32]

Sisters Maura Clarke and Ita Ford, later murdered in El Salvador, illustrate Maryknoll's changes between 1950 and the early 1970s. Maura, short for Mary Elizabeth, applied to Maryknoll not long after finishing high school and was accepted in 1950, part of a wave of women joining religious communities. Born in 1931 to Irish immigrant parents, she grew up in Queens.[33] Her background was typical. New Maryknollers in the 1940s and 1950s were usually from working-class or lower-middle-class "ethnic communities." Nearly one-third came from New York, Pennsylvania, Massachusetts, and Illinois.[34] In describing Clarke's time as a novice, another sister noted that "she simply believed what she was told, dealt with what was evident, and only seldom, if ever, doubted anyone or anything."[35]

Thirty-one-year-old Ita Ford, by contrast, joined Maryknoll in 1971 when women were leaving religious life in droves. Though her age was unusual, her background as an Irish American from Brooklyn was not. Ford originally entered in 1961 but left for health reasons just before taking her vows in 1964. In the intervening years, she worked for a Catholic publisher, protested the Vietnam War, and visited Japan to reflect on the atomic bombings. During her senior year of college, she visited Russia and was struck by the lack of religious freedom she witnessed.[36] Ford's life experience, more typical of women entering after Vatican II, contrasted sharply with women like Maura Clarke, who joined Maryknoll in the 1950s out of high school.

In addition to reconceptualizing laity's role, Vatican II also fostered a new approach to mission. As the congregation's biographer Penny Lernoux points out, two conciliar documents profoundly impacted Maryknoll. The first was *Gaudium et Spes* (The Church in the Modern World). The second was the call for all religious communities to reexamine the charism, or spirit of their founders, and update themselves in light of contemporary times, the Gospel, and Vatican II guidelines. For Maryknollers, this process involved a reconsideration of mission's meaning.[37]

The sisters adopted this challenge at their 1968 Chapter, a meeting of representatives from around the world. The 1964 General Chapter had concluded that missionary work should mean more than establishing a local church; it included addressing oppression's causes and recognizing the poor's role in evangelization. But the 1968 debate was still contentious as the women grappled with how to prioritize their life as nuns versus this new missionary work. On one side of the debate, some prioritized religious life and envisioned a more traditional view of mission. Were they, as one sister asked, "religious missioners" or "missioners who happened to be religious"?[38]

Sisters missionizing in Latin America championed the contrary outlook. Compared with sisters elsewhere, they were "more outspoken about the need for social change." They worked and lived among the poor, whereas most sisters in Asia and the Pacific ran institutions such as hospitals and schools. Latin America also exposed sisters to new ways of thinking about the relationship between evangelization and social justice. Sisters began to see mission as learning more about the Gospel through administering to others, rather than imposing the sisters' view of Catholicism. Barbara Hendricks, who joined Maryknoll in 1945 at age twenty and began work in Peru in 1953, described this new outlook. "We felt that we had gone to help revive an old church which had fallen on bad times because of neglect. We were to teach the faith and its doctrines, restore sacramental life, and strengthen the structures. It was kind of a revival mission. But it soon became apparent—the situation and cry of the poor was startling—that much more than revival of doctrine and structures and sacraments was taking place." Things had changed. As she noted, "The people were telling us what mission was about in Latin America. It was the people who in a very real sense evangelized us."[39]

Maryknollers like Hendricks were not the only ones rethinking mission. In a 1967 article in the Jesuit magazine *America*, Father Ivan Illich called on U.S. Catholics to "do some honest thinking about the implications of their help."[40] Illich ran a center for prospective missionaries in Cuernavaca, Mexico, attended by more than twelve hundred priests and other missionaries from the United States, Canada, Europe, and Australia in the 1960s. Promoted as an orientation program, the Center for Intercultural Formation encouraged missionaries to insert themselves into the local reality rather than impose their culture. Illich wanted them to consider their role, and the church's, in Latin America.[41]

To Illich, the focus should not be "how to send more men and money, but rather why they should be sent at all." U.S. missionaries were propping up a struggling Latin American church, effectively making it "a satellite to North Atlantic cultural phenomena and policy." U.S. Catholics also needed to examine their missionary project's relationship to the U.S. government. U.S. missionaries' arrival coincided with the Alliance for Progress, which aimed "to maintain the status quo," thereby giving the impression the church sanctioned U.S. policy. Instead, Illich asserted, the church needed to consider its "complicity in stifling universal awakening too revolutionary to lie quietly."[42]

Over time, more missionaries began to question their association with the U.S. government. Initially, missionaries shared the Alliance for Progress's interest in combating communism and promoting economic development, which led them to share information with the U.S. government.[43] The CIA sought out "socially progressive" missionaries, such as Jesuits and Maryknollers, because they were more likely to have information about issues of CIA concern, such as "urban labor unrest or attempts to organize estate workers and peasant farmers." But some missionaries began to reject the U.S. approach for failing to address poverty's root causes. As U.S. Catholic Conference Latin

America Advisor Tom Quigley explained, they "learned that development, as practiced, benefited the rich at the expense of the poor, and that containment of communism was often simplistically equated with protecting an unjust and unchristian status quo."[44]

A few Maryknollers who questioned mission's meaning and their role, especially as Americans, turned to armed revolution. In 1967 Maryknoll expelled two priests, brothers Thomas Melville and Arthur Melville, and Sister Marjorie Bradford from Guatemala for involving themselves and others "in plans for starting an armed revolution."[45] Although the Melvilles and Bradford were the public focus, two other Maryknoll nuns and a priest were also part of what became known as the "Melville incident."[46]

Although their acceptance of armed revolution was atypical, the Melvilles illustrate how living in Latin America prompted some Maryknollers to reexamine their anticommunist views and their understanding of what it meant to be Catholic. In 1954, Bradford and Tom Melville separately arrived in Guatemala with the sense that both communism and inferior Catholic practices needed to be eradicated. Bradford saw President Arbenz's overthrow as freeing the country from communism. Born in Mexico to a Mexican mother and an American father,[47] she grew up feeling "very proud to be an American" and that "Mexicans owed much to us Americans." Likewise, Tom, from Boston's "west Roxbury Irish ghetto," dreamt of becoming a missionary and sent his saved lunch money to Maryknoll every month. In Guatemala, Tom saw his role as instilling "true" Catholicism. As he recalled, "I was determined that these people were going to learn about Catholicism and that I was going to save their souls in spite of themselves, even if I had to knock people down or get myself killed in the process."[48]

The two met in 1966.[49] Over time, Marjorie, and then Tom, began to question the status quo. As a teacher of wealthy Guatemalans, Marjorie was shocked to learn through her participation in *cursillos*—"short courses" in Christianity—that most Latin Americans lived in poverty. Then, as she described, during her return to Maryknoll for studies in 1964 she "was coming more and more to realize that religion consisted, not of a collection of doctrines and church rituals, but of living with other people and sharing meaning and direction with them."[50] In Guatemala, Marjorie helped found a student group, the Crater, which grew out of Maryknoll-sponsored "consciousness-raising courses" and retreats centered on "social awareness and Christian social doctrine."[51]

Tom admonished Marjorie for her sympathy with the guerrillas, whom he regarded as communists and terrorists.[52] Eventually, though, the guerrillas prompted him to consider how he lived his faith on a day-to-day basis and what role he played in addressing people's needs, rather than pacifying their misery. This questioning led Tom to reexamine U.S. foreign policy. As he concluded, "Powerful interest groups in Washington were influencing or making decisions in terms of what was good for the United States without understanding or concern for the Guatemalan people." Meanwhile, Marjorie became more militant as the Guatemalan government and church leaders labeled Crater members communists and as government-backed death squads targeted other social reformers.[53]

Tom and Marjorie concluded that change demanded drastic action, not incremental reform, and they organized a meeting of "like-minded Christian radicals" in November 1967. They, along with others, broke from larger Maryknoll discussions about how Vatican II applied to their situation in Guatemala after they realized the stark differences in opinion. This smaller group wondered, "Does a Christian have any role in revolutionary times? Do foreigners in Guatemala, particularly Americans—since our government was helping to suppress the revolutionary movement—have any role to play in Guatemala's revolution?"[54] Using code names, the group discussed starting a "Christian revolution," as Tom explained, "based on an organization of self-defense, to reoccupy lands that had been stolen from [the peasantry] by generations of white men."[55] The group wrote a "manifesto" inspired by the papal encyclical *Progress of Peoples* and the Gospels.[56]

The group's approach was not novel. The year before, former priest Camilo Torres Restrepo died fighting with the Colombian guerrillas. Torres, from an upper-class family, aimed to create a mass organization to overthrow the government. His efforts led to conflict with his country's ecclesial hierarchy, the most conservative in Latin America. Torres left the priesthood rather than face excommunication. Several months later, in the midst of assassination threats, he joined the National Liberation Army, believing it was better to die in armed struggle than at the hands of an unknown assassin.[57] Torres's message resonated with these Maryknollers who worked with the poor but saw no improvements.

Upon discovering the meeting, the Maryknoll regional superior demanded that the three he could identify—Bradford and the Melvilles—leave the country. While he regarded them as a threat to Guatemala, U.S. ambassador John Gordon Mein stressed that their safety might also be at risk. Maryknoll later identified and expelled three others from the country: Sisters Marian Pahl and Catherine Sagan, and Father Blase Bonpane.[58]

Tom and Marjorie, who married after their departure from Guatemala, defended their actions. In a statement sent to the *National Catholic Reporter* and the *Washington Post*, Tom proclaimed that if the Guatemalan government and oligarchy continued to maintain the peasantry "in their position of misery, then they have the obligation to take up arms and defend their God-given rights to be men." In response to accusations that he was a communist, he proclaimed, "I am a Communist only if Christ was a Communist."[59] In writing to some Maryknoll sisters, Marjorie explained that through her involvement "in guerrilla activities," she was "trying to live up to my ideals and to what my conscience demands of me." She saw herself in the "vanguard" of a "revolution beginning in civic society as well as in the church" that she must not back away from because of fear.[60]

While the Melvilles challenged Catholics to consider their obligation to the Guatemalan poor, other Maryknollers distanced the congregation from the group's actions. A month after the Melville group's removal from the community, all 102 Maryknollers serving in Guatemala defended the expulsion and condemned what they regarded as political behavior. As they wrote in the Mexican press and the *New York Times*, "Since they [the Melville group] took part in politics—a field closed to them as missioners and priests—we found ourselves forced to expel them from Guatemala."[61] But Tom disagreed. "Our sin was not that we mixed in politics as such, but that we were on the wrong side—one may respectfully serve as a 'dupe' of the landowners but not of the peasants."[62] The Maryknoll regional superior in Guatemala also disapproved of the Melville group's approach, but he privately acknowledged that many Maryknoll priests agreed there was a "tragic lack of justice" and a need for real political, economic, and social change.[63]

The Melville incident led the Guatemalan government and press to see Maryknollers generally as armed revolutionaries. The secret police surveilled the congregation, and the government linked it to revolutionary violence. News about the Melvilles first appeared in Guatemala's *Imparcial* on January 16, 1968. After guerrillas killed two U.S. military attachés the same day, headlines spoke of "Maryknoll guerrilla priests" for more than three weeks. The coverage then continued for two months.[64] High-ranking Guatemalan ministers, including the vice president and the former secretary of information, condemned the congregation. The kidnapping of the Guatemalan archbishop in mid-March displaced Maryknoll from the front pages, though one theory held "adherents of the Maryknoll fathers who were expelled from Guatemala" were responsible.[65]

The episode drew attention outside Guatemala as well. Mexico's dailies featured front-page photos of brothers Tom and Art, with one headline proclaiming, "Guerrilla Priests Hiding in Mexico."[66] U.S. papers, including the

Baltimore Sun, Washington Post, and *Chicago Tribune,* covered the story, and the *New York Times* mentioned the Melvilles in an editorial criticizing the Alliance for Progress.[67]

Although a year later the Melville incident was out of the news, the episode led many conservative Latin American and U.S. Catholics to see Maryknoll as troublemakers, or even guerrilla fighters. In January 1969, the Maryknoll regional superior noted that Guatemalans no longer discussed the incident and Maryknoll would "go along alright" unless there was another issue. He still believed, however, that the government would "be keeping an eye" on Maryknoll. He posited, correctly, that "any time the Church is attacked it [the incident] will be brought up."[68] In the 1980s, conservative U.S. and Salvadoran Catholics evoked the Melville incident to falsely claim the murdered Maryknoll sisters ran guns from Nicaragua to El Salvador.

The Melville incident also showcased how U.S. missionaries' experiences in Latin America led them to protest U.S. foreign policy upon their return. Less than six months after leaving Guatemala, Tom and Marjorie Melville were back in the headlines. They, along with seven other Catholics, burned 378 draft files with homemade napalm outside a draft board in Catonsville, Maryland. Although the act by the "Catonsville Nine" became known as an anti–Vietnam War protest led by Fathers Daniel Berrigan and Philip Berrigan, such a characterization overshadowed the group's other members and broader message.[69] Three were former Maryknollers who served in Guatemala. Tom and Marjorie Melville wanted to primarily protest "not Vietnam but U.S. military interference in Guatemala."[70] James Hogan sought to condemn the Guatemalan government and "the marriage of U.S. economic imperialism to exploitative native oligarchies."[71]

The Catonsville Nine pushed for justice in the church and in U.S. foreign and domestic policy.[72] The draft board the group targeted was housed in a Knights of Columbus hall. As reporters watched the protesters burn the draft files, Tom said, "Our church has failed to act officially." Therefore, individual Catholics needed "to speak out in the name of Catholicism and Christianity." The group hoped to "inspire other people who have Christian principles to act accordingly to stop the terrible destruction that America is wreaking on the whole world." He noted, "Not only are we killing people through violent physical war, but we are also killing them through the extension of our economic-political empire. Let us pray for all those people that are dying from hunger and starvation throughout the world so that Americans can have a higher standard of living." The group then held hands and recited the Our Father.[73] In referring to the U.S. government as "we," Tom invited his listeners to assess their own complicity.

Catholic pacifists like Dorothy Day criticized the group's use of violence, while conservative Catholics condemned the behavior. Conservatives saw the protest as proof that Vatican II reforms had gone too far, echoing critiques of Catholics' participation in the civil rights movement. Some said the Berrigans engaged in behavior inappropriate for priests. As one working-class Boston Catholic noted, Phil Berrigan "should go back to being a *priest*, and stop this political agitation business." Another proposed the Berrigans had been "brainwashed."[74] In the long term, however, the Catonsville Nine's actions introduced a "new cultural identity" for Catholics. As the epitome of "good Catholics"—religious and former missionaries—the group challenged a government that was acting unjustly. No longer was the good Catholic about "respect for law and order and an unhesitating support of U.S. foreign and military policy."[75] Just as the Melville incident exposed divides over what it meant to be a Catholic missionary, the response to the Catonsville Nine exposed divides over what it meant to be a U.S. Catholic.

The Church in Latin America

As some U.S. Catholics, like the Melvilles, reconsidered their relationship to the poor and the powerful, the Latin American bishops discussed these issues as well. Pope Paul VI's 1967 *Populorum Progressio* (On the Development of Peoples) was the first encyclical to specifically address Third World problems. The pope condemned development's singular focus on eradicating poverty. Instead, he argued, development should mean "building a world where every person, no matter what his race, religion, or nationality, can live a fully human life, freed from servitude imposed on him by other men or by natural forces over which he has not sufficient control."[76] Latin American developments also affected the bishops. Latin Americans began to contemplate how societal and international structural inequalities contributed to poverty. Professors and university students, inspired by the Cuban Revolution, applied Marxist analysis to the study of poverty.[77] Small groups called Christian base communities encouraged members to *conscientization*, a process of self-reflection in which people develop an awareness that their situation is not fated but due to human-created societal structures of injustice.[78]

In the fall of 1968, the Second General Conference of CELAM (Latin American Episcopal Church) met in Medellín, Colombia, to adapt Vatican II's findings to their countries. In their concluding documents, the Latin American bishops stood with the poor over the powerful. The bishops condemned "institutionalized violence" as oppressing the majority of people, and they targeted both domestic and foreign social institutions as perpetuating inequality, poverty, and injustice.[79] To address the situation, the bishops supported a "preferential option for the poor," which meant not simply working to alleviate poverty but also recognizing unequal social systems and seeking to transform them. The bishops proposed that people be liberated from oppression through *conscientization*.[80]

In condemning institutionalized violence, the bishops rejected modernization, the dominant theory of development, and implicitly critiqued U.S. economic influence. Modernization theory, which regarded countries as on a single path of development, inspired the Alliance for Progress. By contrast, the Medellín statements reflected dependency theory, which held that dominant global powers used economic influence to subordinate the region. Latin America's few exports depended on prices set in international markets, allowing foreign investors and local elites to control the economic and political structures. This dependency stifled the region's economic growth as imports outpaced exports, and it fostered coups because authoritarian governments could impose tough economic measures international creditors required. Dependency theorists focused on international actors' influence, especially that of the United States.[81] In echoing dependency theory, the Latin American bishops critiqued both the powerful of Latin America and the United States.

The bishops' stance was nothing short of revolutionary. As Nicaraguan Jesuit Fernando Cardenal explained, before Medellín "my concept of sin was something exclusively personal. I had never seen the concept of sin applied to a social and economic situation."[82] The bishops' move had far-reaching impacts, as Latin American Catholics sought new ways of pursuing change rather than simply following the old path of "Catholic political parties and trade unions."[83] Drawing inspiration from the Medellín documents, in December 1968, the Golconda group, composed of nearly fifty clergy from Colombia, Argentina, and Ecuador, called for "a revolution which will overthrow the ruling classes of our country, through whom our foreign dependence is maintained."[84]

Conservative Catholics, however, saw a worldwide communist attempt to divide the church, and many blamed Vatican II. One Catholic, writing in French, alleged that postconciliar changes facilitated the establishment of a "parallel doctrinal authority" through which communists sought "the integral subversion of the Catholic Church." As evidence, the author noted that after the council, progressives dominated the church, the agitation of clergy—the "principal agent for revolutionary subversion"—began, and an international network of religious reporters and information and action centers started to corrupt Catholic language by giving it a communist meaning.[85] After a parish moved an altar so that the priest could face the people, conservative Argentine Catholics alleged that "violence and destruction" described how Vatican II's mandates were being instituted, and they charged they were "part of a 'massive conversion of man to communism.'"[86] Meanwhile, members of Tradition, Family, and Property (TFP) in Brazil, Argentina, Chile, and Uruguay condemned what they regarded as communist infiltration and called on the pope to "purge" the church. TFP, started in Brazil in 1960, soon spread to the United States, Canada, and Europe. For TFP members, communism threatened "elite rule, private property, the status quo, and Catholicism."[87] In Brazil and later Chile, TFP supported right-wing dictatorships. In the late 1960s, conservative Brazilian Catholics "regularly sprayed churches with machine-gun fire and daubed with slogans condemning alleged Communist infiltration." In 1969, a right-wing paramilitary death squad left Father Antonio Henrique Pereira Neto dangling from a tree after riddling his body with bullets and cutting his throat. Pereira, a sociology professor and youth worker, had criticized the regime.[88] To conservative Catholics, nothing less than the fate of the country and the Catholic Church was at stake.

The U.S. Government

The U.S. government was slow to share these conservative Catholic concerns and continued to promote Catholics as cowarriors on the anticommunist front lines. In 1967, the United States Information Agency (USIA) distributed comic books featuring the Catholic Church as U.S. ally. In *Arriba Muchachos*, university student Timoteo abandons his communist ideals and learns that nonviolent change facilitated by the Alliance for Progress is the best way to work for social justice (figure 1). Initially, an angry Timoteo, dressed in a red shirt and pants to convey his communist sympathies, promotes strikes to bring about revolution. Taking a different approach, Alliance supporters work with local people to expand a store. Rejecting charges that they are imperialists, the university students explain that the Alliance for Progress is the spark that brings everyone together. After Timoteo unsuccessfully bombs the completed project, he realizes the error of his ways. Timoteo asks for forgiveness before a church and congratulates everyone on the new project. By adopting the Alliance's approach, Timoteo rejects communism, accepts the church, and gets the girl.[89]

Even the Melville incident later that year did not shake the U.S. government's public portrayal of Catholics as U.S. Cold War allies. The Alliance for Progress's public information office downplayed the episode as an aberration

FIGURE 1.   From *Arriba Muchachos*, USIA, May 1967, NARA.

by highlighting Maryknoll's positive contributions. The office noted: "Controversy aside, Maryknoll's 26 years of widespread and diverse missionary programs in Latin America are representative of the important work being done by a number of church-related organizations in this hemisphere in harmony with alliance goals."[90]

Behind the scenes, however, U.S. officials acknowledged that the Melville incident compromised American support for U.S.-Guatemalan policy, and they divided over how to proceed. The U.S. ambassador to Guatemala complained that "frustrated priests" (a reference to the Melvilles), among other factors, such as the "present frame of mind of the people in the U.S., the frustrations over Viet-Nam, and the general attitude toward the administration," were turning Americans against U.S. support for Guatemala's antiterror campaign. Nevertheless, Ambassador Mien advised against inducing the Guatemalan army to end its clandestine operations because the army had the "enemy on the defensive." He worried that a change in U.S. policy vis-à-vis the army might suggest the United States "changed our position . . . no longer support[ed] the government and . . . disapprove[d] of its security measures," or "no longer opposed the cause of the guerrillas." Additionally, people might believe the change resulted from the Melville incident, giving further credence to the Maryknollers' position.[91] Six months after the memo, Guatemalan guerrillas kidnapped and then murdered Mien.

By contrast, another State Department official argued the incident provided an opportunity to reconsider an ill-advised approach. Viron "Pete" Vaky, formerly second-in-command of the Guatemalan embassy, contended that the priests' decision to adopt radical means illustrated the profound anger Guatemala's policies provoked. While it was debatable whether the priests were naive—Vaky spoke only of priests—he insisted "one should not discount the depth of the emotion and the significance of the reaction." Guatemala's "brutal" counterterror tactics "blurred" the line between communist and noncommunist in many people's minds and instead "convert[ed] it into an issue of morality and justice." Vaky argued that Guatemala's approach posed a political liability for the United States in Latin America and at home. For these reasons, the United States should reconsider its policies and stop deluding itself regarding its role. As he insisted, "We *have* condoned counter-terror; we may even in effect have encouraged or blessed it. We have been so obsessed with the fear of insurgency that we have rationalized away our qualms and uneasiness. . . . Murder, torture and mutilation are all right if our side is doing it and the victims are Communists."[92] Scholars often cite Vaky's memo as evidence that a State Department official questioned U.S.–Latin America policy.[93] It also reveals the Melville incident's high profile in government circles.

If U.S. leaders were not worried about revolutionary Catholics, Colombia's president insisted they should be. In a June 1969 meeting with President Richard Nixon, President Carlos Lleras Restrepo explained that Latin America faced "two radical trends": communism and "revolutionary priests and even bishops." Both groups linked ideas about social change to anti-U.S. views, namely charges of U.S. imperialism. Lleras warned that radical priests posed a potential danger because their "simple, unsophisticated" ideas about economics could easily be conveyed to the masses.[94]

In elaborating the next day, Lleras explained that subversive clergy held anti-U.S. views and some (Maryknollers) were also Americans. Both clergy and Marxists spoke of "imperialism" and "capitalist exploitation." Colombia's foreign minister added that some clergy adopted violent, revolutionary means, and Lleras noted that these included foreign missionaries, namely Maryknoll priests. The Colombian president concluded there might not be communist infiltration, but a "convergence of discontent, slowness in reform and desire to improve things which led the churchmen to simplistic thinking and to sympathy with the simplistic scapegoats the extremists suggested."[95]

Maryknoll was the only congregation Lleras named, suggesting the Melville incident's notoriety among Latin Americans, or at the very least, the Colombian president's attempt to show how U.S. clergy fostered instability in Latin America. Lleras's eagerness to blame foreigners was not without merit, as U.S. Catholic missionaries in Latin America grew 2,400 to 3,4000—an increase of nearly 42 percent—from 1960 to 1968.[96] In Argentina alone, 25.3 percent were foreigners in 1968.[97] Yet while Colombian representatives pointed to U.S. clergy's involvement in revolutionary activities, they did not cite their own "guerrilla priest" Camilo Torres or the Golconda Group. Lleras also did not mention how, just months before, the country expelled Spanish Jesuit Domingo Laín, a Golconda member. Lleras told the Colombian people that Laín allegedly worked to obtain weapons and supplies for nascent guerrilla groups.[98] Lleras may have emphasized Maryknollers' role to grab Nixon's attention and solicit U.S. assistance. The U.S. president was likely more open to Lleras's charges of radicalism within the clergy given U.S. priests' and nuns' involvement in antiwar protests, including at Catonsville.

Lleras's charges led Nixon to request three government reports. First, Nixon called on the State Department to analyze what led some Catholics "to become radical."[99] Second, at the administration's first National Security meeting on Latin America, Nixon raised his doubts that the Catholic Church was a force for stability and he asked the CIA to study the issue.[100] The president wanted a "country-by-country analysis" of the church's role, its leaders, and current trends. He also ordered an assessment of the role and importance of both "foreign clergy and non-Catholic groups and missionaries."[101] Finally, the president requested Nelson Rockefeller investigate the church's role in Latin America as part of his evaluation of U.S.–Latin America policy,[102] which the governor had begun six months earlier.[103]

The State Department, CIA, and Rockefeller did not agree on whether revolutionary trends in the church posed a problem for the United States. The State Department's report, submitted under contract by the RAND Corporation, downplayed radical trends and argued that anti-U.S. sentiment was less about the United States per se; it reflected Catholic teaching and Latin America's colonial past. RAND authors concluded that Camilo Torres and the Melvilles were outliers who demonstrated "the unrest within the Church and the limits of its political radicalization." Additionally, Latin American Catholics were wary of "foreign" influence on the church. Many associated foreign clergy with colonial and neocolonial practices. Some Latin Americans considered U.S. Catholics in Latin America to be "unwitting agents of U.S. imperialism" and an attempt by the U.S. church to impose its "brand of Catholicism."[104] The State Department report echoed Illich's warnings against U.S. missionaries acting as colonial agents for the church and being regarded as U.S. government accomplices.

In its report, the CIA warned that if Catholics turned to revolutionary means, those might be directed toward the United States. The agency concluded that progressives' influence was "irreversible," though conservative forces still held power. The CIA cautioned that if frustrated by their inability to bring about societal change, progressives and "radical churchmen" might turn to "increasingly disruptive" means. The agency argued these changes held implications for the United States because progressives blamed "foreign domination" for impeding Latin America's economic development. According to the CIA, progressives would likely view the United States as the "principal scapegoat" in this regard.[105]

The *Rockefeller Report*, by contrast, characterized revolutionary change as a positive movement the institutional church led. The publicly released report noted that the Catholic Church and the military—two pillars of the status quo—were "moving rapidly to the forefront as forces for social, economic, and political change." Associated with the government since the conquest and later with the powerful, the Catholic Church was now "more responsive to the popular will." The report concluded that the church was "a force dedicated to change—revolutionary change if necessary" and cited the Latin American bishops' statement at Medellín. In describing the church's new outlook, the report stressed the church's good intentions but warned that naiveté made it "vulnerable to subversive penetration."[106]

Although none of the reports determined that radical trends in the church were inevitable, Nixon concluded that a strong Marxist current existed in the Latin American church. Meeting with several advisors in the spring of 1971, Nixon described himself as "the strongest pro-Catholic who is not a Catholic" and noted that one-third of Latin American Catholics were Marxists. Nixon referred to "the deterioration of the attitude of the Catholic Church" but welcomed the U.S. church's decision "finally . . . [to] condemn . . . an awful lot of Catholics in Latin America and everyplace else."[107]

U.S. religious protesters' alleged associations with communists abroad may have affected Nixon's assessment. The president made the comments months after six people, including Josephite Phil Berrigan, were indicted for plotting to kidnap Secretary of State Henry Kissinger and blow up federal buildings, and *Time*, which a decade earlier had featured Mother Columba, showcased the Berrigan brothers—"rebel priests"—on its cover.[108] Additionally, the U.S.

government continued to hear that priests with alleged communist ties threatened government stability. In 1970, Imelda Marcos, the Philippines' first lady, charged that Catholic laity and clergy who supported socialist movements aligned with communists to back opposition candidates. If the United States did not financially assist her husband in the upcoming elections, she argued, these church-chosen candidates would be elected and the country would move toward either socialism or communism.[109]

Chile and the CIA

Conservative Catholics' worries about ties between Catholics and socialists, even communists, became reality after Salvador Allende's 1970 election in Chile. The U.S. government had long opposed Allende. In 1964, it aided his opponent, Eduardo Frei, a Christian Democrat. In cooperation with the Christian Democrats and the Catholic Church, the CIA warned that an Allende victory would bring communism to the country. Through its Scare Campaign, the CIA funded propaganda, including posters and radio and television ads. U.S. officials believed the democratic election of an "avowed Marxist" might lead other countries down the same path and would compromise U.S. policy in the region. Allende lost, with the United States spending more per Chilean voter than the two U.S. presidential contenders—Lyndon B. Johnson and Barry Goldwater—did per U.S. voter that year. In 1970, the CIA again ran the Scare Campaign,[110] but Allende won a plurality with 36.6 percent.[111]

Though the church hierarchy promoted Frei's cause in concert with the U.S. government, not all Catholics believed Allende posed a danger. After the 1970 election, eighty priests (Los Ochenta) declared their support for the government and worked to end the "mistrust" between Christians and communists. This task required no longer seeing communism as "intrinsically evil," or conversely, religion as the opiate of the people. Even more controversial, Fidel Castro met with the group and said: "I tell you without hesitation: we see revolutionary Christians as strategic allies of the revolution. Not fellow-travellers—nothing of that sort . . . we have to construct socialism with revolutionary Christians. Without Christians any revolution in Latin America will be partial."[112] By that time—December 1971—Los Ochenta included women and Protestant members and called itself Christians for Socialism (Cristianos por el Socialismo, or CpS). Castro's call for cooperation and his blessing fueled fears that Catholics were welcoming communists into the church.

Four months later, in April 1972, four hundred Christians from twenty-six countries, including those from North America and Europe, held the first CpS international meeting in Chile and expressed their desire to establish socialism in Latin America and abroad.[113] The group's manifesto asserted that socialism was the only Christian way and that Christians were obligated to participate in the revolutionary process. The church needed to endorse class struggle; otherwise, there could be no unity within the church. CpS urged closer cooperation between socialism and Catholicism and the creation of a new, less institutionalized church.[114]

A handful of Maryknollers were involved with CpS and the promotion of Allende's socialist project abroad. Five Maryknoll priests, including Charles Curry and John Wiggins, attended the CpS April 1972 meeting. Curry and Wiggins's home served as a gathering place for Leftist activists and church workers as well as the headquarters for the Missioners' Committee on International Awareness, later renamed the Project for Awareness and Action: U.S. Christians in Chile (PARA). Curry, former Maryknoller Margaret Schuler, Methodist pastor Joseph Eldridge, and Patricia Ahern led the ecumenical group of U.S. Christians that promoted Chilean socialism to their home communities.[115]

As part of its efforts, PARA challenged U.S. business and government actions in Chile. In 1971, after the Chilean legislature certified Allende as president, seventy Catholic and six Methodist missionaries wrote President Nixon asking that the United States not interfere in Chile, but instead allow the country to "work out its own destiny." The next year, the group wrote the International Telephone and Telegraph (ITT) president after U.S. press reports claimed the company and the CIA considered initiating a military coup to prevent Allende's election. The missionaries condemned ITT's "plotting" to "decide Chile's future, or that of any sovereign people."[116] They also sent a letter to Nixon disapproving of U.S. policies hostile to Chile and of ITT/CIA ties.[117] Six months later, in a widely circulated letter, PARA implored U.S. Christian leaders, on the basis of the Gospel, to pressure Nixon not to interfere with Chile.[118]

Unlike the Melvilles, PARA did not advocate violence, but its stance was controversial. By supporting Allende, a man the United States worked to keep from the Chilean presidency, the missionaries opposed U.S. policy. After Allende's election and before his certification by the legislature, the Nixon administration attempted to bribe Chilean legislators not to certify the election results. When this failed, the CIA supplied guns and money to sympathetic military and strove to create "a coup climate" by generating "a sense of political crisis and confrontation" and by destabilizing the economy.[119]

To those already critical of Maryknollers' "communist sympathies" after the Melville incident, the missionaries' position added another log to the fire.

Although seventy-six missionaries protested U.S. policies, the *Washington Post* and the *New York Times* mentioned one individual by name—Maryknoller Charles Curry, suggesting either that Maryknollers led these critiques or that they were the only ones involved. But Maryknollers like Curry were the minority in critiquing U.S. policy until Allende's overthrow on September 11, 1973, just months after the Watergate hearings began. In the wake of General Augusto Pinochet's installation as president, the government arrested 50,000 people and engaged in torture and summary executions. Under Pinochet, Chile murdered 3,197 of its own citizens and detained an estimated 100,000–150,000 political prisoners.[120] The coup and subsequent events led many Maryknollers to question U.S. Cold War policy.

In a less confrontational manner than PARA, Maryknoller Ita Ford challenged the idea that Pinochet saved the church and nation from communism. She highlighted how the government was turning on Catholics. In letters to family and friends, Ford invited her recipients to question what a communist threat was by describing her experience in La Bandera, a *población* of seventy thousand to eighty thousand people surrounding Santiago. Ford had arrived in Chile in the spring of 1973. Just weeks after the coup, she wrote: "Try to imagine a company of approximately one hundred soldiers and about two dozen FBI [Federal Bureau of Investigation] agents surrounding a working class neighborhood of two thousand families at dawn. No one may enter or leave." Ford highlighted how the state threatened to tear families apart: "Try to imagine the children frightened by the soldiers with machine guns standing at the corners and accompanying the FBI men to each house. Some begin to cry, 'Daddy, don't let them take you away.'" Even Chileans' reading materials were scrutinized, Ford explained. "Try to imagine the FBI entering your home to do a thorough search without any reason given. One has an iron pipe in his hand. Imagine having the contents of your bookshelves evaluated, book by book, for their approval." The soldiers searched Ford's home three times, she revealed. But she and her neighbors withstood the "arbitrary 'fishing expeditions' and organized terror" through a shared concern and "deep faith . . . in a God who cares for his people."[121]

Ford's work with Chilean refugees led her to see U.S. policy as hypocritical. In a late November 1973 letter to Senator Edward Kennedy (D-MA), she and another Maryknoll sister pointed to the contradiction between U.S. offers of refuge for Chileans and the visa application required for entrance. Applicants feared the information they provided would be used to target their friends and relatives. Additionally, the way the information was solicited could disqualify applicants who appeared to be "subversives" or "agitators" likely to work against the U.S. government. As the sisters asked Kennedy, "Does the United States consider the plight of the refugees serious enough to make the humane offer of refuge?" As matters stood, "those in less serious circumstances, and with the possibility of several options, will be the only ones eligible for our hospitality." As the women wondered, "Is that what we really want to convey to the people of Latin America?"[122]

By 1974, Ita Ford was not alone in questioning the moral implications of U.S.-Chilean policy. The Maryknoll Sisters, along with other Christian missionary groups, declared their opposition to U.S. meddling. In October 1974, leadership of U.S. Catholic and Protestant groups, including Maryknoll, protested all CIA interference.[123] In a letter to President Ford, they explained that based on their time in countries subject to these interventions, CIA actions did not benefit the "majority of the citizens." Instead, "CIA covert actions in the Third World frequently support undemocratic governments which trample on the rights of their own people." Such "gangster methods undermine world order and promote widespread hatred of the United States." Ultimately, the missionaries asserted, these CIA actions were "blatantly incompatible with the ideals we hold as Americans and Christians."[124] The sisters also sent a separate letter to Ford, described earlier, which revealed how, prompted by U.S. covert action in Chile, Maryknollers' questioning of U.S. Cold War policy on moral grounds had grown from a few, such as the Melvilles, to many.

Although foreign press, including that in Mexico and Kenya, covered missionaries' objections,[125] the U.S. secular press did not pay them much heed, and the Ford administration did not respond.[126] The press only took up the story with the publication of two books.[127] In *Inside the Company*, former agent Philip Agee described CIA methods and named 250 CIA agents.[128] *The CIA and the Cult of Intelligence* outlined CIA influence over International Catholic Student and Catholic Action as well as collaboration with the U.S. Agency for International Development (USAID) and through USAID, missionary groups.[129] "Catholic and Protestant mission agencies" received U.S. government supplies and "unwittingly provided information to the CIA" in the process.[130] Exposés like these heightened missionaries' concerns about the separation of church and state, how the cloud of suspicion endangered their safety and credibility, and "the morality of using persons as unwitting accomplices."[131]

In the midst of these debates, Maryknollers in Bolivia disassociated themselves from the U.S. embassy. In May 1975, they canceled U.S. ambassador William P. Stedman Jr.'s talk. Maryknollers had invited him to speak at their annual meeting because of their growing concern that U.S. foreign policy was compromising their work. But Stedman had brought an unannounced guest:

John LaMazza. Though listed as a labor official attached to the U.S. embassy, LaMazza had been described as "very helpful" in CIA efforts to provide "information about certain priests" as part of Bolivia's Banzer Plan.[132]

Named for Bolivia's president Hugo Banzer, the plan advised the military to crack down on Catholic activists but "never attack the Church as an institution." The military was to focus "above all" on foreign clergy. As the plan explained: "Insist continuously that they are preaching armed warfare; that they are connected with international communism and have been sent to Bolivia with the exclusive goal of moving the Church toward communism." To avoid public perception that there was "systematic persecution," the plan advised the military to "maintain a friendly relationship with some bishops," Catholics, and "native priests." State forces should arrest priests "on the outskirts on rarely used streets, or late at night" and "plant subversive materials" in their belongings or home (a weapon if possible) and prepare a story to disgrace them. The plan said the CIA "promised" to provide "information about certain priests." A Bolivian government minister leaked an edited version of the plan to *Justicia y Pax* (Justice and Peace) of South America.[133] The plan circulated within Latin America and the United States, appearing in San Salvador's *Orientación* and the U.S. *National Catholic Reporter*.[134]

The Banzer Plan was not unusual. To conservative Latin American Catholics, any leadership training or grassroots organizing was subversive. Anyone involved in these efforts was a Marxist or, minimally, being used by communists. Under the 1972 Bilateral Intelligence Agreement, the Argentine and Paraguayan militaries agreed to contain threats to "the military, political, economic and/or psychological power" of South America, namely student groups and Third World Priests, which advocated a position between capitalism and communism.[135] In 1974 and 1975, congresses of the Latin American Anticommunist Federation meeting in Brazil and Nicaragua warned of the "subversive action of the clergy." The 1977 congress in Paraguay pledged to support "Christian anticommunist governments" and clergy working against communist infiltration attempts and to financially support priests "deprived of work or marginalized" because they resisted "Marxist tactics." They also resolved to ask Latin American governments to keep the Vatican informed of infiltration and to intercede on behalf of clergy "unjustly removed from their activities." The group vowed to "send pledges of support, confidence and solidarity" to those who worked to preserve "our Western democratic Christian civilization," namely "Christian anticommunist governments of Latin America."[136]

Knowing of LaMazza's connection to the Banzer Plan, Maryknollers voted against allowing him inside. The ambassador refused to speak alone, and the two men left.[137] After the incident, Maryknoller Charles Curry wrote to Senate Intelligence Committee Chair Frank Church (D-ID), describing what happened and enclosing a copy of the Banzer Plan. Curry stressed that the incident was not isolated, and he encouraged the senator to investigate it as part of his committee's inquiry into "the many questionable facets of CIA activity."[138]

Maryknollers in Bolivia were not the only ones trying to break CIA ties. In July 1975, Maryknoll Sisters President Barbara Hendricks, a woman elected by her fellow sisters rather than appointed, wrote to CIA Director William Colby condemning the CIA's use of missionaries. As she explained, missionaries had not been immune from Third Worlders' suspicions that the CIA had infiltrated "all phases of their society." CIA activities were "wholly inconsistent" with missionaries' purposes; therefore, Maryknollers "categorically denounce any involvement conscious or unconscious" with the CIA, either past or future.[139]

But to Colby, missionaries who worked with the CIA were true Catholics and patriots. "As a practicing Catholic and one who personally knew a number of missionaries in various situations around the world I find no basis for 'shame and disappointment' with respect to their role." Instead, "I have had the highest regard for the moral integrity and patriotism of these missionaries."[140] As the Hendricks-Colby exchange highlighted, Catholics disagreed over missionaries' relationship to the U.S. Cold War project. These differences grew in importance as Catholics both shaped U.S. policy from within the government, like Colby, and challenged it, as Maryknollers did.

While the U.S. government saw missionaries who worked with the CIA as patriotic, missionaries struggled to determine how to situate themselves vis-à-vis both the U.S. government and those they served abroad. The same month Hendricks wrote to Colby, Curry organized Protestant and Catholic mission-sending groups to discuss the matter and the "possibility of issuing a joint statement." The group proposed formulating a code of ethics, and their brainstorming questions reflected the group's uncertainty. What "rights and responsibilities" did they have to the two governments? What was the relationship of mission to human rights? Were covert activities good or bad?[141]

To some Maryknollers, it was not enough to condemn CIA activities; they began outing CIA agents. Two Maryknollers "reportedly" alerted *Counter-Spy* magazine that a Peruvian newspaper identified Richard Welch as a CIA officer.[142] The CIA station chief was later murdered in Athens.[143] In the summer of 1976, eleven Maryknoll priests in Bolivia released CIA agents' names to warn other missionaries the agency was using Maryknollers for its own ends.[144] At the time, Maryknollers were among many naming suspected agents in Western Europe, Africa, and Australia. By the end of 1978, Agee and his copycats had published an estimated one thousand names of CIA officers worldwide.[145] For Maryknoll, what began in the early 1970s as condemnation of CIA activity in Latin America grew into a refusal to cooperate with the agency and, eventually, attempts to hamper the CIA's work.

Critiques of Maryknoll

Maryknollers' counterspying received little U.S. attention.[146] Conservative U.S. Catholics focused on communist infiltration of the church. They saw Maryknoll as the problem and argued that instead of using their international connections to evangelize around the globe, Maryknollers employed those channels to spread anti-American ideals and Marxist trends. One woman asked to be removed as a *Maryknoll* subscriber in 1973 because "every time I read it I become more provoked at the anti-American sentiment in most of the articles. I'm very happy to be a citizen of capitalist America. If it weren't for this country, the rest of the world would have collapsed long ago."[147]

It was not just perceived anti-U.S. views some Catholics saw as problematic. Conservative U.S. Catholics also denounced liberation theology and Maryknoll's support for it. Maryknoll introduced many Americans to liberation theology through its publishing house Orbis, formally launched in 1970 to produce books on Catholic thought. Orbis was rooted in the Medellín conference and Maryknoll director of social communications Father Miguel d'Escoto's push for a religious publishing house that magnified "the voices of the church in the Third World."[148] By enlisting Third World theologians as authors, Orbis was revolutionary.[149] One priest and former expert for the U.S. Catholic Conference of Bishops contended that Orbis's contribution to the church and society rivaled, if not surpassed, that of Maryknollers abroad. "Without in any way denigrating the importance of Maryknoll's explicitly apostolic work in the foreign mission, I, for one, would be prepared to argue that, in terms of long-range significance, its sponsorship and continuing support of Orbis ranks near the very top of the list of Maryknoll's very enviable contributions to Church and society." Without Orbis, he doubted Catholics would have learned about topics such as liberation theology.[150]

Orbis gained attention in 1973 with its English translation of Peruvian Gustavo Gutiérrez's *Teología de la liberación*.[151] The book became Orbis's best seller, putting the publishing house on the map, and tethering it to a controversial Christian current.[152] Orbis was the primary U.S. source of liberationist literature.[153] As Robert Ellsberg, Orbis director beginning in 1987, explained, "Liberation theology didn't just introduce a few new books for the shelf, but it called into question *all* the books on the shelf. It offered a challenge to rich, privileged, powerful Christians, a call to conversion, an invitation to see from the eyes of the poor." Ellsberg was no stranger to controversy, having been named, at age thirteen, as coconspirator for helping his father Daniel copy the Pentagon Papers.[154]

Conservative U.S. Catholics criticized Maryknoll for spreading liberation theology instead of the Gospel. An editorialist in the traditionalist *Wanderer* railed against church figures that failed to condemn liberation theology after a 1976 Gustavo Gutiérrez talk in Denver. Even worse, he proclaimed, Maryknoll promoted "the works of the 'liberationists.'"[155] Similarly, a Jesuit argued that U.S. Catholics needed "to do battle" against the arrival of "heterodox imports from Latin America" and noted that Maryknoll already published similar "propaganda" through Orbis.[156] The militarist language revealed that conservative U.S. Catholics like these saw liberation theology's growth as a threatening challenge to the U.S. church, especially given Latin America's proximity.

Conservative U.S. Catholics worried that Latin American developments like liberation theology were infecting the church worldwide. In the mid-1970s, the conservative U.S. Catholic press condemned attempts at dialogue between Marxists and Christians. Readers of the *Wanderer* and the *National Catholic Register* learned that communist infiltration of the church posed a global threat, and throughout 1976, the *Wanderer* reported that bishops in Italy, France, and Portugal sought to counter Marxism and the Communist Party in their countries.[157] To these conservative Catholics, Maryknoll was part of a larger problem.

In the 1950s, Maryknollers, especially those martyred for the faith in Asia, were the model anticommunist, Cold War Americans. They were Senator McCarthy's darlings. But beginning in the 1960s, missionaries began to question, and challenge, U.S. foreign policy. During their time in Latin America, missionaries witnessed U.S. policy's impact on Latin America, and they were exposed to changing ideas within the Latin American church. These experiences led many to reconsider their role as Catholics, as missionaries, and as Americans. For some, a new understanding of mission emerged. Others, such as the Melvilles, proposed a more radical approach. Maryknollers' doubts over anticommunist government policies increasingly led them to challenge unequal societal structures and U.S. foreign policy. Conservative U.S. and Latin American Catholics, disturbed by these developments and their association with Vatican II, condemned Maryknollers and other foreign missionaries. The U.S. government, especially under Nixon, began to wonder if Catholics still shared U.S. Cold War goals.

During the late 1970s, Catholics' disagreements over liberation theology and Marxism intensified as Central America grew more volatile. U.S. Catholics' understanding of their church's role in the world shaped how they viewed developments in Central America. As the region garnered more U.S. attention, Maryknoll played a key role in shaping U.S. Catholics' views of Central America and of U.S. policy. In doing so, Maryknoll increasingly came to the attention of non-Catholic U.S. officials and other conservatives.

CHAPTER 2

Religious or Political Activists for Nicaragua?

In June 1977, Representative John M. Murphy (D-NY), speaking on the floor of the House of Representatives, questioned Maryknoll Father Miguel d'Escoto's status as a priest. D'Escoto, Murphy argued, was "simply a political activist in sheep's clothing" who supported communist revolutionaries' attempts to overthrow Anastasio Somoza, the U.S. ally whose family had governed Nicaragua since 1936.[1] For Murphy, a devout Catholic who according to his sister, "lived his faith, and saw to it that everyone who came into his circle did also,"[2] the priest's involvement in Nicaraguan political discussions was irksome. Even worse was d'Escoto's challenge to Somoza, Murphy's friend from military prep school and West Point.[3] While any threat to his friend may have bothered him, Murphy's focus on d'Escoto revealed Maryknoll's prominence in transnational Catholic disagreements over U.S.-Nicaragua policy and the key role religious figures played in shaping them.

Whereas conservative U.S. Catholics in the late 1960s and 1970s bemoaned some Maryknollers' opposition to Latin American governments and support for socialist ideas, as this chapter argues, by the later 1970s, conservative non-Catholics in the United States adopted these concerns as well. Maryknollers' leadership in opposing Nicaraguan president Somoza was the reason why. Though Father Miguel d'Escoto became the focus of attention, the Maryknoll congregation collectively opposed Somoza. It marked a shift from the 1960s and early 1970s when individuals, such as the Melvilles or Charles Curry, took controversial stances. Maryknollers' involvement in Nicaragua debates reflected larger shifts in what it meant to be a Catholic missionary and showed the growing strength of religious witness in the name of human rights.

The Somozas

Though U.S. attention turned toward Nicaragua in the late 1970s, U.S. involvement in the country, characterized by sporadic military invasions, had begun over one hundred years earlier. In 1855 U.S. filibuster William Walker and fifty-seven U.S. mercenaries entered Nicaragua. Remembered today by many Nicaraguans as the beginning of U.S. intervention, Liberal Nicaraguan elites had hired Walker to defeat their Conservative rivals. But Walker soon became an unwanted guest as he gained control of the country and assumed the presidency. After Walker's 1858 defeat, the next nearly seventy years saw a pattern: Nicaraguan revolt or civil war and subsequent U.S. invasion. The United States sent the Marines in 1910 to support a revolt, in 1912 at Conservative elites' request, and in 1926–1927 in the midst of civil war.[4]

After the civil war, two figures that loomed large in Nicaraguan history—Augusto Sandino and Anastasio Somoza García—came to prominence. With the war's end, the United States gained the power to administer Nicaraguan elections and to establish the Guardia Nacional (National Guard), an armed force. The Guardia consolidated the state's power in rural areas, established control over elections, and assumed both police and judiciary roles. From 1927 to 1933, the Guardia and U.S. forces also fought Sandino, the only local rebel leader who did not sign the treaty ending the war. Only after U.S. troops departed in January 1933 did Sandino agree to lay down his arms. By fighting U.S. forces, he became an international icon of anti-imperialism (see figure 2). Conversely, Anastasio Somoza García became inextricably tied to U.S. power when he became Guardia head upon U.S. withdrawal. This contrast between the anti-U.S. Sandino and the U.S.-backed Somoza further cemented in 1934, when Guardia officers executed Sandino.[5]

From 1936 until 1979, the Somoza family ruled Nicaragua, using the Guardia Nacional to maintain its political power and to enrich itself and its cronies, while most Nicaraguans lived without an education and in poverty. By the 1950s, only 0.59 percent of Nicaragua's college-age population attended university. Educational attainment at lower levels remained shockingly low, despite increased school attendance. By the early 1960s, the average rural Nicaraguan received a year and a half of schooling, while those in urban areas boasted only one year more—two and a half years—on average. Among

FIGURE 2.   "Sandino Vive," León, Nicaragua, 2016. Photo by author.

countries in the Western Hemisphere, Somoza's Nicaragua bested only Haiti for education spending.[6] Economic inequality was equally appalling. The malnutrition rate for children under six doubled from 1965 to 1975. In the 1970s, the richest 5 percent of households held 30 percent of the country's income, while the bottom 50 percent of Nicaraguans held only 15 percent.[7] Even if Nicaraguans wanted to protest, the Somozas eliminated any challengers, leaving opposition anemic or nonexistent.

The Somozas were staunch U.S. allies. Anastasio Somoza allowed U.S. forces to use Nicaragua as a base for the overthrow of Guatemalan president Arbenz. After Somoza's 1956 assassination, his son Luis, a Louisiana State University graduate, assumed leadership of the country. He too allowed the United States to launch the failed 1961 Bay of Pigs invasion from Nicaragua. Beginning in 1967, Luis's brother Anastasio Somoza Debayle led the country.[8] Known affectionately as "Tachito," Somoza attended a Long Island military prep school before West Point, and later married an American. As one former U.S. ambassador remarked, "It's been said that Tachito is the only West Pointer in history to have received an army as a graduation present."[9]

Like the U.S. government, the Maryknoll Sisters were initially supporters of the Somoza family. When the sisters first arrived in Nicaragua in 1944, Somoza hosted the women at the presidential palace. Later the same week, he sent his private limo to take them to his country home to dine with his family and the U.S. ambassador. When they heard stories of the Guardia Nacional torturing, killing, and disappearing people in the 1950s, the nuns had difficulty reconciling the information with the man they knew. Their approach to mission also contributed to their blindness. The women, including Maura Clarke, taught in Siuna, a tiny village where gold miners lived in "rat-infested company houses," in contrast to the Canadian officials who enjoyed a suburban lifestyle, complete with golf courses. The women's work focused on fostering the laity's faith, not addressing the causes of societal inequalities.[10]

Growing Opposition in Nicaragua

The Somoza family faced no real political opposition in the 1960s, yet some Catholics explored options for restructuring the church that challenged the institution and, in the long term, fostered political activism. These new approaches developed as religious grappled with how to implement Vatican II. Maryknollers and Jesuits were at the forefront of these efforts in Central America.[11]

Perhaps the most revolutionary change was the development of Christian base communities (*comunidades eclesiales de base*, or CEBs), which cultivated leadership among those not traditionally looked to as leaders. Through reading, study, and discussion, CEBs led poor people to apply scripture to their lives. CEB members learned that it was not God's will for people to be poor, that God supported the oppressed, and that all people had the human right to organize and improve their lives.[12] The method grew out of the European Catholic Action slogan of "see, judge, act" and Brazilian teacher Paulo Freire's emphasis on conscientization.[13]

CEBs were radical because they envisioned an empowered role for the poor, with profound political implications. Local people created CEBs, decided their focus, such as a community improvement project, and led them, while priests and nuns served only as facilitators.[14] CEBs often led to political action by developing lay "leadership and organizing skills," by fostering a sense of collective identity, and by promoting notions of democracy, which led to questioning institutional structures and authority.[15]

Nicaragua was in "the vanguard of progressive CEB formation."[16] A priest and four Maryknoll sisters started the first Nicaraguan CEB—San Pablo Apóstol—in Managua in 1966.[17] Also in the mid-1960s, Father Ernesto Cardenal organized a CEB at Solentiname, an island on Lake Managua. Cardenal published the group's discussions in which they compared the Gospel with their lives. *The Gospel in Solentiname* served as a "road map" for other CEBs.[18]

The U.S. Capuchin Fathers also fostered leadership by training laity in the countryside to be *Delegados de la Palabra* (Delegates of the Word), or DPs. DPs led Bible-centered celebrations for communities without priests to celebrate the Eucharist. To address the clergy shortage, the Capuchins encouraged laity to assume leadership roles and, in the process, to think critically about their communities and society.[19]

Nicaraguan students asserted themselves as well, often with the assistance of religious. Just as university students in many other countries protested in the late 1960s,[20] in 1970 Nicaraguans occupied the Jesuit-run University of Central America after administrators rebuffed their demands for discussion. Then, after the Office of National Security arrested some student leaders in September, the student government and several priests, including Jesuit Fernando Cardenal (Ernesto's brother), protested via letter. Seeing no change, about a week after the arrests, Cardenal, five other priests, and nearly one hundred students occupied Managua's cathedral and began a hunger strike.[21] In support, students occupied other churches throughout the country for three days.[22] Eventually, Somoza acceded to their demand for the prisoners' release.[23]

While these protests were directed at the government, the incident also exposed divides among Catholics. Five bishops, including Managua's Miguel Obando y Bravo, denounced the occupations as political and threatened to

suspend the priests who supported them. Once Somoza released the prisoners, the controversy continued. In one letter, "several hundred" Nicaraguans
denounced the bishops' actions, and separately, Ernesto Cardenal compared
them to the Pharisees. He lectured the bishops that the church was "the
people of God," not buildings. But the bishops answered back and had their
own defenders. In the opposition paper *La Prensa*, Bishop Pablo Vega blamed
Cardenal for the critiques of the episcopacy, calling him a follower of Castro.[24] In addition, nearly two thousand Nicaraguans signed a letter in *Las
Novedades*, the Somoza-supported newspaper, siding with the bishops. According to one signer, the men took the step after Somoza asked prominent
members of *cursillos* (short courses to cultivate lay leadership that predated
CEBs) to do something to counter "the growing 'leftist' influence within the
Church, especially that emanating from the *cursillistas*."[25] Somoza's move was
unsurprising. He described all opponents, even priests, as communists, as one
priest informed the U.S. embassy.[26]

One Maryknoller's response to the protests revealed how some sisters'
thinking about the church's role in Nicaragua had changed. As Maura Clarke
wrote to her parents, the protest was "very peaceful and disciplined." She was
encouraged by the priests who stayed in the cathedral because they showed
how the church "was committed to the poor and the suffering." But she was
disheartened by the bishops who condemned the protests because they sided
"with the government against most of the people of God who stood with the
protestors."[27] Clarke's viewpoint contrasted with Maryknollers of the 1950s,
who focused on teaching and preparing communities for the sacraments, not
on societal inequalities.

Clarke's understanding of Maryknoll's role evolved along with her own
work. In 1960, at age twenty-nine, she began teaching second grade in Siuna.
As sister superior in the early 1960s, she expanded Maryknollers' role from educating girls to empowering them as leaders. The work then grew to community development. At the same time, Clarke was exposed to new ways of
Christian association through the San Pablo Apóstal CEB, which she saw develop during frequent visits to Managua.[28]

Clarke continued to expand her commitment to assisting spiritual growth
and human rights. She spent 1969 at Maryknoll in New York, where she read
the Medellín documents and protested against the Vietnam War. In 1970, she
returned to Managua, where she and others established a CEB in the Miralagos
neighborhood. Clarke also advocated for religious to support human rights
as the Maryknoll delegate to the Conference of Religious of Nicaragua (CON-
FER), an organization of nuns and priests. Clarke was careful to support Nicaraguans, not lead them. While Nicaraguans occupied the Managua cathedral

for three days leading up to Christmas Eve 1972 to demand the release of political prisoners, Clarke and the other U.S. sisters stayed away. As a Nicaraguan priest and nun insisted, Nicaraguans should make the demands; the sisters should not risk deportation and the ability to carry on their work.[29]

In the midst of the protest, an earthquake rocked Managua and changed the political landscape. After the disaster, Somoza assumed responsibility for distributing all relief supplies and gained enormous personal profit through his purchase of interests in industries involved in rebuilding, such as construction, concrete, and demolition.[30] Seeing the president enrich his coffers while others suffered led many, including members of the church hierarchy, to question the dictator. A broad-based resistance grew.

The December 1973 Mass to commemorate those killed by the earthquake demonstrated the growing rift between the church hierarchy and Somoza. Though the hierarchy began to publicly challenge the regime after 1970, Somoza's handling of the earthquake intensified those critiques. At the Mass, Managua's archbishop Obando condemned repression and called for a more equitable society. Some worshipers held anti-Somoza placards. In response, Somoza left the Mass and ordered Guardia members to unplug the speakers. He later tried to persuade the papal nuncio to remove Obando as archbishop.[31]

While the archbishop critiqued societal inequities, some Maryknoll sisters took a more confrontational stance in defense of human rights. In 1974, the Guardia Nacional arrested Amada Pineda, member of the Socialist Party and the farmworkers' union, as a subversive. They beat her, raped her seventeen times, and tortured other prisoners in front of her. Though the Guard's actions were not unusual, Pineda's were. She told La Prensa and brought a case against the perpetrators. Prompted by Sister Kay Kelly, other Maryknoll sisters, including Clarke, supported Pineda by attending the trial, even though other religious, including CONFER, refused to associate with Pineda due to her political views.[32]

Faced with this kind of state repression, more Nicaraguans grew sympathetic to the armed guerrilla movement. Founded in 1961 and named for Augusto Sandino, the Frente Sandinista de Liberación Nacional (FSLN) embarrassed the government by invading the 1974 Christmas party of a wealthy Somoza supporter and former agriculture minister, and taking government officials and Somoza family members hostage. The episode was a public relations disaster because it revealed the government's vulnerability and the public's sympathy for the rebels. After the raid, Somoza imposed a state of emergency, consisting of press censorship and Guardia crackdowns, including the brutal torture and killings of *campesinos* (peasants) in the countryside.[33]

With the imposition of martial law, Maryknollers continued to side with Nicaraguans against the government. Under the nighttime curfew, the Guardia rounded up any teenager, and groups of them were considered particularly suspicious. To protect those in Operación Permanente de Emergencia Nacional (OPEN 3) camp, sisters, including Clarke, took in the youths. Their actions prompted guardsmen to ask teens, "Why are you hanging out with Sr. Comunista?,"[34] revealing how merely offering protection placed the sisters on the wrong side of the regime.

The sisters also aligned themselves with OPEN 3 members' efforts to pursue human rights, which the women saw as linked to their work of developing Christian communities. Clarke described how CEBs fostered greater liberation: "By developing lay leaders and having them take on the responsibility of their mission in the world, the 'comunidad de base' raises man to his proper dignity and helps him to liberate himself." OPEN 3 strove "toward the integral liberation of man . . . through the development of cooperatives and by making greater efforts to 'concientizar,' to face our reality, and together do what we can united with other Christian communities to improve and change what dehumanizes man."[35]

As an outgrowth of these efforts to develop a consciousness of their surroundings, in the summer of 1976 OPEN 3's Mother's Club wrote a letter insisting the water company change its prices. The camp paid twice what the wealthy Managuan suburbs did. A subsequent meeting at Cruz Grande, the local church, drew a thousand people. The group, which was larger than just CEB members and parishioners, held demonstrations in the face of the Guardia Nacional. To counter censorship, OPEN 3 distributed its own newspaper and operated its own radio station, set up by Maryknoller Margaret "Peggy" Healy. Some engaged in an eight-day hunger strike inside the Red Cross, as others outside, including Clarke, joined in.[36] After nearly three months, water prices were reduced.[37] But to the government, the damage was done: OPEN 3 confirmed its "reputation for militancy,"[38] and by association, so did the Maryknollers living there.

Opposition in the United States

While Somoza faced opposition at home, some clergy criticized the regime through international channels. In June 1976, thirty-five U.S. Capuchins in Nicaragua sent an open letter to Somoza documenting 350 cases of northeastern campesinos that the Guardia had disappeared, tortured, or mistreated over two years.[39] "Church leaders, especially the Delegates of the Word," were often targeted as the Guard sought to eradicate all FSLN members and collaborators. The priests went public after Bishop Salvador Schlaefer, president of the Episcopal Conference, held three private conversations with Somoza that led to nothing.[40] The Capuchins' motivation to speak out, as they told Schlaefer, came from "the power of the Gospel which we preach and which we try to live with the Nicaraguan people."[41] But Somoza saw things differently. When U.S. Capuchin Evarist Bertrant attempted to return to Nicaragua, he was denied entrance because he had engaged in "subversive activities."[42]

The Capuchins were not Somoza's only problem. Representative Donald Fraser (D-MN) chaired hearings, *Human Rights in Nicaragua, Guatemala, and El Salvador: Implications for U.S. Policy.* Jesuit Fernando Cardenal's testimony reiterated what the Capuchins had documented. He described "concentration camps," torture, and rape. He explained that special forces patrolled cities "carrying machine guns and light artillery pieces." He noted the persecution of union leaders and the lack of civilian courts and freedom for the press. Cardenal pointed to the United States as the cause, contending, "what has produced the most harm to Nicaragua, is without a doubt, the constant military aid given out by the U.S. Government."[43] Nicaragua's human rights record mattered because Section 502(b) of the Foreign Assistance Act of 1961, passed in 1974, prohibited military aid to countries that engaged in a "pattern" of human rights abuses unless the president concluded U.S. national security necessitated it. Likewise, Section 116 of the act, passed in 1975, banned U.S. economic aid to countries that engaged in "gross violations" of human rights.[44]

Like the Capuchins, Cardenal explained that his priestly duties mandated that he testify. As he told Mexico City's *Excélsior*, "To work for justice is a profoundly Christian and priestly mission. The condemnation of injustice is something inherent in the preaching of the gospel. To represent the oppressed and the weak—'to be the voice of those who have no voice,' as was stated in the documents of the Latin American Episcopacy in Medellín—is a mission of the Church in Iberoamerica."[45] But Somoza and his paper *Las Novedades* did not see it that way. One editorial argued that Fernando and his brother Ernesto "use the pulpit as a platform for subversion. . . . If by day they are officiating the Sacred Ways, by night they take off the mask and act as preachers of Marxist-Leninism."[46] The paper tried to delegitimize Somoza's clerical critics by claiming they were not really priests.

Though the hearings did not change U.S. aid, Somoza's religious critics prompted the United States to quietly encourage reform. In a July meeting with Somoza, U.S. ambassador James Theberge stressed the "mounting" evidence of Guardia Nacional abuses, including the Capuchins' letter. Although some of Somoza's opponents might have alleged human rights abuses,

Theberge argued "not all of the charges could be dismissed as politically in-spired." As examples, the ambassador pointed to "the sincere concern of moderate Catholic priests and others." He explained that the United States cared about human rights violations abroad "because it runs counter to our conviction that governments draw their legitimacy from their respect for in-dividual rights and human dignity." Though Somoza agreed "human rights abuses could not be tolerated," he stressed that Cuban-supported guerrillas challenged him at home and "opposition elements, including some priests" encouraged use of the "human rights issue" abroad to destabilize his regime. He charged the Catholic Church, "or parts of it," with being "up to its ears in politics."[47]

A month later, the situation was the same. As Theberge pointed out, So-moza had not replied to the Capuchins' letter, supplied information about missing persons as the government said it would, or investigated the Guardia's behavior. The ambassador again stressed the sincerity and trustworthiness of Somoza's religious critics and the need for action. As he argued, "There was increasing criticism of moderate church groups acting out of reasons of con-science and pastoral duty, that could not be dismissed as politically-inspired or irresponsible."[48] Ultimately, there was no real pressure from the State De-partment, and few in Congress cared because Somoza faced "no serious challenge."[49]

The situation soon changed, as Somoza faced stronger opposition at home and from the U.S. Congress in 1977. On New Year's Day, the seven Nicaraguan bishops condemned "the use of humiliating and inhuman methods: tortures, rapes, and even executions without previous civil or military trials."[50] To avoid press censorship, the bishops read their message during Mass and distributed leaflets, while the Capuchins circulated the text in the United States.[51]

The bishops also condemned those who sought change through violence, highlighting the divide among religious. Although the bishops took aim at what they called "so-called liberating movements," they did not stop priests and sisters from supporting, or even joining, the guerrillas. Ernesto Cardenal declared that he and Solentiname CEB members had joined the FSLN.[52] Like-wise, Sacred Heart priest Gasper García Laviana of Spain, who lived in Nica-ragua, joined, as he explained, "as a soldier of the Lord and as a soldier of the National Liberation Front."[53] García's move was significant. According to San-dinista Sergio Ramírez, García "was an icon for the dozens of priests, mis-sionaries, nuns, deacons, and representatives of the Word who preached rev-olution, who worked to support the Sandinista guerrillas in slums and rural areas, who transported weapons, who secured clandestine safe houses, and who were at times themselves combatants."[54]

It was not just the bishops who turned on Somoza; his long-term ally, the United States, challenged him. The State Department criticized Nicaragua's human rights record for the first time, and Congressman Edward Koch (D-NY) called for an end to U.S. aid in March 1977.[55] In response, Somoza's congressional supporters, known as the "Nicaragua lobby" or the "Somoza lobby," defended him. Led by Murphy,[56] they included Charlie Wilson (D-TX), Larry McDonald (D-GA), and George Hansen (R-ID).

For his part, Somoza hired lobbyists, including former congressman William Cramer (R-FL), to aid his cause on the Hill.[57] Somoza also employed the newly formed Nicaraguan Government Information Service (NGIS) for public relations.[58] NGIS used Catholic anticommunist language in a steady drumbeat of charges that Somoza's clerical opponents were communist infiltrators or communist pawns. Somoza was the savior who could protect Nicaragua and the church from these so-called priests. NGIS tried to turn Catholics toward the regime by employing conservative U.S. and Latin American Catholics' fears.

Somoza adopted this approach because to him, "Leftist Jesuit priests" directed the opposition in Nicaragua and abroad. They "preached Communism," and they "indoctrinated" upper-class children in a manner akin to "brainwashing," leading youth to turn against their parents. Realizing that their efforts alone would not lead to his destruction, Somoza argued, these priests turned to the United States and worked with "known Left-leaning" Congress members to use "Human Rights" to run an anti-Somoza "campaign." Somoza credited these priests, both Nicaraguans and foreigners in Nicaragua, with prompting Congress to propose an end to U.S. military aid.[59]

In charging Jesuits with being part of a powerful cabal, Somoza echoed centuries-old accusations. Beginning in the mid-1700s, numerous European countries cracked down on the order. In 1767, Spain expelled more than two thousand Jesuits from the Americas. To Charles III, the wealthy international order threatened the power of the crown, and, the king charged, Jesuit conspiracy had already ousted a government minister.[60] Portugal, too, suppressed the Jesuits for supposedly inciting revolt.[61] In 1773, the Vatican abolished the order altogether; it was not restored until 1814. Somoza's critiques evoked these historical fears, but just as Jesuit suppressions of the 1700s revealed competing "visions of Enlightenment Catholicism,"[62] his accusations revealed deepening contemporary divisions among Central American and U.S. Catholics over the meaning of Catholicism and the proper role of religious. To Somoza, priests had no place critiquing the government, while to men like d'Escoto and Cardenal, priestly responsibilities called them to defend endangered human rights.

Somoza's charge that Jesuits were causing upper-class children to reject their place in the economic and social order was also not far-fetched. Since coming to Spanish America in the late 1500s, the Jesuits had focused their educational efforts—from primary school to the university—on elite creole boys.[63] But four months before Medellín, the Jesuit superiors of Latin America met and concluded that their educational institutions "should accept their role as active agents of social justice in Latin America." Societal conditions required "radical change: to develop in our students first of all an attitude of service to the society in whose transformation they should collaborate, and an effective concern for marginal people for whose development they should labor." Gone were the days of Jesuit education maintaining the status quo. And, as the Jesuit superiors predicted, the upper classes—the schools' traditional base—likely would not support this development. The Jesuits' new approach, however, was consistent with larger church trends. At Medellín, the Latin American bishops stressed schools' importance in promoting social change and the need for students of all economic classes to access Catholic education.[64]

Somoza was also correct that religious critics played an influential role in the United States, though he incorrectly labeled all his priestly opponents "Jesuits." Among the most visible advocates of ending U.S. support was Maryknoll Father Miguel d'Escoto. D'Escoto was born in Los Angeles to Nicaraguan parents who soon returned the family to Central America.[65] After spending much of his childhood in Nicaragua, d'Escoto attended a U.S. high school and later joined Maryknoll. It was d'Escoto who proposed the creation of Maryknoll's Orbis Books—the bane of conservative U.S. Catholics—and served as its first editor until the late 1970s, as discussed in chapter 1.[66] He also edited *Maryknoll* magazine.

D'Escoto, like many Maryknollers, underwent a change in his view of both U.S. Cold War policy and the institutional church. He initially condemned "atheistic communism" and supported the 1973 overthrow of Chilean president Allende. But his frequent travels to Nicaragua in the late 1970s led him to oppose the U.S. role in the country, to see the church as an "accomplice" for its support of capitalism, and to condemn the Vatican for not calling for Somoza's removal in the early 1970s.[67]

In the spring of 1977, d'Escoto advocated an end to U.S. aid. On the fiftieth anniversary of the Guardia Nacional's creation, he asked President Carter to withdraw support for the force and any aid "likely to benefit the Somoza regime more than the people." D'Escoto recounted U.S. involvement in the creation, training, and continued support for the Guardia, which he described as "the guardian of the oppressive Somoza dynasty." U.S. involvement mattered, d'Escoto asserted, because without it, "the Guardia could not have maintained its monopoly over Nicaraguan politics." While criticizing the United States, d'Escoto acknowledged that the Nicaraguan "upper classes and the traditional 'opposition' leaders" were also responsible for the people's plight. They remained silent about "Somoza's excesses" because they benefited. While Somoza and his supporters enjoyed prosperity, the average Nicaraguan lived in poverty and experienced high rates of disease, homicide, and alcoholism. Because the Guardia Nacional was the "key to maintaining this corrupt system of exaggerated social and economic inequality," d'Escoto contended that the withdrawal of U.S. support was the only way to institute change. Some Guardia officers had misgivings about Somoza, but d'Escoto explained that they would not act as long as the United States backed him. Ultimately, "the role of the United States remains pivotal to the future of the Somozas, the *Guardia Nacional*, and Nicaragua itself."[68] Eighty-six others, mostly U.S. Catholic religious leaders, along with professors and press representatives, co-signed the letter.[69]

When d'Escoto reiterated these views before the House Appropriations Committee, he stressed his status as a priest. He introduced himself in both religious and political terms: "I come before you today as a citizen of Nicaragua and a Roman Catholic priest." He testified about his motivation. "As a priest, I believe that actions on behalf of justice and the denunciation of injustice are 'constitutive elements of the proclamation of the Gospel.'" For d'Escoto there was no choice. "I cannot therefore but strongly denounce the seemingly insatiable greed of a family that has turned our Nation into its own private estate and amassed an almost incredible fortune by graft and coercion, even while it jails our patriots and kills our defenseless peasants." D'Escoto called for the United States to "immediately suspend" all aid on the basis of what Carter "called the consciousness of" the United States, the nation's heritage of "Judeo-Christian values," and U.S. laws requiring the "suppression of aid to countries that systematically violate human rights."[70]

D'Escoto publicly linked Maryknoll to anti-Somoza activism. He submitted a copy of *Guardians of the Dynasty: A History of the U.S. Created Guardia Nacional de Nicaragua and the Somoza Family.*[71] Historian Richard Millett's book was significant not only because it was the first substantial English work on the Guardia,[72] but also because Maryknoll's Orbis published it. While the press already had a controversial reputation for introducing U.S. audiences to liberation theology, publishing Millett's book associated the press and its congregational sponsor with critiques of U.S.-Nicaragua policy.

D'Escoto's introduction further underscored the connection between Maryknoll and the book's contents. Hardly one to mince words, he was damning in his assessment of the U.S. role. As he explained, the Guardia "was fathered by arrogant American interventionism and corrupted by the egotistical genius of the United States-picked *Jefe Director*, Anastasio Somoza García." D'Escoto argued that Millett's work "should make it abundantly clear that United States responsibility for the agony which that country has experienced in the last forty years can hardly be overemphasized," although he acknowledged that the United States was not solely to blame.[73]

Though Millett's book was published in the United States, religious circles in Latin America used it to legitimize their push for U.S. policy change. Forty professors from a Baptist seminary in Mexico pleaded with U.S. church members to stop U.S. support for Somoza. While the U.S government cited anticommunism as the reason it defended Somoza, the professors contended this was pretext for "its defense of business interests," and they argued "the real threat" to Latin Americans was the "military governments," trained, armed, and supported by the United States.[74] They cited Millett's book as evidence of the U.S. role in the creation of and continued support for the Guardia. Their appeal reached U.S. and European Christian circles via Protestant missionaries James and Margaret Goff, who translated Latin American church documents of note for their U.S. and European subscribers.

D'Escoto, meanwhile, enlisted the help of other Christians. In 1977, he encouraged Pax Christi USA, the U.S. branch of the international Catholic peace organization founded in 1945, to advocate for U.S. policy change.[75] With Maryknoll's support, d'Escoto appealed for "Christian[s] and . . . responsible American[s]" to request the suspension of U.S. aid in telegrams to President Carter and key Congress members, and to send copies to him.[76] Although d'Escoto did not use Maryknoll letterhead, the Maryknoll Justice and Peace Office distributed his request, which the congregation "fully support[ed]" because it was "a clear cut case of U.S. support of a corrupt regime." Maryknoll believed that efforts for Nicaragua could "serve as a prototype for future" actions against "other repressive governments." Maryknoll also asked recipients to seek others' support.[77] D'Escoto and other Somoza critics were initially successful; in May 1977, a House subcommittee suspended $3.1 million in military credits to Nicaragua because of human rights violations, and the House Appropriations Committee affirmed the move one month later.[78]

But Somoza's congressional supporters successfully fought back by challenging the basis of their opponents' credibility: their status as religious. On June 21, Representative Murphy argued that Congress was misinformed. Murphy identified three key oppositional figures: Pedro Joaquín Chamorro, *La Prensa* editor and face of the moderate opposition; Father Fernando Cardenal; and Father Miguel d'Escoto. Murphy acknowledged that d'Escoto's influence was a force to be reckoned with, as the Maryknoller's "letter and lobbying campaigns have advocated precisely what this Congress has done—cut off aid to Nicaragua." To discredit him, the congressman noted that d'Escoto was editor of Orbis books and *Maryknoll* magazine, and according to Murphy, d'Escoto believed violence and guerrilla warfare was the only way to bring about a new kind of noncapitalistic society. Accordingly, Murphy concluded d'Escoto was "simply a political activist in sheep's clothing." To Murphy, d'Escoto could be a priest or politically involved, not both.[79]

Murphy contended that the image of Nicaragua that Cardenal and d'Escoto presented was untrue. He inserted into the record a letter, which had been included in congressional hearings two months earlier, by twenty-eight Nicaraguan priests. The men claimed the Nicaraguan government supported "ample and unrestricted freedom of worship" and "always" had a "profound respect and sincere appreciation towards the Church and its ministers." In fact, contrary to allegations, "for some time the Church has been working in the country among the peasants and lowest income sectors of the cities, with freedom and help of the authorities."[80] According to these priests, a friendly, even cooperative, relationship existed between church and state.

To accentuate the danger d'Escoto posed, another Congress member tied him to the Melville incident. Larry McDonald, well-known anticommunist and future John Birch Society president,[81] argued that self-described "human rights advocates" for Nicaragua were Marxists, and he highlighted two men associated with Maryknoll. First, he mentioned ex-Maryknoller Blase Bonpane, who played a key role in the U.S. advocacy group Non-Intervention in Nicaragua. As McDonald explained, Maryknoll expelled Bonpane and others from Guatemala for "working in and with terrorist" guerrillas—the Melville incident. McDonald then charged d'Escoto with employing "inflamed rhetoric unsubstantiated by documentation" in his congressional testimony.[82] By mentioning Bonpane, the Melville incident, and d'Escoto, McDonald insinuated that all Maryknollers engaged in armed revolutionary activity. For Catholics already concerned with Maryknoll's promotion of liberation theology and critiques of U.S. foreign policy, d'Escoto's anti-Somoza lobbying efforts provided further confirmation of the order's communist-leaning sympathies. Methodist McDonald also showed how U.S. conservative Catholics' concerns about Maryknoll had expanded to conservative non-Catholics.

Congressman Wilson also questioned the motives of Somoza's religious opponents. A member of the House Appropriations Committee that controlled the State Department and AID budgets, Wilson argued that Nicaragua was "not a gross violator of human rights." If it were, there would not be opposition newspapers like *La Prensa*, nor would Nicaraguans be permitted to travel to the United States to testify against it. He was "suspicious" of "allegations" by "radical preachers." Just "because some dissident bishop came up here and said these things about Nicaragua does not make them true." U.S. lawmakers should rely on the State Department for assessments, not "religious opinion," especially when it "has a stake in the results." As Wilson contended, "before the present government took power in Nicaragua, the church was much more powerful and . . . owned much more land," though he did not explain his implication. Besides, Wilson argued, it made no sense to "single out one country" when they all had problems, and especially when Nicaragua was "one of our best friends in this hemisphere."[83] Wilson won the day; the House restored aid by a vote of 225–180.[84]

The Somoza lobby's approach was no accident; it complemented the dictator's campaign at home. By misrepresenting d'Escoto's testimony, the government-supported *Las Novedades* portrayed the Maryknoller as making baseless claims and proposing violent revolution. As the paper explained, Congressman Bill Young (R-FL) forced d'Escoto to reveal that he had no "details" of supposed Guardia Nacional repression. He also cornered d'Escoto into admitting that the end of U.S. military aid "would contribute to Nicaragua's liberation," and the only "fight that remained was a bloody one."[85] The paper altered the exchange. D'Escoto told Young he provided information about Guardia atrocities to Congress. He also stressed the need to end U.S. military aid, and explained that his appearance before Congress was so that we could "make every effort to stop" the "only alternative that is being allowed" to Nicaraguans—"the bloody" one.[86]

Consistent with *Las Novedades*'s false claim that d'Escoto proposed violence, weeks later police director William Cranshaw argued "certain priests are preaching revolution and violence from the pulpit and in the schools." Flanked by military authorities, Cranshaw told forty national and international reporters that priests "are leading our youth to believe that violence and the recourse to arms is the only way to bring about changes." He spoke after the capture of his Sandinista daughter Martha. Cranshaw blamed the church for not controlling priests who inspired her behavior. Instead, he proposed "the same priests take to the hills with machine guns and do the fighting themselves." Martha was convicted in absentia for "criminal conspiracy and illegal acts to subvert the constitution."[87] She first participated in a teachers' strike at age fifteen, and by the time of her father's press conference, she was in her early twenties.[88]

But unlike U.S. Congress members who criticized religious, Cranshaw proposed violence. As he explained, "We have to begin killing priests," and he revealed his intention to do so. He accused specific priests of engaging in offensive behavior. Cranshaw's remarks received further publicity as "small planes and helicopters" dropped leaflets with his statement throughout Nicaragua. Besides leading the police, Cranshaw served as head of the Anticommunist League of Nicaragua. Two days after the press conference, Robert Cranshaw, general secretary of the league, repeated his father's views. Robert named more priests, including Archbishop Obando and the Cardenal brothers, as well as "some Capuchins, Jesuits and Sisters of the Assumption." He also announced that the "White Hand" guerrilla organization, which he said was composed of "military personnel, civilians and members of private enterprise," kept a list of persons whom it intended to kill.[89] The Cranshaws' calls to violence were consistent with anticommunist congresses across Latin America that warned of "subversive action of the clergy" and sought to expose "communist infiltration of the Church," as discussed in chapter 1.

Threatened by the Cranshaws' words and aware of the Guardia Nacional's targeting of DPs and CEB members, priests demanded the government respond. Nicaraguan members of Archbishop Obando's advisory council wanted to know if the government agreed with the "tendentious and visibly organized campaign of threats, slander, libel, defamation and persecution against the Church and its hierarchy (especially against certain priests and nuns)." If it did not, the priests demanded the government stop the agitation "before it produces more unfortunate consequences for the whole nation." In addition to the Cranshaws, the priests condemned *Las Novedades* for running articles and headlines "against the Catholic hierarchy, the Nicaraguan clergy, the Jesuits, Capuchins, etc." If the campaign did not end, the priests said, they would publicize the problem internationally through civic and religious organizations.[90]

Maryknollers' Activism

At the same time Somoza complained that "leftist Jesuit priests" were both a religious and political problem at home and abroad, U.S. conservatives made similar charges about Maryknoll. In 1977, the libertarian *Human Events*, "perhaps the most influential conservative journal in the Washington political community" during the Nixon years,[91] argued that Maryknoll's Orbis "pours out revolutionary tracts." Maryknoll's publishing complemented its missionary activity, the magazine alleged, as "over the past decade, country after country has jailed or expelled Maryknoll priests and nuns for revolutionary activities."[92] As with McDonald's congressional remarks, *Human Events'* coverage showed how conservative U.S. Catholics' concern with Maryknoll's promotion of liberation theology expanded to a wider circle of conservatives.

Human Events exaggerated the extent, but it was not wrong that some Maryknollers ran afoul of foreign governments in the name of human rights. In November 1976, the Filipino government expelled Father Ed Gerlock after a seven-minute trial. Gerlock was arrested after he, along with bishops and other Christians, supposedly presented a letter to the South Korean embassy requesting clemency for a South Korean poet. Three years earlier, Gerlock was acquitted on charges of possessing subversive literature and providing financial assistance to the wife of an official of the Federation of Free Farmers, the group of poor peasants for whom Gerlock served as chaplain.[93] Significantly, as in Latin America, Gerlock found himself in conflict with a government in a predominantly Catholic country, unlike the Maryknollers communist governments tortured and imprisoned in the 1940s and 1950s.

The year after Gerlock's expulsion, Rhodesia's white minority-led government jailed and then expelled thirty-five-year-old Sister Janice McLaughlin for publishing subversive literature. As press secretary of the Catholic Commission for Justice and Peace in Rhodesia, McLaughlin interviewed blacks "tortured and imprisoned" in government-created "protected villages" and family members who lost loved ones at the hands of security forces.[94] Upon her return to the United States, on college campuses and before Congress, McLaughlin critiqued Rhodesia's political situation, and she encouraged the U.S. government to do the same.[95]

McLaughlin's U.S. activities reflected Maryknollers' expansive sense of mission. Known as "reverse mission," Maryknoll's U.S.-based activities included speaking to parishioners, appealing to U.S. bishops to take specific actions, and communicating through *Maryknoll* magazine.[96] The practice grew out of Vatican II; by 1975, the congregation saw reverse mission as "an integral part" of its work.[97] Gone were the days when Maryknollers asked for funds to save pagan babies or build hospitals in the jungle. Instead, members invited U.S. Catholics to denounce foreign governments' behavior, to question U.S. foreign policy and the role of U.S. actors abroad, and to provide financial support to enable Maryknoll to do the same. As part of this effort, the Sisters' World Awareness Program (WAP) sent missioners to share their experiences with high school and college students, religious communities, and parish groups, encouraging participants to reflect on their role as global citizens intellectually, spiritually, and morally, and then, to act.[98]

Maryknollers' congressional activities were an outgrowth of reverse mission and part of a broader religious and secular human rights movement that grew during the 1970s. On the Right, Captive Nations groups focused on Soviets' human rights violations, while the most well known group on the Left was Amnesty International.[99] Maryknollers were one of the religious, especially transnational, groups active on the Hill. The World Council of Churches used transnational networks to highlight state human rights abuses in Brazil and Chile in the 1970s.[100] The ecumenical Washington Office on Latin America (WOLA) monitored how U.S. policy impacted human rights in Latin America.[101] U.S. sisters, many of whom had worked as missionaries or in poor areas of the United States, founded the lobby NETWORK in the early 1970s.[102] For their part, the Maryknoll Fathers and Brothers established personnel in Washington, DC. Besides d'Escoto, Maryknollers testified about human rights violations in South Korea and the marketing of infant formula, among other issues.[103]

Maryknoll got the ear of key Congress members, which *Human Events* and the Somoza lobby recognized. Senator James Abourezk (D-SD), credited with proposing "the first general human rights legislation to pass Congress" to ban aid to countries with political prisoners,[104] encouraged the Maryknoll Fathers and Brothers to establish a permanent presence in DC. He noted the vital and "positive" role missionaries could play in influencing U.S. foreign policy. As Abourezk explained, missionaries understand U.S. policy's impacts and "many . . . are sensitive to the plight of the people and the poor . . . [and] to the basic human rights and freedom which the local governments sometime violate—often with the support of the U.S. government." Congress needed this "firsthand information."[105] Likewise, Donald Fraser, "liberal human rights' advocates most tireless political advocate in the mid-1970s,"[106] commended Maryknollers' work and influence on him. In a letter to Maryknoll after his 1978 electoral defeat, Fraser stressed that church "assistance" to the Committee on International Relations was "important." He specifically praised Maryknoll for its "record of service and concern for human rights," which "has made a deep impression on me."[107]

The End of Somoza

Feeling the growing pressure at home and from the United States, in September 1977 Somoza ended censorship and revoked the state of martial law, which had been in effect since the Sandinista Christmas raid nearly three years before.[108] But things got worse for Somoza in October when d'Escoto, Fernando Cardenal, and ten other prominent Nicaraguans signed a letter supporting armed insurrection. Known as Los Doce (The 12), the group argued that "until new avenues for a real solution are opened up we cannot contemplate any alternative to war." They called on Nicaraguans "to realize that a solution which will guarantee a permanent and effective peace cannot be achieved without the participation of the FSLN."[109] Los Doce "also wanted to prevent the U.S. government from imposing a solution without taking the Sandinista Front into account," according to Cardenal.[110] The group's spokesperson, d'Escoto, noted that though he was "a great believer in nonviolent protest and civil disobedience," it was "not a real option" under Somoza. Characteristic of his blunt political assessments, d'Escoto alleged, "Anyone who supports Somoza is a murderer."[111] Los Doce gave the Sandinistas credibility, particularly among the moderate opposition.[112]

FSLN members who were part of the Insurrectional Tendency—known as the Terceristas—sought out Los Doce. The Terceristas pushed for military action to inspire the populace to rise up. The other two FSLN factions, by contrast, were against allying with the "bourgeois elements" and they opposed major military efforts. The FSLN split after party founder Carlos Fonseca's death in 1976.[113]

Somoza tried to silence Los Doce. The members were convicted in absentia of inciting rebellion.[114] In the United States, NGIS critiqued Miguel d'Escoto, pointing to his support for the FSLN as evidence of his Marxist sympathies and the church's loss of credibility in Nicaragua. In a November 1977 *Washington Post* op-ed, NGIS's Ian R. MacKenzie alleged that since March, a "sustained" media and congressional campaign worked to discredit and topple Somoza and to end U.S. aid. But MacKenzie referred only to clergy. He charged the church with becoming "politicized and compromised," and he singled out d'Escoto. Echoing Congressman Murphy, MacKenzie argued that d'Escoto "openly advocates violence and guerilla warfare, the overthrow of the Somoza government and the imposition of a 'new, noncapitalist system.'"[115] Although MacKenzie mentioned other clergy, his conflation of the church with d'Escoto demonstrated the degree to which the Maryknoller had become synonymous with anti-Somoza opposition for Somoza's U.S. supporters.

NGIS zeroed in on d'Escoto and Maryknoll rather than the Jesuits for a reason. Maryknoll was a U.S.-based order, unlike the Society of Jesus, founded in Spain. In Maryknoll's less than seventy-year history, the order had become an emblem of U.S. Cold War ideals. Now, Maryknoll seemed to be rejecting this identity. For conservative Catholics, Maryknollers' support for liberation theology and opposition to Somoza were a betrayal of the church and the congregation's past. This pain was raw, while charges of heresy and even treasonous behavior levied against the Jesuits were nothing new in the Americas.

Future president Ronald Reagan took aim at d'Escoto the next month, underscoring non-Catholic conservatives' concern with the Maryknoller's efforts. In one of his radio commentaries, former California governor Reagan cited d'Escoto among those attempting to destabilize the Nicaraguan government and bring about revolution. Reagan wrote the shows himself, which an estimated fifty million people heard every day by 1980.[116] Reagan noted that during the past spring, d'Escoto led a "letter-writing and lobbying campaign" to end U.S. economic aid.[117] The governor's concerns about the Maryknoller's ability to marshal political activism through letter writing and lobbying foreshadowed the Reagan White House's concerns with Maryknoll in the 1980s.

While d'Escoto faced criticism from Somoza's U.S. supporters, Maryknoll sisters in Managua were beaten for their defense of Nicaraguans. Three months after Somoza ended martial law, university students and OPEN 3 members occupied seven area churches demanding the release of political prisoners. On the third day of the 1977 Christmas Campaign, Guardia threw tear gas into the church and beat students. When a priest attempted to intervene, Guardia knocked him down and, while kicking him, shouted, "You're the cause of all this disorder and subversion, you communist priest." The next night, the Guardia beat a Spanish Jesuit outside the Maryknoll sisters' home. When Maryknollers Peggy Healy and Peg Dillon stepped in, Guardia turned on the women in view of the U.S. press.[118] After the incident, the sisters asked Maryknoll headquarters to publicize the events "to get international pressure applied."[119] They also relayed what occurred to the U.S. embassy, Archbishop Obando, and the press. Although the women revealed that they did not necessarily agree with the students, they felt the need to be with them. "We have always been present to try to avoid violence and when necessary, to mediate before the authorities to defend our people."[120] With the use of "our," the sisters claimed membership in the Nicaraguan community and underscored their decision to side with the weak.

In the midst of this growing opposition, the January 1978 murder of editor and moderate opposition leader Pedro Joaquín Chamorro lit the spark that accelerated protests and eventually led to the regime's downfall. Outraged by his murder, Nicaraguans spontaneously rioted for weeks, prompting business leaders to call for a general strike to oust Somoza.[121] The turn of events brought the armed struggle to the cities, and many Christians, including DPs, CEB members, and students, increasingly supported the insurrection or joined as combatants.[122]

Despite growing tensions, the country was not a priority for Carter. In fact, the administration had "no specific policy" in its early days; it followed its overall human rights strategy and applied it to Nicaragua.[123] Instead, Carter saw the Panama Canal treaties as the centerpiece of his Latin America policy. In September 1977, Carter and Panamanian president General Omar Torrijos signed two treaties that mandated the canal's neutrality and the end of U.S.

control on December 31, 1999. According to Secretary of State Cyrus Vance, the treaties "were an indispensible part of the Carter administration's strategy to forge a new and more constructive relationship with the nations of the Western Hemisphere and the Third World."[124] Concerns that anti-U.S. violence or terrorism in the Canal Zone would spread and possibly necessitate U.S. intervention also prompted the treaties.[125]

The impetus for change came from both Democratic and Republican administrations. Lyndon Johnson started conversations after a 1964 anti-U.S. riot in the Canal Zone. These led to a 1967 treaty that was never presented for Senate ratification. The Nixon and Ford administrations continued discussions, and Secretary of State Henry Kissinger reached an agreement on the key points with his Panamanian counterpart in early 1974.[126]

But the canal was contentious. Opponents, led by Senators Strom Thurmond (R-SC) and Jesse Helms (R-NC), argued the treaties symbolized the retreat of U.S. power and provided an opening for Soviet expansion in the Western Hemisphere, given Torrijos's ties to Fidel Castro.[127] During the 1976 Republican presidential primary, candidate Reagan used his treaty opposition to distinguish himself from incumbent Gerald Ford and win the North Carolina primary.[128] Consequently, discussion of the treaties consumed the attention of the Carter administration, the Senate, and lobbyists in 1978.[129]

In responding to the Nicaraguan situation, Carter faced critiques from all sides. The president wanted Somoza gone without leaving an opening for communists. Nicaraguan moderates, including the church hierarchy, shared this view. Carter hoped to combine human rights with U.S. nonintervention. But his cabinet and the public complicated his plans. National Security Advisor Zbigniew Brzezinski argued the United States needed to support Somoza to fend off communist revolution, whereas Secretary of State Vance contended the conflict was not an East-West matter but grew from problems endemic to Nicaraguan society and the Somoza family's rule.[130] Outside the White House, the U.S. press carried stories of human rights abuses, and advocates like Miguel d'Escoto saw Carter as not living up to the human rights rhetoric he espoused. Conversely, Somoza and his supporters argued that human rights concerns were a smokescreen for U.S. attempts to abandon an ally, leaving the country vulnerable to communists.

While the Carter administration tried to thread a difficult needle, Somoza lobby member Wilson saw an opening. In May 1978, he threatened, as a swing vote on the Appropriations Committee, to tie up the 1979 foreign aid bill unless the administration changed its tune. Carter caved. Nicaragua received $160,000 for a military hospital and $12 million in economic aid that had been suspended for human rights reasons.[131]

Carter then made things worse. On June 30, he sent Somoza a letter. As Carter wrote, the "steps toward respecting human rights you are considering are important and heartening signs; and, as they are translated into actions, will mark a major advance in answering some of the criticisms recently aimed at the Nicaraguan government."[132] Though designed to prod him to continue making changes, Somoza viewed the letter as a stamp of approval. When the letter became public, Carter lost face for appearing to praise Somoza.[133]

In Nicaragua, Los Doce's return from Costa Rica in July fed growing opposition. The group was greeted by 150,000 supporters at the airport. By mid-August, Los Doce had traveled throughout one-third of the country airing its views.[134] For his part, Miguel d'Escoto publicly stated his purpose was to end the Somoza regime.[135] In late August, the Sandinistas took over the National Palace, where Congress sat, along with 1,500 hostages.[136] Soon afterward, a general strike was announced, and the government arrested more than 700 suspected organizers. The strikes continued. The Sandinistas called for a general uprising. People armed with "Molotov cocktails, homemade bombs, revolvers, and hunting rifles" fought in the streets. Somoza then reinstated martial law on September 12 and ordered bombings, including napalm, of his own people.[137]

D'Escoto continued to hammer away at the U.S. government's role, and he prodded U.S. Christians to act. As he explained to the *Wall Street Journal*, "We have an awful mess here and it's a mess we inherited from the United States. We are very aware that our people are being slaughtered by guns supplied by Americans and by soldiers trained by the U.S."[138] D'Escoto also promoted Los Doce's position in the U.S. Catholic press. To stress that he was no outlier, d'Escoto told the *National Catholic Reporter* that "at least 85 percent" of "religious personnel" in Nicaragua supported the Sandinista cause. He encouraged U.S. readers to ask Congress to end aid, to educate themselves about Nicaragua and tell others, and to form solidarity committees.[139]

D'Escoto was not the only Maryknoller appealing to Americans on Nicaraguans' behalf. During a 1978 visit to the United States, Peg Dillon wrote to the State Department relaying a request by CONFER and the Archdiocesan Priests' Council.[140] The signers implored Carter to suspend all aid immediately and respect Nicaraguans' attempts to create a new path. As they explained, "Even the non-military aid in the long run is used for repression." The signers represented the 132 members of Managua's Priest Council and the 1,500 members of CONFER.[141] Not long after, the newly formed Protestant Latin American Council of Churches, "representing 110 Protestant denominations in 20 countries," expressed solidarity with the Nicaraguan people and in a telegram to Somoza called on him to stop the violence and resign.[142]

The religious community's pleas were the basis for a renewed push for aid reduction. Hours after Mark Hatfield (R-OR) led the charge to reduce training funds for the Guardia Nacional by $150,000,[143] Catholic Democrats Frank Church and Ted Kennedy proposed reducing economic aid by $8 million. Church cited an article featuring the letter by priests and missionaries that Dillon relayed to the State Department.[144] Kennedy included a letter to Carter from the president of the New York Province of U.S. Jesuits. The Jesuits detailed their five-week visit to Nicaragua during which they witnessed "shocking repression." As they told Carter, they saw "students and bystanders being machine-gunned on the streets, [and] innocent people in barrios killed and wounded while literally asleep, when the *Guardia Nacional* fired through the walls of their homes in arbitrary reprisal for public protests." They "watched with our own eyes young people hounded by soldiers with sub-machine guns. We spoke with priests and nuns who had been beaten with rifles while trying to protect young people during peaceful student protests." Like the signers Senator Church referenced, the Jesuits argued that Somoza used U.S. economic aid for repression.[145] The bill passed. Somoza's religious critics were influential, as the Somoza lobby, NGIS, and Reagan recognized.

The Somoza lobby responded with a multipronged approach in the United States and Nicaragua. On the House floor, Congressman Murphy argued that Nicaragua was experiencing not a "popular uprising against a repressive government" but an attempt by international communist outsiders to orchestrate change. He attempted to discredit the religious opposition by reinserting his June 1977 remarks criticizing Fathers d'Escoto and Cardenal. In a public plea, Somoza's congressional supporters also published their September 22 letter to Carter in the *New York Times*. Led by Murphy and McDonald, seventy-eight representatives asked Carter to support Somoza, arguing that "irrefutable evidence" showed that Havana- and Moscow-trained revolutionaries engaged in "the campaign of violence, urban terrorism and near civil war in Nicaragua" in the hopes of establishing a second Cuba.[146] Seeing no change from Carter, in November Congressmen Wilson and Murphy flew to Nicaragua on their own dime.[147] Flanked by a rocket launcher and grenades taken from the Sandinistas, the congressmen echoed Somoza's calls for a plebiscite rather than immediate resignation, as his opponents wanted.[148] In doing so, Wilson and Murphy fought the U.S.-Guatemalan-Dominican efforts, begun after the September fighting, to mediate between Somoza and opposition groups.[149]

Though a public relations headache for the White House, the real problem was the Somoza lobby's threat to sabotage the canal implementation legislation. After the Senate ratified the treaties in April 1978, Carter requested that Congress pass legislation regarding the treaty's implementation.[150] Treaty ratification was the main political focus of 1978, and for nearly the first six months of 1979 the White House was consumed by garnering legislative support for implementation legislation.[151] The Somoza lobby saw an opportunity. Instead of primarily challenging religious critics and human rights activists, they tied Nicaragua to treaty implementation legislation. In early December 1978, Wilson threatened to "torpedo" the legislation, despite his earlier support for the treaties, because Carter failed to support Somoza.[152] For his part, Murphy used his position as chair of the Merchant Marine Committee, which had oversight over the Panama Canal Commission responsible for the operations and management of the canal, to change the treaty. He proposed that rather than have a civilian head the commission, it should be under the Defense Department in times of peace and the U.S. military in times of war. He also wanted canal revenues to pay the United States for its investment in the Canal Zone, plus interest, making it "almost impossible" that Panama would see any of the remaining profits.[153]

Despite the focus on Panama, tensions continued to rise in Nicaragua. In May 1979, the FSLN announced its "final offensive,"[154] and days later the Nicaraguan church hierarchy endorsed armed revolution as just.[155] In weeks, the Sandinistas had the "major cities, virtually all the countryside, and half of Managua."[156]

With Somoza under siege, his congressional supporters pushed Carter on Panama's aid to the Sandinistas. At a June 11 meeting to gain the support of one hundred Congress members for the canal legislation, the lobby instead asked about Panama's alleged arms shipments.[157] Congress members urged the president to change U.S. policy in a letter they also published in the *New York Times*. House members called on him to stop the arms flow and "logistical support" from Cuba and Panama.[158] Two days after the letter appeared in the press, the House held closed-door hearings on accusations that Torrijos was gunrunning to Nicaragua.[159] Though true, the Carter administration "downplayed" the issue in an effort to get the treaties passed.[160]

Panama was not the only issue distracting the administration. Even as fighting engulfed all of Nicaragua in June, the White House was "absorbed" with other foreign policy matters deemed "of far greater importance," according to Robert Pastor, director of Latin American and Caribbean affairs on the National Security Council. Officials focused on the signing of the SALT II treaty and traveled to Asia to attend a meeting of industrialized nations.[161]

Events in Nicaragua intervened. On June 20, a Guardia Nacional member shot ABC news reporter Bill Stewart as his cameraman filmed. The next day, U.S. news broadcast the guardsman firing into Stewart's head after forcing him to lie down on his stomach.[162] There was no denying the Guardia's brutality, contrary to what Somoza's supporters claimed. The day after Stewart's murder, the House passed the treaty implementation legislation.[163]

The Carter administration tried again to pursue a middle path. While the House debated treaty implementation legislation, Secretary of State Vance stood before an emergency meeting of the Organization of American States (OAS) and, for the first time, publicly called on Somoza to resign. He proposed the OAS aid Nicaragua in forming a transitional government and send a peacekeeping force.[164] In response, the Carter administration faced blowback from two opposing Catholic quarters: Congressman Murphy and Father d'Escoto.

Murphy impeded U.S. attempts to encourage Somoza to step down. When Ambassador Lawrence Pezzullo met with Somoza to demand he leave office, Murphy, whom Somoza repeatedly referred to as his "associate," sat by his side along with Nicaragua's foreign minister.[165] Murphy's questionable behavior was not new. During the height of the crisis from 1977 to 1980, Murphy said the old friends spoke "maybe two or three times a week. And I made many visits to Nicaragua."[166]

While Murphy charged Carter with abandoning a longtime U.S. ally, Maryknoller d'Escoto criticized the administration for not recognizing the Sandinistas as Nicaragua's new leaders. D'Escoto's condemnation mattered not only because he was Los Doce spokesperson,[167] and later the provisional government's "ambassador to all nations,"[168] but also because he was a member of a U.S. missionary order. D'Escoto saw Vance's OAS proposal as a power play. "The United States is not as concerned with what is happening in Nicaragua as it is afraid that it will lose control of what will happen in the future."[169] After the Sandinistas proposed an outline for a nonaligned, democratic government that they envisioned leading post-Somoza, d'Escoto contended that U.S. delay was blocking democracy's development.[170] As he argued, the United States was "trying to bargain with the blood of our people."[171]

Though d'Escoto was in the spotlight, he was not the only Maryknoller working to change U.S. policy. Maura Clarke had been speaking about Nicaragua as part of Maryknoll's WAP since the fall of 1976.[172] Margarita Jamias, who also served in Nicaragua, led reflections for adult parish groups on the East Coast. After the May 1979 offensive, Jamias cautioned her New York listeners not to judge how Nicaraguans worked to overthrow Somoza. As she explained, "As North Americans, it is not our path to choose if they should use violence. We know many of the people in the Sandinista [sic] and we know they are fighting for their brothers' and sisters' future." She implicitly endorsed the church's doctrine of just war when she contended, "they have tried every peaceable means possible to win their freedoms."[173] That same month, Clarke, together with Sister Annette Mulry, organized a hunger strike in front of the

United Nations to push the United States to break ties with Somoza and to recognize the provisional government.[174] Not just an individual effort, the Maryknoll Sisters collectively declared, we "support our Nicaraguan brothers and sisters in their struggle for justice and self-determination." They called on the United States to "withdraw recognition" of Somoza, to "stop all intervention in Nicaragua," to "recognize the provincial government of reconstruction as the choice of the Nicaraguan people," and to provide "generous" economic aid once fighting ended.[175]

Days later, on July 17, Somoza and his close advisors fled the country for Florida; and two days later the FSLN entered the capital triumphant.[176] The war exacted a large civilian toll and left the country in shambles. An estimated 45,000 Nicaraguans died and 160,000 were wounded. One million were without food and 25,000 without shelter. The country had no real financial resources because Somoza had borrowed $1.5 million to defend the regime.[177] The Government Junta of National Reconstruction included FSLN leader Daniel Ortega, Los Doce member and writer Sergio Ramírez, guerrilla leader and mathematics professor Moisés Hassan, and non-FSLN members businessman Alfonso Robelo and Violeta Chamorro, widow of murdered journalist Pedro Joaquín Chamorro. Priests were later included, with Fernando Cardenal as education minister, his brother Ernesto as culture minister, Edgard Parrales as OAS ambassador, and most significantly for U.S. observers, Maryknoller Miguel d'Escoto as foreign minister.

To U.S. conservatives, Maryknollers, and especially d'Escoto, personified the danger of the Nicaraguan revolution and its spread. As *Human Events* argued in "Priests Preach Pro-Marxist Gospel to the Third World," d'Escoto was no outlier but representative "of mainstream thinking within the Maryknoll Fathers." As the magazine contended, the role of foreign minister and the former editor of *Maryknoll* magazine and Orbis books revealed "the extent to which radical priests—and the Maryknoll missioners in particular—have been involved in efforts to oust anti-Communist governments not only in Nicaragua but in other third world countries as well."[178] In a companion piece, *Human Events* questioned d'Escoto's legitimacy as a priest by placing quotation marks around "Father." Echoing Representative Murphy, the paper explained that d'Escoto, the "hard-line radical who embraces revolutionary violence" and "supposed disciple of Christ, doesn't bat an eyelash when condoning terror as a means of altering Nicaragua's economic system."[179] The next month, the traditionalist Catholic periodical the *Wanderer* reprinted "Priests Preach Pro-Marxist Gospel to the Third World," showing how non-Catholic periodicals were leading the charge against Maryknoll.[180] Through these pieces, *Human Events* and the *Wanderer* challenged Maryknoll's credibility by contending the order was a political, not religious, organization that influenced countless Catholics.

By the late 1970s in the United States, both conservative Catholics and non-Catholics argued that Maryknollers were involved in "politics" as a way to delegitimize their views. It was not Maryknollers' lobbying efforts or congressional testimony per se that bothered conservatives; it was Maryknollers' U.S. foreign policy opposition. Political activity was acceptable when it meant Maryknoll support for U.S. Cold War aims, as in the 1950s. Maryknoll's calls to end the Somoza regime pushed U.S. conservatives over the edge. Similarly, Nicaraguan Catholics accused religious, especially Jesuits, of "taking sides" in political debates. In doing so, they ignored the church's prior alignment with the state. Those inspired by liberation theology who opposed Somoza and U.S.-Nicaragua policy were not moving from a neutral position to one side, as conservative critics claimed. Those priests and nuns—as part of the church—were now switching from standing with the powerful to speaking out for the poor. Conservatives' accusations of inappropriate political activity increased as pressure grew on Somoza to step aside. In the United States, conservatives' association of Maryknoll with Marxist revolution outlasted Somoza and shaped their understanding of events in and U.S. policy toward El Salvador.

CHAPTER 3

Subversives in El Salvador

In 1976, the Salvadoran government accused Maryknoll priests John Halbert and Ron Michaels of being "subversives." As evidence, officials pointed out that the two men "taught small seminars, celebrated Mass in people's homes, and ran a tuberculosis clinic" in Santa Ana, one of El Salvador's fourteen departments.[1] The following year, Father Bernard Survil, a diocesan priest from western Pennsylvania who went on mission with Maryknoll, was arrested on similar grounds in the department of La Libertad. Survil arrived in El Salvador in 1975 and embraced liberation theology. While he saw his CEB work as furthering human rights, one of the arresting officers disagreed, asking, "Why is it that you priests are preaching hatred? Why aren't you preaching love?"[2] To this officer and Salvadoran elites, the priests encouraged class conflict because they prioritized one group—the poor—over the powerful. But these priests, like other religious, were following liberation theology. They were not attempting to foment revolution. The officer recognized the potential consequences of the priests' work with the poor.

Liberation theology was a security threat. By the late 1970s, half of Salvadorans were illiterate, 60 percent of families had no access to water, and "less than 1 percent of the population owned 40 percent of arable land."[3] If the Salvadoran poor—the majority of Salvadorans—saw themselves as equal to the powerful in God's eyes and inequity as the result of sin, not divine sanction, it would upend society. Halbert, Michaels, and Survil survived their encounters with state forces; other priests, religious, and laypeople were not so fortunate.

The priests' arrests obscured both U.S. support for the Salvadoran government and the dangers Maryknoll sisters also faced in standing with the poor. Despite El Salvador's rampant violence in the late 1970s, Nicaragua received more U.S. attention. Unlike the Somoza family, in El Salvador there was no figure—or single family—leading the country that was also a long-term U.S. ally. While Nicaragua's economic elite turned against Somoza, the Salvadoran oligarchy stood by the government. Nor did El Salvador have a block of congressional allies, like the Somoza lobby. Even after President Jimmy Carter proclaimed the importance of human rights in shaping U.S. foreign policy, there was no discernible change in U.S. relations toward El Salvador.

This chapter argues that priests, brothers, and nuns in El Salvador and the United States played a crucial role in aiding Salvadorans' push for societal change. Maryknollers, like other religious, approached the situation from a faith-based perspective, but their decision to side with the poor had political implications. Like Salvadoran campesinos, religious suffered violence and death. Like Nicaraguans, Salvadoran Catholics divided over the church's role after Vatican II. Maryknollers and other religious, most notably San Salvador's archbishops Luis Chávez y González and Óscar Anulfo Romero, advocated for El Salvador's poor and tried to persuade Carter to accentuate human rights in U.S. policy. The Nicaraguan revolution made El Salvador a U.S. priority. By 1980, El Salvador was a major conflict between the White House and the religious community, and life for Salvadorans and Maryknollers in the country was becoming increasingly more dangerous. Though Maryknoll sisters in El Salvador were not yet known in the United States for their advocacy, unlike Miguel d'Escoto in Nicaragua, they were no less important in accompanying the poor and in pushing for change in U.S. policy.

Inequality and Attempts at Change

Conflict existed in El Salvador because of inequality, particularly in land distribution. The Somoza family controlled Nicaragua for over forty years, whereas the native oligarchy held power in El Salvador. The group—referred to as *las catorce* (fourteen families)—built its fortune on coffee, El Salvador's key crop. The *catorce*, though composed of dozens of families, consolidated power in the late nineteenth and early twentieth centuries during the coffee boom.[4] Inequitable land distribution coupled with overpopulation also increased societal tensions and prompted emigration from the country.[5]

Hope for land reform in the 1930s ended in massacre. Promising to enact reforms, coffee planter Arturo Araujo won the "first free and fair presidential election" in 1931.[6] The army overthrew him and installed General Maximiliano Hernández Martínez. Six weeks later, in January 1932, several thousand people, primarily in the western region, targeted local power holders, gained control of over a dozen municipalities, and in the process killed about fifty people.[7] Those uprising—rural and urban, literate and illiterate, *ladinos* and indigenous, communists and noncommunists—complained about falling coffee prices and the decrease in wages precipitated by the Great Depression, and the inability of reforms to address the country's political and social inequalities.[8] They sought "radical agrarian reform" and an end to the current government and oligarchy's grip on the country.[9] The army put down the rebellion, killing between ten thousand and thirty thousand in what became known as *la Matanza*, one of the deadliest episodes of state-sponsored violence in modern Latin America.[10]

The year 1932 left an indelible mark on the country's psyche. The lesson for the Left was that Salvadoran elites were so unwilling to consider change that they joined "with the military to use violence of a colossal scale in defense of the status quo." Elites and the military saw 1932 as the tale "of gullible peasants being manipulated by crafty communist organizers from the cities, like [Augustín] Farabundo Martí, who in turn were tied to international communism through organizations like the Comintern."[11] Martí, from a Salvadoran landowning family, helped found the Central American Socialist Party and served as Nicaraguan Augusto Sandino's personal secretary. He was arrested before the uprising and later executed by firing squad.[12] This 1932 narrative blamed communists, ignored Salvadorans' grievances, and discounted campesinos' ability to assess the situation. To the Salvadoran right, the lesson was clear: international communist forces caused the uprising, so all communist influences must be eradicated. In the late 1970s and 1980s, armed Rightist groups evoked 1932 by naming themselves after General Maximilian, while guerrilla revolutionaries took Martí as a namesake.

The Cuban Revolution only increased these Salvadoran fears of a communist-inspired uprising, and it also prompted greater U.S. desire to affect Salvadoran politics. Salvadoran president José María Lemus López accused university students and faculty of being Cuban influenced and of attempting to overthrow his government. The U.S. ambassador agreed, proposed U.S. military aid to handle the dissenters, and supported the president's September 1960 military crackdown. The next month, Lemus was overthrown. But the new civilian-military junta's days were numbered. U.S. diplomats called junta intellectuals "communists" and denounced the government for not breaking diplomatic ties with Castro's Cuba. In January 1961, military officers, "encouraged by the US Military Group," overthrew the junta.[13]

These events mattered for both Salvadoran domestic politics and Salvadorans' perceptions of U.S. influence. Within a month of taking power, the new Civilian-Military Directorate instituted martial law. In response, communist intellectuals established the United Front of Revolutionary Action (Frente Unido de Acción Revolucionaria or FUAR), "the first armed left movement" since 1932. Besides critiquing the oligarchy and the country's "feudal labor relations," FUAR warned U.S. coup involvement was the first step in making El Salvador a U.S. "colony." To the two thousand–member FUAR, the U.S. Military Group controlled the Salvadoran army and security forces. The U.S.-supported coup inspired a generation of university students and faculty to turn toward more radical nationalist politics. This shift, historian Joaquín M. Chávez explains, "marked the beginnings of the insurgent and counterinsurgent politics that characterized El Salvador in the subsequent three decades."[14]

The U.S. government also aimed to redistribute land as part of the Alliance for Progress. Announced two months after the Salvadoran coup, the plan was ambitious. In 1961, "less than 1 percent of landowners owned more than 50 percent of the arable land."[15] The oligarchy opposed the plan, leading U.S. aid to focus on disparate projects "from schools and clinics to basketball courts."[16] Land tensions grew. By 1969, three hundred thousand Salvadorans had immigrated to Honduras.[17] As Honduras attempted land reform, Salvadorans there were forced out, leading to the "Soccer War" between the neighboring countries. The conflict resulted in the return of about one hundred thousand Salvadorans, further increasing land tensions.[18] By 1971, three times as many people were landless as when the Alliance for Progress began.[19] El Salvador was the "only country in Latin America without even a semblance of agrarian reform legislation" by the early 1970s.[20] At the same time, increased U.S. investment entrenched the oligarchy's power. While it profited from agricultural exports, the country was one of the world's five most malnourished.[21]

Although El Salvador's powerful contained the impact of the Alliance for Progress, they could not squelch the church's support for change, led by San Salvador's archbishop Luis Chávez y González. Inspired by Vatican II, the archbishop funded a "network of student organizations, cooperatives, peasant training centers, and radio school programs." Peasants learned reading and mathematics through radio schools, which numbered about four hundred in just the departments of San Salvador and San Vicente.[22] Peasant training centers—known collectively as *universidades campesinas* (peasant universities)—promoted "self-help" by educating peasants in "modern agricultural techniques, cooperative formation, and planning, along with theology and religion."

Students participated in activities to increase their confidence in public speaking, and they learned from priests and outside lecturers, including Ministry of Agriculture representatives. About fifteen thousand people attended these seven centers throughout the country from 1970 to 1976. The peasant university's purpose was not to create rebels. Instead, the church sought lay helpers to address the ratio of thirty thousand persons per priest in rural El Salvador.[23]

Upon their return home, catechists trained others. "Peasant intellectuals" like Fabio Argueta, who helped others use religion to better understand their social and economic situation, described the results. "Through the Bible [the poor would] discover themselves as human beings with the capacity to transform their own history, not [to have to live] as slaves or as persons condemned to die young or be illiterate."[24] CEB members underwent a religious conversion of sorts that shifted their understanding of faith as an interior piety to social obligation.[25] Argueta's neighbors then tackled "collective projects," such as road building. He organized three catechist centers within three months of leaving the peasant university.[26]

Under the archbishop's leadership, the church adopted controversial positions, including land reform. In January 1970, President-Colonel Fidel Sánchez Hernández held the country's First National Congress on Agrarian Reform. The church argued for "massive expropriation."[27] Members of the oligarchy left the meeting in disgust.[28]

The church paid a price for its stance. After the meeting, Father José Inocencio Alas, founder of a peasant university, was arrested. As he recalled, he was drugged and "abandoned, stripped, on a high mountain in the country." He was at death's door for nine days.[29] Months later, Nicolás Rodríguez, who supported a Chalatenango peasant cooperative, endured machete and knife cuts to the point of disfiguration, and was left, dead, with one hand. Locals insisted security forces murdered the priest for supporting campesino organizing efforts.[30]

The archbishop persisted despite the opposition. The same year as the agrarian congress, Chávez y González convened a pastoral meeting to discuss how to implement Vatican II's and Medellín's changes, as Pope Paul VI requested of all Latin American bishops.[31] About two hundred bishops, clergy, nuns, and laity agreed the church needed to do more to advance people's liberation and to develop CEBs and lay leadership.[32]

Not everyone was happy. San Vicente's bishop Pedro Arnoldo Aparicio y Quintanilla critiqued the outcome.[33] He and the bishops of the other four dioceses maintained a conservative stance.[34] Institutionally, they were more in line with the Latin America church hierarchy, which also worried about liberation theology's spread. CELAM elected Bishop Alfonso López Trujillo secretary-general in 1972. The liberation theology opponent consolidated CELAM training institutes into one in Colombia, hampering the preparation of pastoral agents. Colombia also housed a center, established by Jesuit Roger Vekemans in 1971, dedicated to critiquing liberation theology.[35] Yet even within the Salvadoran dioceses led by conservative prelates like Aparicio, priests, nuns, and catechists trained at peasant universities fostered the progressive church's growth.[36] This divide within the Salvadoran church widened over time.

Maryknollers positioned themselves on the archbishop's side, as *Maryknoll* coverage revealed. The sisters first arrived in El Salvador in 1969.[37] In the spring of 1973, *Maryknoll* magazine showcased their changing mission. An article described how Sisters Patricia Murray and Teresa Lilly were "working on a pastoral team and visiting people at home." Rather than assign the women a job, superiors instructed them to "see what has to be done and how you can help." The two Maryknollers, living a few miles from the capital in Ilopango, "tried to expand the meaning of religion from simply praying and honoring God to include the everyday activities of parishioners. They are emphasizing the training of lay people to carry on their work."[38] The article did not say so, but the women were facilitating CEB development. The approach mirrored Maura Clarke's call for sisters in Siuna, Nicaragua, to shift from teaching girls to fostering leadership skills and community building. The article's title, "Are They Real Sisters?" (complete with a question mark), captured the novelty of the women's work. Instead of focusing on the more traditional missionary activities of baptisms, conversions, school teaching, or hospital work, the women accompanied campesinos as they reconsidered their understanding of themselves and their place in the world.

The article's title anticipated that the sisters' work might surprise readers; it did not convey how this work affected campesinos. Maryknoller Joan Petrik, who arrived in 1973,[39] witnessed CEBs' transformative effect. "When I first arrived in Tamanique [La Libertad], every time a child died the family would say 'It's the will of God.' But after the people became involved in the Christian communities that attitude began to change. And after a year or so I no longer heard people in the communities saying that. After a while they began to say, 'the system caused this.'" CEB members even carried themselves differently. "They walk upright, their heads held high, with self-confidence," while the others bowed their heads.[40] CEBs taught campesinos to live a faith of emancipation, which instilled a sense that they had a right to participate in society.

The article also did not highlight the implications for Salvadoran society. To stand with the poor entailed a political choice because it meant choosing "one social class against another." As liberation theologian Gustavo Gutiérrez explained, "The 'poor person' is not the result of an act of fate; his existence is not politically neutral or ethically innocent. The poor person is the by-product of the system to which we live and for which we are responsible."[41] In El Salvador, this stance had deadly consequences, as the sisters soon learned.

Growing Tension and Violence

Once campesinos viewed their circumstances differently, there was no putting the genie back in the bottle. Campesino consciousness translated into social action in Aguilares, about eighteen miles from San Salvador where sugarcane plantations occupied the best land. Jesuits espousing liberation theology, including Rutilio Grande, arrived in September 1972.[42] In the nine months from September 1973 to June 1974, priests helped organize 37 CEBs and trained 326 lay leaders in the town and surrounding countryside. In May 1973, 1,600 sugar mill workers went on strike. Many workers belonged to CEBs, and many strike leaders were CEB leaders. The Christian Federation of Salvadoran Campesinos (Federación Cristiana de Campesinos Salvadoreños or FECCAS), which worked to protect campesino rights, also participated. FECCAS set up its base in Aguilares before Grande arrived, and it then extended its reach into the country during 1973 and 1974. In witnessing the strike, Grande struggled to reconcile his pastoral mission with the radical action that often resulted from campesinos' consciousness of their situation. The powerful were uninterested in ambiguity. They saw religious as responsible for encouraging campesinos and, therefore, for the unrest. The government and oligarchy blamed Grande for the strike and FECCAS's growth.[43]

As peasants began to organize through CEBs, the state cracked down, leading many CEB members to turn to guerrilla organizations. In 1974, the National Guard began surveilling CEB meetings in Morazán, prompting many peasants to join the ERP (El Ejército Revolucionario del Pueblo [People's Revolutionary Army]) for protection.[44] The ERP advocated a military offensive to inspire the masses to join, echoing Che Guevara.[45] Similarly, after soldiers killed six at La Cayetana, San Vicente, campesinos, including their priest, David Rodríguez, turned to the FPL (Fuerzas Populares de Liberación [Popular Liberation Forces]). Initially a Marxist organization, the FPL welcomed "progressive priests and Christians" in 1974.[46] In contrast to the ERP, the FPL proposed a "prolonged popular war"—à la Vietnam—that aimed to build mass militancy before attacking the government. The three smaller guerrilla groups consisted of the RN (Resistencia Nacional [National Resistance]), which split from the ERP in 1975; the PRTC (Partido Revolucionario de los Trabajadores Centroamericanos [Revolutionary Party of Central American Workers]), which formed in 1977 and also included former ERP members; and the FAL (Fuerza Armadas de Liberación [Armed Liberation Forces]), the Communist Party's armed wing. The groups began in urban areas, then built ties with campesinos in different areas of the country.[47]

Father Rodríguez joined the FPL after concluding the armed movement fit the church's theory of "just war." The people had exhausted all peaceful and democratic means; they had been met with violence. He felt responsible for training catechists who were being killed. A week before soldiers entered the village, "informants" falsely told Bishop Aparicio that Rodríguez was inciting armed rebellion. Rodríguez concluded he should accompany them on their path and he regarded the FPL as a way to protect himself.[48] Rodríguez became a guerrilla priest.

In the capital, others took a different approach. In the summer of 1975, students in Santa Ana objected to El Salvador's hosting of the Miss Universe Pageant and its use of funds for the event, rather than on the country's people. The National Guard killed protesters. Students from the University of San Salvador marched in protest on July 30. Again, state forces gunned down students. Catholics in San Salvador, led by the archbishop, condemned the state violence. On August 1, the archbishop, auxiliary bishop Arturo Rivera y Damas, and thirty-eight other priests concelebrated a Mass for the dead. Then, about forty people, including priests and nuns, occupied the cathedral for six days. The group condemned state repression, including the killing of peasants and students, and among other demands, they called for the release of both arrested students and the bodies of those killed. During the occupation, a collection of groups—teachers, university students, artists, and the federation of rural workers—formed the BPR (Bloque Popular Revolucionario [Revolutionary Popular Block]), the largest grassroots-popular organization.[49] As the organization showed, state violence against protesting students prompted some church leaders to take a more confrontational position and inspired disparate groups to work together.

The powerful did not back down. As support for land reform increased, so did opposition. Arturo Armando Molina, who assumed the presidency after the fraudulent 1972 election, proposed modest land reform in March 1976. The Jesuit-run Universidad Centroamericana "José Simeón Cañas" (UCA) was the only institution to publicly support reform.[50] Consequently, the Right blamed the church for Molina's position and persuaded him to abandon it. UCA rector Ignacio Ellacuría criticized Molina in a scathing piece, "A sus ordenes, mi capital," a play on the Latin American address to superior officers, "At your orders, my captain." The Jesuit accused the president of bending to the wishes of economic elites like FARO (Frente Agrario de la Región Oriental [Agricultural Front of the Eastern Region]) and ANEP (Asociacíon Nacional de la Empresa Privada [National Free Enterprise Association]).[51] In response, a Right-wing group bombed the UCA for the first of six times that year.[52] Just as it did with campesinos, the Right attempted to silence dissent through violence. Merely speaking out risked a vicious response.

In 1977, political-religious tensions reached new heights as conservative Catholics took aim at religious. In *campos pagados*, paid political press advertisements, the Salvadoran Women's Front argued that some priests "dedicated themselves to preaching class warfare, violence, pillage and crime," not "teaching the authentic Gospel."[53] FARO, a lobbying group landowners established to pressure Molina to abandon land reform,[54] said Jesuits incited the masses to break the law. FARO "severely censured the criminal, anti-Christian, and illegal conduct of THOSE PRIESTS who preach hate, violence and incite the masses to commit criminal acts." Priests were out of line; FARO aimed to preserve the church.[55] More than seventy "prominent" laity of Santa Ana, El Salvador's second-largest city, turned to the Holy See. They wrote the papal nuncio, underlining their claim that "the church has taken over from professional revolutionaries and leadership of the subversive movement."[56] Like conservative Nicaraguan and U.S. Catholics, these Salvadorans equated clergy social activism with communism.

Even the president used his bully pulpit to call liberation theology a national security threat. Molina criticized those he referred to as "liberationist priests" in 1975.[57] By early 1977, he classified liberation theology as El Salvador's "number one" enemy. In a televised campaign pitch for his potential successor, Defense Minister Carlos Humberto Romero, the president drew a line down a blackboard to separate the country's "enemies" and "friends." He wrote "liberation theology" first under enemies.[58] To Molina and others like him, campesinos' sense of self-worth inspired collective action that threatened to upend the country's entire social structure. Even worse, many in the church supported and aided this change in perspective.

The government answered with repression. Besides violence against peasants, it arrested and deported priests, including Americans. In February, an unnamed person accused Maryknoll associate Bernard Survil of "working day and night instilling class hatred to incite violence and discredit the government," declaring that blood would flow on the upcoming presidential election day, and calling for violence during Masses he celebrated. When Survil denied the charges, the Salvadoran government canceled his visa. Sixteen days later, five "unknown men" took Survil "violently" from his home as he was "screaming for help."[59] He was charged with "subversive activities and . . . activism in FECCAS-UTC" (Unión de Trabajadores del Campo [Union of Rural Workers]) and then deported to Guatemala.[60]

Maryknoll insisted Survil broke no laws; he was carrying out his priestly duties. In a memo to San Salvador's archbishop, Maryknoller John Spain denied the charges. Survil "was developing a completely pastoral work that is within the law and within the doctrine of the Church."[61]

Survil was not the only priest targeted. Officials charged Maryknoller Lawrence McCulloch with "subversive activities and . . . activism in FECCAS-UTC," along with Salvadoran Guillermo Alfonso Rodríguez.[62] In 1977 alone, El Salvador expelled eight priests and refused reentry to seven. Three left the country after being threatened. Others suffered a worse fate. Two priests were imprisoned, one was beaten, one was tortured, and two were murdered.[63] In El Salvador, accompanying the poor often meant putting one's life on the line.

The Election and Human Rights Violations

The presidential election that the Salvadoran government insisted Survil interfered with was marred by fraud and followed by violence. During the February 20 voting, "amateur radio operators" overheard police and military give coded messages to commit fraud at polling stations.[64] In protest, people occupied San Salvador's main plaza. On February 24, opposition presidential candidate Colonel Ernesto Antonio Claramount called for occupation until the election was annulled. The next morning, "youths armed with sticks" had "blocked" the plaza "with small barricades." By that night, the crowd numbered over fifty thousand. Molina then addressed the nation via television and radio and announced his party's nominee, General Romero, as the winner. On February 28, National Police equipped with "armored personnel carriers, fire hoses, tear gas, and small arms" moved in. About a thousand people ran to a church for refuge. In the morning, National Police fired on crowds gathered near the plaza. The government declared a state of siege and closed La Crónica, an opposition paper.[65] Claramount was forced into exile; his running mate José Antonio Morales Ehrlich sought asylum in the Costa Rican embassy. While the government claimed five were killed, Morales argued the number was over one hundred.[66] Estimates of those injured were as high as two hundred and those detained ranged from two hundred to five hundred.[67] The presidential election, just like that of 1972, demonstrated why change through the ballot box was impossible.

The Episcopal Conference of El Salvador condemned the violence and lamented the country's overall climate. In a March 5 letter, the bishops recounted
how since the election, there was an increase in "repression against the peasants and all those who accompany them in their just cause," in "the number
of dead persons and those disappeared," and in "torture as a means of intimidation." The church, too, was subject to attack. FARO and ANEP engaged in
a media "publicity campaign." There were "threats and intimidation of priests,
laymen, institutions and publications of Christian orientation," and "foreign
priests . . . deported from the country without any explanation."[68] Though the
bishops did not mention it, there was at least tacit government approval for
the press attacks because under the state of siege, free speech was suspended.[69]

The election grabbed the attention of the U.S. Congress. In March, the
House held hearings on electoral fraud and its potential implications for U.S.
policy. As Chair Donald Fraser explained, Congress was interested not only
because fraud potentially violated the right to take part in free and fair elections under the UN Declaration of Human Rights, but also because U.S. military equipment might have been used to carry out fraud and suppress people.[70]

A State Department representative admitted U.S. aid could have been involved in internal repression. First, even though the United States sent equipment to fend off external enemies, the military was "frequently involved in
'internal security' activities" because those matters were "considered
Communist-inspired and externally influenced, thus a responsibility of the military force." Second, the Ministry of Defense supervised "all military, paramilitary and police forces." Finally, U.S. equipment did not remain with the
units it was sent to assist. It "frequently transferred between and among units,"
so any military unit involved in "any activity, law enforcement or internal security," might use U.S. materiel.[71]

Despite this, the State Department insisted military aid should continue. A
representative acknowledged that there were "sporadic instances of torture,
inhumane or degrading treatment or punishment" and that the department
was "disquieted by the suspension of certain rights following the election."
But these did not constitute 502(b)'s "consistent pattern of gross violations"
necessitating aid suspension.[72]

Although Congress focused on electoral fraud and the violence surrounding it, Maryknollers and other missionaries raised the issue of religious persecution. In between the first and second day of hearings, leaders of the
Maryknoll Sisters and of the Fathers and Brothers, together with Jesuits and
other Catholics, wrote to Congressman Fraser expressing their "distress." Besides electoral fraud, they were "disturbed" by the inability of religious "to

exercise their Christian ministry." In particular, the group cited Maryknollers' and others' expulsion and denial of their reentry "without any specific charges being made or without the elementary right of self-defense." Even worse, a Salvadoran priest was tortured, and on March 12, in the midst of the hearings, Father Grande, a teenager, and a seventy-two-year-old campesino were murdered. The writers believed these were not isolated incidents but "the beginning of an organized, well-planned and concentrated attack against the Church in El Salvador." As they explained, they wrote "to affirm our concern for missionaries of all nationalities and above all to unite ourselves with the entire Church in El Salvador as they struggle, not against people, but rather against enslavement by sin, hunger and injustice for which people often unconsciously are responsible."[73] What the writers did not explain was *why* religious were being targeted. What priests and nuns saw as support for the poor and defense of their human rights, El Salvador's powerful saw as communism. Just as in Nicaragua, the situation was simultaneously a religious and political conflict. Maryknollers' defense of the poor explained both their critique of U.S. support for a Salvadoran government that abused human rights and why they were government targets.

Maryknollers' ability to establish themselves as credible information sources, at least in Fraser's view, gave the impression that all U.S. missionaries wanted change in Central America and in U.S. policy. But Maryknollers were atypical. Only a minority of the 2,234 U.S. missionaries in Central America took this position. In 1978, there were thirty Catholic missionaries in El Salvador; nine were associated with Maryknoll.[74] Maryknoll faced backlash both in Central America and in the United States for charting a new path. In El Salvador, the state and elites regarded those who advocated for the poor as turning on the rest of society and encouraging revolt. The missionaries were security threats. Similarly, conservative U.S. Catholics objected to Maryknoll's approach. Missionaries should spread the Gospel, not critique U.S. policy or U.S. corporations. But to Maryknollers, reverse mission—educating Americans and aiming to change U.S. policy that negatively affected the people they served—was integral to their role as missionaries. Their work was not unidirectional; their service in Central America prompted them to "missionize" Americans as well.

Besides hoping for congressional action, Maryknollers may have turned to Fraser because both the Catholic Church hierarchy and the U.S. Foreign Service seemed unreceptive. No member of the hierarchy visited Survil as he sat in a Guatemalan prison. Bishop Emmanuel Gerarda, papal nuncio for Guatemala and El Salvador, admitted to the Maryknoll regional superior that this was because President Molina "advised the Cardinal not to visit the priest-prisoners."[75] The Vatican seemed to be bending to Salvadoran government pressure.

The U.S. embassy response was just as problematic. While Survil was held in Guatemala, the U.S. consul said to Maryknoller John Spain: "I think he did this . . . because he wanted to create a situation where he would be arrested or expelled and later on complain that his human rights were violated." After Survil returned to the United States and described his ordeal, the consul continued to insist that something was amiss. "Bernie, I think, is not interested in the violation of his human rights; he just wants to get something into the press." Spain was furious. He pointed to the consul's statement as evidence of "prejudice against Bernie, by the very person who is assigned to look after the best interest of the American citizens here in El Salvador."[76] To Spain, the consul, like the papal nuncio, showed an unwillingness to challenge the Salvadoran government in defense of human rights.

Maryknollers were not the only ones disheartened by the U.S. government's failure to respond to human rights violations. U.S. ambassador Ignacio Lozano Jr. claimed the Carter administration did little to pressure El Salvador, even when it came to U.S. citizens. As evidence, the Ford nominee pointed to African American Ronald J. Richardson's disappearance. The United States did not push, Lozano explained, because Carter wanted "a more friendly relationship" with incoming president General Romero.[77] Another potential reason Lozano did not mention was that during its early months, the Carter administration was formulating how to integrate support for human rights into U.S. foreign policy.[78]

Confusion surrounded the Richardson case. In 1976, the twenty-four-year-old "drifter from Philadelphia" disappeared in El Salvador.[79] Richardson had caught the eye of authorities in Belize for allegedly offering to serve as a mercenary for El Salvador in its ongoing border dispute with Honduras. Belize then deported him to El Salvador and notified the U.S. embassy.[80] Salvadoran authorities said they deported Richardson, while Lozano claimed he died while in custody.[81] Unbeknownst to Lozano, National Guardsmen took Richardson and "hung him up by the arms to some device like a mill which stretched his arms. They tied his arms and the chain stretched him," according to a solider who witnessed the event. They gave Richardson electrical shocks. Blood poured from Richardson's nose and ears as the soldier saw him being taken away.[82]

U.S. pressure did nothing to clarify what happened. In early 1977, the State Department recalled Ambassador Lozano to convey U.S. "dissatisfaction with official explanations regarding the Richardson case." Lozano was back in DC on March 7.[83] By that time, Maryknoll associate Survil had been kidnapped, taken to Guatemala, and deported. Two days after Lozano returned to DC, tension between the U.S. and Salvadoran governments escalated when Fraser opened hearings on the Salvadoran presidential elections. The Salvadoran government charged the United States with meddling in its internal affairs and rejected U.S. military aid the day before the House finished the hearings. The move allowed El Salvador to save face if Congress terminated aid in response to Grande's murder, but did not affect any U.S. military aid already in the pipeline or U.S. military advisors in the country.

Soon after, the deputy assistant secretary of state for inter-American affairs reported that "evidence" suggested El Salvador "intend[ed] to stonewall on the Richardson case" and that the human rights situation was likely to worsen. The United States sent Lozano back to convey to President Molina both the "growing concern over the Richardson matter" and the "current human rights situation," specifically, "the recent treatment of American clergymen and the trend" regarding "other foreign clergy." Additionally, Lozano gave Molina a deadline: if no progress was made by the time the ambassador left El Salvador (because of the new Carter administration), the U.S. military group would be cut from ten to six people.[84] The reduction happened,[85] but little else changed. As Lozano cabled the State Department in late April, once El Salvador rejected military aid, U.S. leverage disappeared.[86] The Carter administration pushed for improved human rights, but its halfhearted attempts were easy for the Salvadoran government to ignore.

The State Department kept pressuring the embassy. In anticipation of Lozano's departure around June 1, 1977, Deputy Secretary of State Warren Christopher instructed him to "carefully and emphatically" raise "salient irritants in our current bilateral relations." The first was the Richardson case. Others included "the more general question of treatment of Americans," particularly "clergymen," including "the questionable treatment of Father Bernard Survil."[87]

Despite DC's repeated instructions to raise the Richardson case, and sometimes the Survil case, Lozano felt unsupported. As he cabled in early May, Salvadoran officials did not take his and others' warnings seriously. They believed embassy officers expressed their "personal biases" because of "the deafening silence that has emanated from Washington." The U.S. government had not made one comment or "single public reference" to the Richardson case, making it difficult for Salvadoran officials to believe it mattered. Lozano questioned not only the U.S. government's commitment to human rights but also its ability to assess Salvadoran conditions. "I feel obligated to register my mounting concern that a basic lack of understanding of local culture and politics continues to plague USG analysis of the nature and dimensions of its problems with the GOES [Salvadoran government]."[88] U.S. policymakers did not get it. In subsequent years, Maryknollers repeatedly voiced the same claim.

Archbishop Romero and Religious Persecution

The Salvadoran government's decision to reject U.S. military aid ushered a change in relations, but it was not the only one. In response to Grande's murder, the Salvadoran archdiocese adopted a more confrontational stance vis-à-vis the government. The priests and two bishops of the archdiocese closed Catholic schools for three days and canceled all Sunday Masses except one in the cathedral. The group mandated the establishment of a committee to continue to "monitor events." The archdiocese also began disseminating information that challenged the state's accounts through bulletins and its radio station YSAX, which "broadcast a combination of Scripture readings, religious and protest songs, official church statements, and its own reflections." These media efforts were particularly important given the press censorship at the time.[89]

For his part, the newly appointed archbishop Óscar Anulfo Romero (unrelated to General Romero) criticized the government, which came somewhat as a surprise.[90] Many, including Jesuits and Maryknollers, initially regarded Romero as backing the oligarchy.[91] Although Romero was a supporter of liberation theology, he believed that while priests could aid and "accompany" people, they must refrain from taking a political position. To many younger priests, this line was untenable.[92] How could they encourage people to organize through CEBs, but then not actively support those dangerous efforts? Grande's murder contributed to Romero's changed outlook.[93]

Romero became the country's main opposition voice. During Sunday homilies broadcast over YSAX, the overwhelming majority of rural Salvadorans—73 percent—and nearly half of those in urban areas listened as Romero listed those killed, tortured, or assaulted during the previous week, regardless of the perpetrator.[94] The archbishop confronted the president. When Molina met with the papal nuncio and the country's bishops and claimed that "international communism" killed Grande, Romero warned him against confusing the church's approach after Vatican II and Medellín with Marxism-Leninism.[95] The archbishop also refused to attend government ceremonies because he did want to appear to be sanctioning the government.[96]

Romero was the lone diocese head to challenge the president; not all Catholics, or even all priests, saw things as he did. Reverend Ricardo Fuentes Castellanos, columnist for the conservative *El Mundo*, blamed Father Grande for his own death. Fuentes argued that "progressive clergy" were carrying out a Marxist campaign. In a familiar argument, he blamed Vatican II. After the council the church "embarked on a socialist adventure that has looked to win over the modern world, profoundly distant from the traditional principles of the Catholic Church." As evidence, Fuentes characterized the bishops' Medellín language about institutionalized violence and social sin as "an attack on bourgeois society, private property, and military institutions" as well as the impetus for liberation theology's growth. The bishops' talk of "community ownership" and "social reform" was the same as Marxist party language. Fuentes also charged Jesuits with engaging in an "intense campaign of Marxist indoctrination" since the early 1970s. They "FOOLED" nuns and through their university, the UCA, influenced youth.[97] As in 1932, the armed forces were the "ONLY" way to save the church and the country.[98]

Fuentes's argument echoed other conservative Catholics' charges against religious, especially Jesuits. Some Salvadoran parents accused Jesuits of corrupting sociology students at Externado, San Salvador's Jesuit *colegio*. As they charged, "When our sons come back from their field work in marginal zones with their teachers, who should be orienting them with a Christian spirit instead of class conflict, they begin to accuse their families of living like bourgeois, as if trying to work hard to improve one's economic position were a crime."[99] The argument that Jesuits were turning children against their social class, their country, and their church was the same in Nicaragua. And Fuentes's appeal to violence came the same month Nicaraguans William and Robert Cranshaw called for killing priests. Their similar proposals revealed how conservative Catholics across political borders shared a sense that communists threatened the church from within and that violence was the only way to eradicate them.

Fuentes got his wish. In May, the Right-wing death squad White Warriors Union (Unión Guerrera Blanca or UGB) murdered Father Alfonso Navarro,[100] along with a fifteen-year-old boy. The group claimed retaliation for the FPL's kidnapping and killing of Foreign Minister Mauricio Borgnovo.[101] UGB was one of several death squads that first appeared in 1975. Backed by elites, such as those in ANEP and FARO, death squads urged the security forces and others to form "independent cells" and eradicate suspected communists.[102]

As hostility and violence against religious increased during the spring at breakneck speed, Salvadorans disagreed over how to interpret it. Some, most notably Archbishop Romero, argued that through violence, the government intended to remove priests committed to serving the poor.[103] Others argued that charges of church persecution were "an utter lie" designed to "blackmail the government" so that "national and foreign priests can do as they wish."[104] The government claimed it was combatting communism by targeting security threats: problem priests. It was not persecuting the institutional church; it was cutting out diseased elements.

Rather than targeting individuals, in May the White Warriors upped the ante by threatening to kill any of the more than fifty Jesuits still in the country on July 21.[105] The White Warriors argued, as other conservative Salvadoran Catholics had, that the problem was individual priests and nuns under communist influence, not the church as a whole. It simply happened that every Jesuit fit this category. "The religious orders and priests who are not agents of international Communism have nothing to fear from us and can continue their work in complete tranquility. Our struggle is not against the Church, but against Jesuit guerrillaism."[106] Anonymous pamphlets appeared in San Salvador that urged people to "Be a Patriot, kill a Priest!"[107]

Unlike the Richardson and Survil cases, the White Warriors' threat attracted U.S. attention. Some Catholics asked the U.S. government to condemn the UGB.[108] As William Guste, Louisiana's attorney general and Carter's "good friend,"[109] explained in a telegram to the president, Jesuits and other Catholics were attacked because they "have emerged as staunch defenders of civil liberties and human rights especially for the poor."[110] They were living the Gospel's spirit. Conservative U.S. Catholics, by contrast, saw these priests and nuns as agents of class conflict who furthered the Gospel according to Karl Marx. *National Review* agreed that the White Warriors' warning was the logical outcome of Jesuits' collusion with Marxists. As the magazine alleged, "it is widely understood that the Jesuit order in Latin America has been radicalized, and many priests and even some bishops have been cooperating with Marxists and even seeking to fashion a philosophical synthesis of Marxism and Christianity." The "harsh secular counterattack" by "the terrorist White Warriors Union" was unsurprising given the priests' involvement with "secular politics."[111] *National Review* implied that Jesuits removed themselves from the religious into the political arena, thereby stripping themselves of their religious identity. In doing so, *National Review* reiterated conservative Catholics' view that socially active priests and nuns were no longer religious but political actors or even communists. As *National Review* demonstrated, the belief that communism infiltrated the clergy was not confined to El Salvador.

Largely prompted by religious groups, the U.S. government responded. On July 8, 1977, Secretary of State Vance met with Georgetown University's president and other Jesuits, a U.S. Catholic Conference of Bishops official, and National Council of Churches representatives.[112] He explained that the United States "had already made protests to the Salvadoran ambassador." In the following days, an assistant secretary expressed concern to the Salvadoran charge,[113] and the deputy assistant secretary of state traveled to El Salvador to reiterate this message to President Romero.[114] The White House did not send a representative to Romero's July inauguration, nor did it fill the ambassador post.[115] The House of Representatives also held hearings, *Religious Persecution in El Salvador*.[116] The danger to Jesuits temporarily ended when the

Vatican's threat to excommunicate Salvadoran officials led President Romero to announce government protection for Jesuit schools and the seminary.[117]

The White Warriors' threat ended, but violence shifted to the laity, especially the rural poor. Salvadorans feared having Catholic Bibles at home, listening to Mass, or associating with the church.[118] Delegate of the word Felipe de Jesús Chacón illustrates the fate that often befell liberationist campesinos. In August 1977, National Guardsmen arrested him, scalped him, and removed "the flesh from his face." They drew and quartered his body, and left it to be eaten by dogs. The Law for the Defense and Guarantee of Public Order, issued in late November 1977, further targeted campesinos. It prohibited government opposition by outlawing "eighteen categories of activities,"[119] including strikes and public meetings. The press was censored and "normal judicial procedures" were suspended. The law "accelerated the spiral of political violence" because it most affected political moderates, not guerrillas. The repression bred animosity, leading to further radicalization and international rebuke.[120]

A January 1978 investigatory team sponsored by the Unitarian Universalist Service Committee concluded there had been no improvement in church-state relations or state-directed violence against the church since General Romero's July inauguration. As the group, which included Jesuit Congressman Robert F. Drinan (D-MA), explained, "We saw an unrepentant government dominated by the military, perpetuating terrorism and a persecution of religion seldom if ever seen in any nation in the Western Hemisphere within living memory." The government's war "against the rural poor" was really "against religion" because priests served as leaders in the struggle for change, particularly land reform.[121] To the investigatory team, the conclusion was clear: the government sought to violently eradicate any spark for change.

The team blamed the government, but Salvadoran leaders identified priests as instigators. Vice President Julio Ernesto Astacio contended "some priests" preached subversive ideas. President Romero alleged that 60 percent of priests in the central zone told campesinos to violently seize land if it was not given to them. He named several priests and revealed that the government tape-recorded homilies. Just as the powerful had concluded in 1932, Romero believed campesinos were incapable of independently questioning Salvadoran society. Priests were planting these ideas and needed to be stopped. Just like Nicaragua's Somoza, President Romero dismissed the *escándolo* (scandalous outcry) arising from "trouble-making" priests like Father Alas, who spoke in the United States, including before Congress. By contrast, Drinan characterized the activity as priests' pastoral mission and angrily retorted that they were following Vatican II.[122] The dispute turned on whether priests should say Mass and perform sacraments, or whether they ought to involve themselves in the country's social conditions. The heated Romero-Drinan exchange underscored how disagreements about the church's role in society aggravated political tensions.

In this atmosphere, Archbishop Romero was unsafe. He faced death threats, but refused bodyguards.[123] Foreigners sought to protect the archbishop through international recognition. Georgetown University awarded Romero an honorary doctorate,[124] while 118 members of the British Parliament and peers across party lines nominated him for the 1979 Nobel Peace Prize.[125]

Charges of religious persecution continued. In January 1979 when journalists confronted President Romero with the OAS finding of religious persecution, he denied it.[126] Archbishop Romero accused the president of lying, especially given that church sources had recorded 1,063 people arrested on political grounds, 147 killed by security forces, and 23 disappeared in 1978 alone.[127] Salvadoran political organizations, such as CUTS (La Confederación Unitaria Trabajadores Salvadoreño [Unitary Confederation of United Salvadoran Workers]), and Solidarity Committees with the People in El Salvador in the United States, based in New York, Los Angeles, Washington, DC, and San Francisco, disputed the president's account through *campos pagados*.[128]

Religion and Revolution

President Romero was not the only one concerned about religious involvement in revolution. Though the Carter administration was not focused on El Salvador, after the Iranian revolution it worried about religion's relationship to revolution and about liberation theology. Carter ordered the CIA to "study and examine" Islamic movements and "dissident" Catholic lay movements in "traditionally Catholic" countries, especially Latin America. In doing so, Carter was responding to Brzezinski's recommendation and the National Security Council's failure to identify leaders or key religious currents in Latin America. Senators on the Foreign Relations Committee learned of this development during early February 1979 closed-door hearings. Troubled by the U.S. failure to identify the role of religion and religious activists in Iran, Congress members warned of the potential for "another Iran" in Latin America, this time Catholic led. Members also inquired about liberation theology and Marxism's influence on dissident religious and lay Catholics.[129]

Though the hearings were closed-door, some media reported on them, and members of faith communities raised objections. The Mexican center-Right *Excélsior* covered the story, leading Brazil's *Temp e Presenca* and the U.S. *National*

Catholic Reporter to do so as well.[130] After the hearing, forty-five Catholic religious and laity attending the Latin American bishops' meeting in Puebla, Mexico, wrote Carter, objecting to his call for CIA surveillance of the church. The group described the U.S. government's approach as "a very grave violation of the most basic human right" and queried, "What would President Carter think if a Latin American government announced a plan to examine and study the churches of the United States, including his own church, the Baptist church?" Referencing Carter's practice of teaching Sunday school while serving as president, the group wondered, "How would Carter like to have a spy in his Bible class?"[131] For those familiar with the Banzer Plan, Carter's orders were further proof of U.S. government attempts to smother Leftist trends in the Latin American church.

The administration's fear of religious revolution grew with the Sandinistas' success. The day after the Sandinistas triumphantly entered Managua, Carter worried about the revolution's impact on nearby countries. In his diary he wrote that the "Nicaraguan question has been substantially resolved . . . but we are concerned about the spread to neighboring countries of the revolutionary impact. El Salvador is weakest, but Honduras, Guatemala, and even Costa Rica could be vulnerable."[132]

Carter's concern was not without foundation. The Sandinista victory "elevated the fighting morale of the left."[133] Salvadoran popular organizations linked Somoza to President Romero. After the Sandinistas entered Managua, Salvadorans chanted the rhyme "Romero y Somoza, son la misma cosa" (Romero and Somoza are the same thing).[134]

The administration tried to "befriend" the Nicaraguan government. Carter hoped to discourage Nicaragua's movement toward the Cubans and Soviets by supporting the "non-Sandinista elements within the anti-Somoza coalition—the private sector, the Church, the independent press." But Congress blocked aid for months because many conservatives saw Nicaragua as a lost cause and "second Cuba." Carter requested $75 million in economic aid in November 1979, but Congress did not approve it until the spring of 1980.[135]

Carter was uneasy about the Sandinista government and anxious about a replay in El Salvador. He was not alone. The Nicaraguan revolution led Salvadorans to evaluate their situation. Many military worried revolution could leave them exiled and without funds, just like Somoza's Guard. For this reason, they supported the October 1979 overthrow of General Romero and the creation of a civilian-military junta. They saw it as a way to preserve the military as an institution in the face of a growing Leftist movement the government could not control.[136] U.S. ambassador Frank Devine came to a similar conclusion. One week after the coup, he described the junta of three civilians and two military as the "last chance of staving off a takeover by the far left."[137] The junta needed public support to prevent the Left from gaining more adherents. Just as the Carter administration regarded the Sandinistas as the biggest threat and tried to isolate them, the White House pursued the same course regarding the Salvadoran guerrillas.

The junta's changes were short-lived. The junta pledged land reform and nationalization of trade in coffee.[138] In theory, the junta broke up ORDEN, an anticommunist "paramilitary network of informers and vigilantes," in existence since 1967 and that at its height had one hundred thousand people.[139] But ORDEN secretly continued, protected by its many members associated with the army and security forces.[140] Violence returned when state forces killed sixty-five people during a peaceful demonstration in November. Afterward, the United States sent $200,000 of antiriot equipment, signaling its support for the junta.[141] In response, Archbishop Romero condemned the government and asked that the United States not provide unrestricted military aid but condition it on "a purge of the country's security forces."[142]

More Attention on El Salvador

Like the archbishop, Maryknollers recognized El Salvador's dire conditions. In December 1979, Joan Petrik, Maryknoll's area secretary for El Salvador, called for sisters to join her and Madeline Dorsey. Petrik worked alone in La Libertad, while Dorsey was in Santa Ana. The women accompanied the "suffering and poor," as Archbishop Romero called for.[143] They worked with CEBs, co-ops, women's groups, and a "community based health program." They taught literacy and accompanied "Christians organized in popular political groups." But Petrik warned, "due to the political situation," only those with "previous mission experience" should come. The work was so difficult that those interested could live in El Salvador for two to three months and receive a "temporary" salary while deciding if they "could accept the challenge." Despite the risks, Petrik argued "the opportunity is unique because the church here has suffered much persecution for her prophetic stand and has grown stronger through that conflict." In El Salvador, "the whole Archdiocesan church [is] struggling to respond," not just the "vanguard of the church" as in other countries.[144] Ita Ford and Carla Piette, who lived in Chile during Allende's overthrow, accepted the challenge and arrived in the spring.[145]

The Maryknoll sisters in El Salvador—and elsewhere in Central America—were under no illusions about the situation they faced. Their work involved health care and religious education; but in keeping with Maryknollers' understanding of mission, they sought to transform people, structures, and systems. The Mexico and Central America delegates to the 1978 Maryknoll Sisters' General Assembly pledged to "address the *cause* of the poor as well as their *needs.*" In the midst of societies dominated by "socio-economic-political systems" that created unjust and oppressive societies, working for justice in the name of God meant siding with the poor and suffering.[146]

The sisters knew the risks. To Maryknollers, "neutrality" meant support for the status quo; therefore, the women concluded, "We cannot remain neutral." The sisters recognized the potential consequences. "By being faithful to the Gospel in denouncing injustice in society, Christians risk misunderstanding, persecutions and perhaps even torture and death. We may be accused of being subversive."[147] The sisters' conclusion revealed how living among the Latin American poor influenced their role as missioners. While they continued Maryknoll's belief in martyrdom's virtue, risking persecution for one's beliefs in the late 1970s was based on the sisters' commitment to the poor, not on the women's status as Catholic nuns, as in the early Cold War. And if they were indeed martyred, it would be at the hands of other Catholics.

Though Maryknollers called for more attention to El Salvador, there was little U.S. knowledge about the country, as early 1980 international solidarity events demonstrated. Organizers planned coordinated activities in Europe and North and South America on World Peace Day, January 12–13, to stress human rights, the right to self-determination, and liberation through nonviolent means. They began plans when the Bishops' Conference of Central America requested solidarity days after the Nicaraguan revolution.[148]

In the United States there were religious vigils, fasting, and educational seminars; planners recognized the need for the latter because even the sympathetically inclined were often only familiar with Nicaragua. St. Mary's parish in Corvallis, Oregon, tried to attract attendees by referencing Nicaragua. As the parish bulletin announced, "You've seen the Nicaraguan revolution on TV. Maybe you've guessed at the weight of oppression and violation of basic rights that can bring on such a conflict. The Central American bishops urgently warn us that the same oppression is at work in Guatemala, Honduras and El Salvador—injustice, exploitation of landless peasants, hunger and malnutrition."[149] Organizers also had to contend with other foreign policy concerns, such as the taking of hostages in Tehran in November and the Soviets' invasion of Afghanistan in December. The ignorance among some Americans betrayed Nicaraguan and Salvadoran immigrant communities' work opposing Somoza and the Salvadoran government for several years.[150]

Even the White House acknowledged its limited focus on El Salvador. As National Security Advisor Zbigniew Brzezinski admitted in January, the administration gave El Salvador "only sporadic attention because we have had so many other demands on our time."[151] But the approach was changing because the administration regarded El Salvador as both a regional problem and a test of U.S. credibility worldwide.[152] In this context, Archbishop Romero's opposition to U.S. policy was an obstacle. Officials characterized the archbishop as biased, seeing him as part of the Salvadoran Left that opposed the U.S.-backed junta.[153] Carter officials, like conservative Catholics, regarded Romero's outlook as inappropriate for a church leader. One of the administration's "basic policy questions" regarding El Salvador in January 1980 was "how to get the church to be neutral."[154]

Romero's opposition to the junta so preoccupied the White House that officials, including Secretary of State Vance and National Security Advisor Brzezinski, repeatedly asked church leaders to intervene. U.S. representatives spoke to the Vatican foreign minister and secretary of state, encouraged Jesuit leadership to speak to Romero's Jesuit advisors, obtained Nicaraguan archbishop Obando's word that he would talk to Romero, and pursued "contacts with a number of Catholic clergy" that might be able to help.[155] Most significantly, Brzezinski spoke to Pope John Paul II about Central America, and he wrote to the pontiff soliciting his assistance.[156]

In a letter drafted by the State Department, Polish-born Catholic Brzezinski requested the Polish pope's support regarding Romero, whom Brzezinski portrayed as compromising U.S. foreign policy, Central Americans' safety, and the church. As Romero abandoned support for the junta and "leaned toward support for the extreme left," Brzezinski argued, Romero veered from promoting the middle path of "moderation and peaceful reforms." The United States attempted through various channels to change Romero's mind, but to no avail. Consequently, Brzezinski implored the pope to "urgently" intervene on Central Americans' behalf "to ensure that the Church plays a responsible and constructive role on behalf of moderation and peaceful change which only it can play."[157] The archbishop's criticism of the junta was problematic because the Carter administration was trying to "bolster the junta" and "split the left and neutralize the right."[158]

It was not unreasonable for Brzezinski to think the pope might be receptive. The archbishop was already on the Vatican's radar screen. Other members of the Bishops Conference of El Salvador complained to the Vatican that Romero was "too political."[159] Bishop Aparicio told the *New York Times* that Jesuits "manipulated" Romero and that his popularity was misunderstood.[160] To counteract Romero's homilies broadcast over YSAX, Aparicio bought full-page ad space to print his.[161] He also prohibited people in his diocese from circulating or reading *Orientación*, the archdiocesan paper.[162]

The Vatican shared these concerns. In their first meeting, John Paul II questioned Romero about his positions. The Holy See considered keeping Romero as titular head of the archdiocese with a Vatican envoy holding actual control.[163] Instead, it shifted personnel to dampen liberationists' influence and improve relations with the Salvadoran government. In late 1977, the two most progressive bishops—Romero and his auxiliary Arturo Rivera y Damas—were separated. While Rivera was sent to head the Santiago de María diocese, conservative Marco Revelo replaced him in San Salvador.[164]

Even if the White House was unaware of Vatican internal politics, the pontiff's statements seemed to conflict with Romero's espousal of liberation theology. At the 1979 Latin American bishops' meeting at Puebla, the pope disputed any notion of a revolutionary church. "This idea of Christ as a political figure, a revolutionary, as the subversive Man from Nazareth, does not tally with the Church's catechesis." He continued, God "unequivocally rejects recourse to violence."[165] Though the pope did not use the term "liberation theology," many interpreted his words as condemnation of it. Liberation theology was significant because 90 percent of Latin Americans were baptized Catholics, and because Latin American Catholics, by early 1979, composed nearly half of all Catholics worldwide.[166]

The White House's endeavors bore no fruit. Carter noted that the efforts "didn't work," and record do not definitively state whether the letter was ever sent to the pope.[167] But its existence demonstrates the administration's perception of Romero's influence and the lengths the White House went to try to muzzle him.

Despite these behind-the-scenes efforts to quiet him, Archbishop Romero continued to criticize both the junta and U.S. military aid. In January 1980, three civilian junta members and ten of the eleven cabinet ministers resigned. The military and Christian Democratic Party (Partido Demócrata Cristiano or PDC), with U.S. encouragement, formed a new junta that again attempted land and bank reforms. But by February, Romero charged the PDC with "covering up the bloody repression against the people and the fact that the country is actually being governed by the right."[168] In a letter to President Carter he also argued that U.S. military equipment would "without a doubt" make the injustice and repression worse. As he explained, the junta and the Christian Democrats were not governing the country; "political power was in the hands of the unscrupulous military," and the "only thing it knows how to do is suppress the people and favor the interests of the oligarchy." Romero asked Carter to "prohibit" military aid and to "guarantee that the United States would not intervene directly or indirectly through military, economic, or political pressure." The Salvadoran people must be allowed to determine their own path, as the Latin American bishops at Puebla recognized that all peoples have the right to self-determination.[169] Romero read this letter during Mass on February 17, and days later, bombs destroyed the archdiocese's radio station.[170]

Romero was correct; the junta was no moderate force. Its PDC representatives were accomplices in repressing people, including their own party members. More Christian Democrats were killed from January to March 1980 than during the prior seven years, according to former PDC member Rubén Zamora. Even worse, PDC members, including José Napoleón Duarte, dismissed the issue when Zamora and others raised their concerns. The tension fractured the PDC. Leftists also lost respect for party cofounder Duarte, who had served as San Salvador's mayor for three terms, been fraudulently denied the 1972 presidency, and subsequently been forced into exile in Venezuela until 1979. Once the face of Salvadoran opposition, Duarte was now in bed with both the military and the U.S. government. And to the guerrillas, even those who initially supported the junta, its failure to institute democratic reforms or stop repression meant war was the only remaining option.[171] The PDC's participation was not evidence of the junta's centrism, as Carter officials insisted.

The White House disagreed with Romero's assessment, but he had supporters among U.S. religious, including Maryknoll.[172] In a letter to Carter, Father Thomas Marti explained that "based on the experience of our missionaries in Latin America," Maryknollers agreed with Romero's conclusion that military arms and training would bring more repression. Marti appealed to Carter's human rights policies. Maryknollers in Latin America witnessed how Carter's "stance on the new Panama Canal Treaties" and the Sandinista government "created a much better view of the United States among the people of Latin America." Marti urged Carter to remain "steadfast on the human rights issue" regarding El Salvador and other countries.[173] Maryknoll also encouraged others to send letters to President Carter and Secretary of State Vance supporting Romero's call.[174] Non-Catholics who joined them included U.S. United Methodist mission officials,[175] the National Council of Churches, and the American Friends Service Committee.[176]

Human rights advocates were heartened when Carter appointed Robert E. White as ambassador to El Salvador. White previously critiqued Chile's human rights record before the OAS in 1976.[177] As ambassador to Paraguay, he defended critics of General Alfredo Stroessner's dictatorship. White regarded his selection for the San Salvador post, as he later wrote, as the Carter administration's reaffirmation of its "conviction that El Salvador could not be saved from revolution by abandoning democratic values and human rights."[178]

But the Carter administration stuck to its guns. In defending continued U.S. military aid, the State Department described the junta as "the best hope for a non-extremist solution" and stressed that "the vast bulk of our contemplated assistance" was economic.[179] The administration's characterization of the junta as caught between Right and Left as well as its emphasis on economic aid was one the Reagan administration later stressed as well.

In March, tensions in El Salvador heightened. The junta reshuffled again and reintroduced land reform, but accompanied it with a state of siege.[180] Romero railed against the violence, and during his March 23 homily, he called on soldiers to disobey orders to kill their fellow citizens.

> No soldier is obliged to obey an order against the law of God. No one has to fulfill an immoral law. It is time to recover your consciences and to obey your consciences rather than the order of sin. The Church, defender of the rights of God, of human dignity, the dignity of the person, cannot remain silent before such an abomination. We want the government to take seriously that reforms are worth nothing when they come about stained with so much blood. In the name of God, and in the name of this suffering people whose laments rise to heaven each day more tumultuous, I beg you, I ask you, I order you in the name of God: Stop the repression!

Romero's words were met with thunderous applause.[181] The next day, the man known as "the voice of the voiceless" was shot while saying Mass.[182] The attack's mastermind, Roberto D'Aubuisson, former deputy director of the central intelligence unit and associated with the White Warriors Union, was not arrested. After the October 1979 coup, D'Aubuisson lost his position when the junta abolished ORDEN. But he continued his fight against subversives. He often appeared on television, naming suspected communists based on centralized intelligence information. Days later, death squads murdered those he fingered.[183]

Unlike in Nicaragua after Chamorro's murder, an eerie calm descended on El Salvador after the archbishop's death. Streets were quiet. Businesses closed. The response was a mix of respect, fear, and for some, a failure to acknowledge what had occurred. In the hours afterward, both radio and television continued their regular programming. Salvadorans had to turn to Nicaraguan channels to learn about the archbishop's death.[184]

Violence returned at the archbishop's funeral. Thirty thousand Salvadorans processed ten blocks to the cathedral. Then, during the service, gunfire rang out and bombs exploded for forty-five minutes. The violence and chaos left thirty dead and hundreds injured.[185] The experience provided many non-Salvadorans at the funeral with insight. As a few Maryknoll sisters said, "It was good for all of us to experience with the people the danger and fear and anger of being subjected to violence." The death, as Ita Ford wrote to her mother, also "started a continental examination of conscience about how each local Church was or wasn't being faithful to the Gospel."[186] She arrived in El Salvador after Romero's murder, in mid-April.[187]

The Religious Community versus the Carter Administration

Romero's supporters took his place as the leading opponents of U.S. policy. Shortly before the archbishop's murder, U.S. Catholics formed the Religious Task Force on El Salvador, later the Religious Task Force on Central America, while in May 1980, Protestants created the Inter-Religious Task Force on El Salvador, later the Inter-Religious Task Force on Central America.[188] Religious from across the United States and the world flooded the State Department with letters and telegrams opposing military aid.[189] Their efforts were unsuccessful. Though in a statement Carter "strongly condemn[ed] the tragic assassination" as "a shocking and unconscionable act,"[190] the administration pushed for—and got—congressional approval to reprogram "non-lethal" aid, including trucks, ambulances, and tear gas.[191] Romero's murder drew battle lines between the U.S. government and the religious community that hardened with time. The two groups were at odds over why there was violence, and what the role of religious and the U.S. government should be.

In an article in *America*, James Connor, Jesuit Conference president in Washington, DC, showed how the liberal U.S. religious community was moving farther away from the U.S. government. Connor recounted a phone conversation the evening of Romero's murder with a State Department official who recently visited El Salvador "at length" and met with Romero. The official expressed regret but also said that "the archbishop had been asking for it" because he aligned himself with the Left and aroused the people by speaking about revolution. Romero should have worked to moderate, calm, or heal the country, as was the proper role for a church leader.[192] Unbeknownst to Connor, the official's response was the same as top Carter officials' desire for Romero's "neutrality."

Connor also explained how his attendance at Romero's funeral led him to reassess U.S. policy. As he described to *America* readers, he was "huddled with 4,000 terrified peasants inside San Salvador's cathedral while bombs exploded and bullets whistled outside in the plaza." Yet the Salvadoran government blamed the people for the violence, a "fabrication," Connor and twenty-one other religious leaders insisted in a signed document. The experience of seeing the United States back a lie convinced Connor that U.S. policy was "badly misguided." He concluded: "It became a choice between Archbishop Romero and the U.S. State Department."[193]

Connor was not alone in his view. At a State Department roundtable on El Salvador for religious leaders in April, disagreement arose over the government's sources. As the Jesuit Missions executive secretary pointed out, the government depended exclusively on the Salvadoran army, whereas the church's sources were more credible, he contended, because they were "from the base."[194]

One voice "from the base," Maryknoller Joan Petrik, expressed frustration with the U.S. government. As she wrote in a May letter to other sisters, friends, and relatives, "When will our embassy get out of their bunker and see things from the point of view of the poor? I do not believe that it can ever happen." As Petrik explained, "The situation . . . has deteriorated rapidly since January 1980." No "section of the country . . . has been left untouched by the political repression." She continued, "Everyday, no matter where . . . trucks . . . full of soldiers or National Guards are seen patrolling the streets." El Salvador was "not only a full fledged but *visible* National Security State now. The army, navy, national police, Hacienda police, National Guard, ORDEN . . . and now the Death Squadron . . . impose fear and repression everywhere. They are like an invading force, feared and hated by the poor."[195]

In response, Petrik and other sisters accompanied Salvadorans. When they heard rumors of a "military operation and search" at the same time as Mass, the women went to the community "to console, encourage and prepare the people for the Mass" because they knew "the people would be terrorized." Earlier, hundreds of soldiers and National Guardsmen arrived in two nearby towns, searching and threatening the people. The violence led Salvadorans to oppose the junta and the U.S. government. As Petrik wrote, "The people believe that the Junta either directs the armed forces in their brutality and massacres or that they have no control over them." And for its military aid, the people "hated" the U.S. government.[196]

Whereas Connor and Petrik saw a misinformed State Department, U.S. policy supporters accused the religious community of the same thing. In a *New York Times* op-ed, former U.S. ambassador to El Salvador Henry E. Catto Jr. charged religious with naiveté. He argued that the United States needed to quickly send aid, but Archbishop Romero's opposition to it and his murder "set off an extraordinary lobbying campaign. The President, members of Congress and State Department officials have been inundated with letters and telegrams—much of the mail is from priests and nuns—from as far away as Hong Kong. Editorials in church newspapers and sermons have kept the pot boiling." But, Catto insisted, Romero and his supporters—"political naïfs"—suffered from "myopia" because they regarded the junta as "repressive" and they failed to condemn the Leftist guerrillas.[197] To Catto, priests and nuns were incapable of understanding political realities. The contrasting views between religious and the U.S. government intensified with time.

While the United States debated policy, Romero's successor, acting archbishop Rivera, organized church efforts to help. The archdiocese formed the Emergency Committee because the undeclared war meant there were no international humanitarian agencies in El Salvador. National groups, such as the Red Cross, were unresponsive and rumored to be "pro-government/oligarchy connected."[198] At Rivera's request, Maryknollers Ita Ford and Carla Piette helped in sixteen parishes in Chalatenango, an area known for its active farmworkers' union and support for the Left.[199] Just two months before, in May 1980, military high command designated the department a "military emergency zone," prompting operations designed to weed out guerrillas.[200] The sisters distributed food, medicine, and aid. They also collected information about the situation for the church and international agencies.[201]

The work was especially dangerous because of the state of undeclared and unrecognized war, something Ford and Piette worked to address. They wrote to the USCC, asking that it "petition the International Red Cross (ICRC), Geneva, to recognize the existing state of war."[202] The distinction mattered because international humanitarian supplies, such as medicine, could not be sent, nor were international norms of behavior regarding warfare observed.[203] The government could seize people seeking protection in hospitals and refugee centers.[204]

Ford and Piette also worried that the United States would militarily intervene, and insisted Maryknoll combat the U.S. public's ignorance of El Salvador. While the U.S. press covered Archbishop Romero's murder, since then, Ford and Piette argued, "news coverage on Salvador has declined to almost nothing." While press coverage suggested nothing was happening, Salvadorans believed there was a serious risk of U.S. intervention "under the guise of 'stopping the subversive' or 'containing communism,' and that all of Central America will be involved." The women insisted, "if we have a preferential option for the poor as well as a commitment for justice as the basis for the coming of the Kingdom, we're going to have to take sides in El Salvador—correction, we have."[205] Neutrality was not an option, no matter the consequences.

The situation took a toll. The women felt "isolated and alone," they told other sisters in Central America, Chile, and Maryknoll, New York. "We are pastoral workers used to having people whom we can visit, meet with, etc.

Now we have no people—we cannot visit because of the times and the very real fear of placing others in danger because of belonging to the Church, which is one of the security forces' biggest enemies." Still, they would soldier on.[206]

Work was dangerous for other Maryknollers as well. Joan Petrik did not return to El Salvador after a seminarian was tortured with electric shocks while being asked about her whereabouts.[207] Teresa Alexander, who arrived in 1980 to take Petrik's place,[208] had been alone in La Libertad. After receiving death threats, she moved in with Madeline Dorsey, hoping there would be safety in numbers.[209] Dorsey, a nurse, had been in El Salvador the longest, since 1976. No stranger to unpopular causes, in 1955 she and other Maryknollers opened the first racially integrated U.S. hospital in Kansas City, and ten years later she marched at Selma.[210] Maura Clarke joined Dorsey and Alexander in August. Clarke spent her days distributing food, "supervising the young religious instructors and visiting sick people."[211]

The threat to Maryknollers increased. In August 1980, Colonel Ricardo Peña told Ford "that Catholic nuns and priests were subversives because they sided with the poor." She and Piette were at the barracks demanding that a few young men be released, as they often did. When one was let go, the sisters drove him to his family in a nearby village. They did not want him staying at the convent because people claimed he was an ORDEN informant.[212] En route, a storm erupted. On their return, the jeep got caught in a flooded river, toppled over, and trapped the women inside. Piette pushed Ford out before the current carried her away.[213]

Clarke took Piette's place. With Ford, she brought food to remote areas and secretly ferried refugees to San Salvador through National Guard checkpoints.[214] The two often worked with Ursuline Sister Dorothy Kazel and lay missioner Jean Donovan, part of the Cleveland diocese's mission team based in the La Libertad area.[215] Forty-one-year-old Kazel arrived in 1974 and planned to return to the United States in the spring, but Romero's murder led her to stay.[216] Donovan, twenty-seven, began training with Maryknoll as a lay missioner in 1978. In 1975, Maryknoll Fathers and Brothers together with the Sisters established the training program for lay volunteers.[217]

The refugee crisis grew as campesinos fled the security forces or ORDEN.[218] By mid-September, the San Salvador archdiocese had seven centers, serving 2,500 refugees. And it was not just to the capital that Salvadorans went. July estimates put the number of refugees in Honduras at 4,100, though some claimed 10,000. Costa Rica and Nicaragua had "at least 3,000." Others sought refuge in Guatemala and Mexico.[219]

In letters to family and friends, Maura Clarke described how the refugee problem resulted from the powerful's opposition to change. Catechists' decision to act as religious leaders was risky, Clarke wrote, "because anyone suspected of being in an organization or attached to the Church is in serious danger."[220] Rather than just targeting those with church connections, death squads instilled fear through indiscriminate violence. As Clarke wrote, "People are fleeing from their houses looking for some kind of safety as the so called 'death squadron' strikes anywhere and everywhere. . . . The cutting up of bodies by machete is one of their tactics to terrorize the organized groups from continuing their efforts. . . . The effort of the oligarchy is to wipe out the farmers and workers who have organized for change and they do this in the name of fighting communism. It is a much more vengeful, confusing and frightening case than that of Nicaragua."[221] For someone who had lived through protests, state violence, and accusations of communist sympathies in Nicaragua, Clarke's conclusion that El Salvador was worse spoke volumes.

Tension was palpable. In the spring, sixteen Leftist organizations formed the Democratic Revolutionary Front (FDR or Frente Democrático Revolucionario), the country's largest political movement. By summer's end, the FDR was underground, concluding violence was the only way forward.[222] The five guerrilla organizations also formed the Farabundo Martí National Liberation Front (FMLN or Frente Farabundo Martí para la Liberación Nacional), named after a leader of the 1932 uprising.[223] In the United States, Salvadoran exiles and allies, supportive of the FMLN-FDR, formed the Committee in Solidarity with the People of El Salvador (CISPES) to educate the public about the situation and to send humanitarian aid.[224]

In the midst of undeclared war, Ita Ford lashed out at the U.S. government. In a mid-October interview, she shared: "As a U.S. citizen I'm highly disappointed and mostly outraged by the type of support we're giving this junta. . . . The government doesn't represent anybody at this point. It's fearful to think of the U.S. now training Salvadoran troops and sending in equipment. It's reprehensible."[225] Just as Archbishop Romero had warned, the junta was no centrist force.

The U.S. government saw things differently. The State Department insisted 502(b) had not been triggered and stressed that U.S. interests outweighed human rights concerns. In a late October letter to Representative Matthew F. McHugh (D-NY), Assistant Secretary of State for Legislative Affairs Brian Atwood admitted that "the pattern of killings seems plain, gross and tragic." But, he insisted, "the question of government responsibility is not as clear," and, since 502(b) also required state responsibility, aid continued. U.S. "long term interest in the area" also tipped in favor of continued aid. The Salvadoran government was trying to remedy the situation, and U.S. aid could help. With better communications equipment, commanders could "exercise better control over field units," leading to "better discipline and less unwarranted violence against the civilian population." Ultimately, Atwood pleaded for understanding. El Salvador should not be evaluated based on its human rights record, but with a keen understanding of its "violent tradition."[226] Atwood characterized violence as an uncontrollable force endemic to El Salvador. A mixture of stereotyping and U.S. Cold War concerns overrode human rights.

Because the Carter administration viewed El Salvador through the lens of Nicaragua, U.S. officials saw the wrong picture. As Atwood's letter revealed, Jimmy Carter's overall focus on human rights meant little to nothing when it came to El Salvador policy. The two countries shared rampant inequality and revolutionary movements largely inspired by liberation theology, but there were key differences. El Salvador saw no middle-class defection, as occurred in Nicaragua. Instead, Salvadoran elites maintained their alliance with the military, sanctioning and supporting state and paramilitary violence against those who pushed for change.

Campesinos and others, such as Maryknollers, who advocated for human rights put their lives at risk. The danger increased over time. Nevertheless, Maryknollers pushed for U.S. attention and policy change. As the sisters often argued, U.S. officials did not understand the situation. It was not a question of communist infiltration but of poverty and inequality. U.S. military aid exacerbated things. The U.S. government's cost-benefit analysis, like the one Atwood explained to McHugh, changed in early December 1980 when National Guardsmen raped and murdered four U.S. missionaries, including two Maryknoll sisters.

CHAPTER 4

U.S. Guns Kill U.S. Nuns

On Thursday, December 4, 1980, U.S. news showed two men using ropes to hoist a female body wrapped in white cloth from a shallow grave and drag it across the dirt. A crowd watched uncomfortably, many standing with arms crossed or hands over their mouths. The bodies of three other women followed. They had been raped and shot at close range. The four were Americans: Maryknoll nuns Ita Ford and Maura Clarke, Ursuline nun Dorothy Kazel, and Maryknoll lay missioner Jean Donovan. They collectively became known as the "four American churchwomen" (figure 3). The coverage introduced many in the United States to El Salvador.[1] By the end of May 1981, six months after the murders, the White House had received ten times more protest letters about their deaths than it did during the Iran hostage crisis, which lasted 444 days.[2]

Three months after the murders, Secretary of State Alexander Haig spoke about the incident before the House Foreign Affairs Committee. Contrary to the evidence, Haig proposed the women tried to run a roadblock and were killed in an exchange of gunfire.[3] Commentators then and scholars since have argued the remarks were designed to bolster the Salvadoran junta's reputation or diminish the murders' impact on the protest movement against U.S. policy, or that they reflected the administration's ignorance of the Catholic Church's role in Latin America.[4] But as this chapter argues, Haig's comments revealed how a contentious intra-Catholic debate became integral to

FIGURE 3.   The churchwomen: Dorothy Kazel, O.S.U.; Maura Clarke, M.M.; Ita Ford, M.M.; Jean Donovan. Photo courtesy of the Maryknoll Mission Archives.

U.S.–Central America policy with Reagan's ascension to the White House. To liberal Catholics, including Maryknollers, the murdered churchwomen symbolized the church's championing of the poor and a U.S. foreign policy that was morally corrupt and politically unsound for training and arming their killers. To conservative Catholics, on the other hand, the two murdered Maryknollers were members of a Catholic order that represented a dangerous trajectory for U.S. foreign policy and the church. This Catholic divide mattered because liberal Catholics played key roles in opposing Reagan's El Salvador policy, while conservative Catholics, such as Haig, shaped it. The dividing line was Catholic versus Catholic. The U.S. government aligned with conservative U.S. and Central American Catholics and amplified their perspective.

Conservative Catholics on the Ascendancy

The Catholic divide the murders exposed was not new. While some Catholics pushed for the United States to stop supporting Somoza and the Salvadoran government in the late 1970s, others lobbied for a strong anticommunist foreign policy that backed them. Tensions also flared over the Panama Canal Treaties. To sell the treaties, Carter worked with religious groups, including Catholics.[5] Before the treaties were signed, a 1975 U.S. Catholic Conference (USCC) administrative board resolution called for a new treaty that provided for the canal's return as "a moral imperative—a matter of elemental social justice." The USCC served as secretariat for the National Conference of Catholic Bishops and proposed policy.[6] The next year, the entire body of bishops called for a new treaty. The USCC broadcast its position through publications and an appearance before the Senate Foreign Relations Committee.[7]

Many conservative U.S. Catholics objected to the bishops' stance. A Catholic from Tonawanda, New York, saw the bishops' position as both heretical and treasonous. He wondered "if the USCC . . . [has] turned from evangelizing for Christ our Lord, to that of church politicizing for Lenin's third phase of world conquest which is the strategic encirclement of the United States."[8] Others mobilized. Richard Viguerie, who pioneered the use of direct mail for conservative causes and congressional candidates, led a mail campaign encouraging people to inform their senators and local media of their treaty opposition and soliciting financial contributions. Of the estimated seven to nine million letters and postcards the anti-treaty camp sent from the summer of 1977 to April 1978, Viguerie mailed four million on behalf of clients American Conservative Union and the Conservative Caucus. His efforts yielded about $1.4 million. Staunch anticommunism served as guiding principle for Viguerie and many of his clients.[9]

In the short term, conservatives lost. In April 1978 by one vote each, the Senate ratified the treaties that mandated the canal's neutrality and provided for the end of U.S. control. But in the long term, opponents gained the upper hand. The treaty fight formed an important basis for cooperation between conservative Catholics and Ronald Reagan, whose opposition led him to victory in the 1976 North Carolina primary over President Ford.[10] The treaty fights also coalesced the Right. Conservative organizations added four hundred thousand new members to their lists.[11] Unlike previous campaigns, the New Right worked through coalitions. Catholics played key roles.[12] Paul Weyrich led the Committee for the Survival of a Free Congress, a political action committee, and Coalitions for America, which served as an umbrella organization for over one hundred conservative lobbying, research, and political action groups. He also helped found the Heritage Foundation. Later, he devised the term "Moral Majority" and encouraged Baptist minister Jerry Falwell to organize the group.[13]

Neither Weyrich's Republican affiliation nor his interreligious efforts were unusual. Since 1968, Catholics had been shifting politically. Except for Dwight Eisenhower in 1956, Catholics went for the Democratic candidate between 1936 and 1968. After 1968, they tilted Republican, nudged by social issues like abortion, school busing, and the Equal Rights Amendment. At the same time, conservative religions gained adherents. More than one-third of Americans described themselves as "born again" by 1975. They also increased their political clout within the Republican Party. Equally as significant, Catholics, Protestants, Mormons, and Jews worked collaboratively—what Andrew Preston terms a "conservative ecumenism"—in the 1970s.[14]

Conservative U.S. Catholics also saw themselves on the ascendancy with Pole Karol Wojtyła's selection as pope. As the first non-Italian pontiff in 455 years, John Paul II's October 1978 election came as a surprise.[15] Many conservative Catholics hoped he would challenge the Soviet Union as they believed Carter failed to do. As the *National Review* declared, "The papacy of John Paul II may help prevent the satellization of the West; may prevent it, in fact, by opening up a huge fault along the Western edge of the Soviet empire, where Catholicism still has immeasurable latent power."[16]

The charismatic pope appealed to people across political and religious divides. Upon his fall 1979 visit to the United States, John Paul II was greeted like a rock star. During his five-day trip, two million gathered for a Mass at Boston Common, more than a million in Philadelphia's Logan Circle, and half a million at Chicago's Grant Park.[17] *Time* featured him on the cover with the caption, "John Paul, Superstar."[18] As *Harper's* managing editor derisively remarked, "To judge what was on television and in the papers, America went Catholic. It was a collective act unrivaled in the annals of crowd psychology since the Beatles' first North American tour in 1964."[19]

Contra their desire for papal intervention against the Soviets, conservative Catholics welcomed the pope's directive that priests stay out of politics. In late spring 1980, the Vatican demanded that Jesuit Robert Drinan, Massachusetts congressman, withdraw his candidacy for another term.[20] Jesuit James Schall applauded the pontiff. As he argued, "priests ought not to be politicians" because "we are not to dilute the Gospel charisms through exaggerated interests in temporal power."[21] But others worried about the potential consequences. *America* warned "reactionary elements" could "exploit" the directive to undermine church human rights efforts.[22] They could use the pope's words to argue socially active priests were out of bounds. And in Nicaragua and El Salvador, conservative Catholics had charged priests with engaging in political activities before torturing or murdering them.

Ronald Reagan seemed another promising ally to conservative Catholics like Weyrich and other New Right members. A 1980 internal memo circulating among the New Right warned the group needed to "bring key leverage upon the Governor before the election" if it hoped to see its policies enacted under Reagan. Among the priorities was an end to Nicaraguan aid, the cancellation of aid to all "Marxist-leaning governments," and the "total reassignment of all American diplomats who favor any socialist political revolution." Recipients included Catholics Weyrich, Viguerie, the National Conservative Political Action Committee's Terry Dolan, and Heritage Foundation president Edwin Feulner, as well as Protestant Howard Phillips, founder of the Conservative Caucus.[23]

While the anticommunist New Right wanted to politically isolate the Sandinistas, conservative Catholics also wanted to do so for religious reasons. They saw Central America as determining the church's future direction, and their fears were not unfounded. Sandinistas stressed the church's role in the revolution, and U.S. religious promoted Nicaragua as a model. Moisés Hassan stated, "Catholic religious men and women have been very important to the success of the revolution."[24] Similarly, Daniel Ortega told the Latin American bishops' conference in 1980, "for us, a church indisputably integrated, participating with the people in their sacrifice, their struggle and their hope is a church which cannot be denied by the revolution because it is a part of the revolution."[25] A Maryknoll priest in Nicaragua described his hopes: "A genuine revolution on behalf of the poor is going on. . . . We want this revolution to be Christian and perhaps a model for all of Latin America."[26] Conservative Catholics saw these developments as proof of communist infiltration. They feared these disturbing trends would have a domino effect on the U.S. church.

The Republican Party agreed Nicaragua was a threat. Its 1980 platform condemned "the Marxist Sandinista take-over of Nicaragua and the Marxist attempts to destabilize El Salvador, Guatemala, and Honduras."[27] Candidate Reagan tied himself to protecting El Salvador from suffering the same fate as Nicaragua. Reagan saw Central America as a battleground between communism and anticommunism, and after the Sandinista takeover of Nicaragua, he feared that El Salvador would be next.

The Churchwomen

Conservative U.S. Catholics were not the only ones supporting Reagan's candidacy. Many Latin Americans followed the presidential race "with unprecedented interest" and even advertised for their candidate in newspapers.[28] Salvadoran Rightists held signs reading, "Reagan is America's Last Hope," "Only Reagan Can Halt Communism," and "Reagan for President" outside the U.S. embassy and Ambassador Robert E. White's home.[29] In October, the Salvadoran foreign minister informed White that the Right was planning a coup in anticipation of Reagan's victory.[30]

In the midst of rising tension, Maryknollers Maura Clarke and Ita Ford faced increasing danger. Colonel Peña Arbaiza, leader of the military detachment across the plaza from where they lived, continually complained to Defense Minister Colonel José Guillermo García that the sisters were subversives.[31] And he told the women the same thing. When Ford and Piette complained of military harassment he reminded them how nuns should act. Maryknollers, along with the rest of the parish house, were behaving subversively, he insisted, and so, generally, was the church.[32]

Then, a rumor began circulating that the women had guns in the convent. On November 3, the day before the U.S. presidential election, the Mauricio Borgonovo Anti-Communist Brigade death squad left a note on their door. Together with a drawing of a knife protruding from a head dripping with blood was the message: "Everyone who enters this house dies. We know that you are communists. If you don't believe this just try it. We know that the military takes no action against you, but we will execute you." Alarmed, Father Ephraím López told the parish team, along with the religious, to work only in Chalatenango. Clarke and Ford were not deterred. They continued just as they had before the death threat.[33]

The next day, sixty-nine-year-old Ronald Reagan, former B-list movie actor and California governor, defeated Carter. Reagan won in a landslide in the Electoral College, besting Carter 489 to 49. On Reagan's coattails, Republicans gained control of the Senate for the first time in nearly thirty years.[34] Salvadorans on the Right welcomed the victory. Two days after the election, bodies riddled with bullets were found on the roadside with signs reading "With Ronald Reagan all of the guerillas and unbehaved in El Salvador will be eliminated."[35]

Among the "unbehaved" were Maryknollers. Like Colonel Peña Arbaiza, the defense minister was convinced some priests and nuns were subversives and communists. In a mid-November presentation, García tried to convince the civilian junta members that religious in Chalatenango, including Clarke and Ford, were working with guerrillas.[36] "We've got to take steps against the missionaries," he insisted.[37]

The violence against "subversives" increased on November 27, when six prominent leaders from El Salvador's largest Leftist political organization, the FDR, were murdered. They were taken from a Jesuit high school during a day-time press conference and shot.[38] In claiming responsibility, the Maximiliano Hernández Martínez Anticommunist Brigade—named for the Salvadoran president who ordered the 1932 massacre—described the FDR men as "communists" and warned that "just executions of the traitors to our country" would continue.[39]

Rightist forces anticipated a change in U.S. policy, a view the Reagan transition team encouraged. On November 28, the day after the FDR murders, Reagan advisors told a Salvadoran business group that the new administration would quickly send aid.[40] At the same time, Reagan's State Department transition team criticized both Carter's aid suspensions on human rights grounds and U.S. ambassadors in Latin America. The December 1 report—leaked to the press—decried ambassadors who acted as "social reformers," namely Ambassador White, and called for their removal.[41] The New Right's attempt to influence candidate Reagan had worked.

The next day in El Salvador, an unidentified man approached the parish sacristan at Ford and Clarke's parish. He presented a list of the parish staff and said, "And tonight, this very night, we will begin," in reference to killings.[42] That evening, Ford and Clarke flew back from a Maryknoll regional meeting in Nicaragua. Jean Donovan and Dorothy Kazel met them at the airport, having already driven Maryknollers Madeline Dorsey and Teresa Alexander home from an earlier flight. Shortly after 7 p.m., National Guardsmen stopped the women's van, arrested them, and drove to an isolated spot. There, they raped and shot the women at point blank range. They left the bodies fifteen miles from the airport in one direction and their burned-out van ten miles in another.[43] After campesinos discovered the bodies and alerted local authorities, two National Guardsmen ordered them to bury the women in a remote area "where killings are commonplace and fresh graves likely to be ignored."[44] Out of respect, the campesinos dressed the naked bodies.[45] Another campesino saw the fresh graves and alerted his parish priest, who contacted the archdiocese and eventually Ambassador White, who knew the women had been missing for thirty-six hours.[46] On December 4, their bodies were exhumed as White and forty television, radio, and newspaper reporters watched.[47] In contrast to the eight thousand to twelve thousand Salvadorans killed in 1980, the church-women received international attention.[48] Part of the reason was their nationality; it was also because the foreign press was in the country to cover the FDR funerals on December 3.

President Carter's and the incoming Reagan administration's response to the murders began running on two parallel tracks. The day after the women's bodies were recovered, the White House announced it was cutting aid and sending a fact-finding mission. When pushed, the State Department press secretary admitted there were larger concerns, but he stressed the "emphasis" was investigating "a circumstantial link between security forces of the government and these killings."[49] The Carter administration created an association in many people's minds between the women and U.S. policy, and it began using the women for political purposes.

Behind the scenes, the White House had other motives. The State Department had been struggling to assert the importance of human rights and to decrease security force violence, especially after Reagan's victory. The murders provided the administration with this opportunity and in particular, as one embassy official explained, to counter "Duarte's strategy to increase his authority by continuing to cover up for the military's wave of killings."[50] Similarly, a National Security Council (NSC) memorandum revealed that part of the intention in suspending aid was to shake U.S. "friends" in El Salvador and the junta's "democratic supporters" outside the country.[51] By contrast, the Carter administration had declined to use Ronald Richardson's disappearance or Archbishop Romero's murder to confront the Salvadoran government.

While Carter reacted, Reagan's silence led to calls for a response, even though president-elects typically do not comment. Senator Ted Kennedy appealed for a "strong public statement condemning such violence as the recent killings and church bombings in El Salvador."[52] Papers from New York to Hawai'i encouraged Reagan to "make an exception for El Salvador."[53] Seventy-one religious leaders added their voices. In an open letter they argued, "military governments in many countries are viewing your election as a green light for suppression of legitimate dissent, and for widespread arrest and imprisonment, torture and murder."[54]

The churchwomen's murders sparked immediate protests, particularly by Catholics. San Francisco's cathedral unfurled a banner reading "U.S. DOLLARS KILL U.S. NUNS." Less than a week after the unearthing of the women's bodies, the *Washington Post* asserted that Catholic "protest activities" were "unmatched by few—if any—reactions to past issues, including the controversy over abortion."[55]

Maryknoll, having sponsored three of the four women, was forced to respond. Sister Annette Mulrey, head of the Sisters' Office of Social Concerns (OSC), said Maryknoll was "besieged with calls from all over the country from people asking, 'What can we do?'"[56] Maryknoll suggested praying, sending supportive letters to the churchwomen's families and San Salvador's apostolic administrator Bishop Rivera, donating in the women's memory, and/or writing government officials to praise the aid suspension and request "immediate withdrawal of U.S. military personnel from El Salvador and the immediate cessation of all military shipments."[57] The OSC sent ten thousand information packets on El Salvador worldwide over the next three months.[58]

Maryknoll emphasized how the deaths brought attention to El Salvador. As President Melinda Roper noted at a memorial service: "The only purpose of an investigation of their deaths is to expose to the world the situation and violent oppression of the poor of El Salvador—to call us and people of good will throughout the world to radicalize our faith and convictions—to do something to change this situation of the oppressed and poor throughout our world today—to create a new future—to beat our swords into plowshares."[59] For Maryknollers, the goal was not only to identify the perpetrators but also to use the tragedy to change the conditions in El Salvador.

Salvadoran religious also stressed the big picture: the churchwomen were four among thousands murdered as part of escalating violence against the church. Bishop Rivera and the religious of the archdiocese noted that in the two weeks before the women's murders, two priests had disappeared and one of them had been presumably assassinated. "These criminal acts of persecution" were the "culmination" of the past four years. The church was targeted because it sided with the poor and spoke "truth which irritates the powerful." The group blamed the "Security Forces and ultra-rightist groups" for the violence, along with the government because it oversaw the military.[60]

Less than two weeks after the White House tied the churchwomen to U.S. aid, it changed course. On December 17, the administration announced immediate resumption of $20 million in economic aid, arguing it was necessary for food and jobs. Although officials reiterated that the murders prompted the suspension, they stressed other developments for the restoration, such as the junta's reshuffling (with José Napoleón Duarte as president), its amnesty offer to those who put down their arms, and, most significantly, its "approach" to the case.[61] However, there were no tangible results in the investigation.

Reagan's nominee for UN ambassador Jeane Kirkpatrick took a different tack. She called Carter's decision to suspend aid "colossally irresponsible." She also questioned the churchwomen's motives: "The nuns were not just nuns. . . . They were political activists on behalf of the Frente," the Salvadoran guerrillas.[62] These comments were consistent with Kirkpatrick's argument in "Dictatorships and Double Standards," the 1979 article that put the Georgetown professor on presidential candidate Reagan's radar. Kirkpatrick scathingly rebuked Carter's foreign policy, taking him to task for critiquing conservative dictatorships while giving socialist leaders free rein to abuse human rights. Carter's human rights rhetoric punished Right-leaning U.S. allies, she contended, while it ignored communist ones. Pushing for this misguided approach were "returning missionaries" and "'reasonable' rebels."[63] For someone who regarded missionaries as key movers in Carter's foreign policy, it was not a far leap for Kirkpatrick to accuse the churchwomen of working with the FMLN.

But the Carter administration's calculus soon changed. In January, the FMLN pursued its "final offensive," declaring: "It is necessary to launch now the battles for the great general offensive of the Salvadoran people before the fanatic Ronald Reagan takes over the presidency of the United States."[64] The move, modeled after Cuba in 1958 and Nicaragua in 1979, failed. The people did not rise up, and the guerrillas realized they were no match for the military, prompting them to focus on protracted war based in the countryside.[65] The offensive, however, led the United States to reinstate military aid on January 14, including arms and munitions for the first time since 1977. Significantly, Carter acted alone. Rather than seek congressional approval, he used an emergency provision under Section 506(a) of the Foreign Assistance Act.[66]

Just as when it resumed economic aid, the administration pointed to reasons unrelated to the churchwomen. It said the junta needed "to replace" supplies lost fighting the rebels.[67] And, it ignored additional U.S. deaths. On December 29, journalist John J. Sullivan disappeared, and six days later, three men involved with El Salvador's land reform—Americans Michael P. Hammer and Mark David Pearlman and Salvadoran José Rodolfo Viera—were shot while dining at San Salvador's Sheraton.[68]

The administration argued circumstances had changed, but Carter had a problem. By linking the churchwomen's case to U.S. aid, the president created an expectation: no aid without progress in the case. Consequently, the decision to reinstate military aid was met with anger, confusion, and disappointment. On January 16, around thirty people, mainly U.S. priests and nuns, protested outside the U.S. embassy in Nicaragua.[69] The group staged a sit-in and held signs, including one that read "U.S. guns kill U.S. nuns," like the San Francisco banner.[70] According to the U.S. ambassador, the Maryknoll Sisters "sponsored" the "peaceful" protest.[71]

Reagan, Conservative Catholics, and Human Rights

Six days after Carter resumed military aid, Reagan was sworn in. The hostages in Iran were released "almost at the moment" Reagan took the oath of office,[72] leading many Americans to credit the Gipper. Simultaneously, others clamored for attention to El Salvador. In Mexico City, forty-three U.S. citizens, including priests, sisters, and ministers, sent a letter to Reagan calling for an end to U.S. aid, and on the day of Reagan's inauguration, some of them stood before the U.S. embassy and read the letter aloud.[73]

The administration planned for Latin America based on two documents: Kirkpatrick's "Dictatorships and Double Standards" and the Santa Fe Report.[74] In May 1980, the Committee of Santa Fe, which included future members of Reagan's foreign policy team, outlined their vision in the *New Inter-American Policy for the Eighties*, also known as the Santa Fe Report. The committee described Carter's foreign policy as "strategic indifference" and proposed a more aggressive approach to save Latin America and the United States from continued Soviet penetration. As the committee argued, "The Americas are under attack."[75]

The Santa Fe Report reflected a conservative Catholic viewpoint, especially its linking of revolutionary activity and liberation theology. In recommending how the United States should address forces of "internal subversion," the committee highlighted religious actors in two ways. First, the committee identified the need for U.S. policy to "insulate itself from propaganda" instigated from "forces explicitly hostile to the United States." Like Kirkpatrick, the committee accused "church-affiliated and other so-called human rights lobbies" of manipulating information that contributed to shifts from "authoritarian, but pro-U.S. governments" to "anti-U.S., Communist, or pro-Communist dictatorships of a totalitarian character." Second, the committee singled out liberation theology. It argued that the United States "must begin to counter (not react against) liberation theology as it is utilized in Latin America by the 'liberation theology' clergy." Although the Catholic Church was "vital to the concept of political freedom . . . Marxist-Leninist forces have utilized the church as a political weapon . . . by infiltrating the religious community with ideas that are less Christian than Communist."[76] Significantly, the committee adopted conservative Central American Catholics' argument that individual religious, not the church as an institution, were the problem.

Although the Carter administration was concerned with liberation theology, Reagan's approach differed in three key respects. First, Reagan made Central America a cornerstone of his foreign policy. He portrayed the region as *the* battleground between East and West where the United States could save the world from communism. Second, the Santa Fe Report's description of liberation theology mimicked conservative Catholic language circulating in 1970s Latin America and the United States. Anticommunist congresses in Brazil in 1974, Nicaragua in 1975, and Paraguay in 1977 warned against the "subversive action of the clergy" and "communist infiltration of the Church."[77] The U.S. *Wanderer* characterized liberation theology as synonymous with violent communism, describing it as "the attempt theologically to justify a worldwide proletarian revolution."[78]

Finally, several conservative Catholics who coauthored the report played crucial roles in shaping Central America policy. Roger Fontaine, a "devout" Catholic,[79] served as Reagan's lead advisor on Latin America during the presidential campaign and then as director of Latin American affairs for the NSC.[80] "Jesuit-educated" L. Francis Bouchey chaired the Council for Inter-American Security,[81] of which Fontaine was a director.[82] The organization had close ties to the White House and was later involved in the administration's Central America public diplomacy campaign. Two of the report's other main authors, Lewis Tambs and Lieutenant General Gordon Sumner, later served as U.S. ambassador to Costa Rica and as special assistant to the assistant secretary of state for inter-American affairs, respectively.[83]

This animosity toward liberation theology mattered because the Reagan administration was riddled with Catholics who, like the pope, were staunchly anticommunist. These included Secretary of State Alexander Haig; CIA Director William Casey; three national security advisors, Richard Allen, William Clark, and Robert C. McFarlane; Treasury Secretary and later Chief of Staff Donald T. Regan; Undersecretary for Security Affairs James Buckley; Communications Director Patrick Buchanan; speechwriters Tony Dolan and Peggy Noonan; Ambassador Vernon Walters; Labor Secretary Raymond J. Donovan; and Naval Secretary John F. Lehman Jr.[84] Faith Ryan Whittlesey, director of the Office of Public Liaison, later converted based on her interactions with Catholics during her White House years.[85] As one reporter at the time quipped, "A list of Reagan's advisers and cabinet members reads like the honor roll of a Catholic high school."[86]

The most powerful people involved with shaping foreign policy were Catholics: Haig, Casey, Walters, Allen, and Clark. More significant than their religious affiliation alone was that they associated Catholicism with rigid anticommunism, a consensus view in the 1950s, but after Vatican II, an increasingly contested stance. As Carl Bernstein explains, these men "saw their Church as the crucible of anti-Communist conviction. Like Reagan, their basic view of the Marxist-Lenin canon was theological: Communism was *spiritually* evil."[87] In this way, opposition to liberation theology reflected an entangled political-religious outlook.

Although Catholics formulated Reagan's policy toward Central America, there was no "Catholic cabal," according to Jeane Kirkpatrick.[88] Even so, non-Catholics like Kirkpatrick echoed conservative Catholic views. Kirkpatrick blamed liberation theology for El Salvador's turmoil. During a *New York Times* roundtable discussion, she claimed liberation theology was an "instrument for very radical change" because people engaged in murder and violence in its name.[89]

The first NSC meeting the day after Reagan's inauguration highlighted conservative Catholics in the cabinet and set the stage for the administration's break from Carter's approach. Three of the big issues were Iran and the return of the hostages, El Salvador, and Libya.[90] Haig stressed Cuba's designs on El Salvador. He also argued that "the first order of business is to show Nicaraguans that we will not tolerate" their interference in El Salvador as the Carter administration did. Reagan spoke about the need to distinguish his Latin America policy from Carter's. "We must change the attitude of our diplomatic corps so that we don't bring down governments in the name of human rights. None of them is as guilty of human rights violations as Cuba and the U.S.S.R. We don't throw out our friends just because they can't pass the saliva test on human rights. I want to see that stopped." Reagan argued El Salvador was where the United States "could set an example" by stopping communism. When CIA Director William Casey argued that the issue was time sensitive, Reagan replied, "We can't afford defeat. El Salvador is the place for victory."[91]

Less than a week later, the secretary of state announced this new outlook with himself at the helm. "International terrorism will take the place of human rights . . . because it is the ultimate abuse of human rights," Haig proclaimed.[92] As part of this new approach, he unceremoniously dismissed White as ambassador to El Salvador.

Haig, the four-star general, chief of staff in the Nixon administration's final days, and commander of U.S. forces in Europe, proclaimed himself "vicar" of foreign policy, "a word with pope-size pretensions."[93] In Haig's mind, he was doing what Reagan said: he "would be the spokesman for the U.S. government" when it came to foreign policy.[94] And, despite his battles with Jeane Kirkpatrick, Defense Secretary Caspar Weinberger, and James Baker, Haig called the shots.[95] Haig had room to maneuver because the troika—Counselor to the President Edwin Meese, Chief of Staff James Baker, and Deputy Chief of Staff Michael Deaver—prioritized domestic issues.[96] In keeping with the troika's wishes, Reagan proposed tax cuts to kick-start the economy two weeks after taking the oath of office.[97] The president also gave no speeches about El Salvador or Nicaragua in 1981.[98] Instead, he dedicated his Christmas message to Poland. He encouraged Americans to light a candle in their windows "to support the brave" Poles under martial law.[99] Poles were good, anticommunist Catholics.

To many, Haig's Patton-like bravado seemed out of place, particularly after the Carter years. His tough talk even scared cabinet members. In the administration's early weeks, discussion turned to Cuba. Haig said, "Give me the word and I'll make that island a fucking parking lot." His remark shocked Mike Deaver and "scared the shit out of Ronald Reagan" according to Deaver.[100] If Haig rattled the chief of staff and the president, it was no surprise that he unnerved some of the public as well.

Haig and the White House wanted to downplay human rights, but many Catholics would not allow this. Shortly before Reagan's inauguration, the CIA found that Western Europeans were largely against U.S.–El Salvador policy. The report cited the Catholic Church's "relatively uniform criticism of the Salvadoran government" as a major reason, especially in West Germany, Ireland, Austria, and Italy. Western Europeans were "particularly incensed" over Archbishop Romero's assassination, and, the report concluded, the murders of the FDR leaders and churchwomen "can only strengthen Western European opposition to the junta."[101] The CIA's warning proved correct. At the end of January, fifteen thousand Germans marched through Frankfurt demanding an end to U.S. military aid.[102] In the spring, the Commission for International Justice and Peace of the Catholic Bishops Conference of England and Wales made the same plea.[103] Later that year, Trócaire, the Irish church's overseas development agency, proclaimed the Salvadoran government "denies human rights, [and] practices a brutal policy which reaches dimensions of genocide."[104]

To Haig, the source of opposition was clear: communists and those they manipulated, including Catholics. In early February, the secretary of state warned all U.S. diplomatic posts that protests and critiques of U.S. policy were part of a Soviet- and Cuban-directed "major worldwide propaganda campaign." Communists were exploiting "assorted left of center political groupings, and several religious groups, particularly liberal Catholics." He ordered mobilization of "the full resources of our diplomatic missions in response."[105] El Salvador was not only a "regional problem that threatened the stability of all of Central America" but also "a strategic problem with global implications." The Soviets were not attempting to start a war; they were interfering in El Salvador "to test the strength of Western determination," he later wrote.[106]

The administration argued that outside communist interference was responsible for El Salvador's unrest. Two days after Reagan took office, he approved Carter's suspension of economic aid to Nicaragua, arguing the Sandinistas were aiding the Salvadoran guerrillas.[107] Aid was terminated three months later.[108] In February, the State Department instructed all embassies in Latin America and Europe that El Salvador was "a textbook case of indirect armed aggression by Communist powers." The State Department then released the white paper "Communist Interference in El Salvador," which outlined Soviet and Cuban involvement.[109] The document was based on evidence from the Carter administration but framed differently by the Reagan White House.[110]

The administration faced pushback. Newspapers, including the *Wall Street Journal*, discredited the white paper.[111] Salvadoran junta president Duarte insisted the troubles were homegrown, not incited by international communist interference. As he explained, "This is a history of people starving to death, living in misery. For 50 years, the same people had all the power, all the money, all the opportunities. Those who did not have anything tried to take it away from those who had everything. But there were no democratic systems available to them, so they have radicalized themselves, have resorted to violence. And of course this second group, the rich, do not want to give up anything, so they are fighting."[112]

Critiques of the Churchwomen

The churchwomen's case seemed to be a casualty of Reagan's de-emphasis on human rights, but there was more going on. The administration continued Carter's move away from the churchwomen. On February 11, a State Department spokesperson said the investigation was "not connected to this administration's consideration of aid to El Salvador" and refused to comment further.[113] Nevertheless, Reagan officials spoke about the women in a way that followed conservative Catholics' criticism of Maryknoll, and in the process, they expressed a particular Catholic view of both U.S. foreign policy and the church.

Some Catholics argued that the murders of the churchwomen, or any priest or nun, should not impact U.S. aid. *Wanderer* editor A. J. Matt stressed that without U.S. assistance, Marxists would take over. And, just because government forces sometimes murdered priests and nuns did not mean religious persecution existed, because both sides were "at least nominally" Catholic. Echoing conservative Salvadoran Catholics, Matt implied that priests and nuns who "openly and actively side with Marxist revolutionaries" did not qualify as religious or even as Catholic. He also charged that U.S. bishops who opposed U.S. aid and encouraged others to do so were allowing themselves to be manipulated by communists and were furthering the U.S. church hierarchy's "politicization."[114] Matt illustrated the interrelationship conservative Catholics saw between U.S. foreign policy and the church: U.S. aid protected both El Salvador and the church from Marxist influence.

In mid-February, Ernest Lefever, later Reagan's failed nominee for assistant secretary of state for human rights, distinguished between "religious leaders being involved in theological thought and nuns and clergymen engaging in activities inimical to the interests of the government." He elaborated, "It's a question where religion is used as a garb for cloaking political activity. . . . Some religious groups have overstepped their bounds." As an example, Lefever referred to "nuns hiding machine guns for the insurgents" but said he was not specifically speaking of El Salvador.[115]

In March, the Council for Inter-American Security (CIS), a group with Catholic leaders and close affiliation with the White House, accused the churchwomen of violence. In a press release sent to the Hill, CIS alleged the churchwomen "may have been working with left-wing guerrillas to overthrow the government" and pointed out that three were associated with Maryknoll, which had "earned a reputation for championing radical politics and 'liberation theology.'"[116] The focus on liberation theology was unsurprising as three CIS members, Fontaine, Sumner, and Bouchey, authored the Santa Fe Report.

CIS tied the churchwomen to the Sandinistas through Maryknoll. CIS pointed out that Maryknoller Miguel d'Escoto was Nicaragua's foreign minister and former editor of *Maryknoll*. CIS implied that the women were involved with gunrunning. As the group charged, "It is unknown what the women were doing in Nicaragua at the time when vast quantities of arms were being sent through Nicaragua to the guerrillas in El Salvador." CIS ignored the Maryknoll meeting in Nicaragua at the time. CIS publications director then asserted, "Leftists in Washington say that one of the nuns had been active in Nicaragua's revolution," presumably a reference to Clarke, the only murdered churchwoman in mission in Nicaragua. As proof, CIS quoted Kirkpatrick's statement that the women were "political activists" and cited "press in El Salvador" on "indications" the churchwomen "were involved with the guerrillas."[117]

CIS may have drawn on Ricardo Fuentes Castellanos's January *La Prensa Gráfica* editorial. In reference to the churchwomen, Fuentes, a constant critic of Archbishop Romero, argued there were "some indications that they were involved to some extent in subversive activities," since they worked in areas noted for "guerrilla" and "revolutionary" priests. To bolster his claims, the priest reminded readers of the Melville incident and he incorrectly charged Jean Donovan with being "reportedly involved" in the early 1970s plot to kidnap Kissinger.[118]

The *Wanderer* escalated matters by alleging the churchwomen died in a shoot-out. The paper cited Kirkpatrick and CIS, and quoted an Accuracy in Media (AIM) report challenging the story of rape and murder. According to AIM, the medical examiner who performed the autopsy on Jean Donovan found "no evidence of rape," and he "theorized that the van . . . was probably moving," suggesting the women ran a roadblock.[119] AIM and the *Wanderer* did not mention that the doctor, who performed the autopsy on Donovan and Kazel at the State Department's request, could not assess whether Donovan was raped. He also could not determine from where Donovan was shot, but based on glass fragments in the wound track, he concluded, "There's a good chance it was an ambush."[120] The *Wanderer* amplified AIM's twisting of the medical examiner's words.

AIM and the *Wanderer*'s claims mattered because the secretary of state repeated them. On March 18, Haig proposed that the churchwomen "may have tried to run a roadblock or may have been accidentally perceived to have been doing so," and they were killed in an exchange of gunfire.[121] His remarks before the House Foreign Affairs Committee received attention not only because he was secretary of state but also because he was a devout Catholic whose brother was a Jesuit. Unlike Protestants Kirkpatrick and Lefever, Haig, as a Catholic, could appreciate how insulting his remarks about nuns would be to some Catholics. By painting a picture of the churchwomen firing guns as they sped through a roadblock and then dying in a hail of bullets, Haig escalated Kirkpatrick's political-activist and Lefever's gun-toting claims, and challenged the churchwomen's victimhood. He also showed, yet again, how Reagan officials placed themselves on the conservative side of Catholic debates about Maryknoll and U.S.–El Salvador policy. In that moment, he embodied the alliance between conservative Catholics and the Reagan administration, as each sought to marginalize liberation theology supporters and contain the spread of the Nicaraguan revolution.

The Salvadoran press also featured critiques of Maryknoll. Besides Fuentes's charges that the churchwomen were involved in guerrilla activity, he also argued Miguel d'Escoto caused Maryknoll's shift from anticommunist crusaders to Marxist propagandists.[122] Fuentes not only echoed conservative U.S. Catholics' claims; his January 1981 editorial appeared the same day as a *Wanderer* article critical of Maryknoll.[123] Both pieces cited the same source: a September 1980 Cardinal Mindszenty Foundation report.[124] Phyllis Schlafly and her sister Eleanor founded the anticommunist organization in 1958 to honor

Hungary's Jozsef Cardinal Mindszenty, jailed by the Nazis and later the Soviets.[125] The similar Fuentes and *Wanderer* pieces underscored how conservative U.S. and Salvadoran Catholics shared viewpoints and, possibly, information sources.

Haig and other officials who blamed the women for their own deaths employed the "asking for it" argument of rape cases even as they did not acknowledge the women were raped. Their rhetoric shifted focus from those responsible—individual perpetrators, the Salvadoran government, and the United States as arms supplier and military trainer—to the women. The implication was that by behaving in ways Catholics, and women, should not, the missionaries brought violence on themselves. The approach had some success, as the press, conservative Catholics, and the government largely stopped talking about the rapes, though their silence provoked anger among Catholic women.[126] The responsibility-shifting comments also upset Maryknoll because they appeared to license violence against religious. Maryknoll President Roper explained that because Haig was secretary of state, his words had "powerful" implications, particularly for Maryknollers abroad. As she wrote to Haig, "My primary concern regarding these statements is that they are communicated publicly in other countries where we have personnel and where the Catholic Church is being persecuted."[127]

Officials' criticism of the churchwomen seemed plausible, if not convincing, to some because it recalled earlier "gunrunning" by Maryknollers. Kirkpatrick's insinuation that Clarke and Ford worked for the FMLN, Lefever's claim of nuns hiding machine guns, and Haig's charges of a shoot-out seemed possible to those familiar with the 1967 Melville incident.

Reagan officials also used stereotypes of nuns to imply that the women were responsible for their own deaths because they engaged in behavior inappropriate for nuns. Caricatures of "the nun" depicted a woman "as the captive of the convent or a stern school marm or starchy floor nurse,"[128] or as Kazel's biographer contends, as "an immature, incompetent, asexual being that floats around in medieval dress and has little knowledge of life in the real world."[129] When pressed about her remarks, Kirkpatrick distinguished Maryknollers from "nuns teaching school children." As she wrote to Senators Charles H. Percy (R-IL) and Claiborne Pell (D-RI): "The nuns, two of whom I said were reported to have just returned from Nicaragua and to have ties with the Santanista [sic] junta, were perceived not just as nuns teaching school children but as political activists on behalf of the Frente. I do not believe that my point was either very original or controversial. Spokesmen for the Maryknoll Order themselves repeatedly make clear their view that in our times their vocation involves them in political struggle."[130] Similarly, when Senator Pell confronted Haig about his roadblock comment, he denied the accusation "with a tone of amazement" and also seemingly distinguished between good and bad nuns.[131] As he responded, "You mean that they tried to violate—oh, not at all. No, not at all. My heavens." When Pell challenged Haig again, the secretary of state replied, "The dear nuns who raised me in my parochial schooling would forever isolate me from their affections and respect."[132] Like Kirkpatrick, Haig referred to the somewhat anachronistic model of sister-teachers. Labeling the women "political" and accusing them of dying in an exchange of gunfire conveyed a sense of power, perhaps even feminist tendencies, deemed inappropriate and inconsistent with the idea of nuns as child-like, innocent creatures, or alternatively, as stern educators with their rulers ready to discipline.

Haig and Kirkpatrick could rely on stereotypes because an image of the naive and meek nun persisted in U.S. popular culture and was personified by Mother Teresa. In late 1970s advertising, companies such as The Gap, Icelandic Airlines, and Volkswagen used the image of the nun as a woman in full habit, "a demure female-yet-neuter someone dedicated to saving souls."[133] The media often presented Mother Teresa as a living example of such a nun: a habit-wearing, modest, apolitical woman.[134] She won the 1979 Nobel Peace Prize for her work among India's poor, bandaging the sick and caring for the dying. Her approach was apolitical because her concern was poverty's immediate effects, not its structural causes.[135] Although Mother Teresa was "the world's best known Roman Catholic nun," *Chicago Tribune* religion editor Bruce Buursma pointed out, she was "hardly typical of the 750,000 nuns scattered throughout the world" because "the watchword among international sisters increasingly is becoming political activism." Buursma described the Maryknoll Sisters as "among the chief symbols of this spirit" of political activism and mentioned murdered churchwomen Maura Clarke and Ita Ford by name.[136]

By the time of the churchwomen's murders, U.S. sisters were challenging their role in the church and were politically active in society. During the pope's 1979 visit to the United States, Sister Theresa Kane confronted him about the church's refusal to ordain women.[137] By 1980, nuns held political office. A sister served in Arizona's legislature, and another was mayor in Iowa. A nun also ran as the 1980 vice presidential candidate for the Social Party, U.S.A.[138] Others, realizing that their retirement fund and other investments gave them power as shareholders, forced corporations to be more socially responsible.[139]

But the Maryknoll Sisters stressed that they were not political activists. When Senator Jesse Helms (R-NC) challenged Melinda Roper to describe Mary-knollers if not with the term "political activists," Roper said their motives were not ideological: "Political motivation many times accommodates itself to political expediency, whereas our motivation, as one that comes from God, does not change. We will denounce injustices; and so let us get more used to looking at reality from a Christian perspective with a gospel that never changes."[140] For Maryknollers, faith, not ideology or arms, was the means to combating oppression.

While condemning the churchwomen, Reagan officials encouraged priests and nuns to engage in political activity consistent with U.S. anticommunist aims. The Reagan administration, together with the Vatican, worked with priests to support the Polish Solidarity movement. Priests conveyed strategic advice to Solidarity founder and leader Lech Wałęsa, and established secret channels for smuggling communication equipment, such as fax machines, telephones, and computers, into Poland.[141] The White House gave the pope "highly classified intelligence," including spy satellite photos, while the Vatican supplied "information and analysis."[142] The White House's support for activities like Solidarity demonstrated that it was liberation theology, not religious involvement in politically related activities, the administration opposed.

Symbolism of the Churchwomen

The White House tried to forget the churchwomen's case, but the women evoked a bipartisan response. In a letter to the president, Democratic senators Pell, Edward Zorinsky (NE), and Joseph Biden (DE) wrote that the murder investigation was "a key determinant of our relationship with the government of El Salvador."[143] Similarly, in opening the hearings, *Situation in El Salvador*, Republican chair Percy said the Salvadoran government "must move to indict and prosecute the murders of the American missionaries. . . . [It] is an important symbol of the government's intention to curb the abuses which have been committed by certain elements in Salvadoran society."[144]

To many Catholics, the churchwomen were examples of living faith: women who followed Jesus by laying down their lives for others. The women were martyrs, not because of how they died but because of their service to the poor and persecuted. The churchwomen forced U.S. Catholics to confront their comfortable lives compared with Salvadorans.[145] They prompted some to become missioners or to visit Central America.[146]

The churchwomen also became a protest symbol. Throughout the spring of 1981, protesters in Los Angeles, New York, Tucson, and Kansas City carried signs with the slogan "U.S. guns kill U.S. nuns!"[147] Protesters recalled the churchwomen during Central America Week, scheduled around March 24, the anniversary of Archbishop Romero's murder. New York's cardinal celebrated Mass in St. Patrick's Cathedral in Romero's honor, and Albuquerque's archbishop did the same in El Paso. A vigil and fast, mostly by Salvadoran refugees, took place in Los Angeles, and in Washington, DC, protesters held a vigil and hunger strike outside the Pentagon.[148] Illinois protesters delivered ten thousand signatures opposing aid to Senator Percy.[149] Minnesota saw its largest antiwar demonstration since Vietnam.[150] Unlike the anti–Vietnam War movement, opposition to U.S. policy toward El Salvador was not student led. And, women seemed to be the majority.[151]

Women religious, especially Maryknollers, toured the country recounting their experiences and detailing how Reagan's policies negatively affected people in the region.[152] To assuage Catholics' concerns about communism and their unwillingness to oppose U.S. foreign policy, missionaries framed their appeals with biblical themes and Catholic social teaching that emphasized the church's long-standing commitment to the poor. In particular, they highlighted similarities between Catholics' persecution and martyrdom in El Salvador and that of Jesus.[153]

When speaking to Catholics, Maryknoll sisters held a position of respect that gave them credibility. Children who attended parochial schools through the mid-1960s were familiar with Maryknoll because the order regularly spoke to students about vocations and organized financial drives to save "pagan babies" in communist China. As some Catholics, later active regarding Central America, noted, this Catholic education exposed them to other peoples and emphasized Catholicism's international nature.[154] In this way, Maryknoll sisters' accounts of Central American atrocities would have been nothing new to Catholics who grew up hearing missionaries.

Maryknollers' efforts had an impact. After missioners expressed their disapproval of Reagan's policies to Representative Thomas Downey (D-NY), he advised them to speak to his constituents. For months afterward, Downey's constituents said "this nun came to talk" as the impetus for their opposition to U.S. policy.[155] Others found missionaries' accounts more credible than the government's. In imploring her Massachusetts representative to oppose military aid to El Salvador, a Sister of Charity wrote, "Surely the missionaries there know the true situation and their testimony should be given top priority—way above reports from 'observers' or political reporters who see only what is to their material advantage."[156]

But opposition did not stop military aid. In March 1981, Reagan sent "four military teams" and $20 million using executive authority. Congress also approved his request to reprogram, or shift, $5 million more from other aid.[157]

The $25 million in new military aid was historic. El Salvador had not gotten that much in total since 1946, and the other countries of Latin America and the Caribbean did not receive that much in 1981.[158]

An assassin's bullet displaced Central America, but not Haig, from the spotlight. The secretary of state's response to the March 30 shooting of President Reagan solidified Haig's reputation as a loose cannon. Reagan underwent surgery, while Vice President George H. W. Bush was not in DC. As the White House press secretary stumbled to explain who was in charge while Reagan was incapacitated, Haig burst in and assumed the podium. He told reporters, "As of now, I am in control here, in the White House pending return of the vice president, and in close touch with him."[159] Haig was wrong about the line of succession. He was never able to live down the episode.

The shooting catapulted Reagan's approval rating to a high of 68 percent,[160] but it did not dampen protests. By late spring, the FBI, State Department, and Congress credited religious protest, centered on the churchwomen's murders, with decreased support for U.S. policy. In a cable to the FBI director, the FBI legal attaché involved with the churchwomen investigation claimed the murders were driving protests, and he acknowledged the religious lobby's strength. As he explained, the "investigation into the murders of the American churchwomen was a most important issue for the United States Government . . . because it was a main issue for the American Catholics and, increasingly, major Protestant organizations who are protesting U.S. military assistance in El Salvador."[161] Similarly, a senior State Department official told the *National Catholic Reporter* the church was largely responsible for introducing "widespread skepticism of U.S-Salvadoran relations." The official clarified: "The killing of the nuns was a critical point and it's hard to believe the message that came from that event was missed [in Congress]." As Iowa Republican Jim Leach acknowledged, "The role of the church and its views of this (El Salvador) matter has taken on great significance." Leach was not alone; many Democratic and moderate Republicans began to voice opposition to U.S.-Salvadoran policy through the budget debate.[162]

Although for many the churchwomen symbolized U.S.-Salvadoran relations, their deaths complicated, but did not always monopolize, discussions of El Salvador. Six years after the United States evacuated the embassy in Saigon, debate also focused on whether El Salvador was "another Vietnam" and whether Reagan violated the War Powers Act in sending military advisors.[163] For others, particularly Democrats who were outnumbered in the Senate but the majority in the House, El Salvador became a way to oppose administration policies generally.

Privately, White House staffers were perplexed about why Catholics opposed U.S.–El Salvador policy. One advisor stressed that "we must take this problem with Catholics seriously" but argued that El Salvador "has no place in a discussion of regular Catholic issues." Luckily, the memo writer concluded, "much of the opposition" centered on Haig, not Reagan.[164]

The memo author was right; protesters saw Haig as the face of U.S.–El Salvador policy. During his commencement address at Syracuse University, twenty individuals dressed in blood-splattered religious habits stood and pointed at the secretary of state. Over one hundred students walked out, and nearly fifty nonstudents heckled him. Protesters interrupted Haig's speech with chants such as "We need Haig like we need the plague!" "Get out of El Salvador!" and "Washington guns killed American nuns."[165]

White House pollster Richard Wirthlin also blamed Haig for the administration's free fall when it came to El Salvador. From April to May 1981, polls showed opposition increased by 8 percent. Wirthlin blamed scary administration rhetoric, particularly Haig's. James Baker responded by ordering officials to scale back aggressive language.[166]

But the problem was more complicated than rhetoric. As Head of the Office of Public Liaison Elizabeth Dole pointed out, Catholics were divided. "Catholic bishops and certain liberal elements of the clergy and laity" "sharply criticized" U.S.–Latin America policy, while "the majority of the Catholic or ethnic communities" supported the White House. To appeal to Catholics more broadly, Dole recommended "a continued strong anti-Communist foreign policy," but she acknowledged, "for reasons not clearly understood, it will be criticized by Catholic clergy insofar as that policy is applied to Latin America."[167]

Dole's confusion contrasted with conservative Catholics' conclusion: the problem was the wrong *kind* of Catholics. A frustrated *Wanderer* columnist wrote, "The irony of the situation is that Haig, a Catholic, finds his anti-Communist stand being opposed by his own Church leaders while their position is now being openly questioned by increasing numbers of Catholic lay groups, whose members were taught the evils of atheistic Communism in Catholic schools."[168] The bishops and Catholics opposing U.S. aid had turned their backs on what it meant to be Catholic. And Haig was the strong, long overdue anticommunist approach the United States and the church needed.

The administration must respond, James Theberge insisted. In mid-April 1981, the former U.S. ambassador to Nicaragua and member of candidate Reagan's Foreign Policy Advisory Council warned Ed Meese that the White House needed to combat the "growing campaign . . . to erode public and Congressional support for the Reagan Administration's policy toward

El Salvador." Theberge cited "various domestic Church and other lobbying groups, liberal Congressmen, and human rights groups." He recommended "a special task force . . . to mobilize public and Congressional support."[169]

But just like the *Wanderer*, CIA Director Casey saw wayward Catholics as the problem. Although he agreed with Theberge, Casey reframed some of his conclusions. In a memo to Haig, his "friend and confidant" with whom he ate breakfast every Tuesday morning,[170] Casey noted the presence of "a strong public campaign" led by "both Catholic and Socialist impetus," rather than just "Church" groups as Theberge claimed. In particular, Casey cited the involvement of "left wing priests" and the need to educate Catholics. As he argued, "The rank and file Catholics will not support the left wing priests when they understand the real danger of another Cuba spreading over three or four countries in Central America."[171] Casey's conclusion was unsurprising, given what his authorized biographer described as Casey's life's purpose: "saving people from the coils of communism." Casey's "secular religion" meshed with his devout Catholicism, leading one friend to conclude, "Bill believed in the American flag, the Catholic Church, and nothing else."[172]

Despite Casey's and other officials' irritation with their fellow Catholics, the powerful symbolism of the churchwomen and the administration's priority on selling its El Salvador policy are likely why Haig responded when it appeared another Maryknoller went missing. In late April 1981, Father Roy Bourgeois traveled to El Salvador as a translator with Chicago's CBS affiliate. He then disappeared. Panic ensued. Believing Bourgeois was kidnapped,[173] Maryknoll activated its network, asking people to contact the Salvadoran embassy and President Duarte, insisting the government reveal where Bourgeois was, guarantee his safety, and release him.[174] Worried supporters asked CBS and Congress members to pressure the State Department.[175] The Maryknoll Fathers and Brothers were in close contact with U.S. officials throughout the incident.[176]

Haig came to Bourgeois's defense. After receiving word of the priest's disappearance, President Duarte said Bourgeois "could have joined the leftists." The remark reportedly led Haig to call and angrily demand the president "fully investigate."[177] The last thing the White House needed was another murdered Maryknoller.

After ten days, Bourgeois walked into the U.S. embassy in San Salvador. He explained that "opposition" members had invited him to the mountains to see what life was like for the people. Bourgeois accepted, but did not inform Maryknoll or the local church, as policy required. He also did not tell the TV crew. Instead, he left a note, but for reasons unclear, it was not publicly released until just hours before he resurfaced.[178]

Whatever Bourgeois's intentions, Maryknoll critics had a field day. An AIM staffer, writing in the *National Review*, argued the incident was suspiciously convenient. Bourgeois's disappearance made the Salvadoran government look poor just in time for a May 3 demonstration at the Pentagon.[179] The twenty thousand who marched against U.S.–El Salvador policy, defense spending, and budget cuts marked the largest antiwar demonstration since Vietnam. In San Francisco, five thousand took part in a similar demonstration.[180]

The episode damaged missionaries' reputation, especially Maryknoll's. After Bourgeois resurfaced, Duarte called for him to be charged with "subversion."[181] In San Salvador, Acting Apostolic Administrator Rivera worried that Bourgeois's actions would "only help those who out of ignorance or self-deception claim that all foreign missionaries are subversives."[182]

Rivera proved correct. In mid-May, Honduras announced that because Jesuits and Maryknollers abandoned their "holy mission" to pursue political activities,[183] those coming from El Salvador and Guatemala would no longer be allowed into the country.[184] Maryknoll temporarily moved its six members in El Salvador—two women and four men—to Guatemala. The State Department cautioned them against return. As Assistant Secretary of State for Inter-American Affairs Thomas Enders wrote to Maryknoll in early June, "I remain deeply concerned about the safety of other religious personnel working in Central America, which can still be jeopardized by this incident. Please call me before you make a decision on returning to El Salvador."[185] In a phone conversation, Enders also noted that San Salvador's *La Prensa Gráfica* argued Bourgeois intended to undermine the government, while *Diario de Hoy* labeled priests, particularly Jesuits and Maryknollers, subversives.[186] The coverage was not new. Since October 1980—before the churchwomen were murdered—an anti-Maryknoll "campaign had been building" in the Salvadoran press. The Bourgeois episode tipped the scales in favor of Maryknoll's departure. As Father John Spain explained in August, "It is impossible to return and do meaningful pastoral work in a country in which one is labeled subversive. . . . Being labeled as subversive is enough to make one a target for murder."[187]

Back in the United States, congressional support for an investigation kept the churchwomen's murders in the spotlight. After eight months of wrangling, in December 1981 Congress passed a spending bill that required the president to semiannually certify that El Salvador (1) was "making a concerted and significant effort to comply with internationally recognized human rights," (2) was "achieving substantial control" over the armed forces, (3) was "making continued progress" to implement reforms, including land reforms, (4) was "committed to the holding of free elections" and "to begin discussions with all major political factions" to find an end to the conflict, and (5) had "made good faith efforts to investigate" the murders of the churchwomen and those killed at the Sheraton hotel.[188] The process ensured that El Salvador returned to the public eye at least every six months.

Ultimate power for funding, however, rested with the president. As former congressional staffer Cynthia Arnson points out, with certification Congress "invited the administration to exaggerate, if not misrepresent, the extent of progress." The standards were vague because the law did not define whether "progress" signified improvement or an absolute standard. At the same time, the exercise allowed representatives to say they placed some restrictions on the president. Notwithstanding the charade aspect of certification, the administration saw it as an irritant. Assistant Secretary of State for Human Rights Elliott Abrams called it "ridiculous."[189]

Each certification brought the same dance: before, the Reagan administration announced progress in the investigation, and after, Congress disputed that human rights were improving.[190] Two days before the January 1982 certification, a Salvadoran general announced there would be developments even though five National Guardsmen had been arrested eight months earlier. The men were soon given to authorities.[191] The administration's desire to show movement underscored the degree to which the churchwomen's case was synonymous with U.S. policy toward El Salvador.

By using the churchwomen's case as the benchmark, the administration downplayed, and even ignored, other human rights abuses. International human rights agencies' estimates of the number of people killed in 1981 were two to three times higher than those of the U.S. embassy.[192] The discrepancy resulted from the embassy's use of the "grim gram"—statistics of dead and wounded according to the Salvadoran press. But the Salvadoran press was conservative to Right leaning and focused on cities, where fewer people were being killed because so many had fled to the mountains in 1979 and 1980.[193] If there were no reports, according to the embassy, it did not happen.

One of those nonevents was a massacre in December 1981. The elite, U.S.-trained Atlacatl battalion murdered 936 people in el Mozote and surrounding areas. The *Washington Post* and *New York Times* featured the massacre on their front pages the day before Reagan delivered certification to Congress.[194] The U.S. government denied the incident and continued to do so until 1992.[195]

Congress and others disputed certification. Representative Gerry Studds (D-MA) and thirty-one cosponsors introduced a joint resolution "declaring the president's certification with respect to El Salvador to be null and void."[196] In a letter to House Speaker Tip O'Neill, Fermán Cienfuegos, member of the FMLN's general command, argued "the document itself seems to constitute only an effort to justify a political decision made a priori apart from any rigorous examination of the facts and any legal substantiation."[197]

While some argued certification was a sham, the process forced the Salvadoran junta to take action, leading some Salvadorans to complain. Jesuits expressed frustration that U.S.-Salvadoran relations centered on the churchwomen's case. In February 1982, *Cartas a las iglesias*, a UCA publication aimed at CEBs and other Catholics,[198] questioned the U.S. government's influence on the Salvadoran junta. As the article explained, on February 10, Duarte and three other junta members appeared on radio and television, suggesting an important announcement, such as the war's end or dialogue. Instead, Duarte said that those accused of the "capture, rape and murder" of the churchwomen had been delivered to the court. The announcement occurred after Reagan's certification, which *Cartas* alleged showed that the junta "complied" with Reagan's insistence on progress in the case. By contrast, Duarte did not follow Bishop Rivera's call for investigations into the murders of Archbishop Romero, priests, and pastoral agents. Nor did Duarte heed the churchwomen's families, who advocated for the institution of justice in the country, or the Maryknoll Sisters, who "demanded" investigations into Salvadorans' deaths. *Cartas* argued that the response to the churchwomen's case showed that political interests, not concern for human rights, drove progress. The churchwomen were worth millions in U.S. aid and attention, while thousands of Salvadorans lay dead and disappeared.[199]

The Salvadoran president agreed with the Jesuits' conclusion that certification dictated junta behavior. As Duarte later complained, "When military aid was conditioned to human-rights improvements, the U.S. ambassador became more powerful than I was as president."[200] Whereas Jesuits clamored for more attention to all human rights abuses, not just those perpetrated against U.S. citizens, Duarte resented how certification made him a lapdog rather than the determiner of El Salvador's policies.

The certification tango—some Congress members challenging U.S. policy and the administration essentially getting what it wanted—was a metaphor for U.S.-Salvadoran funding overall. Opponents prevented the Reagan administration from having free rein, but they did not stop the White House. Reagan funded El Salvador without congressional approval. In February 1982, El Salvador received $55 million in military aid through the emergency powers Carter used. Just as Carter argued funds were necessary after the FMLN final offensive in early 1981, Reagan sent aid after the FMLN attacked the Ilopango air base.[201]

One reason opponents did not stop the White House was because not all Democrats were spoiling for a fight. Senator J. James Exon (NE) expressed the views of many when he worried about options. As he explained, "If we turn down the additional aid, we could be helping the Communist guerrilla take-over of the country. But on the other hand, we'd be aiding a Government we're not happy with. The bottom line is, which is the lesser of two evils?"[202] House Speaker Tip O'Neill tried to thread the needle: placate Democrats against Reagan's Central America policy but not lose conservative Democrats sympathetic to the president's anticommunist aims. He feared a conservative defection on El Salvador would spell the loss of those Democrats to Reagan permanently.[203]

Although Democratic leaders dragged their feet, the administration still could not get in front of the Catholic-led protest movement. U.S. ambassador to El Salvador Deane Hinton privately cited Catholic Church opposition "as the main obstacle" in the push for military aid.[204] Democrat Michael Barnes (MD), opponent of Reagan's Central America policy and chair of the Subcommittee on Inter-American Affairs, similarly described the church's influence. "The group that has the most credibility and that I sense is listened to most by my constituents is the Catholic Church. I'm not sure how they mobilize people, but they are certainly well-mobilized."[205]

The problem grew worse for Reagan as faith communities flouted the law. On the second anniversary of Romero's murder, six churches in Arizona and California declared themselves sanctuaries for Central Americans unlawfully in the United States. The Refugee Act of 1980, modeled on the UN refugee definition, required a "well-founded fear of persecution" based on a person's race, religion, nationality, political opinion, or membership in a particular social group. Because most Central Americans left to escape "the generalized climate of violence," they did not satisfy the strict definition, leading Reagan officials to classify them as economic migrants under U.S. law, not as refugees. Sanctuary members saw U.S. policy as "illegal and immoral" and in violation of the Refugee Act of 1980 and international law for returning Central Americans.[206] The interfaith movement grew to more than forty-five sanctuaries—churches, synagogues, and homes—in early 1983 and about two hundred by January 1985.[207] It stretched across Mexico, the United States, and Canada.[208]

From Haig to Casey

Haig—the personification of the administration's tough anticommunist El Salvador policy—left the White House in June 1982 when Reagan asked him to resign.[209] The new secretary of state, George Shultz, changed the tenor on

Central America, though not the policy. While Haig seemed to obsess over Central America, Shultz looked to the Middle East and NATO (North Atlantic Treaty Organization) during his first six months on the job.[210]

Haig's departure did not mean anticommunist aims disappeared; Haig's friend Casey had been pursuing the crusade through covert action. Less than three months into his term, Reagan authorized $19.5 million for Casey's covert plan to stop the arms flow into El Salvador from Nicaragua and Honduras.[211] The move built on Carter's authorization for the CIA to work with Sandinista opposition.[212] Then, in December 1981, Reagan approved efforts to build popular support against the Sandinistas and train teams in paramilitary activities. The goal was to pressure the Sandinista government, causing it to suppress its people and thereby decrease its international support.[213]

The U.S. government did not create the disgruntled Nicaraguan guerrilla fighters. Not long after Somoza's overthrow, former National Guardsmen formed guerrilla units to oppose the Sandinistas. Argentine special forces advised the counterrevolutionaries, or Contras, and by early 1981, the United States assumed the responsibility.[214]

The CIA was involved, however, in creating specific Contra groups and training, arming, and paying them. In August 1981, Casey's division chief for operations in Latin America, Duane R. Clarridge, together with Argentines, met in Honduras to create the Nicaraguan Democratic Force (FDN), the largest of the Contra groups.[215] The FDN brought together wealthy Miami exiles and former National Guardsmen.[216] Some Nicaraguans joined the FDN because they were disgruntled with FSLN economic policies, needed money the U.S. government provided, or were kidnapped into service. Most often, they joined because they regarded Sandinistas as godless communists. While the FDN was based in the north, on the Atlantic coast the Miskito, Sumu, and Rama ethnic communities formed their own opposition forces, which sought independence or more political freedom. Finally, in the south, former Sandinista fighter Edén Pastora Gómez led the Democratic Revolutionary Alliance (ARDE).[217]

The White House's covert Contra plan was not so secret, and as details leaked out, its purpose seemed at odds with what the administration said publicly. The press began featuring stories in the spring, and in November 1982, a *Newsweek* cover story detailed CIA support for overthrowing the Sandinistas.[218] A worried Congress tried to put the brakes on. Passed in December 1982, the Boland Amendment prohibited the CIA and the Defense Department from using U.S. funds to overthrow the Nicaraguan government or to provoke military engagement between Nicaragua and Honduras. Nonlethal aid to the Contras was still permissible, as were CIA attempts to stop arms moving from

Nicaragua to El Salvador.[219] Despite the Boland Amendment, Casey's CIA forged ahead.

With their rape and murder in December 1980, the four churchwomen came to symbolize U.S. policy toward El Salvador. Their deaths were a call to action, particularly for liberal Catholics critical of U.S. Cold War policy. For conservative Catholics, however, the murders were the logical result of Maryknoll's misguided activities that threatened U.S. foreign policy and the church. The Carter administration fostered the link between the women's case and U.S. policy by saying their deaths ended U.S. military and economic aid to El Salvador. Though the Reagan administration tried to unlink the case, it was to no avail. The White House faced a robust protest movement, largely led by liberal Catholics, while conservative Catholics shaped U.S. policy, thereby strengthening the conservative side in intra-Catholic debates. In the first two years of Reagan's presidency, the administration funded its El Salvador aims either with begrudging congressional support or through presidential action. But overall, the White House and its conservative Catholic allies found themselves on the defensive: backtracking from controversial comments or explaining a lack of progress in the churchwomen's murder case. With the approaching 1984 election, the administration shifted tactics.

CHAPTER 5

Reagan and the White House's Maryknoll Nun

Running for reelection in July 1984, President Ronald Reagan addressed Catholics at St. Ann's Festival in Hoboken, New Jersey. Reagan listed four "Catholic" concerns that distinguished his campaign from Democratic candidate Walter Mondale's: abortion, tuition tax credits, school prayer, and Central America. As Reagan explained, "We're rather more inclined to listen to the testimony of His Holiness the Pope than the claims of Communist Sandinistas" in Nicaragua. Reagan accused the Sandinistas of "trying to abolish the Church of Rome and replace it with a so-called popular church."[1] More than an attempt to garner Catholic votes, Reagan's remarks revealed how his administration took sides in the "ecclesiastical guerrilla warfare" occurring among Catholics.[2]

Reagan promoted himself as defender of the Nicaraguan Catholic Church to win support, especially among conservative Catholics, for U.S. policy and his reelection bid. As this chapter argues, the White House tried to move the public focus from human rights in El Salvador (and the churchwomen's case) to Nicaragua by alleging that the Sandinista government persecuted religion and was trying to create a fake church. The public diplomacy campaign involved cooperation with religious conservatives,[3] and its design and execution reflected conservative Catholic viewpoints and language, continuing the pattern begun when Reagan officials criticized the murdered churchwomen. While the administration aimed its criticism at the Sandinistas, Catholic allies, including former Maryknoller Geraldine O'Leary de Macías, critiqued Maryknoll and liberation theology at home and abroad. Maryknoll's prominence revealed the enduring role the murdered churchwomen had on U.S.–Central America policy discussions.

Conservatives and the White House

Reagan and his supporters regarded Nicaragua as an international pariah; others saw a beacon of hope. For liberationists, "Nicaragua became a living laboratory."[4] Liberation theology influenced the revolution against Somoza and its attempts to create a new Nicaraguan society. For this reason, liberal Catholics saw U.S. policy as derailing their hopes for a new direction in Central America and the church. Nicaragua's appeal also reached beyond those who supported liberation theology. As Father Ernesto Cardenal noted, "Nicaragua became a mecca for thousands of people who wished to see social change in their own countries and who came to be inspired and help us move forward." Besides nationalizing the financial system, the mines, and foreign trade, the Sandinistas reformed agriculture and made education free.[5]

Their most celebrated endeavor was the National Literacy Crusade. The campaign's goal—eliminating illiteracy—was ambitious. In 1980, 70 percent of Nicaraguans living in urban areas, but only 25 percent of those in the countryside, were literate. To the Sandinistas, the literacy crusade was integral to the revolution. Literacy would help the new economy and ensure that campesinos could not be exploited as they had been by Somoza.[6]

International bodies recognized Nicaragua's success. In 1980, the United Nations Educational, Scientific, and Cultural Organization (UNESCO) awarded Nicaragua for reducing the illiteracy rate from "roughly 50" to 13 percent.[7] Three years later, the World Health Organization and the United Nations Children's Fund (UNICEF) called Nicaragua a "model country for health."[8] UNESCO also found that the working classes' standard of living had increased owing to the literacy campaign, together with other government programs, including "expanded health services, price controls on 'basic foodstuff,' and a 'subsidy for certain essential goods and services.'" But the Nicaraguan government shifted its resources away from programs like these and more toward national defense in response to U.S. policies, including the Contra war.[9]

The U.S. government engaged in a multipronged approach to pressure the Sandinistas. In its first three years, the Reagan administration blocked or vetoed international loans to Nicaragua.[10] In early 1983, the U.S. military conducted exercises—Big Pine—involving sixteen hundred troops.[11] At the same time, both the *Washington Post* and Contra leaders on Nicaraguan television challenged Reagan's claim that the Contras sought to stop the arms flow to El Salvador. Instead, they insisted, the Contras were fighting to overthrow the Sandinistas.[12] The news called into question the Boland Amendment. And the Nicaraguan government agreed. As it charged in the spring of 1983, Reagan was carrying out an "undeclared war." The Nicaraguan government called on the people to "defend the fatherland" in the face of "invasion" by the Honduran army and increased attacks by the Contras—the "genocidal counterrevolutionary forces" the United States "financed and directed."[13]

None of this was enough for U.S. conservatives. In the spring of 1983, leaders met to address the White House's failed approach and to devise a plan to eliminate "communist influence in the western hemisphere."[14] The Conservative Caucus and the Coalitions for America, both led by Paul Weyrich, spearheaded the effort.

Weyrich's faith shaped his political agenda, and he charted a new course religiously and politically. He left the Roman rite for the Melkite Greek Catholic Church because he wanted "to remain a Catholic," but he "could not stomach" Vatican II's liturgical reforms.[15]

Like other conservative Catholics, Weyrich contended the U.S. church was in a state of "advanced decline" because bishops prioritized "temporal politics" over spiritual life. As evidence, he pointed to the bishops' support for the Panama Canal treaties.[16] His disillusionment served as a key impetus for the Moral Majority's formation. Weyrich coined the term and encouraged Baptist Jerry Falwell to organize the group. Besides offering a political opening for Catholics disappointed with the post–Vatican II church, Weyrich hoped the Moral Majority could organize blue-collar Catholics to be "the Achilles heel of the liberal Democrats."[17]

The Central America PR strategy Weyrich and others proposed recognized Catholics' role on both sides of the Central America debate. To counter U.S. policy opponents, the group recommended developing spokespeople, arguing that Catholics would be "particularly helpful." Among others, they suggested Heritage Foundation president Ed Feulner, future national security advisor Richard Allen, William F. Buckley, Phyllis Schlafly, Father Enrique Rueda, future White House communications director Patrick J. Buchanan, the NSC's Roger Fontaine, *Wanderer* editor A. J. Matt, and the former editor of Nicaragua's opposition paper, *La Prensa*, Humberto Belli.[18] The list highlighted the influential positions Catholics held in both the administration and outside organizations.

The White House worried about Weyrich's grumbling because it feared his influence. A few months into Reagan's presidency, Office of Public Liaison

Elizabeth Dole met with Weyrich to assess his views and solicit his support for the president's economic policies. A memo preparing Dole for the meeting described Weyrich as "the key organizer of a surprising number of the conservative organizations and coalitions responsible for political activity not supporting the President" and warned that he played the same role in fighting the Panama Canal treaties and labor reform in the Carter years.[19] By appeasing Weyrich, the administration hoped to neutralize a powerful critic and expand its share of Catholic votes in 1984.[20]

The White House and its conservative Catholic allies saw Catholic votes as key. In 1983, the memo "The Northern Campaign and the Catholic Problem" circulated in the White House and among conservative Catholics.[21] In it, a 1976 campaign strategist for Carter asserted that *"when Catholics vote as a block, they vote Democratic. When their block voting declines, Republicans win."* The author stressed that Catholics were "concentrated in big states" in the North and that they "are not *in* the Democratic party; they *are* the Democratic party." Although the memo was written for the 1976 election, one White House official working on Reagan's reelection effort called it a "brilliantly written memo" containing "excellent advice."[22] Another strategist proposed that "the time is ripe" for the GOP to promote itself as "the Catholic Party." In comparison with Democrats, Republicans were more aligned with Catholics "on many major social issues," and more Catholics voted for the Republican presidential candidate in two of the past three elections. Republicans needed to capitalize on the Catholic vote's "state of flux."[23]

To address conservative Catholics and attract more Catholic votes in 1984, the White House initiated a Central America public diplomacy program. Reagan also wanted the campaign to "relieve" congressional restrictions on U.S. aid, namely certification for El Salvador and the Boland Amendment on Nicaragua.[24] The campaign became organized in late spring/early summer even though Reagan had approved it in January 1983.[25] In May, officials stressed the need to "immediately" organize public diplomacy efforts.[26] In response, the administration created the White House Outreach Working Group on Central America (OWG) and the Office of Public Diplomacy for Latin America and the Caribbean (S/LPD).

The Office of Public Liaison's Faith Ryan Whittlesey led the OWG and Chief of Staff Jim Baker oversaw it.[27] In directing Whittlesey to establish the group, Baker envisioned its purpose as "coordinat[ing] the Administration's efforts to increase public awareness of and support for the President's Central American policies in the country and the Congress."[28] The inside and outside OWG groups met weekly.[29] The interagency inside group included representatives from the State Department, AID, the Office of the U.S. Permanent Representative to the OAS, and the Office of UN Ambassador.[30] The outside group held Wednesday White House briefings for nongovernmental groups, created the White House *Digest* to communicate U.S. policy, and sent presenters to "interested audiences across the country."[31] Speakers addressed groups as wide-ranging as the Latin American Chamber of Commerce, the National Republican Hispanic Assembly, Catholic anticommunist organizations, diocesan priests, and university students.[32] Within two months, representatives from "more than *145 organizations*" had attended White House meetings, which the administration credited with prompting "millions of issues of publications" containing editorials and "hundreds of thousands of letters" supporting U.S.–Central America policy.[33]

Although the White House wanted support, the OWG was not designed to convert opponents. Instead, the group was "a Presidential public outreach effort to supportive and uncommitted groups."[34] Whittlesey believed Central America was a good issue "to reinvigorate conservative support."[35] At the same time, opponents got the message. Thomas Quigley, advisor on Latin America for the U.S. Catholic bishops, described his experience with the Wednesday OWG meetings as "mostly a waste of time, dog-and-pony shows, with low levels of real information. They did succeed, however, in solidifying the support of more conservative clergymen."[36]

Whittlesey's approach responded to and worked with conservatives eager to see the White House push its Central America agenda. The OWG tapped Paul Weyrich to establish a "Campaign Calendar," which included "a proposed completion date for full aid to Central America."[37] Just months into the OWG's work, Weyrich's Coalitions for America spent millions promoting U.S. policy through direct mail campaigns, TV specials on religious stations, newsletters, "educational trips" to Central America for church groups, and lobbying efforts for incumbents facing challengers opposed to U.S.–Central America policy. The group received most of its information from the OWG. As Weyrich revealed, "They do the informing and we do the work. It's a nice team effort."[38]

Like the OWG, the S/LPD promoted U.S. policy and cooperated with White House supporters, but the S/LPD used illegal methods. The S/LPD was part of the CIA's efforts to circumvent legal prohibitions on domestic propaganda and lobbying. Under the National Security Act of 1947 and Presidential Executive Order 12333, the CIA could not engage in domestic activities or attempt to "influence United States political processes, public opinion, policies, or media."[39] The S/LPD reported to the NSC but was ostensibly part of the State Department to remain in legal compliance. The S/LPD paid outside contractors to write articles for the press, distributed propaganda to organizations, monitored the media, harassed journalists who wrote unfavorable stories, and targeted Congress members. S/LPD contractors spoke before Wednesday OWG meetings and the S/LPD declassified information for White House *Digests* the OWG distributed. The S/LPD also worked with outside groups in activities the executive branch could not legally do.[40] As the comptroller general concluded in September 1987, the S/LPD engaged in "prohibited, covert propaganda activities."[41]

U.S. Pressure on Nicaragua

In keeping with its attempts to reflect conservative Catholics' concerns, administration officials accused the Sandinistas of attempting to replace the Catholic Church with a fake or "popular church" and of persecuting the Catholic Church—and all faiths. The tactic catered to both conservative U.S. and Nicaraguan Catholics.

The U.S. government's approach exploited existing divisions among Nicaraguans. In the late 1970s, many put aside religious differences to oust Somoza from power.[42] After the revolution, these ruptures resurfaced with a vengeance. The social upheaval caused by the revolution aggravated tensions among the laity as base communities tended to support the revolution, while conservative Catholics did not. Religious and political conflicts overlapped as conservative Catholics accused base communities of being communist cells that wanted to divide the church by spreading class hatred.[43] As one Maryknoll lay missioner explained, "The economic and political sectors that . . . lost power . . . desperately sought to regain it" by "convincing the people that their religious beliefs and traditions are being threatened" by the Sandinistas.[44]

These divisions were not unique, as Nicaraguan Jesuit José Arguello explained. They existed "just below the surface in every local church in the world" because everywhere "there are Christians committed to change and others who are committed to the status quo."[45] In Nicaragua those divisions overlapped with political views on the revolution. Those who sought change in the church tended to support the revolution, while the status quo group opposed it. What made the Nicaraguan intra-Catholic conflict different and intensified it, Arguello insisted, was that "a large part of the episcopacy," particularly Archbishop Obando, aligned themselves with "wealthy elites who have created a political project to oppose the revolution."[46] These church leaders saw the revolution as dangerous for ushering in "an undesirable, albeit powerful, Christian political and Marxist theory and practice." To counter Sandinista influence, the hierarchy transferred or expelled religious, critiqued lay organizations that supported the revolutionary project, and encouraged groups that opposed the Sandinistas.[47] Not to be outdone, Sandinista leaders appeared at religious processions.[48] These divisions among Nicaraguan Catholics became so entrenched, Arguello argued, that by August 1983 "healthy criticism" of the church was not even considered. Instead, it was "branded" as "popular church,"[49] further driving a wedge among Nicaraguan Catholics and highlighting that the conflict was not as simple as church versus state.

"Popular church," "parallel church," and "people's church" were contentious terms that derived from Catholic circles outside the United States, dating at least as far back as the late 1960s. As discussed in chapter 1, conservative European, Latin American, and U.S. Catholics concluded that Vatican II's changes facilitated the establishment of a "parallel doctrinal authority" through which communists worked to subvert the church and set up "the totalitarian tyranny of atheistic communism."[50] In Latin America, the term "popular church" originated in the mid-1970s in Brazil to refer "to the new forms of expression of the church," such as Christian base communities. Catholics opposed to these developments used "popular church" to accuse other Catholics of attempting to create a separate or parallel church.[51]

Catholics used the term differently, as one French Dominican explained in *Le Monde*. While Pope John Paul II criticized the "popular church" as a challenge to the hierarchical church, the phrase had a unique Latin American meaning. Latin American bishops developed the idea of church as people, as espoused at Vatican II, by stressing the church's obligation to speak for the poor. In this context, "The Church is the church of the people because it is the church of the poor."[52] Whereas one group of Catholics saw "popular church" as the rightful recognition of the role of the laity, and especially the role of the poor, other Catholics saw "popular church" as threatening the church's top-down structure.

By the late 1970s, conservative U.S. Catholics adopted the link among the "people's church," liberation theology, and subversion in Latin America. The U.S. publication of Brazil's *The People's Church* and Spain's *The New Libertarian Gospel: Pitfalls of the Theology of Liberation* prompted a U.S. Jesuit to warn that liberation theology "devotees" were "not really Catholics at all." Instead, they were "atheistic Marxists, disguised as Catholics, who, working from within the Church, are attempting to remake the Catholic Church into a tool for socialistic revolution."[53]

In Nicaragua, government opponents, such as Managua's Obando, condemned the "popular church," whereas the Sandinistas celebrated it. Both camps hoped the pope would validate their position during his March 1983 visit. Standing below "red and black mural portraits of FSLN founders,"[54] John Paul II celebrated Mass in the Plaza of Revolution before over six hundred thousand people. Many had waited in one-hundred-degree heat. In his homily, he denounced the people's church and the existence of a "parallel magisteria," and he called for church unity. The pope's plea to support the Nicaraguan bishops was controversial. Mothers of Heroes and Martyrs, the mothers of fallen Sandinista combatants, were seated near the pope, clutching "posters with photos of their dead children." They began chanting "We want peace," which others repeated. The call for the pope to condemn the Contra war was even more sensitive given the location. In the same plaza the day before the government had commemorated seventeen Sandinista youth killed by Contras a week earlier. The pope responded that "the first to want peace is the Church," but after the murmurs continued, he shouted *"Silencio."* In response to continued chants, the pope shouted twice more. Eventually, Sandinista party and government leaders raised clenched fists and shouted "People's Power!" with the crowd. Sandinista opponents saw the episode as the Vatican described it—a "premeditated political provocation"—while revolution supporters were disappointed with the pope's failure to understand the church in Nicaragua and to recognize those the Contras injured or killed.[55] Years later, former Sandinista Sergio Ramírez admitted the government regarded the pope's words as "hostile" and provocative because it opposed negotiating with the Contras at the time.[56]

Reagan seized on the incident. In his first address to the nation on Central America, in April 1983, he spoke of repression and said the Nicaraguan government "insulted and mocked the Pope."[57] The month before, Reagan gave his first speech focused on El Salvador. The moves signaled a shift from the president's first two years when he stayed in the shadows on Central America to his role as main spokesperson in 1983. Instead of Haig and his confrontational rhetoric, Reagan had become the administration's smooth salesman.

Complementing Reagan's portrayal of an aggrieved pope, the administration, especially the OWG, stressed religious persecution. The administration pointed to how the Sandinistas curtailed the archbishop's ability to say Mass on television, restricted publication of the church's newspaper, and deported priests. The focus on religious persecution as the key human rights issue followed an approach, dating back to James Madison and emphasized during the early Cold War, which characterized religious freedom as the "prerequisite" to all freedoms.[58] The theme tapped into many people's understanding of the Cold War as a battle against godless communism and Catholics as synonymous with anticommunism. The OWG hosted speakers who described the religious persecution of Catholics as well as Jews, evangelical Protestants, and Miskito Indians. The administration invited Americans to wonder, how could the religious protest movement support a government that aimed to eradicate religion?

By arguing the Sandinista government persecuted religion, the White House echoed conservative U.S. and Nicaraguan Catholics' understanding of religious freedom as the right to worship. The *National Catholic Register*'s Joan Frawley described a persecuted church. As those she described as "Nicaraguan Catholic leaders" explained, "Direct and indirect Sandinista attacks on the organized Church are part of the regime's program to transform the nation's culture." Despite the oppression, Frawley reported that "practicing Catholics" believed religious persecution would purge "the local Church of heterodox theologies as well as nominal Catholics."[59] Frawley's message was clear: real or "practicing Catholics" were Sandinista opponents.

Frawley's sympathetic account of conservative Nicaraguan Catholics was unsurprising given her father's background. Nicaraguan-born Patrick J. Frawley Jr., *National Catholic Register* owner and publisher, was a friend of Somoza's who gave to anticommunist candidates and causes, including Ronald Reagan and Young Americans for Freedom.[60] *Time* magazine credited the former chair and CEO of Paper Mate Pen, Technicolor, and Schick Safety Razor of turning the *National Catholic Register* into "an effective voice of Catholic conservatism."[61] Maryknollers were not the only Catholics with strong Central American ties who shared their perspectives with U.S. Catholics.

In contrast to the White House's and conservative Catholics' framing of religious freedom, liberal Nicaraguan and U.S. Catholics contended context mattered. The Nicaraguan government took action, its defenders insisted, in the midst of both a political feud between bishops and the state and an undeclared war with the United States. Additionally, religious freedom was more expansive; it included the church's ability to exercise its "social ministry."[62] The church was free to do so in Nicaragua. There were "problems" and "mistakes," a group of Protestant and Catholic missionaries in Nicaragua recognized, but "we must not confuse errors with systematic repression." In neighboring El Salvador, by contrast, Catholics inspired by liberation theology were routinely met with Rightist violence.[63]

U.S. officials' reference to the "people's church" also mirrored Nicaraguan bishops' rhetoric, exacerbating tensions among Nicaraguan Catholics. Managua's Obando declared, "That church that they call 'popular' is a church wedded to Marxist ideology."[64] Those who belonged to the true church followed the bishops and the pope. Prominent Sandinista opponent Bishop Pablo Antonio Vega argued, "The Popular Church is neither a church, nor of the people: it is not a church because it does not promote man's reference to a superior being, and it is not of the people, because it cultivates people's worship of the State."[65] Though common language between Reagan and the bishops did not mean coordinated efforts, many Sandinista supporters saw treasonous behavior when their bishops used Reaganesque language.[66]

Reagan's charges hit a nerve because Nicaraguans spoke of the "people's church" or the "popular church." As one former Sandinista leader acknowledged, "radical revolutionary discourse" often referred to the "popular church," which made Reagan's charges seem valid. The Sandinistas did not aim to create a separate church in the way opponents claimed; "people's church" meant the poor were the church. Despite this, the idea of "official support for a parallel church . . . became the most sensitive accusation against the FSLN."[67]

The Reagan administration's position was also in line with the pope's. John Paul II prioritized human rights, specifically freedom of worship, in a way unseen since Vatican II's *Dignitatis Humanae*. In his first encyclical, *Redemptor Hominis* (The Redeemer of Man), the pontiff declared that religious freedom was first among the "objective and inalienable rights" of people. Seven months later before the UN General Assembly, the pope continued this theme. He argued that weapons were not the biggest risk of war; it was injustice, sometimes government sanctioned, which deprived people of their human rights and in turn endangered world order. The most important right was "freedom of thought, conscience, and religion, and the right to manifest one's religion either individually or in community, in public or in private." As biographer George Weigel points out, John Paul II's emphasis on religious repression as human rights abuse called into question "communism's claim to be the twentieth century's true humanism and the true liberator of humanity." At the same time, this backdoor approach allowed him to avoid being labeled "an ecclesiastical politician allied with the West."[68]

Religious persecution charges allowed the Reagan administration to appeal to conservative Catholics without appearing to cater to them. The White House needed Catholic votes but feared losses in the Bible Belt and the Deep South. One strategist insisted stealth was key. "Perhaps the best way to *disguise* this maneuver is to make it appear as part of an overall moral tone of the administration rather than a specific appeal to Catholics." Among the recommendations, the author suggested Reagan use "correct Catholic terminology at all times. This would entail forms of address as well as liturgical and cultural designations. These designations would instantly be recognized by all Catholics but would go essentially unnoticed by most Protestants."[69] Officials' charges that the Sandinistas created a fake church and persecuted religion fulfilled this need by both resonating with Christians and holding a deeper meaning for Catholics.

The religious persecution charge also avoided any theological debates that critiques of liberation theology might raise. In a May 1983 meeting, OAS ambassador J. William Middendorf proposed a White House *Digest* on liberation theology because he used the topic "with good effort to arouse" evangelicals.[70] In addressing the graduates of Pat Robertson's Christian Broadcasting Network University (now Regent), Middendorf argued that "in addition to exporting their revolution, the Sandinistas are attempting to bring the Church to its knees." Inspired by liberation theology, some priests joined armed revolutions, while others advocated the idea to their congregations. Middendorf drew on Americans' fears of another Iran. Liberationists "portray[ed] the United States as the grand archvillain," employing "a tactic similar to the one used by Muslim fundamentalists to rally public opinion in the Middle East."[71] In short, liberation theology threatened national security.

Despite Middendorf's positive reception, the NSC and White House counsel recommended against publishing a *Digest* on liberation theology. As one official wrote, "It would be unprecedented for any President, *qua* President, to become involved in a religious controversy of this nature in any way that even approached the level of detail presented in this proposed release." Although counsel did not state so explicitly, by condemning liberation theology the publication might have implicated the Establishment Clause. Instead, if the president wanted to address liberation theology, he could, "in an appropriate speech to an appropriate audience, note his disapproval of attempts to use religion to foster revolutionary purposes in Central America—perhaps by quoting Pope John Paul II."[72] This memo suggests why Reagan and other officials often quoted the pope to promote U.S. policy. The tactic—and religious persecution charges—allowed the White House to sidestep open theological debates but still comment on the Catholic Church's relationship with the Sandinista government.

Reagan officials' Catholic appeals were overlooked because they were designed to be. Scholars and observers have noted how the administration employed or "manipulated religion" to push U.S. policy,[73] missing why the White House adopted these tactics and why this approach resonated with Catholics. Because the White House needed to balance soliciting Catholic votes with maintaining Protestant support, the administration used rhetoric so specific that only Catholics likely appreciated it. The term "popular church" held special meaning and signaled the administration's support for conservative Catholics. At the same time, the term "parallel church" heeded advisors' warnings to disguise overtures to Catholics. Non-Catholics could understand the term "parallel church" as communist efforts to infiltrate and destroy religion, while conservative Catholics also heard a reminder of the church's wayward post-Vatican drift.

The White House believed it could speak to Catholics with "popular church" but not alienate other Christians, as evidenced by officials' remarks before Catholic and non-Catholic audiences. Reagan officials, such as Jeane Kirkpatrick and Whittlesey, neither of whom was Catholic, argued the Sandinistas sought to create a "puppet popular church" or a "fake popular church" because the government failed to silence the (real) Catholic Church.[74] Similarly, Nicaraguan Arturo J. Cruz warned in *Foreign Affairs* that the Sandinistas used the popular church "to mortify the traditional Church" and to defraud the revolution's supporters in Nicaragua and abroad into seeing "the Revolution through Pollyanna's eyes."[75] The former Los Doce member's disillusionment with the Sandinistas led him to resign his positions as junta member and, later, ambassador to the United States. Finding common cause with the Reagan White House, Cruz was on the CIA payroll by 1983.[76]

Even Protestants pointed to the pope's treatment and the "people's church" as reason to support U.S. policy. On the front page of its fall 1983 newsletter, the Institute on Religion and Democracy (IRD) concluded that one cause of church-state tension was the Sandinistas' attempt to create an "alternative church."[77] Founded in 1981 "to explore the ways in which the values and practices of U.S. Religious organizations help or hinder the development of democratic institutions in the world,"[78] the IRD gained attention as a Protestant—led and focused—organization despite its Catholic board members, such as neocon Catholic Michael Novak.[79] The choice of the IRD—a largely Protestant organization—to portray the pope as victim was remarkable.

In contrast to the IRD, the Ecumenical Committee of U.S. Church Personnel in Nicaragua, composed of Catholics and Protestants, disputed charges of religious persecution. The conflict between the church hierarchy and the government was "being confused with persecution and thus used by external interests as a pretext for destabilizing the Revolutionary Government." There were "isolated abuses," the group conceded, but they were not based on "Christian belief"; it was because a person was "suspected of a particular political position or action." And, local officials or organizations, not government policies, were "generally" responsible for those abuses. There was no religious persecution, the group charged.[80]

The response of the IRD and the Ecumenical Committee highlighted how U.S.–Central America policy revealed interreligious collaboration. Conservative Protestants, Jews, and Catholics stood together more than they did with people of their own faith communities, just as liberal Protestants, Jews, and Catholics did. This interreligious cooperation was part of a larger post–World

War II trend.[81] In the case of Nicaragua, however, the White House focused on charges of Catholic religious persecution the most, as Nicaragua was predominantly a Catholic country and Reagan sought Catholic votes in the 1984 election.

And rhetoric was not the only tool the administration used to challenge Nicaragua; the White House also turned up the heat militarily. After the House voted against Contra aid for the first time in July 1983,[82] the administration initiated Big Pine II. The six-month operation, "the longest and the largest U.S. military exercise in Central America history," involved "amphibious landings" and "mock bombing raids." Big Pine II aimed to pressure the Nicaraguan government into ending its support for the Salvadoran guerrillas and its attacks on Contras in Honduras. The military operation also sought to create a siege mentality. Constant threats of attack, the U.S. government expected, would require the Nicaraguan government to shift resources from economic to military needs and to show its response if attacked. The state of siege would also unnerve the people, thereby undermining the Sandinistas' base of support.[83]

In the midst of Big Pine II and the continued Contra attacks, the Nicaraguan government proposed a military draft. Although designed to counter increasing U.S. and Contra military actions, the draft aggravated tensions between the church hierarchy and the government and between the bishops and other Catholics. Perhaps more than any other issue in the 1980s, the draft tore Nicaraguan Catholics apart.

Nicaragua's bishops rejected the call for military service, and in doing so, challenged the government. The Episcopal Conference argued the conscription bill was "partisan" and "totalitarian type legislation." It was one thing for a state to request military service; it was another when the party and the state were one and the same. The army would not protect and defend the people; it would be the "obligatory center of political indoctrination." Consequently, those who did "not share the Sandinista Party ideology," the bishops argued, should be conscientious objectors and not "be punished, persecuted or discriminated against for adopting this position."[84]

Catholic Sandinista supporters challenged the Episcopal Conference in paid newspaper advertisements. Whereas the bishops argued the draft's purpose was to further party interests, the advertisements charged the Episcopal Conference's aim was to attack "the legitimacy of the present Nicaraguan state and the legitimacy of our Revolutionary Process." The group, which included CEBs, the Conference of Religious of Nicaragua (CONFER), university students, and youth groups, contended the bishops' statement "defends the interest of Imperialism" because it critiqued the Nicaraguan government yet said nothing about U.S. ships on Nicaragua's coasts, Contra and Honduran army invasions, or U.S. interference in Nicaragua's political affairs. The bishops were not promoting civil disobedience; they were encouraging "general and generalized disobedience."[85] Another Catholic group argued the bishops were hypocritical. While the bishops accused the Sandinistas of creating a one-party state and using the army to promote party ideology with no room for dissent, the bishops were "deny[ing] the same right within the Nicaraguan Church" because they mandated a single Catholic response.[86]

In the midst of Nicaraguans' draft debates, the U.S.-trained Contras attacked "industrial and transportation targets inside Nicaragua," rather than guerrilla operations along Nicaragua's northern border with Honduras.[87] In September, Contras targeted Managua's airport and Nicaragua's oil terminal.[88] The following month, fires were set at Corinto, the main port for imported fuel,[89] destroying "five large storage tanks" and forcing twenty thousand people to evacuate. One of the Contra groups—the Nicaraguan Democratic Force—claimed responsibility, and Reagan officials admitted that the CIA instructed Contras "in sabotage techniques and commando tactics and helped plan a series of attacks."[90] The offenses led Exxon, which brought 75 percent of Nicaragua's oil, to stop shipments.[91] The government announced plans to further ration gasoline and to "strengthen the military reserves and plans for civil defense."[92] The loss of gasoline had a ripple effect, compromising transportation and production capabilities. The country was also without spare parts necessary for harvesting cotton, coffee, sugar, and rice.[93]

The switch to striking inside Nicaragua had two goals, according to U.S. officials. First, the Reagan administration hoped to force Nicaragua to stop aiding the Salvadoran rebels. Second, the moves aimed to showcase Contras' ability to carry out successful attacks. At the time, the Contras held no "strategically important territory" and did not have the Nicaraguan public's support. With effective military moves inside Nicaragua, U.S. national security officials hoped to convince skeptical U.S. Congress members of the Contras' competence and earn support for Contra funding.[94]

The atmosphere in Nicaragua got worse in late October when 4,600 U.S. forces invaded Grenada, the island in the West Indies.[95] Though the U.S. public overwhelmingly supported the invasion, many members of the religious community were outraged. In a joint statement, some Nicaraguan Catholics and Protestants condemned the invasion as dress rehearsal for Nicaragua.[96] Religious in Nicaragua also pleaded with U.S. religious to lobby and to send medical and humanitarian supplies.[97] Maryknoll Sisters conveyed their message to the United States, which led the Quixote Center to coordinate

Quest for Peace, which sent $27 million in aid to offset the same amount of U.S. Contra aid.[98] U.S. religious activists also pledged that in the event of a major U.S. escalation in Central America, they would nonviolently occupy congressional offices until it ended.[99] About seventy-five thousand people signed the Pledge of Resistance.[100]

Reagan's approach sowed internal discontent, as it was designed to do. The Contra war "completely derailed the Revolution from its goal," which was "the people's well-being." The government rationed "rice, beans, sugar, and grains," while "groceries, medicine, toilet paper, [and] gasoline" were "scarce." As former member of the revolutionary government Gioconda Belli explained, "the Revolution's main base of support began to erode, slowly but irrevocably," in the face of what the CIA called a "low-intensity war."[101]

By early 1984, Nicaragua was faltering, and the Sandinistas played right into Reagan's hands. Belli and other high-level party members raised concerns about the war's strain on the people. In response, the party closed ranks. As she explained, "Paradoxically, the United States gave the Ortegas the perfect excuse to silence the debate raging within the Sandinista movement." The Sandinista Directorate moved from a nine-person body with divergent views to a two-man show: the Ortega brothers, Daniel and Humberto. Dissent now raised questions about one's loyalty to the party and the revolutionary cause. As a result, the Contra ranks grew with "disgruntled *campesinos*, young people who refused to serve in the army, and soldiers who defected." At the same time, the upper classes felt more and more alienated.[102]

The Churchwomen and Maryknoll

Despite the administration's attempts to focus on Nicaragua, many people still clamored for justice in the churchwomen's case in El Salvador. Though the administration publicly kept silent, unlike in its early days, it supported allies that critiqued Maryknoll at home and abroad. For its part, Maryknoll quietly defended itself.

In September 1983, Senator Arlen Specter (R-PA) proposed that Congress withhold 30 percent of military aid to El Salvador until those accused of murdering the churchwomen were brought to trial. Nearly three years after the murders, Specter explained the urgency to the secretary of state: "As you know . . . many members of the Foreign Operations Subcommittee regarded the nuns' case as pivotal on whether the El Salvadoran government was proceeding adequately on the human rights issue. Given the current status of the record, this case could be determinative in some or many members voting against aid for El Salvador."[103] Specter demanded measurable action, unlike certification's vague requirement of "progress."

As Specter's bill moved through Congress, conservative Catholics attacked Maryknollers by tying them to liberation theology and by questioning their patriotism and loyalty to the church. Just as conservative Catholics insinuated that the churchwomen's failure to behave as nuns justified their rape and murder, they implied that Maryknollers' failure to behave as Catholics should negate efforts to tie U.S. funding to the churchwomen's case. In a *Wall Street Journal*–commissioned piece, Joan Frawley charged Maryknoll with fueling a political movement of U.S. Catholics to oppose Reagan's policies as well as inspiring "the reassessment of the church's role and political alignment in Latin America—and ultimately Catholicism's future in the U.S." Frawley alleged that "radicalized by their exposure to right-wing violence, Maryknollers increasingly reject democratic capitalism and traditional Catholicism in favor of liberation theology." Describing the effect of Maryknoll's shift she wrote, "For many members and supporters of Maryknoll, it comes as a shock that an order whose missionaries were once imprisoned and tortured by Chinese and Korean Communists could accommodate a Marxist government."[104] A reporter for her family's *National Catholic Register*, Frawley gained a wider audience for her claims in the *Wall Street Journal* that Maryknoll was a national security threat.[105] Her critique underscored conservative Catholics' turn away from the order. In mailing Frawley's article to friends, her father Patrick noted how as "old friends of Maryknoll," his daughter's revelations "saddened him," especially given his family's $600,000 gift to the sisters' hospital in the late 1950s.[106]

Maryknollers worried that Frawley's comments might endanger their members in Latin America, just as they were concerned after Haig's remarks eighteen months earlier. As Maryknollers explained to *Wall Street Journal* editorial representatives, the charges were false. More disturbingly, Frawley's claims would "undoubtedly be accepted as factual by intelligence organizations and embassies throughout Latin America."[107] As Maryknollers knew, comments like Frawley's often foreshadowed violence against religious in Latin America.

Less than two weeks after Frawley's article, witnesses before the Senate hearings, *Marxism and Christianity in Revolutionary Central America*, alleged that Maryknoll's ties to liberation theology led its members to support, if not participate in, revolutionary violence.[108] The argument was no accident, as both the committee chair Jeremiah Denton (R-AL) and the majority of witnesses were Catholics with close ties to the White House.

Denton was a conservative Catholic worried about liberation theology. The first Catholic senator from Alabama credited his strong faith with aiding his survival as a prisoner of war in Vietnam.[109] The Moral Majority backed Denton's candidacy after Paul Weyrich encouraged him to run and provided the "campaign its first $1,000."[110] Once in office, Denton worked closely with the organization and the White House on Central America, including meeting with non-Sandinista leaders in Nicaragua and serving as elections observer in El Salvador.[111] Denton also spoke out against liberation theology, making the familiar claims that "the priests and nuns who get caught up in" liberation theology were communists' "useful idiots."[112]

Denton's brand of conservative Catholicism was on full display in his opening remarks. He and Vermont's Patrick Leahy, another Catholic, debated the propriety of the hearings and showcased the divide among Catholics. Denton asserted: "We cannot ignore the involvement of religious institutions, which under the influence of some theologies of liberation follow a new avenue to achieve radical socioeconomic changes; namely, violent Marxist revolution." The hearings focused mainly on Nicaragua because, as Denton asserted, it was the "first Marxist revolution on the mainland of the Americas." When Leahy argued that the hearings involved the government in investigating religious belief, Denton objected. As he insisted, "We also are not interested in the beliefs, in the theological sense" of the witnesses, nor was the Senate "trying to hold a theological hearing." Instead, the concern was Marxist influence on churches and what influence, if any, religious may have exerted in parallel with Marxists.[113] The hearings' premise—that liberation theology was a national security threat—was the same conclusion drawn by Reagan advisors in the Santa Fe Report and Ambassador Middendorf in his commencement address.

Leahy likely took aim at Denton because no opposing witnesses testified and because of Denton's association with the Moral Majority. In the spring of 1981, Leahy charged the "radical right," particularly the Moral Majority, with hijacking Catholicism. In a *Washington Post* op-ed "The Church We Love is Being Used," the senator argued that the "political alliance" between Christian evangelical groups and the Catholic Church threatened to derail "nearly all that the Catholic leadership and laity have stood for in this country." Leahy pointed to the most visible manifestation of this alliance: the prolife movement. It was a "stalking horse for the right" that "manipulated" Catholics into acting counter to church teaching. Christian teaching promoted "compassion for the weak, support for the poor, aid for the hungry and love for all mankind," not reductions in federal programs and support for unlimited defense spending, as "the religious shock troops of the radical right" claimed.[114]

Leahy used the same reasoning that conservative Catholics like Denton used to contend that communists manipulated priests and nuns.

At the hearing, witnesses stressed the dangers of liberation theology and Maryknoll's connection to it, echoing the conservative Catholic refrain of the late 1970s. Cuban-born Father Enrique Rueda contended that Congress should care about liberation theology because it threatened the West's religious, political, and economic foundations. Imprisoned during the Bay of Pigs invasion, he became a priest after he left the country in 1961.[115] Rueda pointed to Nicaragua as "the blueprint for revolution of liberation theology." Cuba and the Soviet Union saw liberation theology as a way "to destabilize and ultimately conquer the 'soft underbelly' of the United States." Supporting this conspiracy, according to Rueda, was "a well-financed network of centers and publishing houses," including Maryknoll's Orbis books.[116] Rueda earlier shared these same concerns as a *Wanderer* contributor.[117]

Rueda identified himself as a priest and CIS Educational Foundation project director, which did not adequately convey either CIS's or his efforts to challenge Leftward trends in the church. In a press release to Congress two years earlier, CIS insinuated the murdered churchwomen worked with the Salvadoran guerrillas, and stressed Maryknoll's support for liberation theology and "radical politics," as discussed in chapter 4.[118] Besides CIS, Rueda led the Catholic Center for Free Enterprise, Strong Defense and Traditional Values. The Catholic Center, part of Paul Weyrich's Free Congress Research and Education Foundation, was formed to combat church leadership's Leftward tilt and, specifically, some leaders' efforts "to turn Latin America into a communist satellite," according to Rueda.[119] The Catholic Center sponsored training aimed to turn "the average conservative Roman Catholic . . . from a passive complainer to an activist capable of helping to reverse the leftward drift of the Church." In the center's first two years, it trained fifteen hundred people across the country.[120]

The second witness, Miguel Bolaños Hunter, also linked Maryknoll and liberation theology. The S/LPD arranged for the testimony of the twenty-four-year-old Sandinista defector who worked with state security.[121] Bolaños characterized liberation theology as a "very important tool" to "establish communism in Latin America" and other predominantly Catholic areas. He charged that the Sandinistas "have used some people that are called priests in Nicaragua," such as foreign minister Maryknoller Miguel d'Escoto. Most controversially, Bolaños accused murdered churchwoman Maura Clarke of hiding "guns, propaganda," and people and of carrying weapons before Somoza's overthrow. Bolaños claimed that after the revolution, Clarke went to El Salvador, where "she was killed because she was with the FMLN."[122] Clarke was not even in Nicaragua at the time. Bolaños's false charges echoed CIS's 1981 accusations against the murdered churchwomen.

A former Maryknoll sister and her Nicaraguan husband continued the same theme. Geraldine O'Leary met Edgard Macías while in Nicaragua with Maryknoll. She left the congregation in 1974, then worked for Protestant social services while he continued his efforts as a public servant. Edgard was Popular Social Christian Party president and a union organizer. In the summer of 1982, the two left Nicaragua after accusations of receiving CIA funds. In the United States, the couple created New Exodus, a nonprofit dedicated to assisting Nicaraguan refugees. The two originally supported the Sandinistas but had a falling out.[123] By the time of the hearing, Denton noted, they were "volunteers for ARDE, the Nicaraguan Democratic Revolutionary Alliance,"[124] one of the Contra groups. Both were also S/LPD contractors.[125]

Geraldine condemned Christians, especially Maryknollers, for their ignorance and naiveté. She asserted: "Since 1979, more than 8,000 Nicaraguans have been arrested by the FSLN and then assassinated." Yet when she sought assistance from church leaders and U.S. groups upon the couple's arrival in the United States, they defended the Sandinista government. As Maryknoll's peace and justice director supposedly told her, "What is your problem? The Sandinistas do not kill anyone." Other Christian leaders discouraged her from publicly criticizing the Nicaraguan government, she claimed.[126]

Foreign Christians with little understanding of Nicaragua frustrated Geraldine. They pressured her to work with the Sandinistas, but had not lived in the country. She classified them into two groups: "committed Marxist-Leninists who parade as Christians in order to influence the social programs of the church, and naive romantics that have no sense of ideologies and understand Marxism only as a vague theory." As for her former congregation, she explained, "I think Maryknollers, in general, are in the latter category." Although Geraldine described the Nicaraguan government as antichurch and anti-American, she reserved her harshest criticism for U.S. religious. As she alleged, "The churches are involved in politics; the churches are involved in a diabolical coverup, and they are directly supporting a Marxist-Leninist government against the wishes of its citizens."[127] Though Geraldine was not the first to critique Maryknoll, her status as a former sister made her words more compelling.

Geraldine's critique implied that one had to support either the government of the United States or Nicaragua, but many opponents of U.S. policy did not see an either-or situation. As Thomas Quigley, head of the U.S. Catholic Conference's Office of International Justice and Peace, explained, "People who disapprove strongly of U.S. efforts to overthrow the government and fund the

Contras can still be quite critical of the Sandinistas."[128] For missionaries in Nicaragua, the situation was even more difficult. Many who had lived through Somoza saw U.S. pressure, including support for the Contras, as destroying the revolution's potential. At the same time, they recognized that the Sandinistas made mistakes in working toward revolutionary goals and in fending off Contra attacks and U.S. pressure. There was not one uniform missionary response; even members of the same religious community held opposing views.[129] But Geraldine and other Reagan allies did not see it that way. To them, anyone who critiqued U.S.-Nicaragua policy was a Sandinista supporter.

Edgard testified after Geraldine, and he stressed Maryknoll *women's* ignorance by revealing how they fit into the "four main Christian currents" in Nicaragua. The conservative current included the Somozas, their cronies, and the oligarchy, while the "critical progressive current," led by Archbishop Obando, condemned Somoza and "a Marxist-Leninist option" for the country. The Maryknoll Sisters were the "prototype" of the "naive progressive current" of Christians complicit in supporting the communist state. Because of their "child-like faith," Marxist-Leninists, the popular church, and the Sandinistas manipulated the women. The fourth current was "Marxist-Leninists" and included Maryknoller Miguel d'Escoto and other priests in government.[130] Edgard implied Maryknoll men understood politics and political ideology, while the sisters did not.

The hearing confused Maryknollers. There was never "a break in relations," yet Gerri, as they called her, turned on the community. When the Nicaraguan media accused the Macíases of CIA ties, Maryknoll sisters in Nicaragua contested the charges before government officials. After the couple's U.S. arrival, Gerri wrote to individual sisters and the Central Governing Board about their difficulties. Her animosity was unexpected, leaving Maryknollers to conclude it sprang from a confluence of factors: Gerri and Edgard's "indignation" at the Sandinista government, difficulties adjusting to U.S. life, and the couple's wish for "Church people in the U.S. to support their statements of systematic persecution of the Nicaraguan Church by the Sandinistas."[131]

After the hearings, Maryknoll privately confronted Macías. President Melinda Roper wrote with surprise and confusion, given that Macías's "letters reflect a deep respect for Maryknoll as well as gratitude for the love and support you received both before and after your leaving the Congregation." She reminded Geraldine that "your clear and exclusive reason [was] your plan 'to marry a very wonderful Nicaraguan man.'" Roper recalled "the concern of the sisters when they realized that you were in love with a married man who had a wife and two small children, and that you planned to live with him in

Managua where you had worked as a religious." Roper also challenged Macías about her self-identification as a former Maryknoller during her Senate testimony. Some people referred to her as "Sister Macías." As Roper argued, this identification and Macías's presence alongside Miguel Bolaños Hunter "gives credibility to his outrageous allegations regarding Maura Clarke." Roper was shocked because Geraldine had worked with Clarke in Nicaragua. But Roper's "gravest concern," just as with Haig's and Frawley's comments, was the potential "spin-offs" from Macías's remarks. U.S. and international press might repeat her claims, "predisposing people against any and all Maryknollers."[132]

Just as Roper feared, the Reagan administration promoted the Macíases' views. In November, the OWG showcased them and Miguel Bolaños Hunter during a three-hour gathering, "Catholic Briefing on Foreign Policy." Attendees also saw a film depicting the pope's 1983 Mass in Managua and heard about Nicaragua, Grenada, arms control, Lebanon, and the Middle East.[133] El Salvador was conspicuously absent.

The briefing was part of a plan to more pointedly address Catholics. Whittlesey hired Robert Reilly as her assistant in the fall of 1983. He had served as Central America expert for the Heritage Foundation, worked on Reagan's transition team, and ran the U.S. Information Agency's grant program.[134] Reilly was also a founder of the Catholic Center for Renewal, which insisted "the danger of a politicized Catholic Church, with its support going almost exclusively to radical political causes, remains great." Opposition to U.S.–Central America policy was among the group's top four concerns.[135]

Reilly selected briefing invitees based on their church alignment. In his notes, he praised individuals for being "100% loyal Catholic," "loyal to Rome," "orthodox loyal Catholic," and "absolutely faithful to the Holy Father & the Magisterium."[136] As Reilly saw it, true Catholics followed the church and U.S. Cold War policy.

Reilly was right. In a thank-you letter to Whittlesey, Jesuit and *National Review* contributor James Schall noted, "I learned a good deal, some very moving as the reports on Nicaragua on the organization of the Papal Mass." He also stressed Catholics' need for education on U.S. policy. "You and Mr. Reilly are to be commended in realizing that this sector needs particular attention to present the rationale of our government's policies."[137] By contrast, the Center for Concern's Jane Blewett expressed frustration. She described the briefing as a "monologue—very one-sided and biased presentation of highly complex issues about which people of good-will differ radically." Blewett continued, "Surely the White House knows that many among the Catholic community are not sympathetic to the view of the Administration on several of the issues presented" because they "have access to alternative sources of information, trusted voices in the parts of the world under discussion who inform us of very different interpretations from those offered by the Government."[138] Schall's and Blewett's responses highlighted Catholics' conflicts over Central America and the White House's attempt to benefit from them.

More disturbing to Maryknoll than the briefing was the government dissemination of Edgard Macías's claims abroad. United States Information Service (USIS) official Maria Luz Skelly wrote "Communism Dominates the Popular Church in Nicaragua," reporting that Edgard said "naive progressives" represented the popular church in Nicaragua. As Skelly wrote, "This group has been the object of manipulation of the Sandinists [sic] . . . and . . . the feminine religious order of Maryknoll is a good example of it." The press secretary at the U.S. embassy in Caracas sent Skelly's piece to Venezuela's *La Religión*, which included Skelly's USIS affiliation on publication.[139] The article suggested a deliberate campaign against Maryknoll.

Maryknollers objected to U.S. government involvement. As Helene O'Sullivan wrote to House Speaker O'Neill, "What is most disturbing is that this article was prompted by the U.S. government against U.S. citizens living abroad and could endanger their lives." She continued, "By actively writing and promoting the article, the U.S. Government (USIS) could be perceived to support the allegations, thereby giving the wrong signal to governments whose human rights records are poor."[140] Though the article attacked the Maryknoll Sisters, because none served in Venezuela at the time, it was the Fathers and Brothers that felt the impact.[141] As they explained to O'Neill, the accusations "directly jeopardized the work of our missioners," as it required "the Cardinal of Caracas to visit two of our works in poor areas in order to dispel any misconceptions concerning the Maryknoll Congregation and a linkage to Communism. Still these misconceptions persist due to the distribution of disinformation circulated against Maryknoll, making working relations with other clergy members extremely difficult."[142]

Maryknoll wanted the embassy to take responsibility for distributing the article, but the ambassador refused. In meeting with Maryknoll, the ambassador said he was not authorized to send a disclaimer to *La Religión*, to explain the situation to the cardinal of Caracas, or to apologize to Maryknoll in writing as he could not "negate something sent by the USIA in Washington."[143] One possible purpose for the article was to defuse religious opposition in Venezuela to that government's support and financial aid to the Salvadoran junta.[144] A more nefarious motive was to stop Maryknoll from objecting to U.S. policy by threatening its members' safety abroad.

While the administration and its allies attempted to undermine Maryknoll's influence through the Denton hearings and the USIS article, Reagan tried to change the narrative regarding military aid to El Salvador. With the Caribbean Base Initiative (CBI), Reagan proposed "aid, trade, and investment" for twelve countries, including El Salvador.[145] Congress saw through Reagan's attempt to bundle his El Salvador request within a larger plan. El Salvador would get more than half of CBI's military aid. Congress approved CBI but with changes regarding El Salvador: no military aid and a substantial reduction to nonmilitary aid.[146] Reagan also attempted to garner support for his Central America policy by appointing a bipartisan committee, popularly known as the Kissinger Commission.[147] It did little to change the congressional conversation, as it offered no new approaches to deeply entrenched opposing sides.[148]

The administration also condemned death squad activity in El Salvador. In the fall of 1983, the embassy leaked the names of Salvadoran death squad leaders. In December, Vice President Bush condemned death squads in a San Salvador speech and privately named participants, insisting "they be exiled or expelled."[149] But at the same time, Reagan pocket vetoed a bill continuing certification, which conditioned U.S. aid on several factors, including progress in the churchwomen's case.[150]

The Reagan administration struggled to put the churchwomen's case behind it because the public would not let it. To coincide with the third anniversary of the women's murders, NBC aired *Choices of the Heart*. The TV movie starred Melissa Gilbert of *Little House on the Prairie* fame as Jean Donovan, Mike Farrell as Ambassador White, and Martin Sheen as the Irish priest who inspired Donovan to become a lay missionary. The movie received rave reviews,[151] and its popularity revealed the continuing interest in the case and kept the story in the public eye.

Also in commemoration of the women, Witness for Peace organized its first official delegation to Nicaragua. Delegates sought to discourage Contra attacks by serving as human shields and, in the process, show U.S. foreign policy's impact. Former Maryknoller Gail Phares, who lived with Maura Clarke in Nicaragua in the 1960s, launched the organization.[152] Over a ten-year period, 4,200 people traveled to Nicaragua with the program.[153]

Nearly three years after Reagan took office, his administration could not neutralize the robust, largely Catholic-led protest movement. The White House regarded "much of the church criticism as naive or unfair," yet one senior administration official admitted that church opposition was "the toughest nut we have to crack." As the *Wall Street Journal* explained, the church "makes its pronouncements with a distinct air of authority and emotion," and returning missionaries, such as Maryknollers, make effective lobbyists based on their firsthand experience.[154] Additionally, the murdered churchwomen—missionaries—evoked protests and served as a rallying cry for the cause of human rights in U.S. foreign policy.

As the Reagan administration seemed to be losing the battle against its religious opponents, some saw Reagan's cozying up to the Vatican as a ploy to hamper Catholic protests. In early 1984, the White House announced the establishment of diplomatic relations with the Vatican, which had been suspended since 1867. As the *Boston Globe* alleged, Reagan sought "to make an end run around the Catholic bishops in the United States" who opposed his Central America policy and nuclear program.[155] The bishops' 1983 pastoral letter *The Challenge of Peace* condemned nuclear war and deterrence.[156]

Like Central America, the bishops' position on nuclear weapons drew conservative Catholics' ire. In response to these "misguided trends in the political direction" of the U.S. church, conservative Catholics formed the American Catholic Committee (ACC). The group, as one planning board member explained, sought to address "nuclear weapons and the morality of deterrence; U.S. involvement in Central America; and the link between theology and economic questions." Though, like Weyrich, they contested the bishops' perceived political involvement, ACC founders like Michael Novak were largely labor-affiliated Democrats.[157] The ACC revealed the multiple levels on which Catholics disagreed about foreign policy and many Catholics' shifting political affiliation from the Democratic Party to the GOP.

Macías versus Maryknoll

To counter opposition by missionaries, especially Maryknollers, and to shift attention away from the churchwomen's case, the administration turned to Geraldine Macías—the White House's Maryknoller. Macías bridged the administration's Nicaragua and El Salvador concerns. She critiqued the Sandinista government and, at the same time, condemned her former congregation, which many people associated with El Salvador because of the churchwomen. Macías illustrated how Catholic Sandinista opponents shared a mutually beneficial relationship with the White House, rather than just held similar views.[158] Geraldine gained a platform to critique the Sandinistas and the U.S. Catholic Church hierarchy. The Reagan administration got a powerful counterweight to missionaries and, in the process, exploited the intra-Catholic conflict. Maryknoll's fear that Macías's views would gain a wider audience was correct. What the sisters likely could not have anticipated was the extent to which the government publicized Macías both in the United States and abroad.

Macías spoke often about the Sandinistas' "betrayal" of the revolution, and just as in her congressional testimony, she attacked the religious protest movement. She argued missionaries and lay people who visited Nicaragua were ignorant of the country's history and present circumstances.[159] She spoke at Wednesday OWG meetings and special briefings to outside groups,[160] and she appeared before religious groups, college students, and conferences on Latin America across the country.[161] Unbeknownst to her listeners, in 1984 the S/LPD paid Macías $9,500 to write about Sandinista "distortions" and "human rights violations," and the following year, she earned $11,200 to produce more documents, including one on church-state relations.[162]

In promoting her, the White House highlighted her role as a former Maryknoller. In doing so, both the White House and Macías tapped into conservative concerns about Maryknoll's and nuns' role in the church. The White House stressed that Macías's authority came from her time as a Maryknoller, not her more recent experience as a nonprofit worker. Even at briefings for non–religiously identified groups, the White House described Macías first as a "former Maryknoll nun" and second as a "political dissident" or "human rights activist."[163]

Macías presented a portrait of Maryknoll sisters that echoed conservative Catholics' views. Maryknollers, she claimed, were naive, as she had been. She told the *Wanderer*, "Looking back on it from my husband's perspective, we were doing political things without admitting it. . . . But since we never studied Marxism and politics we didn't often realize what we were saying and doing." Her words were misleading, as since the 1960s Maryknollers increasingly studied topics such as economics and politics. Macías also suggested that only a man could understand politics since she needed her "husband's perspective" to see the error of Maryknoll's ways. She agreed with the interviewer that many Maryknollers harbored "an intense hatred for their own country," which grew from ignorance of Cold War politics.[164]

Macías's explanation for leaving Maryknoll mimicked conservative Catholics' disillusionment with the community. Although Geraldine told Maryknoll's Central Governing Board in 1974 that she was leaving to marry, in the 1980s she often gave the impression it was due to Maryknoll's political leanings. She said she grew "tired" of those Maryknollers "who wanted to keep moving forward toward a more secular kind of existence." And, some sisters seemed to want "a revolution for revolution's sake." Despite this criticism, Geraldine replied "yes" when asked if she still had "a genuine feeling for Maryknoll—

affection perhaps."[165] Her response suggested she knew her continued access to a platform depended on critiquing Maryknoll.

The White House and the conservative press promoted Macías perhaps more than any other OWG speaker.[166] Besides featuring her at briefings, the White House distributed copies of Macías's published articles.[167] Both the religious and secular press covered her talks and described her as credible and persuasive.[168] Conservative Catholics endorsed Macías as a true authority on Nicaragua, in contrast to missionaries and bishops.[169] The U.S. government also sponsored Macías in Europe. In January 1984 she addressed audiences in Ireland, Germany, Norway, England, France, Holland, Denmark, and Iceland through USIA auspices.[170] Europeans' disapproval of U.S.–Central America policy mattered because it fueled opposition to U.S. nuclear weapons in Europe.[171]

Macías's visit to Ireland illustrated how liberation theology worried conservative Catholics in the administration, how Catholics fueled international opposition to U.S.–Central America policy, and how the Maryknoll-Reagan debate over Central America spread beyond U.S. borders.

Conservative Catholic officials had long cared about Irish opposition to U.S. policy. Less than three months after Reagan took office, National Security Advisor Richard Allen noted in a memo ahead of Vice President Bush's meeting with Irish opposition leader Garrett FitzGerald, "The Irish attitude on El Salvador is the single sticking point in an otherwise smooth relationship."[172] By late 1982, U.S. ambassador Peter H. Dailey expressed his frustration with Catholic opposition. In a letter to National Security Advisor Clark, a friend since their days at Catholic high school,[173] Dailey complained that Irish church leaders "criticized" U.S. policy and their views influenced the press.[174] Dailey blamed liberation theology. The NSC staffer responsible for Latin American affairs, Alfonso Sapia-Bosch, agreed. In his cover letter to Clark introducing Dailey's letter, Sapia-Bosch noted that during his 1981 trip to Ireland to discuss U.S.–Central America policy, he "was greeted by the same criticism Ambassador Dailey mentions."[175]

Just as in the United States, Irish missionaries were key opponents of U.S. policy. As one Dáil member observed, "Religious orders and lay missionaries in Central America . . . are the main movers in opposing American policy."[176] Trócaire, the church's overseas development agency, established projects in Latin America in the 1970s and used 20 percent of its funds for "raising awareness" in Ireland.[177] The Irish El Salvador Support Committee, formed by religious and others in 1979,[178] disseminated information from missionaries, lobbied Irish officials, and organized protests at the U.S. embassy.[179] Additionally, the churchwomen's murders were "an enormous story" in part because

Jean Donovan studied at University College, Cork, in 1973–1974.[180] There she met an Irish priest who helped start a mission in Peru and inspired her to go to El Salvador.[181] Donovan returned to Cork shortly before her murder to speak at a youth Mass.[182]

To counter Irish disapproval, in October 1983 Dailey proposed a plan. To Secretary of State George Shultz Dailey argued the administration needed to sell its Central America policy in Europe. Among other recommendations, Dailey stressed that people with "firsthand experience in Central America" should be sent to speak. These people should be "former Sandinistas, Centrists from El Salvador and most importantly 'real' Roman Catholic priests from the mainstream Church to help us counter the 'liberalist' theological view being propounded here and in the U.S."[183] Dailey's use of the adjective "real" revealed his sense that only true Catholics opposed liberation theology and supported Reagan's Central America policy.

Geraldine Macías was one of the "real" Catholics the Reagan administration sent. Macías gave a private briefing at the U.S. embassy in Dublin on January 23, 1984. She argued the Sandinistas had betrayed the revolution. They "massacred" "tens of thousands," set up "a national spying network," and reorganized the country "to produce a Marxist-Leninist model society."[184] She told the only newspaper to cover her visit that "organizations like Trócaire" were "naive," just like U.S. religious, when it came to Central America.[185]

It is unlikely Macías converted any Irish. According to a Trócaire representative at the meeting, Macías's "session went very badly for her." Several priests who had recently traveled extensively in the region "and who are very familiar with the stance of the U.S. Bishops and the Maryknolls . . . in favour of social justice" challenged her.[186] When asked for evidence, Macías "admitted she had no documentation" because she could not afford photocopies. She also revealed the U.S. government was paying her and her husband's expenses. In her defense, the U.S. public affairs officer noted Macías's information came from "a sincere and convinced woman and should be viewed as being valuable as such." He also "complained" the Irish media disregarded U.S. statements about Central America.[187]

The Trócaire representative's conclusion was consistent with the State Department's assessment of its own efforts. As the public affairs advisor for European Affairs explained four months after Macías's visit, Ambassador Dailey spent two years trying "to change Irish thinking on Central America." Even though it was "a number one priority," the former head of advertising for the Nixon, Ford, and Reagan campaigns had "little success."[188]

What the USIA officer likely did not know was that Maryknoll had quietly warned Europeans about Macías. Maryknoll sent a "dossier" on Macías to its international contacts, including Trócaire, Galway's Bishop Eamonn Casey, and London's Catholic Institute for International Relations.[189] The dossier was passed along in Germany to "leaders of Nicaragua solidarity groups," as well as "key people in the social democratic party" and "political circles."[190] Though the S/LPD post-trip review boasted that in Denmark, Macías "was so successful she merited a special attack in the local Communist newspaper,"[191] a Danish ally of Maryknoll said that Nicaragua solidarity groups refused to meet with her and concluded it was because they had read Maryknoll's dossier.[192] Maryknoll and the Reagan administration extended their battle over U.S.–Central America policy to Europe.

The Catholic Candidate

While the administration enlisted Macías's help at home and abroad to counter missionaries' influence, disagreements about what it meant to be Catholic took center stage in the presidential campaign. Democratic candidate Walter Mondale announced Geraldine Ferraro as his running mate at the party's convention in July 1984. To conservative Catholics, Ferraro was the poster child for what was wrong with the church. She personally opposed abortion but was against removing the option for others. In response, New York's cardinal, John O'Connor, chastised Ferraro, along with Governor Mario Cuomo, who shared her views.[193] But to a *Wanderer* editorialist, the stakes were higher than the next election. "Geraldine Ferraro personifies to a high degree the Modernist rot which infects large segments of the Catholic Church in America today. By that I mean she manifests, in a clear and living manner, those characteristics which comprise the Modernist heresy."[194] Unlike JFK, Ferraro did not enjoy overwhelming Catholic support. Her status as a Catholic was not the issue; it was the *kind* of Catholicism she represented.

The same month as Ferraro's selection, Catholic debates over Central America came to the fore. Controversy erupted when New York's Mario Cuomo linked the Reagan administration to the churchwomen's murders during his keynote address at the Democratic National Convention. Praised by some for delivering an "electrifying" speech,[195] Cuomo asserted that the president had created a tale of two cities, the haves and have-nots, not a city on a hill. In condemning Reagan's foreign policy, Cuomo asserted, "We give money to Latin American governments that murder nuns and then lie about it."[196]

The timing of Cuomo's comments was surprising, given Salvadoran developments. In May, Salvadorans elected their first civilian president in over fifty years. In a runoff, University of Notre Dame graduate José Napoleón

Duarte defeated Major General Roberto D'Aubussion, former National Guard major, death squad leader, and Archbishop Romero assassination architect.[197] Weeks later, five National Guardsmen were found guilty of murdering the churchwomen. Because the case was so linked to U.S.–El Salvador discussions, many believed the convictions would end protests. As the conservative Catholic *Crisis* posited, "Nothing remains to prevent American Catholics from enthusiastically supporting the efforts of that budding democracy."[198] Congress seemed to share *Crisis*'s perspective. Hours after the convictions, the House approved $61.7 million in supplemental aid, totaling $196.6 million for the year, almost two and a half times the amount El Salvador received the year before.[199] Despite Congress's shift, Cuomo's remark showed that many still considered the churchwomen's case emblematic of Reagan's foreign policy.

Reagan and Bush resented Cuomo's inaccuracies and his "demagoguery."[200] The president and vice president noted the women were murdered and El Salvador aid was reinstated during the Carter-Mondale years, while the guardsmen's trial and conviction occurred on Reagan's watch.[201] Bush also insisted that Mondale apologize for Cuomo's remarks that "accused us by inference of having nuns killed."[202]

While Cuomo focused attention on El Salvador, Reagan stressed Democrats' failures to address human rights violations in Nicaragua. In a speech before Colorado Republicans, Reagan insinuated that he deserved Catholics' votes because Mondale "has been silent about the humiliation of the Holy Father . . . but this president and this vice president will not forget."[203] Reagan repeated the same theme—Mondale's failure to condemn religious repression in Nicaragua and the pope's treatment—during fall campaign rallies in Illinois, Oregon, Washington, Ohio, Pennsylvania, and West Virginia.[204] Reagan's appropriation of the church-defender mantle was astonishing given that a member of the Democratic ticket was Catholic.

Human rights, and specifically religious freedom, became a key pillar of the Reagan administration's attempts to sell its Nicaragua policy ahead of the 1984 presidential election. Though the Reagan White House accused the Sandinistas of persecuting religion, officials' ultimate goal was to sway Catholic voters and satisfy key conservative allies who pushed for a more aggressive stance regarding Central America. While conservative Catholics believed that U.S. policy might combat what they saw as the wayward trend in the church and communism's growth, liberal Catholics saw U.S. policy ruining their hopes for a new direction in Central America and the church. The White House also continued to exploit the divides among Catholics by focusing on Maryknoll. But rather than target the murdered churchwomen's reputation as Reagan officials did in late 1980 and 1981, the campaign became more general and extended abroad with allies like Geraldine Macías. The continued focus on Maryknoll revealed both conservative Catholics' influence in shaping U.S. policy and the power of Catholic opposition, particularly by missionaries, to U.S. policy.

The White House's campaign to appeal to conservative Catholic voters through its Central America policy proved successful. In Reagan's landslide victory over Mondale, the president increased his share of Catholic votes from 51 percent in 1980 to 58–61 percent.[205] At the same time, the administration did not alienate Protestant supporters. In fact, a month before the election the White House discussed how to defuse charges that it was captive to the Protestant Right.[206] But while Reagan gained more Catholic support, he likely did not anticipate that Maryknollers' influence on Central America debates was far from over.

CHAPTER 6

Real Catholics versus Maryknollers

A story circulates among Washington insiders that during a meeting about funding the Contras, Ronald Reagan grew frustrated with Democrat Tip O'Neill, Speaker of the House. Reagan reminded O'Neill that his views were supported by CIA intelligence. "Well," quipped O'Neill, "my information is much more accurate than that. I get mine from nuns."[1] O'Neill, a Catholic, sought the counsel of Maryknoll sisters in framing his views of Nicaragua. Whether the two men had this precise exchange is less important than what the story's existence indicates: Washington insiders perceived that O'Neill depended on nuns for his understanding of Central America and that he considered the women better information sources than U.S. intelligence.

Though many in the U.S. and international press characterized O'Neill's reliance on Maryknoll sisters as unusual and silly,[2] to conservative Catholics the connection between the Speaker and the sisters was powerful, even dangerous. O'Neill was already persona non grata in conservative Catholic circles because he avoided vocal pro-life advocacy.[3] When he associated himself with the Maryknoll Sisters, O'Neill legitimized both the women's opposition to U.S. policy and their view of what being Catholic meant. Scholars have noted this connection but not what it reveals about the relationship between gender and religious identity, and the conduct of U.S. foreign relations.[4] Catholics' gendered critiques of O'Neill and Maryknollers were the connective tissue that linked their concerns about the direction of U.S.-Nicaragua policy and of the church. At their heart, these gender-based critiques were about who could fight the Cold War, shape U.S. foreign policy, and define what it meant to be Catholic.

As this chapter argues, O'Neill's decision to oppose U.S.-Nicaragua policy based on Maryknoll sisters' advice led the Reagan administration and its supporters to question O'Neill's authenticity as a Catholic and his masculinity. Conservative Catholics close to the president, such as White House Communications Director Patrick Buchanan and Republican Congressman Henry Hyde (IL), repeated a familiar refrain of Maryknoll critiques. Whereas Reagan portrayed himself as defender of the pope during the 1984 campaign, after his reelection, the president and his allies also attacked Catholics for not defending their church. Non-Catholics, including the president, argued that true Catholics backed Reagan's Contra policy because, as they incorrectly asserted, the pope supported U.S. policy. While twenty-five years earlier presidential candidate John F. Kennedy faced questions about his primary loyalty as a Catholic, Reagan and his allies promoted the stereotype that Catholics should fall in line behind the pope. Catholics' loyalty to Rome was no longer a liability but a true test of being a patriotic American. Likewise, the Maryknoll Sisters were bad nuns for failing to obey those among the male church hierarchy who supported the Contra cause. By opposing U.S.-Nicaragua policy, the Maryknoll Sisters challenged the shared male culture, or "imperial brotherhood," of the U.S. foreign policy establishment and of the Catholic Church.[5] The Maryknoll Sisters, like Nicaragua's foreign minister Maryknoller Miguel d'Escoto, were misguided, while the true Catholics, according to Reagan and his allies, included Managua's Archbishop Miguel Obando y Bravo.

O'Neill and Nuns

Reagan may have clobbered Mondale at the polls, but he faced a Congress that had circumscribed his Nicaragua agenda a month before the election. In October 1984, Congress immediately cut off Contra funds after Republicans postponed the issue rather than risk a potentially bruising political fight a month before the election.[6] As part of the House-Senate compromise, the White House could request additional funds on or after February 28, 1985, but any new funds required both chambers' approval. Congress also passed the second Boland Amendment, which prohibited funds for any "agency or entity of the United States involved in intelligence activities" from being used to support "directly or indirectly, military or paramilitary organizations in

Nicaragua."[7] Part of the support for Boland II came from senators' frustration over the discovery that the CIA played a role in mining Nicaragua's harbors without fully briefing Congress and while publicly claiming the Contras were responsible. Then, just days before the U.S. presidential election, the press reported on the Freedom Fighters' Manual, a CIA-issued comic book that advised the Contras on psychological operations.[8] The manual disputed administration claims that it did not seek the Sandinistas' overthrow.

Congress's moves set up a postelection showdown between the executive and legislative branches. As Speaker of the democratically controlled House, O'Neill was the main impediment to Reagan fulfilling his Nicaragua agenda. El Salvador was largely out of the spotlight and no longer a problem for the president. Congress did not challenge U.S. policy after the election of Duarte as president, the convictions of the churchwomen's murderers, and the defeat of key congressional opponent Clarence Long (MD) in 1984.[9]

The Speaker's opposition to Reagan's Nicaragua policy was unusual. O'Neill generally supported Reagan's foreign policy; Central America was among a "few key exceptions."[10] O'Neill gradually became an outspoken opponent of Reagan's Nicaragua policy, leading conservative columnists Rowland Evans and Robert Novak to describe O'Neill in April 1983 as "emerging as a behind-the-scenes power shadowing."[11] But by September 1984, a New York Times reporter wrote, "No one in Congress has been more caustically critical of the Reagan Administration's policies in Central America than the Speaker of the House, Thomas P. O'Neill."[12]

O'Neill did not draw attention, however, until his source of opposition was disclosed. In early fall 1984, New York Times reporter Philip Taubman revealed the Maryknoll Sisters as the reason, and Taubman suggested that the Speaker was a bad Catholic for listening to the women. Taubman characterized Maryknollers as out of step with the Catholic Church. As the reporter explained, "While some members of Congress base their foreign policy positions on elaborate briefings by aides, consultation with colleagues or public opinion polling of their constituents, Mr. O'Neill depends on the activist nuns and priests to help shape his views on Central America." Taubman then inaccurately contended, "the church hierarchy has not been outspoken" on Central America policy, suggesting that the "activist" nuns and priests acted neither appropriately nor in accordance with church hierarchy.[13]

In justifying his confidence in Maryknollers and his opposition to the Contras, O'Neill argued that the missionaries' perspective was more accurate because it was not politically motivated. As he told Taubman, "I have great trust in that order. When the nuns and priests come through, I ask them questions about their feelings, what they see, who the enemy is, and I'm sure I get the truth. I haven't found any of these missionaries who aren't absolutely opposed to this policy."[14] In his 1987 autobiography, O'Neill elaborated, "People often ask me where my passion about Central America comes from. In fact, I have a special source—the Maryknoll priests and nuns, who are there as missionaries and health care workers. These people don't care about politics; their only concern is the welfare of the poor. And I haven't met one of them who isn't completely opposed to our policy down there."[15] With these remarks, O'Neill could have been arguing that these religious sought to live out their faith, not pursue political goals, or that given their status as priests and nuns, they were incapable of thinking in political terms.

Although the press and O'Neill cited Maryknollers as the reason he opposed Reagan's policies, his biographer contends it was not the only one. Other explanations included the Vietnam War and Eddie Kelly, one of O'Neill's friends from Cambridge, Massachusetts. Kelly went to Nicaragua as a Marine in the 1920s during the U.S. military intervention. When O'Neill asked why the Marines were there, Kelly responded, "We're taking care of the property and rights of United Fruit."[16] On at least one occasion, O'Neill publicly mentioned Kelly as a reason for his opposition to U.S.-Nicaragua policy, yet the Reagan administration and its allies focused on O'Neill's ties to Maryknollers and on one sister in particular: Peggy Healy. O'Neill connected with Healy, his main source on Nicaragua, through his Aunt Annie. Aunt Annie, or Sister Eunice, entered Maryknoll in 1920 and died in 1981. O'Neill maintained contact with his aunt no matter where she served, including her time in China. He wrote in 1987, "I continue to be inspired by her convictions."[17] Aunt Annie visited O'Neill's office to share her experiences abroad, and she encouraged other Maryknollers to do so.[18] Peggy Healy continued this Maryknoll connection with legislator O'Neill after Sister Eunice's death.

Healy kept the Speaker informed about Nicaragua by sending him materials and by visiting him whenever she was in the United States.[19] From Long Island, New York, Healy served as a health worker and assisted Christian base communities outside Managua from 1975 to June 1978. Though she returned to the United States for a planned year of studies focused on theology and economics, she stayed until 1981. During that time Healy worked with church and human rights organizations, including the Washington Office on Latin America (WOLA). WOLA monitored how U.S. policy impacted human rights in Latin America,[20] yet its critics decried the organization as "an apologist for the Sandinistas."[21] Healy organized fact-finding missions for journalists and Congress members. She also spoke to congressional representatives and staff.[22]

Healy's congressional testimony and public writings offer insight into the advice she gave O'Neill. She criticized U.S. support for Somoza, highlighted Latin Americans' negative perceptions of U.S. power, and questioned communism as the source of the region's turmoil. In testifying before Congress for WOLA in September 1979, just two months after the Sandinista revolution, Healy pushed for economic aid. Though she acknowledged WOLA had opposed aid for Somoza, she contended that U.S. support for the new Nicaraguan government would help the war-torn country rebuild and have "the potential for reversing the U.S. image in Nicaragua." As Healy explained, "Having backed Somoza for so long, the United States now has a moral obligation to undo the damage wrought in the war to oust him."[23]

In the press, Healy urged Americans to look beyond communism as a source of Central America's problems. In a 1980 *Newsday* op-ed, she criticized Americans' tendency to see "the false specter of Cuban subversion" while overlooking the hunger, sickness, and joblessness that plagued the region. Healy saw the Senate Budget Committee's decision to freeze government spending, including aid for Nicaragua, as a missed opportunity. As she contended, it was another example of "the extraordinary case of myopia which has afflicted this country in its dealings with Nicaragua and with Central America as a whole." Instead, the United States should help Nicaragua rebuild its economy and, in the process, "be on the right side for once in Latin America."[24]

Looking back more than twenty years later, Healy described how her commitment to Central Americans motivated her. "Your job was not to change US foreign policy because it was entirely unenlightened, although it was entirely unenlightened. Your job was to try to be a voice for people who were suffering because of it. It had to be changed because of the day-to-day results of it. Not once in a while, not in some vague way, but every single day it affected their survival. It needed to be changed, and in the end that was the reason for why we did it."[25]

O'Neill's decision to follow Maryknoll sisters' recommendations appears to have rested on the power of personal relationships and O'Neill's lifelong connection to and respect for nuns. In his autobiography, nuns loom over nearly every significant experience in O'Neill's early life. O'Neill recognized some nuns' stern attitude, yet he never strayed from a respectful tone. In describing his childhood, O'Neill noted that grammar school "discipline was pretty strict," as "the nuns would hit you on the hand with a piece of rattan" for tardiness or failing to know catechism. At the same time, he observed, "All through my childhood, the nuns, knowing I didn't have a mother, kept watch over me." In high school, O'Neill went to his teacher Sister Agatha with his problems. She introduced O'Neill to Millie Miller, his future wife, "was responsible for getting" him into Boston College, and was instrumental in persuading him not to run for governor of Massachusetts.[26]

Nuns played a prominent role in the Speaker's description of key political events. In 1928, fifteen-year-old O'Neill worked for Al Smith's presidential campaign. Although he noted that his neighborhood supported Smith, a fellow Democrat and Irish Catholic, O'Neill specifically mentioned nuns' role. "The nuns in school were praying for his success, and they urged all of us to make sure that our parents were registered to vote." O'Neill also described nuns' involvement in the 1960 presidential race. While campaigning with John F. Kennedy in Missouri, O'Neill saw nuns standing outside a Catholic school "holding their Kennedy signs." In response, JFK said, "Stop the car" and then left to shake "hands with all the sisters." As O'Neill wrote, "I loved him for it."[27]

O'Neill's respect and affection for nuns and priests continued during his time in Congress from 1953 to 1987. When asked about their visits to the Speaker's office, O'Neill's longtime personal secretary Eleanor Kelley "rolled her eyes at all the priests and nuns who dropped by over the years" as the Speaker catered to their requests. Kelley noted how the arrival of religious at the office "shattered the Speaker's schedule" or prompted a lunch "with the handiest available aide."[28]

Administration officials could not believe the Speaker listened to Maryknollers. The State Department complained that O'Neill took Central America briefings from the sisters rather than its officials.[29] The Speaker's trust in Maryknollers so infuriated Assistant Secretary of State Elliott Abrams that he described O'Neill's reliance on Peggy Healy as "ludicrous" and "irresponsibly narrow."[30]

The Speaker's dependence on sisters for foreign policy information aggravated the government's fears that it was losing the public relations battle over the Contras. The administration and its allies regarded this as key to gaining public support. As an advertising agency explained to the Contras' corporate arm, the Nicaraguan Development Council (NDC), in August 1984, "It is clear Nicaraguans are losing their freedom more because of words than because of bullets." Yet, the agency argued, the NDC had not found a way "to counter the Sandinistas, the liberal media, and the outlandish charges of political leaders like Tip O'Neill." In promoting its services, the agency concluded that without "a major public relations and lobbying campaign," the Contras could not be successful.[31] Given the battle for hearts and minds, any interpretation that challenged the administration's portrayal of Nicaragua threatened the president's program.

Attacking O'Neill and Maryknoll

To challenge O'Neill's reliance on the Maryknoll Sisters, U.S. policy supporters used stereotypes of nuns and of women in politics as well as challenged
O'Neill's manhood. Reagan officials and their allies undermined Maryknollers'
presence in foreign policy debates by relying on two different caricatures of
the nun. At times, Contra supporters evoked images of the nun as "an immature, incompetent, asexual being that floats around in medieval dress and has
little knowledge of life in the real world."[32] They argued—just as Geraldine
and Edgard Macías did—that nuns were well intentioned but naive, childlike
creatures subject to communist manipulation. Critics contended Maryknollers
critiqued U.S. actions in Central America, condemned the Contras, and supported liberation theology because they did not understand what they were
saying. The women were communist puppets, not real nuns or real Catholics. Those who followed Maryknollers' advice, like Tip O'Neill, were not authentic Catholics or true Americans either. At other times, Reagan officials
and their allies evoked images of the nun as the "stern school marm."[33] Nuns
were powerful, but only regarding their influence over Catholic schoolchildren.
In heeding Maryknollers' advice, Tip O'Neill was not a man but a child blindly
following nuns' orders as he presumably did in parochial school. Rather
than defend Maryknollers, conservative Catholics employed these tropes, revealing how their concerns about the church and U.S.-Nicaragua policy were
intertwined.

At the same time, the sisters' participation in foreign policy debates dis-
rupted the image Reagan projected of himself as an exemplar of masculinity.
Pointing to the 1979 Iranian and Nicaraguan revolutions, and the Iran hostage
crisis, presidential candidate Reagan offered himself as a strong U.S. global
leader in contrast to President Jimmy Carter's "weak" approach. As president,
Reagan turned first to Central America to demonstrate this strength. The Cold
War required manly men to battle communism, as the government's antigay
purge (the Lavender Scare) decades earlier demonstrated.[34] In this context, Reagan's foreign policy approach left no room for the Maryknoll Sisters, whose
analysis of Central America challenged the factual substance of U.S. policy and
Reagan's more "masculine" approach.

More recently, the 1984 campaign, featuring the first major-party female
vice presidential candidate, Geraldine Ferraro, highlighted the issue of women's
ability to conduct foreign policy. O'Neill, whom Ferraro described as playing
the role of "mentor and father figure" to her, was instrumental in her selection.[35] Views of Ferraro, like those of Maryknollers, vacillated between a

threatening figure and a weak woman incapable of handling the job. Barbara Bush referred to Ferraro as "that $4 million . . . I can't say it, but it rhymes with rich." Despite Bush's later claim that she meant "witch," George H. W. Bush's press secretary said Ferraro was "too bitchy." Reagan campaign manager Ed Rollins characterized Republicans' depictions of Ferraro as "a macho game we play." On the other hand, some reporters implied Ferraro's gender made her unable to do the job. During a vice presidential debate Ferraro was asked, "Do you think in any way that the Soviets might be tempted to try to take advantage of you simply because you are a woman?" Three days later, *Meet the Press* co-moderator Marvin Kalb asked Ferraro if she could push the button. As a reporter reflecting on the exchange opined, "The assumption behind Mr. Kalb's question has to be that somehow a woman is less capable than a man of making the tough decisions about national security and defense."[36] As the *Washington Post* declared, Ferraro's candidacy "reopened and accented" the contentious debate over women's role in society and politics.[37]

As the administration fought congressional opposition to its Nicaragua policy and as Americans debated women's ability to conduct foreign policy, Contra supporters pounced on O'Neill's relationship with the Maryknoll Sisters. They stressed Maryknoll's danger and challenged O'Neill's masculinity and his Catholic credentials. The *News-Sun* of Waukegan, Illinois, argued that O'Neill's position was naive, not well reasoned, and based on an "emotional" attachment to Maryknoll. The editorial board challenged Maryknoll's Catholic authenticity by describing it as "radical-tinged." The paper noted that Maryknoll supported liberation theology, which the Vatican "condemned as Marxist," and equated the congregation's concern for the poor and oppressed with Marxism.[38] Ultimately, the board characterized O'Neill as subject to the sway of naive nuns who did not understand the realities of Central America. In doing so, the paper implied that O'Neill was blindly following the stereotypical nun like a parochial schoolchild.

Conservative Catholics warned that O'Neill was the tip of the iceberg; Maryknoll was the real problem. As Michael Novak, Reagan's former ambassador to the UN Human Rights Commission asserted, O'Neill's confidence in the sisters demonstrated liberation theology's growing influence in the United States. Maryknollers who returned from Latin America infected U.S. Catholics with communist doctrine masquerading as Catholicism. Even worse, Maryknollers brought liberation theology "to many Catholics in Congress," including the Speaker.[39] In stressing Maryknollers' sway over Catholic politicians, Novak implied that Maryknoll simultaneously threatened to derail church and nation.

Just as Novak warned, O'Neill was not the only Catholic congressman who drew inspiration from the congregation. To *Maryknoll* magazine Representative James L. Oberstar (D-MN) described his lifelong connection to Maryknoll and the community's impact on his work. "For years I have been reading *Maryknoll* at my parents' home in Chisholm, Minn." Its articles are "a bountiful and powerful insight into the problems of Third World countries and a constructive inspirational influence on my legislative work in Congress, particularly on the issues of Central America." In fact, Oberstar revealed, "I can truthfully say that my first inclination to visit El Salvador was inspired by articles in *Maryknoll* which brought home in a graphic and unforgettable way the cruel toll human rights abuses have exacted on an innocent civilian population."[40]

A Kidnapped Maryknoller

Besides persuading Congress members and other Catholics to oppose U.S.–Central America policy, Maryknoll became a bigger problem for the White House when Contras kidnapped Sister Nancy Donovan. In January 1985, members of the Nicaraguan Democratic Force (FDN) detained fifty-two-year-old Donovan for six hours. After the ordeal, the missionary with twenty-nine years of experience in Central America said of the Contras, "It appears that they have directions to kill, to terrorize civilians."[41] She also provided a list of Contra atrocities against civilians, and she criticized the U.S. government for funding them. Donovan explained that her faith and her patriotism prompted her to speak out. "As a Christian and as a U.S. citizen I am deeply pained by the fact that my government has been responsible for arming and training these forces which have caused the deaths of so many. I continue to join my voice and my prayer to that of the U.S. Catholic Bishops, and of the churches and faithful across the U.S. who have protested the U.S. government's covert war against Nicaragua, and who are calling for a peaceful solution to the conflict."[42] Upon returning to the United States, Donovan traveled the country speaking out against U.S. policy. Both she and Peggy Healy appeared on *The Phil Donahue Show*.[43]

The Contras rejected Donovan's allegations and criticized Maryknoll in a familiar way. In a press release, the FDN "question[ed] the authenticity of the reports, given the history of open Maryknoll Order support for the FSLN." FDN leader Adolfo Calero renewed charges of Maryknoll involvement in guerrilla activity, specifically gunrunning. As he argued, "Members of the Maryknoll order have been helping the Sandinistas as messengers, as weapons carriers.

They used their convents as safehouses." He continued with a veiled threat that the sisters might face violence, as the murdered churchwomen had. The Maryknoll Sisters "are now helping the Sandinistas who are our enemies. They have no business going around with armed troops. I just hope they don't run into our bullets."[44] Calero's false claims evoked Reagan officials' and conservative Catholics' allegations that the murdered churchwomen were gunrunners who died in a shoot-out and Sandinista defector Miguel Bolaños Hunter's accusations that Maura Clarke hid guns, propaganda, and people in Nicaragua.

The uncanny resemblance of the FDN's statements to Reagan officials' earlier comments was no accident, given the U.S. role in the creation and maintenance of the FDN. As former FDN official Edgar Chamorro admitted, "The name of the organization, the members of the political junta, and the members of the general staff were all chosen or approved by the CIA" in 1981. The next year, the CIA helped the FDN restructure and rewrote the press statement announcing the changes. It also instructed FDN members on how to deal with the press,[45] and hired a public relations firm to market the Contras globally. Still unsuccessful in its attempts to gain support for Contra funding, the CIA pushed for another FDN facelift in 1984.[46]

Donovan was not alone in her accusations against the Contras. Eighty-eight Catholic and Protestant priests, pastors, and women religious in Nicaragua wrote to the U.S. Congress urging an end to the Contra war and highlighting its humanitarian toll. The group, which hailed from Nicaragua, the United States, and Europe, argued that though the United States described the situation as a "low-intensity war," for those in Nicaragua, "it was very high-intensity." In four years of war, 2,767 civilians lost their lives, close to 150,000 Nicaraguans fled, and 6,236 children were orphaned. To illustrate the devastation, the group noted that the same proportion for the U.S. population would have meant 232,000 deaths, not the 58,000 suffered in the Vietnam War.[47] Similarly, Americas Watch and the Lawyers Committee for International Human Rights released reports detailing human rights abuses by the Contras.[48] Reed Brody, former New York assistant attorney general, issued a powerful report based on sworn affidavits of 145 witnesses.[49]

Accusations like Donovan's complicated the Reagan administration's ability to present itself as promoting human rights in Nicaragua, especially after the president admitted in late February 1984 that the United States sought to overthrow the Sandinista government. The stated policy was no longer to stop the arms flow or to pressure the Sandinistas into negotiations. To sell its position, the administration pursued a two-track strategy. First, the White House argued that the Contras defended Nicaraguans against the Sandinistas' human rights abuses. To underscore this point, on April 15 Reagan attended the dinner of the Nicaraguan Refugee Fund, which raised money for refugees and educated the U.S. public.[50] A photo-op featured the president and a young "refugee," born in the United States to international civil servants.[51] Second, Reagan officials and their Catholic supporters questioned Donovan's standing as a Catholic and portrayed the Contra cause as the true Catholic one. The task, however, was difficult because Donovan challenged the moral righteousness of U.S. policy.

Before the House Committee on Foreign Affairs, the Maryknoller called U.S. Contra aid "an evil, inhumane, and illegal policy." She also stressed that her motivation came from faith, not communist manipulation. As she clarified: "I do not owe my faith, convictions, nor my mission, to any ideology, economic or political system but to the life and message of Jesus Christ and the living tradition and teachings of the Catholic Church. Together with my Sisters in Maryknoll I have chosen to understand and interpret our world today in the spirit of the Gospel and from the point of view of the poor with whom we live and work."[52] Donovan disputed the president's claim that the Contras were the moral equivalent of the Founding Fathers.

Because Donovan's experience gave her credibility and her status as a nun provided her with an air of moral authority, it fell to another Catholic—Henry Hyde—to challenge her. Hyde described his Catholicism as a "combative faith." Like many Catholic supporters of Reagan's Nicaragua policy, Hyde lamented what he saw as the "drift of the Activist Church in America," and he criticized church leaders for this move "towards the secular Left." In particular, Hyde cited some Catholics' tolerance for liberation theology and their failure to "recognize communism as the mortal enemy of Christianity."[53] Hyde's faith was inseparable from his actions in Congress. As he noted, "I have great difficulty in justifying a sequestration or separation of public life from private life and private convictions." Hyde could not see how others could make such a distinction. "I find it hard to understand people who claim a religious affiliation, who claim to personally believe things but do not seek to implement their beliefs or act out their beliefs."[54]

In his questions, Hyde reiterated conservative Catholics' charge that Maryknoll was a religious and political problem. First, Hyde inferred that because Donovan criticized the Contras, she supported the Sandinistas, whom he believed sought to corrupt the church. Hyde pointed to Managua's Iglesia Santa María de Los Angeles, which featured a mural "of Christ as a guerrilla" behind the altar and ended all Sunday Masses with "Hate America," according to "a regular attendee." The political talk did not seem to bother Hyde, but rather the animosity toward the United States. Second, Hyde stressed Donovan's status as a Maryknoller and he connected her to Miguel d'Escoto,[55] Nicaragua's foreign minister and editor of Maryknoll's press, Orbis, the largest U.S. publisher of liberation theology works.

Besides Hyde, the White House used its own religious figure to undermine Donovan: Father Thomas Dowling. Oliver North of the National Security Council arranged for the priest to testify before Congress. Dressed in a Roman collar, Dowling introduced himself as "a Catholic priest" even though he was a member of the Old Catholic Church, a schismatic group not in communion with Rome.[56] Unlike Donovan, Dowling praised the Contras. He stressed that they were Christian in an implicit contrast to the allegedly godless Sandinistas. As he explained, "The Contras are overwhelmingly religious. One sees tremendous artifacts of Christianity, both Catholic and Protestant, tremendous amounts of Bibles, crucifixes, et cetera." Nor did the Contras commit human rights abuses; it was Sandinistas dressed in Contra uniforms. Although Dowling admitted that his knowledge came from what he heard at a press conference, no Congress member challenged him.[57] The flimsiness of Dowling's testimony revealed the White House's desperation to neutralize Catholic Contra opposition.

The president himself implied that Contra aid opponents were at odds with the Vatican and, therefore, bad Catholics. In the midst of the congressional hearings, Reagan informed attendees at the Conference on Religious Liberty at the White House, "I just had a verbal message delivered to me from the Pope urging us to continue our efforts in Central America."[58] The conference brought together two hundred delegates from seventeen countries.[59] The next day, Reagan said that Pope John Paul II "has been most supportive of all our activities in Central America," yet both the Vatican and its U.S. ambassador denied any endorsement.[60]

The tactic of accusing Catholic Contra opponents of not being true Catholics likely came from a Catholic. Renowned conservative strategist Paul Weyrich encouraged the argument as one of the nine "classic elements of strategy" he proposed conservative Catholics use to counter liberal Catholics' claims. In training workshops sponsored by his Catholic Center, Weyrich told attendees to label their Catholic opposition as people "who do not follow the pope" because doing so "takes the moral high ground away from them."[61] Ironically, when employed by non-Catholics, Weyrich's strategy turned on its head the old stereotype that Catholics placed their loyalty to Rome ahead of the United States.[62] Reagan and other non-Catholics criticized Catholics for *not* following the pope.

Reagan's move to align himself with the pope revealed not only his desire to appeal to conservative Catholics but also how respect for John Paul II transcended Catholics. Although some challenged the White House's establishment of diplomatic relations with the Vatican on First Amendment grounds, Gallup polls suggested that most Americans approved because of John Paul II. As Moral Majority Vice President Ronald Godwin declared, Protestants' traditional concerns "about recognizing the Vatican are no longer seen as relevant or as important as they did years ago." Given "the important contributions that the Vatican and this Pope have made to world peace in the last several years, it seems to be an appropriate time in history to extend this recognition and to enhance his efforts." Leaders from the National Association of Evangelicals and the Southern Baptist Convention shared these sentiments.[63]

Despite his efforts, Reagan lost the April House vote on aid, leaving his Catholic allies to blame fellow Catholics, especially Maryknollers. In a letter on the hearings' final day, Michael Novak shared his frustration with Henry Hyde: "A number of Congressmen have expressed to me their doubts about voting to cut off funds to the revolutionaries in Nicaragua, although they feel under pressure from activist Catholic clergy to do so."[64] CIA Director William Casey was more specific; the problem was Maryknoll sisters. As he remarked, "If Tip O'Neill didn't have Maryknoll nuns who wrote letters, we would have a Contra program."[65]

Masculinity and the Contra Fight

Two months later, on June 12, 1985, the House approved nonlethal aid to the Contras for the first time. Several developments helped the administration's cause. First, Nicaraguan president Daniel Ortega's visit to the Soviet Union frustrated Contra opponents' claims that it was not a shared communist outlook but U.S. behavior that drove the Sandinistas into Moscow's arms. Second, Reagan asserted in a letter to Representative David McCurdy (D-OK) that he desired a political solution, that the United States did not seek the "military overthrow of the Sandinista government," and that the United States condemned "in the strongest possible terms, atrocities by either side." The letter provided an opening for Congress members to support Contra aid for a reason "other than intimidation." Unbeknownst to Congress, McCurdy and a pro-Contra lobbyist wrote the letter for the president's signature. Finally, Reagan successfully targeted southerners, who composed twenty-one of the twenty-six Democrats who switched sides on Contra funding from April to June.[66]

To mobilize congressional support, Reagan appealed to southern notions of manhood, implicitly contrasting himself with O'Neill, who presumably exhibited a feminine weakness by relying on the Maryknoll Sisters. The White

House engaged in a southern "media-blitz" that, according to Tom Turnip-seed, southerner and staffer on George Wallace's presidential campaigns,[67] exploited "the most deep-seated and dangerous psycho-cultural flaw in white Southern manhood—a fear of defeat that dates back to Dixie's greatest lost cause, the Civil War." Although congressmen were swayed both by their "fear of dark-skinned hordes swarming across the Rio Grande and forming a political coalition with Jesse Jackson . . . together with various white scalawags" and of upsetting defense contractors in their region, Turnipseed opined that the notion of Dixie manhood won the day for the president. For white southern men, Turnipseed alleged, manhood since the Civil War meant not appearing afraid to fight. Playing on those fears, Reagan argued that southern congressmen who voted against the Contras would be labeled "soft on communism."[68] The success of Reagan's gender-based campaign was surprising as polls from late May and early June revealed that southerners cared little about Reagan's Central America policy, ranking it last out of six domestic and foreign policy issues.[69]

Reagan's allies aided his efforts by attacking O'Neill's masculinity and his Catholicism. In his June 1985 nationally syndicated column, Moral Majority Vice President Cal Thomas urged O'Neill to abandon his opposition to Contra funding. After reminding readers that during a presidential debate Jimmy Carter revealed that he and his twelve-year-old daughter Amy discussed nuclear weapons, Thomas charged that O'Neill "has gone Carter one better" by relying on Maryknoll nuns. Evidently the sisters were more naive than a twelve-year-old on foreign policy matters. Thomas also described O'Neill as a "San Francisco Democrat," a slur Republicans used to question a politician's heterosexuality and suggest that he was weak on defense. Thomas also continued the trend of non-Catholics challenging Catholics' fidelity to the church. Like other Contra supporters, Thomas implied that O'Neill was a bad Catholic for following the counsel of illegitimate Catholics: the Maryknoll Sisters. Instead, O'Neill should listen to "Sister DeMacías."[70] Thomas somehow missed Geraldine Macías's departure from Maryknoll. His use of her former title, though, showed the evangelical Thomas did not object to Tip O'Neill's decision to listen to nuns; it was the *wrong* nuns that were the problem.

Thomas and others, including the president, could challenge Maryknollers' standing as nuns because the missionary Mother Teresa served as a high-profile alternative. In the midst of battles over Contra funding, Reagan honored Mother Teresa. In June 1985, he awarded her the Presidential Medal of Freedom—the nation's highest civilian honor—and six months later, the White House hosted a showing of a documentary about her life.[71]

Reagan, meanwhile, bolstered the contrast between him as tough and masculine and O'Neill as "emotional" by linking himself with the movie character Rambo. In 1985's *Rambo: First Blood, Part II*, Rambo embarks on a top-secret
mission to investigate prisoners of war in Vietnam. He decides to rescue them
himself, battling communist Vietnamese and Russians as well as corrupt U.S.
officials in the process. A month after *Rambo's* release, Reagan watched it at
the White House while waiting to hear the fate of thirty-nine U.S. hostages
held in Lebanon.[72] After learning of their release the president joked, "Boy, I
saw *Rambo* last night. Now, I know what to do next time this happens."[73] Three
months later, Reagan quoted Rambo when discussing his tax plan: "In the spirit
of Rambo, let me tell you, we're going to win this time."[74] In October 1985,
fiction and reality came together when the president invited the film's star Sylvester Stallone to a state dinner at the White House.[75]

Both Reagan's friends and foes associated his Nicaragua policy with Rambo.
U.S. and international press, including the *Wall Street Journal* and England's *Observer*, connected the two men through headlines like "Rambo Rides High in
Washington" and "Reagan Promise on Rebel Aid Has Signs of Rambo Rhetoric."[76] Contra aid critics decried the president for his "Rambo tactics,"
"Rambo-style intervention," and "Rambo-like causes."[77] Even the Soviet Union
denounced Rambo as reflecting the bullying nature of the United States.[78] By
contrast, Reagan's Catholic supporters praised the movie character as a model
for a strong post-Vietnam United States. As Phyllis Schlafly explained, "Rambo
expresses the collective outrage of Americans that we let a two-bit backward
country in Southeast Asia defeat us," how the United States "has allowed our
POWs and MIAs to languish," and how "brainwashed U.S. citizens" spat on
veterans and "called them 'baby-killers.'"[79] Supporters of U.S.-Nicaragua policy saw Rambo as such a role model that they implored Sylvester Stallone to
attend a Miami rally for the Contras. As Paul Weyrich wrote, he hoped the star
would appear "because of the roles you have played and the perception that
you also are sympathetic to these roles." As additional incentive, Weyrich enclosed letters from Republican senators Peter Wilson (CA) and Robert Dole
(KS) asking Stallone to appear.[80] It is unclear whether Stallone attended the
rally, as press coverage does not mention him.

Conservative U.S. Catholics were not the only ones who appropriated
Rambo for the Contra cause. Nicaraguans living in the United States tried to
use a sexualized image of Rambo mixed with Catholic symbols to attract U.S.
support. Two Nicaraguan exiles paid $4,000 for posters depicting a Nicaraguan
woman, "María," wearing a wet camouflage tank top and holding an M-16
draped in a rosary. Behind her in the jungle were the words, "I love Nicaraguan

Freedom Fighters." The plan was to sell the posters, along with a rosary, for five dollars to raise money for the Contra youth group. Rene Quiñones, the poster's producer and Somoza's former attorney, saw Comandante María as "our Ramba, representing Christ, sex appeal and *la lucha* [the struggle]." As he noted, the best shot "was when we wet the shirt so that her sex appeal could show through." To Quiñones, the poster united Nicaraguan and U.S. ideals. "Our María stands for a return to values, for Nicaragua and the American way." While Quiñones conflated Comandante María's sexuality with Catholicism to sell U.S. support for the Contras, FDN spokeswoman Marta Sacasa described her as "inauthentic" and complained that she wore "nothing beneath her shirt."[81]

Maryknoll Challenge from Nicaragua

Reagan's challenge to O'Neill's masculinity and authenticity as a Catholic may have helped him win House approval for nonlethal aid, but many Nicaraguans objected to the president's characterization of the United States as defending Nicaraguans from religious persecution. The Baptist Convention of Nicaragua disputed Reagan's supposedly Christian motivations after the United States announced a full trade embargo on May 1, 1985. The move was the culmination of administration efforts to destabilize Nicaragua economically.[82] In a pastoral letter, the Baptists condemned the embargo as "anti-Christian, anti-biblical, inhumane, unjust, illegal and arbitrary." The embargo contradicted Reagan's claims of defending people of faith. As they declared, "We cannot conceive how the same President who was sworn in with his hand on the Bible can issue a decree that goes totally against the Bible and is aimed at annihilating an entire people."[83]

Nicaragua's foreign minister Maryknoller Miguel d'Escoto was even more aggressive in his challenge. Beginning on July 7, d'Escoto embarked on a twenty-six-day fast, which he called "Fast for Peace, for the Defense of Life and Against Terrorism."[84] As d'Escoto explained, the *ayuno* (fast) was "an expression of Christian rejection of the policy of state terrorism imposed by the U.S. government against Nicaragua" and "a religious expression of condemnation of the systematic kidnappings and assassinations of our sisters and brothers by the counterrevolutionaries whom the U.S. government finances and directs."[85] With the fast, d'Escoto challenged not only U.S. policy but also Reagan's use of religion to justify it. The foreign minister pursued the fast to counter Reagan's "theological war" against Nicaragua. As the Maryknoller explained, Reagan sought "to appropriate for himself the struggles of the religious right in the United States: His speeches are full of religious allusions."[86] The fast was necessary, d'Escoto insisted, because "the government as a government cannot find an answer to a theological war."[87] By challenging Reagan's method, d'Escoto aimed to reclaim the true Christian voice for U.S.-Nicaragua policy opponents.

The fifty-two-year-old priest hoped the fast would be a *chispa* (spark) to ignite an "evangelical insurrection" in Central America, the United States, and Western Europe.[88] As he told members of the Nicaraguan armed forces, he sought to create "a movement of nonviolent struggle . . . to complement our legitimate military defense."[89] Though the Nicaraguan government announced d'Escoto's actions reflected "a personal expression of Christian faith,"[90] not his official role, the government declared a National Fast Day on July 26.[91]

The U.S. government was not d'Escoto's only target; he called out U.S. and Nicaraguan church leaders. The U.S. bishops were "guilty of sins of omission" because as d'Escoto charged,[92] "they could stop Reagan, but they are allowing him to get away with murder."[93] Likewise, d'Escoto critiqued Cardinal Obando's association with Reagan and his failure to condemn the Contra war.[94]

D'Escoto's attack on Obando was part of an ongoing battle; the two Miguels represented competing views over the church's direction, the Sandinista government, and the Contra war. Tensions increased in January 1985 when the Nicaraguan Bishops Conference called on d'Escoto and all priests in government to resign.[95] They refused. The situation reached a stalemate when the conference announced no further action would be taken so long as the men did not engage in priestly duties. In essence, d'Escoto and others were suspended.[96]

Maryknoll supported d'Escoto. The foreign minister felt that resigning would mean turning his back on his people in a time of war when he might use "the charisms of the priesthood, which includes peace and reconciliation," to work for peace. As the Maryknoll superior general explained to the Vatican and other Maryknollers, the congregation was stuck "in an extremely delicate position." Expelled d'Escoto could be viewed as support for U.S. policy. Maryknoll felt strongly that d'Escoto's denunciation of the Contra war was important because the Nicaraguan Bishops' Conference "had not yet condemned the war against the people and the atrocities being perpetrated."[97]

While the Bishops Conference and the Vatican pushed for priests to leave the Nicaraguan government, the pope seemed to side with the hierarchy and against the government when he elevated Obando to cardinal in the spring of 1985. Many interpreted the promotion as another sign of the pope's support for the hierarchical church rather than the people's church and for the Contras rather than the Sandinistas.[98] While most Nicaraguans, including Daniel

Ortega, enthusiastically cheered the first Nicaraguan named cardinal, Oban-do's decision to celebrate his first Mass in Miami with Contra leaders quickly changed the mood. When questioned about Contra leaders being seated in places of honor, Obando remarked, "I do not object to being identified with the people who have taken up arms." His response led Contras to proclaim him as one of their own.[99] On the other hand, in an open letter to the cardinal, 105 Nicaraguan Christians explained that Obando's decision regarding the Mass was particularly upsetting given his failure to deliver "a prayer for our mar-tyrs nor the slightest protest because of the atrocities that the counterrevolu-tionaries commit." He had turned against Nicaraguans, they insisted, as his "unconditional position in favor of the United States Government situates you publicly against our people and causes bloodshed and suffering for the very poor."[100]

In this context, d'Escoto's fast exposed fissures among Catholics in and out-side Nicaragua. In Nicaragua, priests showed their support by fasting and concelebrating Mass,[101] and six thousand representatives of base communities declared their support.[102] On the other hand, Radio Católica, the church's of-ficial station, condemned d'Escoto. The station cited biblical passages that called for fasting for the right reason and criticized Pharisees who fasted pub-licly for attention. The Contra station in Costa Rica, Radio Impacto, also broad-cast these critiques.[103] In Mexico, seven hundred priests, including a few bishops, fasted in support.[104] By contrast, the Mexican Bishops' Conference de-scribed d'Escoto's action as "a misuse of Christian practice."[105] International supporters, representing twenty-eight countries and numbering more than five thousand people, visited the Maryknoll priest.[106] Europeans in France, England, Italy, and West Germany fasted,[107] and people in thirty U.S. cities held prayer vigils and fasts.[108]

In the United States, conservative Catholics disparaged the fast and con-nected it to larger concerns about Maryknoll. Michael Novak called d'Escoto's fast "a wonderful propaganda ploy" by Maryknoll to challenge U.S. policy.[109] Likewise, Father Enrique Rueda, former director of Paul Weyrich's Catholic Center, dismissed the fast as a communist-controlled "show, to galvanize the masses in support of the Sandinistas and the Revolution." Popular church members and others who supported d'Escoto, including church hierarchy members, were "enemies of the Faith." As Rueda argued, the debate was big-ger than Nicaragua; there was a "war going on within the Roman Catholic Church between those who still believe in the teaching and tradition of 20 cen-turies and those for whom this is not acceptable in the 20th century." The battle pitted faithful Catholics like himself who worked to save fellow Catho-lics from communism's grip and from religious persecution against those who "infiltrated the Church" and aided in its destruction.[110] In this way, Maryknoll threatened more than the U.S. Catholic Church or U.S. foreign policy.

Instead of addressing the fast, Reagan stressed a victimized church the United States needed to defend. In a December 1985 radio address, Reagan condemned Nicaragua's October state of emergency that restricted civil liberties, and the president extolled Obando's virtues. Reagan described Nicaragua as "an imprisoned nation" in which churches—collectively—were "the enemy" in the government's eyes. Reagan detailed government actions against Protestants, Jews, and Catholics, and he singled out Obando as "a great hero of truth and courage." The Sandinistas needed to be stopped, Reagan insisted. "These men are nothing but thugs, a gang of hard-core Communists to whom the word of God is a declaration of liberation that must be stamped out."[111]

In response, d'Escoto challenged Reagan's use of religion to justify and sell U.S. policy. In February 1986, d'Escoto continued his evangelical insurrection with the *Vía Crucis* (Stations of the Cross), which commemorate Jesus's carrying of the cross, suffering, and death. D'Escoto called "for a halt to the manipulation of religion against Nicaragua," referencing Reagan's use of religious rhetoric to defend and promote U.S. intervention.[112] From February 14 to 28, d'Escoto walked from Jalapa, a town near the northern border of Honduras that twice repelled Contra attempts to overtake it, to Managua, home of Obando's diocese.[113] At each stop, or station, the group commemorated those killed by the Contras, and d'Escoto asked the United States to stop "crucifying" the Nicaraguan people.[114] Eighty people, including ten war veterans in wheelchairs, made the 190-mile journey.[115]

Just as with d'Escoto's fast, the response to his *Vía Crucis* revealed the deep ruptures within the Nicaraguan church. While the bishop of Estelí greeted d'Escoto with open arms,[116] in Tipitapa, the parish priest threatened to excommunicate anyone who participated and even enclosed the chapel in barbed wire.[117] Upon reaching the capital, more than ten thousand Nicaraguans attended Mass concelebrated by seventy-two priests—one-quarter of all those in the country.[118]

At the end of his journey, d'Escoto scathingly condemned Reagan and Obando, as he had after his fast. During his homily, the foreign minister challenged Reagan's portrayal of himself and the United States as defender of the church. As d'Escoto asserted: "That poor mortal, possessed by the demon of intervention, by the demon of death, invents and proclaims to the world that what he is doing in Nicaragua he is doing in order to save the Christian faith. The assassin suddenly becomes the protector of the faith!" Reagan's position led people to look to Nicaragua's bishops for guidance. But, d'Escoto explained, the bishops were accomplices in the U.S. slaughter. They went "to the United States to calm the conscience of the legislators, many of whom had said that Reagan's policy was not only illegal, but immoral." Obando, in particular, "betrayed" the priesthood and had "been the principal accomplice" of the aggression against the Nicaraguan people. D'Escoto called on Obando to repent immediately.[119] The Maryknoller's words were "broadcast over 17 radio stations."[120]

In assessing these Nicaraguan developments, CIA analysts concluded that the fight over faith was a major battleground. "The regime consistently portrays this proregime group as the 'real' Nicaraguan church and uses sympathetic clergy to counter charges of persecution leveled by the traditional hierarchy."[121] The CIA accused the Sandinistas of using the same argument Reagan and his Catholic cronies did to belittle Contra aid opponents: they were not real Catholics. The similarity of language underscored how battles over the church and what it meant to be Catholic overlapped with and influenced debates over U.S.–Central America policy.

The 1986 Aid Battle

Though Reagan gained House support for nonlethal aid in June 1985, he wanted Congress to approve more aid, including military aid, in 1986. To push his agenda, Reagan continued some of his earlier tactics. He ignored the Nicaraguan foreign minister's protests and accused the Nicaragua government of persecuting religion. He praised Obando. Administration officials and allies maintained their attacks on Tip O'Neill's masculinity and his status as a true Catholic. They praised Obando and disparaged d'Escoto and Maryknoll. But the administration and its allies' 1986 response differed in one key aspect: non-Catholic Contra supporters promoted themselves as more concerned with the church's fate than Catholic Contra opponents.

U.S. government rhetoric characterizing the Catholic Church as victim and praising Cardinal Obando was not simply about selling U.S. policy. The White House regarded the church as the most viable opposition force. As CIA analysts concluded in early 1986, "Inside Nicaragua, Cardinal Obando y Bravo will remain the principal rallying force for opposition to the regime. . . . We judge the regime will be unable to discredit Obando, and his immense popular base in Nicaragua will give the prelate the credibility and the forum that elude other opposition leaders."[122] By shoring up Obando, the Reagan White House believed it was strengthening non-Contra opposition to the Sandinistas. At the same time, the administration sought to discredit U.S. Contra aid opponents, namely O'Neill and Maryknoll.

As part of this campaign, White House Communications Director and Catholic Pat Buchanan targeted Maryknollers. In a *Washington Post* op-ed, "The Contras Need Our Help," Buchanan challenged "San Francisco Democrats" to stand up to communism. He questioned their patriotism, arguing they could side with either Reagan and freedom or Daniel Ortega and communism. Buchanan warned of the peril should Nicaragua fall to communism. He recounted the Sandinistas' crimes against their fellow Nicaraguans, which even Lenin's "useful idiots"—"liberated nuns and Marxist Maryknolls"—could no longer defend.[123] Buchanan's accusations that Democrats supported communism generated controversy, but scholars have overlooked how he singled out Maryknoll.[124]

Buchanan's reference to Maryknoll revealed how the congregation brought together conservative Catholics' fears of a wayward church and a weak foreign policy. To Buchanan, Maryknoll represented how the church—or as he called it, "The Church I Knew, That Is No More"—had gone astray since the 1950s. A self-described "traditionalist" who occasionally attended Latin Mass at a Greek Melkite Catholic Church, Buchanan saw himself as a "pre-Vatican II Catholic."[125] As he explained, while Maryknoller Bishop Walsh was tortured and imprisoned in China in the 1950s, Maryknollers of the 1980s "seemed permanently enraged" that the U.S. government worked to stop the Sandinistas from inflicting "the same evil system" on Nicaraguan Catholics. The change was not due to an external enemy; the church had been "surrendered from within." Buchanan cataloged the changes he witnessed: how the Liturgy was now "a communal meal celebrated in the vernacular" and many nuns were "in acrimonious rebellion against the 'patriarchal' Church." Buchanan recounted his frustration over seeing a priest give "half the congregation" the sign of peace: "As he went on and on, shaking hands, hugging people, smiling up a storm, it was all I could do to contain myself from shouting, 'Get back up on that altar!'"[126]

The church he loved was gone. As Buchanan wrote, "Visiting the modern churches today is like coming back to the town where you grew up and finding the oldest landmark, the great mansion on the hill, has been gutted and rebuilt to fit in architecturally and devotionally with the bustling suburban scene. Outside a sign reads UNDER NEW MANAGEMENT."[127]

Maryknollers privately confronted Buchanan, just as they confronted Alexander Haig, Joan Frawley, and Geraldine Macías. Father John Geitner admonished Buchanan for the "potential harm you have done to Maryknoll missioners working in authoritarian nations such as Chile." Buchanan's position was particularly disturbing given that his late brother Bill had begun studies to join Maryknoll but left before ordination. While Geitner praised Buchanan for his professional accomplishments, he characterized his Contra support as contrary to what being a Catholic meant: "It's quite a tribute to your ability and character coming from your sound Catholic education to be so close to the President. But it's one thing to be conservative on economic and foreign policy issues and another thing to resort to the use of armed thugs to try to enforce U.S. control of Central America, especially when the Catholic bishops of the United States have spoken out so clearly against this policy."[128] Both sides of the Contra debate claimed they represented the true Catholic position.

Though other Catholics shared Buchanan's frustration,[129] as White House communications director he had the platform to voice his concerns about Maryknoll and to influence the packaging of U.S. policy. Whereas during Reagan's first term Deaver, Baker, and Communications Director David Gergen steered Reagan clear of Central America whenever possible for fear of alienating voters or jeopardizing his reelection chances, with Reagan's reelection, things changed. Donald T. Regan became chief of staff, and more importantly, Buchanan stepped in as communications director. The shackles on Reagan's pro-Contra talk were off, and he found a willing partner in Buchanan. Reagan's "tough rhetoric" on Nicaragua came from Buchanan. He controlled the speechwriters and crafted Reagan's characterization of the Contras as the moral equivalent of the Founding Fathers.[130]

Echoing Casey's conclusion that Maryknollers' letter writing prevented a Contra program, Buchanan saw the congregation as the key impediment to U.S.-Nicaragua policy. He was not alone. A *Dallas Morning News* cartoon depicted Daniel Ortega holding an AK-47 emblazoned with the word "propaganda" and featuring a "G" that was the Soviet sickle and star. The first two bullets in Ortega's propaganda gun were "Maryknolls."[131] Similarly, Enrique Rueda again singled out Maryknoll among those who stood in the way of U.S. policy.[132] Aid to the Contras was "perfectly moral," Rueda insisted, because it was the only way to "save" Nicaragua and the church from the communist Sandinistas and their presumed takeover of Central America. To address this problem, Rueda encouraged Catholics to inform Maryknoll they were withholding contributions because they disapproved of the so-called missionaries' behavior.[133] Rueda provided a template by reprinting his letter to Maryknoll in the *Wanderer*.[134]

Rueda's tactic was effective, as other Catholics sent their own disapproving letters to Maryknoll and copies to Rueda.[135] Some used his language. An unsigned editorial (presumably written by the pastor or with his approval) in a Rhode Island parish bulletin mimicked Rueda's condemnation of Maryknoll and other Contra opponents.[136]

The White House encouraged conservative Catholics like Rueda in their efforts. Before the March 1986 congressional vote, Reagan met with leaders whose organizations had been spearheading grassroots campaigns to "educate both Congress and the general public on the importance of the restoration of democracy in Nicaragua." As a preparatory memo informed the president, most attendees had been working for nearly a year and were about to begin an aggressive lobbying campaign. While the meeting's stated purpose was "to give inspiration," Reagan's appearance also communicated the importance of the group's efforts to the White House. The invitation list included Catholics, such as Paul Weyrich, Phyllis Schlafly, the Heritage Foundation's Ed Feulner, the Knights of Columbus's Virgil Dechant, and Lew Lehrman of Citizens for America,[137] a recent convert.[138]

Despite conservative Catholics' work, the U.S. press portrayed the 1986 battle over Contra funding as a personal struggle between Reagan and O'Neill ahead of the Speaker's upcoming retirement. Reagan delivered eleven speeches urging support for the Contras in the two and a half weeks before the House vote.[139] In fact, Reagan's 1986 speeches on Nicaragua totaled more than all the addresses he gave on South America during his presidency.[140] But the debate was much more than executive versus legislative or Republican versus Democrat. The two men represented two opposing camps in Catholic fights over the church's direction. By following Maryknollers' assessment of the region, O'Neill elevated what conservative Catholics regarded as communist sympathy among Catholics. Non-Catholic Reagan, on the other hand, promoted the conservative Catholic viewpoint by alleging the Nicaraguan government persecuted religion and by praising Obando as leader.

Reagan cited Obando to bolster his claim that U.S. policy aligned with the Catholic Church. In his March 16 address to the nation imploring Congress to approve $100 million more in Contra aid, Reagan quoted Obando. "The Catholic primate of Nicaragua, Cardinal Obando y Bravo, has put the matter forthrightly, 'We want to state clearly,' he says, 'that this government is totalitarian. We are dealing with an enemy of the church.'"[141]

While Reagan cited the Nicaraguan cardinal to stress the moral righteousness of U.S. policy, non-Catholics used Obando to lecture O'Neill on the proper way to be Catholic. On the morning of the House vote, Ben Wattenberg, cofounder and chair of the neoconservative Coalition for a Democratic Majority, accused O'Neill of being a bad Catholic for relying on Maryknollers. In an op-ed, Wattenberg praised the Speaker as "a great American" but determined that O'Neill was "making a great mistake." Wattenberg concluded that O'Neill did not understand what Maryknoll stood for, especially "within the deeply divided Catholic community." As Wattenberg asserted, "Tip O'Neill—who is as far from Marxism as you can get—has never gotten the word." Though "many" Maryknollers served the poor, according to Wattenberg they also "praised" Castro's Cuba, supported communist guerrillas in the Philippines, and backed the Sandinistas. By contrast, Managua's Cardinal Obando described the Nicaraguan government as "totalitarian." Though O'Neill claimed Maryknollers "are not going to mislead me," Wattenberg implied that Maryknoll's influence blinded O'Neill to the Nicaraguan reality, which Catholics like Obando recognized.[142]

While Wattenberg's claim that O'Neill's reliance on Maryknollers made him less of a Catholic was not new, the visual attack on O'Neill by the *Washington Times* was. The paper accompanied Wattenberg's piece with a cartoon of O'Neill in a dress resembling a pilgrim's and a habit inspired by the *Flying Nun's*. His hands rested piously atop one another. In a stark contrast to Reagan as Rambo, O'Neill was not just listening to nuns; he was one.

Despite the attacks, O'Neill's "impassioned speech to close the debate" in March, and his early vote against funding (a break with his previous practice),[143] the House voted against Contra aid. Henry Hyde then intensified his attacks on the Maryknoll Sisters. While Buchanan served as the White House's Catholic attack dog, Hyde assumed the mantle in Congress. Echoing Buchanan's charge that Maryknollers were Lenin's "useful idiots," Hyde contended that the sisters blocked U.S.-Nicaragua policy, which sought to save the Catholic Church and the Western Hemisphere from communism's spread. To Hyde, U.S.-Nicaragua policy did not affect the Catholic Church; the policy *was* a Catholic issue.

Hyde authored a letter by congressional Catholics to their colleagues, urging fellow Congress members to follow two Catholic bishops and support Contra aid. Referring to themselves as "members of Congress who are Roman Catholics," the twenty-two representatives contended, "Religious persecution is not a peripheral issue as we resume debate on aid to the Nicaraguan democratic opposition." In support, they attached a letter from Bernard Cardinal Law of Boston and John Cardinal O'Connor of New York acknowledging that the Sandinistas persecuted all faiths, but arguing, "no group has suffered persecution on as great a scale as the Roman Catholic Church."[144] Even the orthodox National Committee of Catholic Laymen described the letter as "blistering."[145] By stressing the U.S.-based bishops as authorities on the matter, Hyde implicitly contrasted the men with Maryknoll sisters who served in Nicaragua and presumably supported the communist Sandinistas.

Hyde's non-Catholic colleagues responded. In advocating for Contra aid, Representative Ronald Marlenee (R-MT), a Lutheran, inserted Obando's *Washington Post* op-ed in which the cardinal declared the Sandinistas had "gagged and bound" the church.[146] In introducing the piece, Marlenee described Obando as "the real leader of the majority of the people" against "the Marxist totalitarianism in Nicaragua." The congressman continued: "Mr. Speaker, you should recognize that. The Maryknoll nuns should recognize that."[147] In directly addressing O'Neill and the Maryknoll Sisters, Marlenee echoed the familiar refrain: they were misguided Catholics.

On the morning of the pivotal June Contra aid vote, Hyde argued that Obando was the true Maryknoller, and he implied that the Maryknoll Sisters, as women, were ignorant about politics. In a *Wall Street Journal* op-ed, Hyde discussed the persecution of the Nicaraguan church and lamented how Maryknoll's support for the Sandinista regime indicated an abandonment of anticommunism. It was not Maryknoll sisters or Father Miguel d'Escoto who embodied the true "heritage of Maryknoll"—it was Miguel Obando, a non-Maryknoller. "Persecution of the Catholic Church by Marxist-Leninists is a constant of our times, only the cast of persecutors changes. It is Cardinal Obando y Bravo—not Miguel d'Escoto, and not those Maryknoll nuns who have, for whatever reasons of confused compassion, systematically misled House Speaker Tip O'Neill about the realities of Nicaragua—who truly represents the heritage of Maryknoll and Bishop Walsh."[148] To Hyde, the Maryknoll Sisters did not understand the Nicaraguan situation, yet they held mysterious influence over Tip O'Neill.

On the same editorial spread, the *Wall Street Journal* board echoed appeals from Congress to ignore wayward Catholic women. O'Neill's opposition to Reagan's Nicaragua policy was "a weak-kneed response" to a national security threat. In arguing that O'Neill was not only misguided but also no longer the party's future, the board wrote, "The influence the Sandinista apologists have been able to bring to bear in the House has been little short of amazing. It owes much to Tip O'Neill, who spends more time listening to the Maryknoll Order than to the pope, a man who knows infinitely more than the Maryknolls seem to about communism. What Democrats should keep in mind today, however, is that Tip O'Neill does not represent the future of the Democratic Party."[149] Besides stressing O'Neill's upcoming retirement, the *Journal's* editors argued that Maryknollers, as women, were not as knowledgeable as the pope, and they suggested that the women failed to act deferentially. Rather than Catholics defending their status as Americans first and Catholics second, the *Wall Street Journal*, like Reagan and other non-Catholic Contra supporters, encouraged them to follow Rome in making policy decisions.

O'Neill got the message: it was the Gipper and his macho men versus the Speaker and his nuns. Just before walking onto the House floor for the vote, O'Neill explained the White House's approach to reporter Jimmy Breslin. "The first time Haig was here, five years ago, he sat right there and said, 'Oh, we have to go in there and show them.'" And with a new secretary of state, the story had not changed. "They have to show they're strong. I don't know what it is, but they have to do it." O'Neill's chief assistant interjected: "And we're left with the ladies in the long dresses." As O'Neill explained, the president says, "Tip listens to the ladies in the long dresses." O'Neill then defended his reliance on Maryknoll sisters: "Am I wrong in listening to women who live in Nicaragua and follow the Sermon on the Mount? Or am I supposed to just sit here and believe generals?"[150] The choice was clear: missionary nuns over the U.S. military.

The 1985–1986 Reagan-O'Neill battle over U.S.-Nicaragua policy pitted two views of U.S. Cold War policy and of the Catholic Church against one another in new ways. Previously, the Reagan administration and its Catholic allies critiqued those who supported liberation theology, especially Maryknollers. These criticisms continued, but in the 1985–1986 debate over Contra funding, Reagan and other non-Catholics contended that Catholics who opposed U.S. Contra funding were not true Catholics. Similarly, Maryknoll, and especially the Maryknoll Sisters, remained front and center in the debates over U.S.– Central America policy. Before, the murdered churchwomen played a symbolic role in El Salvador debates. In 1985–1986, sisters with Nicaragua missionary experience became a powerful influence in Nicaragua discussions. Sisters such as Peggy Healy and Nancy Donovan gained notoriety for opposing U.S. Contra support. Although Maryknoller and Nicaraguan foreign minister Miguel d'Escoto also challenged Reagan's characterization of himself as defender of the church, Reagan ignored him. The contrast between Reagan's seeming obliviousness to d'Escoto's public religious acts and the ink spilled over O'Neill's reliance on Maryknoll sisters underscored how the battle over Contra funding was about more than U.S. foreign policy. The Reagan-O'Neill standoff, and the gender-based critiques at its center, showed again how U.S.– Central America policy debates overlapped with and influenced debates among Catholics over the Cold War, U.S. foreign policy, the church's direction, and the role of nuns—and women generally—in the church.

In the summer of 1986, Reagan won House and Senate approval for Contra funding.[151] But in September, the White House still lamented religious communities' influence. The memo "Public Diplomacy Plan for Explaining U.S. Central American Policy to the U.S. Religious Community" noted "church-based supporters of the Sandinistas have been able to frame much of the public debate on Nicaragua." The memo cited religious communities, rather than the media, as influential sources of information: "These networks have been successful in dominating the flow of information to local churches, parishes, and synagogues." To counter these views, public diplomacy efforts should "increase the U.S. religious community's awareness of the experiences and situation of their religious brethren in Nicaragua."[152] While still acknowledging religious communities' role, the memo's omission of the Maryknoll Sisters perhaps reflected Reagan's success in gaining congressional support for Contra funding and Tip O'Neill's retirement at the end of the 1986 term. The success was short-lived. Once news of a secret arms-for-hostages scheme surfaced, the White House moved from focusing on its policy opponents to damage control. For some of the president's Catholic defenders, however, the Maryknoll Sisters and Tip O'Neill remained part of the story.

CHAPTER 7

Maryknoll and Iran-Contra

In August 1987, Henry Hyde was part of the joint Senate-House congressional efforts to investigate Iran-Contra, the scheme to sell arms to Iran in exchange for U.S. hostages and, later, to transfer the excess funds to the Contras. During the questioning of CIA Central America Task Force Chief Alan Fiers, Hyde lashed out at Congress for forcing the White House to make an end run around the Boland Amendment. Hyde maintained that the "Iranian arms hostages operation," which was "goofy off-the-wall," was Congress's fault. He characterized Congress's behavior as "stupidity" and said the legislative body played "partisan politics," even "visceral politics." But Hyde reserved his anger for one member: fellow Catholic Tip O'Neill. When he was Speaker, according to Hyde, O'Neill held Reagan in "visceral contempt" when it came to the Gipper's Central America policy. More than once O'Neill proposed the president would not be satisfied until U.S. troops were fighting and dying in Nicaragua. As Hyde proclaimed, "I don't know how you deal with somebody who feels that way or who gets their intelligence from the Maryknoll nuns on Central America."[1] Without Maryknollers' influence on Tip O'Neill, according to Hyde, Reagan would not have been forced to find another way to arm the Contras. Even after the Speaker's retirement, the sisters and their influence on O'Neill were still part of U.S.-Nicaragua policy debates.

Despite the Iran-Contra revelations, the Reagan administration still pursued a take-no-prisoners approach when it came to its Contra policy. The White

House's focus, however, shifted from U.S. Contra aid opponents to undermining Central Americans' peace attempts. As the administration said little regarding Iran-Contra, conservative Catholics outside the White House, especially Congressman Hyde, strenuously defended officials, as this chapter argues. Conservative Catholics held up Catholic William Casey and former Catholic Oliver North as symbols of true Catholic patriotism in contrast to Maryknollers, whom they blamed for causing Iran-Contra. But to those Catholics opposed to U.S.-Nicaragua policy, these men were pariahs and Maryknollers were true heroes. The missionaries condemned the Contras' human rights abuses and argued it was U.S. influence Nicaraguans needed saving from. The focus on North was not a U.S.- or Catholic-based conversation, as North was associated with an apparition of the Virgin Mary in Nicaragua and as evangelical Protestants also labeled North a model patriot and Christian. Ultimately, the charges against Maryknoll did not pack the same punch because they were not coming from the White House. Key conservative Catholics had left the administration or died.

Iran-Contra

When the House approved military aid for the Contras in June 1986 and Tip O'Neill retired, Reagan's Nicaragua policy seemed to be turning a corner. But four months later, the administration's secret and illegal efforts to aid the Contras unraveled. In October, a plane carrying ten thousand pounds of U.S.-supplied materiel and U.S. mercenary Eugene Hasenfus was shot down over Nicaragua by a "shoulder-launched surface-to-air missile." Disobeying instructions, Hasenfus parachuted from the plane. His three companions—"two former CIA pilots" and a Nicaraguan radio operator—died. Hasenfus told the Nicaraguans about CIA efforts to aid the Contras, which the plane's flight logs from Miami to Ilopango, El Salvador, supported.[2] The Nicaraguan government disseminated photos "of Hasenfaus, a bear of a man, being led on a thin little rope by a teenage captor," alleging he was part of secret U.S. efforts to aid the Contras.[3] The Reagan administration denied the accusations.[4]

Less than a month later, the White House faced another public relations crisis. The day before the U.S. midterm elections, Lebanon's *Al Shiraa* charged the United States with selling arms to Iran in exchange for the release of U.S. hostages held in Lebanon. Just as it did after the Hasenfus allegations, the White House disputed the charges or declined to comment.[5]

The two seemingly unrelated developments were connected, originating early in Reagan's first term. In 1981, the CIA, with Reagan's approval, provided covert aid to the Contras. After Congress prohibited Contra funding to overthrow the Nicaraguan government with the first Boland Amendment in 1982, Reagan ordered National Security Advisor Robert C. McFarlane to "keep the Contras together body and soul." The United States persuaded its ally Saudi Arabia to contribute to the Contra cause, aid that totaled $1 million a month for two years. McFarlane appointed his subordinate Lieutenant Colonel Oliver North to help with the effort. North assisted the Contras by raising money, advising them on military tactics and strategy, and obtaining arms through retired U.S. military personnel.[6] When confronted with *Miami Herald*, *Washington Post*, and *New York Times* reports of North's activities in 1985, North and McFarlane altered documents and then McFarlane lied to Congress.[7]

During Reagan's second term, the illegal Contra aid scheme merged with an effort to release U.S. hostages held in Lebanon and involved more illegal activity. In its simplest terms, the United States traded arms to Iran in exchange for the Iranians persuading Hezbollah to release the seven U.S. hostages taken in Lebanon. The hostages so preoccupied the president, his biographer H. W. Brands contends, that "no matter what else he was working on, Reagan never forgot" them. For Iran, the desperately needed arms aided its war against Iraq. The scheme violated the Arms Export Control Act, which prohibited arms transfer to Iran without presidential approval and congressional notice. Although Reagan gave permission, the administration did not inform Congress. The scheme also went against the United States' professed neutrality in the Iran-Iraq War. In the initial phase, Israel served as go-between by providing Iran with arms from its own stockpiles. Israel wanted to support Iranian moderates to offset its closer neighbor, Iraq. Later, the United States sold arms directly to Iran. Because there were no more congressionally approved Contra funds, in early 1986 the United States sold the weapons at inflated prices. The extra funds were channeled into Swiss bank accounts for the Contras. Oliver North served as the U.S. point person. While Poindexter claimed that Reagan was not informed about this diversion scheme, North argued the contrary. Despite multiple weapons shipments, only three U.S. hostages were released,[8] and three more were taken in what Secretary of State Shultz frustratingly referred to as a "hostage bazaar."[9]

For a week after the *Al Shiraa* revelations, the White House denied the accusations. Finally, in a November 13, 1986, address to the nation, Reagan admitted the selling of arms. He continued, however, to deny that the activities were illegal or that there was an exchange for U.S. hostages. As the president argued, "The actions I authorized were, and continue to be, in full compliance with Federal law." He was adamant. "We did not—repeat—did not trade weapons or anything else for hostages, nor will we."[10] Meanwhile, Attorney General

Edwin Meese offered to investigate the matter. Many NSC staffers then destroyed evidence. North allegedly shredded a stack eighteen inches high.[11] North also doctored documents and told his assistant "to prepare new documents to replace the originals."[12] During a November 25 press conference, Reagan told the American people he was not "fully informed" about the venture. He also revealed that he had fired North and that Poindexter had resigned.[13] After the president's departure, Attorney General Meese clarified: "The only persons in the United States government that knew precisely about this—the only person—was Lieutenant Colonel North. Admiral Poindexter did know that something of this nature was occurring but he did not look into it further."[14] With this, the White House began its campaign to isolate North as a rogue agent who acted without higher-ups' knowledge.[15]

The Iran-Contra revelations prompted several investigations. In December 1986, Reagan asked former senator John Tower, former national security advisor Brent Scowcroft, and former U.S. senator and secretary of state Edmund Muskie to look into the matter. The Justice Department appointed retired federal judge Lawrence E. Walsh as special prosecutor, and the Senate initiated an investigation. Congress held joint Senate-House hearings into the matter, but the exercise was limited in scope. With no appetite for possible impeachment proceedings, Congress decided not to focus on Reagan's potentially illegal activities. Congress also gave itself a ten-month deadline for its work to avoid spillover into the 1988 campaign season.[16]

Casey's Funeral

In identifying the problem for the U.S. government and the church, many conservative Catholics echoed a common refrain: Maryknoll. To them, Catholic William Casey and former Catholic Oliver North were model citizens and Christians because they took whatever actions were necessary to combat the Sandinista government's alleged persecution of religion and to beat back communism in the Western Hemisphere. True Catholics were anticommunists, in contrast to Maryknollers, who promoted liberation theology and played a leadership role in the protest movement against U.S.–Central America policy. As the Iran-Contra scandal unfolded, a familiar cast of characters defended the administration and critiqued Maryknoll: Catholics Phyllis Schlafly, Henry Hyde, Patrick Buchanan, and Fr. Enrique Rueda.

Public focus centered on North because CIA Director William Casey's death largely removed him from scrutiny. In December 1986, Casey collapsed from a seizure. He resigned two months later and died in May 1987. Just hours before Casey's death, Congress learned from retired Air Force Major General Richard V. Secord that he and Casey discussed the plan to obtain illegal arms for the Contras.[17]

Casey masterminded many of the efforts and directed North. In 1984, worried about an end to congressional funding, Casey advised McFarlane to "explore funding alternatives with the Israelis and perhaps others." Casey also suggested creating a "foundation" for nongovernment funds.[18] He pledged to the Contras that aid would continue, and he, along with Duane "Dewey" Clarridge, presented North as their U.S. contact in July 1984. The CIA director also recommended that Secord and Contra leader Adolfo Calero meet. North arranged the encounter and Secord subsequently organized three arms shipments in early 1985.[19] Finally, Casey ordered the CIA Central America Task Force chief to arrange for private funding to the Catholic Church after Congress members worried that discovery of CIA money would compromise Archbishop Obando's standing in Nicaragua. North sent private donor money to the church through the Heritage Foundation, and Obando tapped into a CIA- and Contra-controlled Cayman bank account.[20]

Although Casey could not answer questions before Congress, his funeral spoke volumes about his dedication to the Contra cause. In lieu of flowers, the family asked that donations be made to the "William J. Casey Fund for the Nicaraguan Freedom Fighters."[21] Mourners included Contra leaders Adolfo Calero and General Enrique Bermúdez, former cabinet members, Ronald and Nancy Reagan, and Richard Nixon.[22] As one (Catholic) reporter wryly observed, "The only touch absent at the funeral was a platoon of Contras serving as pallbearers and firing a 21-gun—CIA supplied—salute at the cemetery."[23]

Without the ability to confront Casey, his funeral became a forum for debates over his actions, and it underscored tensions among Catholics over Reagan's Contra policy. Casey and the funeral officiant, Bishop John McGann of Rockville Centre, New York, held contrasting positions. McGann set the tone for a funeral focused on U.S.-Nicaragua policy when he supplied reporters with a one-paragraph statement deploring U.S. Contra aid as causing the "violence wrought in Central America."[24] The bishop believed he needed to say something because otherwise people might conclude he no longer opposed U.S. support for the Contras.[25] McGann knew Casey well. He described the former CIA director, a man he "respected," as a "dedicated public servant." McGann linked Casey's faith to his actions as CIA chief: "Given the world as he saw it, Bill was seeking to do what was best for the United States and the freedom that allowed him to worship God openly as a Catholic." Yet the friends had a "fundamental disagreement" over U.S.-Nicaragua policy. As McGann admitted,

"Bill must have thought us bishops blind to the potential for a Communist threat in this hemisphere as we opposed and continue to oppose the violence wrought in Central America by support of the Contras."[26]

Since the 1960s McGann had disagreed with U.S. military interventions abroad,[27] and more recently, he encouraged Catholics to oppose U.S.–Central America policy. In anticipation of the July 1983 El Salvador certification, Mc-Gann urged his flock to contact their elected representatives, expressing their opposition to military aid and pushing Congress to work toward dialogue, a ceasefire, and a negotiated settlement. The issue was also personal. Murdered Maryknollers Maura Clarke and Ita Ford were from nearby Brooklyn, and Clarke's mother and sister lived on Long Island. The diocese also saw an influx of "nearly forty thousand Salvadoran refugees." Yet a voice against certification was more than a tribute to the murdered churchwomen and Archbishop Romero; McGann urged Catholics "to respond to the cry of the poor and oppressed of El Salvador by raising our voices." As he argued, "to remain silent" in the midst of recertification "dishonors the memory of all of the martyrs of El Salvador, and serves only to fuel the violence and hatred consuming that country and its people."[28]

In contrast to McGann, Jeane Kirkpatrick, Casey's friend and former UN ambassador, stressed Casey's faith. As she noted, Casey "was a God-fearing man, and he knew that the beginning of wisdom is the fear of the Lord; before Whom, one firmly believes, those who struggle against the totalitarians will confidently appear."[29] Indirectly responding to McGann—and her only reference to U.S.-Nicaragua policy—Kirkpatrick argued Casey's actions were legal. "Supporting Nicaragua's freedom fighters had a special priority for him, no question about it. But that had no more priority than law."[30] For her defense of Casey, Kirkpatrick received a standing ovation, a rare occurrence during Mass.[31] She also earned the title "St. Jeane" from the National Review, an unusual moniker for a non-Catholic.[32]

The funeral took on a life of its own as Catholics tussled over the propriety of McGann's homily. Washington Post columnist Colman McCarthy applauded the bishop's comments as "refreshing in their candor" and "not out of place." After all, McCarthy charged, "this was the funeral of a man who advocated violence as governmental policy and was under investigation for possible violations of the law in carrying out that policy." If "village priests" in Nicaragua could speak about U.S. policy "at the funerals of women and children murdered by the Contras, it can be preached too at the funerals of the Caseys who sanction the killing." The divide was about more than U.S. Cold War policy; McCarthy saw himself as a different kind of Catholic. He critiqued Casey's "old way" of Catholicism, in which "bishops built schools and hospitals, not moral cases," and he condemned "the dated anticommunist obsessions that drive the William Caseys to fund thugs in Nicaragua."[33]

While to McCarthy the situation demanded remarks like McGann's, to Catholic feminist scholar Phyllis Zagano the bishop was grandstanding. McGann, "an unknown bishop," raked Casey, a "senior citizen" and "unparalleled civil servant," through the mud over the Vietnam War, nuclear deterrence, and the Contras. Even worse, McGann "was fundamentally wrong," Zagano charged. He misread the bishops' statement on Nicaragua while claiming Casey misunderstood it. McGann "tongue-lashed a dead man in front of his wife, family, friends and, not incidentally, his President." Zagano's condemnation included a broader critique of priestly power. McGann's move was typical "in the United States, where bishops are silent about pederasty and pornography in their own institutions, and where good old boys can still get parishes independent of their emotional or professional status."[34] Her jab highlighted the complex fault lines among Catholics; both a feminist like Zagano and an antifeminist like Phyllis Schlafly supported U.S. Contra policy.

Zagano's challenge for the bishops to look inward was more insightful than her readers were likely aware. By the time of her writing, U.S. bishops knew of serial abusive priests. In October 1985, Louisiana's Gilbert Gauthe entered a plea deal for crimes involving the molestation of at least thirty-seven children, though "depositions and psychiatrists' reports" put the number in the hundreds. He became the first U.S. priest indicted for multiple crimes of abuse. Also that year, "a church bureaucrat, a lawyer and a psychiatrist" drafted a ninety-two-page report outlining how to deal with abuse allegations, advising the establishment of "committees to aggressively prevent abuse," and warning that left unchecked, the church would face hundreds of abusive priests and legal settlements of $1 billion. Their prediction was too low. The bishops ignored the report.[35] And it was not just the U.S. church turning a deaf ear and a blind eye, as Catholics later learned. The Congregation for the Doctrine of the Faith, with Cardinal Ratzinger (later Pope Benedict) as head, disciplined theologians, not abusers. From the Vatican's perspective, the real danger was liberation theology.[36]

The controversy over Casey did not end with his burial; it spilled over into a Beverly Hills memorial service for the former CIA director. Two months after the New York funeral, the pastor of the Church of the Good Shepherd stressed that he would celebrate "a purely spiritual ceremony instead." He canceled planned eulogies by the Los Angeles County supervisor and a local television news commentator. He also noted that the church would distribute a disclaimer to attendees that the Catholic Church did not associate itself with the service's sponsors,[37] which included an array of conservative groups from the California Republican Assembly and Voice of Americanism to the Hungarian Freedom Fighters Federation, Junta Patriotica Cubana, and Cruzada Anticomunista.[38] The priest acted because the planned services conflicted with the U.S. bishops' resolution calling Contra aid immoral. Despite his best efforts, the service still carried political overtones as Contra aid opponents held a prayer vigil outside the church.[39]

Even in death, Casey kept the Contra cause alive with the Freedom Fighters Fund. One Catholic contributed because of McGann. As he explained in a letter to Reagan, "I'm a Catholic, but Bishop McGann certainly didn't speak for me when he condemned aid to the Contras at William Casey's funeral service." He asked the president to "forward" his ten-dollar check to the fund.[40] Casey's wife Sophia presented the Contras with $140,000 in December 1987 to build a rehabilitation center for wounded Contras "at an undisclosed location in Central America." According to Sophia, most people gave ten or fifteen dollars, although a few, such as former president Nixon, contributed larger amounts.[41] In 1988, the fund received $45,000; in 1989, it saw a drastic reduction, which Sophia Casey believed was the result of the Central America peace process.[42]

Oliver North

While memorials to Casey exposed Catholics' divided views on U.S.–Central America policy, it was Oliver North who provoked a longer discussion about morality, Catholicism, and foreign policy. On May 5, 1987, the day before William Casey died, the Iran-Contra hearings, convened by the House Select Committee to Investigate Covert Arms Transactions with Iran and the Senate Select Committee on Secret Military Assistance to Iran and the Nicaraguan Opposition, began. The most anticipated and controversial witness during the forty-one days of hearings was Oliver North.

The hearings catapulted North into a darling of the Right. Clad in his Marine uniform, the Vietnam veteran defended his actions as necessary and patriotic. Testifying under immunity, North insisted that many in the White House were intimately acquainted with his actions. He was not a rogue agent; he followed orders. He named CIA Director Casey, National Security Advisors Poindexter and McFarlane, Assistant Secretary of State for Inter-American Affairs Elliott Abrams, head of the CIA's Central America Task Force Fiers, and the Joint Chiefs of Staff representative on the Restricted Inter-Agency Group on Latin America, Vice Admiral Arthur Moreau. North claimed his efforts were also "fairly well-known" to Secretary of State Shultz, Secretary of Defense Weinberger, and Chairman of the Joint Chiefs of Staff General John W. Vessey Jr.[43]

To Contra supporters, North became a sacrificial lamb. Television networks carried his six-day July testimony live, interrupting regularly scheduled daytime soap operas.[44] To stress North's public support, his lawyer placed some of the fifty thousand telegrams and letters North received beside him at the witness table.[45] "Olliemania" swept the country, with people even proposing that the lieutenant colonel run for president.[46] Others rushed to barbershops for "Ollie North" haircuts.[47]

Phyllis Schlafly was among those who saw North as a hero who should be thanked because he tried to stop communism's spread. She encouraged her Eagle Forum members to "spread the truth about Nicaragua" to family and friends with the aid of Eagle Forum videos.[48] One video featured a "super speech" by Robert Reilly, former White House Catholic liaison, and Oliver North's "famous SLIDE SHOW" that he used to solicit Contra contributions. For a tax-deductible donation of eighty-seven dollars, Eagles could obtain videos in tribute to Ollie—"our Man of '87."[49]

Other conservative Catholics repeatedly referred to North as a patriot and model Christian whose behavior was "moral." North's actions to stop communism were so important, Henry Hyde alleged, that the "moral dilemma" North faced was similar to Truman's decision to drop the atomic bomb. As North noted and Hyde agreed, the choice was "Lies or Lives."[50] In admitting he lied to Congress, North argued, "I want you to know that lying does not come easy to me . . . but I think we all had to weigh in the balance the difference between lives and lies."[51] Patrick Buchanan, who left his post as White House communications director earlier that spring,[52] insisted that Congress placed North, the "patriotic son of the republic," in a "moral dilemma" through its own "immoral act": the Boland Amendment. North, a "genuinely moral man," possessed a "faith deeply rooted in Christian tradition," while his congressional questioners—"pharisees"—were without it. As Buchanan contended, "In a single week, Ollie not only put God and country and the Constitution, and all the splendid values he represents, back on the side of the president and the Nicaraguan Resistance; he held up a mirror to the ugly face of the Inquisition."[53]

Both Hyde and Buchanan used a Catholic moral framework to justify North's actions. North was a model citizen and Christian because he employed whatever means necessary to fight communism, the greatest evil. Buchanan chastised those who expressed "moral horror over" North's shredding of documents as "4,000 unborn children are daily shredded in the abortuaries [*sic*] of the United States."[54] Buchanan charged Contra opponents with caring more about shredded documents than fetuses. But to North's opponents, the issue was destruction of government records that revealed illegal government action.

Likewise, Hyde wondered why there was so little support for the Marine, yet applause for those who engaged in civil disobedience to protest other aspects of U.S. foreign policy. North was the exemplar, not those who "trespass on military installations, splash animal blood on draft records, illegally picket within 500 feet of the South African Embassy, conduct sit-ins to obstruct C.I.A. university recruitment, and deliberately violate our immigration laws to provide sanctuary to a chosen few."[55] Several of Hyde's examples involved Catholics whose faith inspired their actions. His mention of military installations likely referred to the Plowshares movement, pouring animal blood on draft files harkened back to the dozens of Catholic antiwar draft office invasions that followed Catonsville, and his final example referred to the sanctuary movement. Like Buchanan, Hyde highlighted how Catholics divided over an array of domestic social concerns and foreign policy matters. According to Buchanan, these were not just disagreements over Central America but were symptomatic of how "Americans of Left and Right no longer share the same religion, the same values, the same codes of morality; we only inhabit the same piece of land."[56]

To Enrique Rueda, North's case revealed not a Right-Left problem but true, traditional Catholics versus impostors. As Rueda saw it, North defended the "beleaguered Nicaraguan people." U.S. Catholics and Nicaraguans, especially those "persecuted for their religious or political beliefs," should be thankful. North's appeal lay in his stance against "liberals" in Congress and his ability to "turn the tables" regarding Contra funding. And North's charm extended beyond Contra funding. Rueda saw support for North as hope that traditional Catholicism would prevail. As Rueda explained, North "has come to represent the very antithesis of the modern spirit," "in which agnosticism prevails and the total certainty of faith is viewed with suspicion." To Rueda, North proudly defended his actions without equivocation. In this respect, "our people's reaction to Oliver North's testimony gives me hope that eventually *Roman* Catholic Orthodoxy—yes, *unchanging* Catholic orthodoxy—will triumph over the Modernism of the *American* Catholic Church."[57] Oliver North was a hero and a sign of hope that traditional Catholicism would overcome modernist decay in the United States.

Rueda was not the only one to associate North with conservative Catholics. Nicaragua's minister of culture Father Ernesto Cardenal derisively linked North to an apparition of the Virgin Mary. In May 1980, Nicaraguan campesino

Bernardo Martínez reported the vision; she instructed him to pray the rosary and use the Bible for reflection.[58] Pilgrims by the thousands flocked to Cuapa on May 8, 1981, to commemorate a year since Martínez's first Marian sighting.[59]

Nicaraguan Catholic reactions to the apparitions fell along familiar lines. Both Bishop Pablo Antonio Vega and Archbishop Obando's decision to celebrate Mass at the site suggested church endorsement.[60] Beginning in April 1981, the opposition newspaper *La Prensa* ran articles promoting the vision as a miracle and a sign that "change" was afoot in the country, implying that God was on Sandinista opponents' side.[61] The press coverage coincided with organized pilgrimages to Cuapa. In December 1982, Bishop Vega declared Cuapa a Marian sanctuary.[62] But critics charged *La Prensa* with ulterior motives; the paper was just trying to aid conservative Catholics' cause against the so-called people's church. As Jesuit James Brockman explained, "In general, political and ecclesiastical conservatives tend to favor the Cuapa devotion. Persons sympathetic to the Sandinista revolution and liberation theology are more inclined to be skeptical of, or even opposed to, the whole development."[63]

Controversy resurfaced when Martínez reported another appearance. In March 1987 he told Bishop Bosco Vivas, an Obando aide, that under the name "Virgin of Victories," Mary instructed him to pray the rosary and burn Sandinista books because they were "agents of Satan." Unlike in the 1980 visions, the Virgin did not command general prayers; she commented on Nicaragua's political situation. In response, conservative Catholics burned books by Marxist authors or those they considered to be. The Contras' radio stations in Honduras and El Salvador proclaimed that "the Virgin wants Bernardo to pass her message on to us: 'Suffering people of Nicaragua, you will soon receive a new life, full of joy.'"[64]

Catholics' attempts to claim the apparitions for the Contra cause both reflected and exacerbated tensions over Catholicism's role in U.S. and Nicaraguan political debates. Bishop Vega's endorsement took on added significance as the Contra war heated up and tensions between some members of the church hierarchy and the Sandinista government increased. Vega, like Obando, was one of the few major opposition voices in Nicaragua. The Nicaraguan government exiled Vega in July 1986 for his seeming defense of the Contras. At a Heritage Foundation event in Washington, DC, earlier that year, Vega appeared alongside Contra leaders and charged the Sandinista government with killing three priests. He admitted the claim was untrue after returning to Nicaragua.[65] In the United States, a 1987 *Wanderer* advertisement for a book about the vision stressed that "the exiled Bishop Vega" had given the "imprimatur."[66] To Nicaraguan and U.S. Catholics, Vega's approval of the apparitions implied that Mary sided with Sandinista opponents. But Minister of Culture Ernesto Cardenal mockingly referred to the apparition as "Our Lady of Oliver North" while another commentator labeled the devotion "St. Mary of the Contras."[67]

Maryknoll in Contra Debates

Conservative Catholics shared Republicans' desire to defend the president and the Contra program. They argued the Iran-Contra hearings were a sham and Congress was at fault for what transpired. There was no legal issue or constitutional crisis; Congress was just playing politics.[68] Buchanan characterized the hearings as a failed coup to oust Reagan from the White House.[69] Schlafly contended that the hearings' purpose was not to determine what happened but for "liberal" Congress members "to embarrass" Reagan and end Contra aid.[70]

Hyde did more than talk; he used his committee position to stand up for North and others. Hyde mocked the charges against Richard Secord, calling them "the high crime of ambiguity of intention."[71] When Democrats accused Poindexter of lying, Hyde defended him for an hour. Likewise, Hyde cited Thomas Jefferson in support of Oliver North's lies. As Hyde claimed, Jefferson stated that "a strict adherence to the written law is doubtless one of the high duties of a good citizen but it is not the highest." A decade later, Hyde's view of lying was different when he served as chief prosecutor in the impeachment trial for President William J. Clinton.[72]

Conservative Catholics also differed from the typical Republican line by blaming their old nemesis: O'Neill and Maryknoll. As Schlafly argued, Congress, especially Tip O'Neill, was guilty of denying aid, which forced the administration to find other ways to fund the Contras.[73] Hyde charged Maryknollers and O'Neill with responsibility for Iran-Contra. As he frustratingly announced during the questioning of Alan Fiers, "I don't know how you deal with somebody who feels that way or who gets their intelligence from the Maryknoll nuns on Central America."[74] Hyde focused on the Maryknoll Sisters' influence on O'Neill, just as he did during Contra debates in 1986.

The O'Neill-Maryknoll connection was just the tip of the iceberg, as Michael Novak charged years earlier. The sisters' influence on the former Speaker was a foreign policy problem, according to Hyde. In "Liberation Theology and American Foreign Policy," written for *Crisis*, Hyde warned of liberation theology and Maryknoll. In a phrase that sounded like it came from Senator Jeremiah Denton's 1983 hearing, *Marxism and Christianity in Revolutionary Central America*, Hyde urged policymakers to examine the often overlooked role of "radical elements in the Catholic Church" in betraying the Nicaraguan revolution. In particular, he argued Marxists used Christianity for their own ends through the guise of liberation theology. Hyde outlined how key Catholics, especially priests who supported liberation theology (such as Miguel d'Escoto) became key players in the Sandinista government. As Hyde pointed out, d'Escoto was a member of Maryknoll, the largest U.S. producer of liberation theology works through its publishing house, Orbis. Liberation theology's danger was real, Hyde asserted, because of "its virulent anticapitalist, anti-U.S., pro-Marxist bias." Echoing U.S. ambassador to the OAS Middendorf, Hyde noted that although there were "many dissimilarities," some liberationists shared the view of "Khomeini's Islamic fundamentalists," who regarded the United States as "the Great Satan" and justified violence in response. "Liberation theology has serious consequences inasmuch as it is now being adroitly exploited by enthusiasts such as Fidel Castro and the Sandinistas as a means of solidifying and exporting their revolutions. It exercises real influence over the imagination of Christians in this hemisphere." Lest Americans thought liberation theology was merely a Latin American or Catholic problem, Hyde stressed how the Maryknoll Sisters persuaded former Speaker Tip O'Neill.[75]

Hyde was not the only Catholic to posit that without Maryknollers' sway over O'Neill, there would have been no Iran-Contra. As one Catholic woman wrote to the *Pilot*, the Boston archdiocesan newspaper, "Maryknoll is now filled with heretical, left-wing friends of Communism. There is never a mention of their loyalty to our Holy Father or to the true faith, Catholicism." Yet O'Neill "took his advice" from Maryknoll, and as the reader alleged, "it showed in his politics." She charged that the former speaker and Senator Ted Kennedy—Massachusetts representatives—"have surely prevented much good that could have been done toward helping the brave men called the Contras. It would have prevented the useless Iran-Contra investigation."[76]

Hyde continued to defend the White House, even as the joint Iran-Contra committee did not. The majority report, signed by all Democratic and three Republican committee members, concluded that "the ultimate responsibility" rested with Reagan, given his constitutional duty to ensure that the laws were faithfully executed. As the committee argued, Reagan "created or at least tolerated an environment where those who did know of the diversion believed with certainty that they were carrying out the President's policies." Reagan should have known what his national security advisors were doing. Among other presidential actions or inactions, the committee criticized his failure to condemn staffers who shredded documents, lied, and concealed their actions, despite public knowledge of these activities. Yet even with these criticisms, the report failed to say what the president knew about the venture.[77]

Consistent with Hyde's condemnation of O'Neill, he and other Republicans pointed to Congress. In the minority report, Republicans concluded that the actions were not illegal, or even a "coverup," but "mistakes in judgment." A "substantial number of the mistakes . . . resulted directly from an ongoing state of political guerrilla warfare over foreign policy between the legislative and executive branches."[78] Hyde and Richard Cheney (R-WY), more than other members of the minority, prepared and publicized the report.[79] The Iran-Contra scandal made the White House less aggressive in challenging opponents, but not Hyde. Hyde's stature as an unofficial government spokesperson for the conservative Catholic viewpoint grew as conservative Catholics left the White House through resignation or death.

While conservative Catholics praised North as the epitome of patriotism, other Catholics saw him as representative of the immoral U.S. foreign policy they worked to counteract. Quest for Peace strove to match U.S. funding for the Contras dollar-for-dollar with its "Oliver North Reparations Shipment." During a lunch break in North's July 1987 testimony, Quest for Peace held a rally across from the Capitol and announced its plans to send a twenty-foot cargo container to Nicaragua. The group worked with over four hundred organizations to collect medical supplies, clothing, and other humanitarian goods.[80] As Iowa senator Thomas Harkin (D), a Catholic, noted, the group was sending "clothing, not uniforms, bandages not bullets, aspirin not ammunition, and Bibles not assassination manuals." Columnist Colman McCarthy contrasted the efforts of Quest for Peace with those of North, "a White House gun-runner who lies and takes the classic I-followed-orders defense, believes that giving money to mercenaries who burn villages, rape women and murder children is the way to peace in Nicaragua." As organizer of Quest for Peace Jesuit William Callahan explained in reference to North: "We don't need a shredder to 'clean up' the program. We don't need to lie about what we are doing."[81]

Instead of attacking North, other Catholic Contra aid opponents promoted Maryknollers as the alternative. Representative James J. Howard of New Jersey explained that all the "talk about heroes" in the Iran-Contra hearings ignored true acts of heroism in Nicaragua. To illustrate his point, the Catholic inserted into the *Congressional Record* a New York *Daily News* article, in which Jimmy Breslin contrasted North's view of Nicaragua with that of Maryknoller Dan Driscoll. As Breslin watched North testify on television, he spoke to Driscoll. On the phone from Managua, Driscoll said he was attending a funeral for Brother Thomas. While he was traveling in a van, a Contra-planted landmine killed Thomas and a woman and injured a priest and another woman. Breslin recalled a comment Driscoll made during McFarlane's testimony: "America says we have to stop communism and all I'm doing is burying Catholics."[82] To Driscoll, the U.S. government and the Contras, not the Nicaraguan government, were Catholics' enemy. In comparing Driscoll with North, Breslin invited readers to question U.S. policy's life-and-death implications for Nicaraguans and U.S. missionaries.

Maryknoll readers shared this sense of Maryknollers as the true heroes. For a woman in St. Petersburg, Maryknoll told "the whole truth," in contrast to the Reagan administration's "disinformation," which, she contended, "borders on criminality."[83] A priest living in Columbia Falls, Montana, wrote in 1987, "Given the false propaganda on the Contras that has been turned loose on the American public in the past six years, you do a fine job of presenting the true story with tactful delicacy."[84] A woman from Chicago noted that this was Maryknoll's purpose. "Maryknoll has a duty and obligation to prod our consciences and those of our elected servants in Washington who prefer to support a terrorist band preying on poor peasants in an effort to overthrow a legally constituted government, and who spend funds on this instead of on caring for our own poor and homeless."[85] Several readers praised Maryknoll's "courage" in opposing U.S. support for the Contras.[86]

On the other hand, Iran-Contra prompted some Catholics to sever their ties with Maryknoll because, they concluded, the congregation was no longer truly Catholic.[87] One Michigan reader insisted that Maryknoll engaged in "revolutionary politics."[88] Some contended the community had lost "sight of true Catholicism" and been "duped" by communists.[89] A Nicaraguan Catholic alleged Maryknoll misused Christian symbols to bring Catholics to the Sandinista cause. "What outrages me is the constant meddling of your order in my country's affairs and your hypocritical use of Christian symbols and words to influence U.S. Catholic opinion in favor of a group of communists who betrayed their own people."[90] These readers' request that Maryknoll remove their names from the rolls was not simply about ending mail; it broke a relationship. Anyone who contributed to Maryknoll, no matter the amount, received the magazine.

Given that *Maryknoll* subscribers saw themselves as sharing the congregation's endeavors, debates turned personal. A reader from Downers Grove, Illinois, asked that Maryknoll remove his name because he opposed the congregation's promotion of liberation theology and "often virulent, anti-U.S. line." To "counter" these Maryknoll tendencies, he donated $100 to the Contras.[91] In response, a woman from Scottsdale reported she was increasing "her normal nominal donation." "He made me mad," she wrote. "Keep up the good work."[92] The timing of these letters suggested the Iran-Contra revelations strengthened some Catholics' ties to Maryknoll, pushed others with doubts to finally leave, and revealed that Catholics' views of Maryknoll and U.S.– Central America policy continued to change, and harden, over the course of Reagan's presidency.

It was not just U.S. Catholics that contrasted Maryknollers with architects of Reagan's Contra policy. A few weeks after the Iran-Contra hearings ended, Senate Minority Leader Bob Dole visited Nicaragua. While there, Dole criticized the government's jailing of two opposition lawyers for participating in a demonstration.[93] President Ortega responded by offering the two lawyers their freedom "in exchange for the liberty of the Catholic priest"—Maryknoller Roy Bourgeois—"who has been jailed because he was protesting against the U.S. policy toward Central America." Dole snapped back, "We don't do that in our country. You've got us mixed up with the Soviet Union."[94]

Nine months earlier, Bourgeois and two other priests were arrested for trespassing onto Hurlburt Field near Fort Walton Beach, Florida.[95] Twenty of the priests' companions protested legally outside. The group targeted the site after the *Washington Post* revealed seventy Contras were in the area for training.[96] Bourgeois, who went unaccounted for into the mountains of El Salvador in 1981, received a nine-month sentence.[97]

Upon hearing of the Dole-Ortega exchange, Bourgeois was shocked and gladdened. As he told a reporter, "The first thing I thought was, hey, the Nicaraguan people know I'm here." The Maryknoller saw a connection between his situation and that of the lawyers: "We are both prisoners of conscience."[98] Although the Nicaraguan government granted amnesty to the lawyers on September 8,[99] Bourgeois served his time.[100]

Bourgeois probably should not have been surprised that Ortega mentioned him, as two former Maryknollers kept the Nicaraguan government informed of U.S. developments. Darryl Hunt and Donald Casey founded the public affairs and consulting firm Agendas International in 1983. The two had known foreign minister Miguel d'Escoto for thirty years.[101] They assisted the Nicaraguan government at his request. For about $25,000 a month, Agendas International organized official trips and public appearances of Nicaraguan government representatives to the United States, assisted with speech writing, and prepared officials for media appearances, including press conferences.[102] The organization also sent Nicaraguan officials an analysis of U.S. media coverage, including press clippings from twenty-two newspapers and network news excerpts, along with recommendations for how Nicaragua should respond.[103] Agendas registered with the Department of Justice as an agent of the Nicaraguan government, as required by law.[104] In addition to Nicaragua's foreign minister being a fellow Maryknoller, Ortega's mention of Bourgeois likely grew out of Agendas' research and its knowledge that Maryknoll was a thorn in the White House's side. It also did not hurt Nicaraguan PR to remind Dole that even priests were protesting U.S. Contra policy.

White House versus Peace Efforts

Even as Congress held Iran-Contra hearings, Reagan was still not ready to abandon the Contras. But the White House had a problem. The scandal not only raised doubts about administration policy but also damaged officials' credibility with Congress. As Republican senator David Durenberger (MN) remarked in reference to Elliott Abrams, who coordinated U.S.–Central America policy, "I wouldn't trust Elliott Abrams any farther than I could throw Oliver North." To address the problem, in July 1987 Reagan enlisted the help of former Republican congressman Tom Loeffler, friend of Speaker James Wright (D-TX) and an expert at wrangling southern Democrats. As the White House's special congressional liaison on Contra aid, Loeffler learned military aid was unwinnable in the House. Congress wanted diplomacy, but because Iran-Contra had damaged the president's credibility, Reagan could not be the architect of any peace proposal. Instead, Loeffler proposed a joint effort between the White House and Speaker Wright.[105]

About three weeks after North's testimony, the administration announced the Reagan-Wright plan. After a cease-fire, Soviet aid to the Nicaraguan government and U.S. military aid to the Contras would be suspended. There would be limits on foreign military advisors and military establishments; Nicaragua would end the state of emergency and restrictions on civil liberties. There would be a program of amnesty for the Contras and of reconciliation in Nicaragua. The announcement was the first the Contras heard of the plan. While publicly Reagan backed it, U.S. officials, including Abrams, tried to sabotage it. In reality, Loeffler's plan was designed partially in the hopes of spoiling Central Americans' peace attempts.[106]

The administration worried that an agreement without U.S. involvement would compromise Reagan's ability to secure Contra funding. As Weinberger remarked at a National Security Planning Group meeting in May 1986, "We just have to make sure that the negotiations do not get out of our control." He continued, "We need to prevent them . . . signing an agreement or we will never get anything out of Congress."[107] As the White House saw it, the United States needed to dictate the terms of any agreement between the Contras and the Sandinistas.

The White House plan backfired. Two days after the announcement of the Reagan-Wright plan, the Central American presidents signed a plan of their own.[108] Under Esquipulas II, the presidents of Costa Rica, Honduras, El Salvador, Nicaragua, and Guatemala agreed to end outside assistance to insurgents and their territories' use for military action against their neighbors. They pledged to work toward cease-fires, dialogue, and democratization.[109] Esquipulas contained the main ideas of the February 1987 Arias Accords proposed by Costa Rican president Óscar Arias Sánchez. Arias objected to his country's support for the Contras, including an airstrip for their resupply and camps. The Contras, in Arias's view, made war in the region more likely and provided a pretext for the Sandinistas to restrict civil liberties and align themselves with Cuba and the Soviet Union.[110]

The Reagan administration undercut the Central Americans' agreement. Reagan recorded a message for Contra radio in late August. He questioned Esquipulas's call for a concurrent cease-fire and the Sandinista reinstatement of civil liberties. He expressed doubt that the Sandinistas would hold up their end of the bargain; simply put, they were not trustworthy. The administration also critiqued the agreement, expressed doubts to Central American leaders, and strong-armed Honduras into not complying. For its part, the State Department delayed $40 million in economic aid for Costa Rica and told Costa Rican officials aid was linked to their response to the peace process.[111]

Simultaneously, Wright and other Democrats worked to support the plan. Wright invited Arias to DC, separately met with Contra leaders and Ortega, and tried to persuade Cardinal Obando to mediate peace talks. The congressman's diplomatic activities irritated the White House.[112] At the same time, however, Wright got nonlethal aid for the Contras in the fall of 1987. The Speaker finagled House rules to add $3.5 million in nonlethal aid to a short continuing resolution, and in another short continuing resolution, an additional $3.2 million.[113]

In January 1988, the Sandinistas offered an olive branch. Ortega agreed to end the state of emergency, free "some political prisoners," and engage in direct talks with Contras, among other measures. But Ortega's position did not change Reagan's stance. Reagan requested $36 million for the Contras, including $3.6 million in military aid. He argued that only the Contras' presence would prompt Sandinista concessions. By contrast, Arias insisted Contra aid compromised the agreement's chances of succeeding.[114]

Reagan's request led to a close House vote that resurrected discussion of nuns' influence on Tip O'Neill. In early February 1988, Democrat Lindy Boggs was the only member of the Louisiana delegation to vote against Contra aid. Her vote was among "the most heavily lobbied and closely watched," according to the *Los Angeles Times*. In the twenty-four hours beforehand, the president, secretary of state, Contra leader Adolfo Calero, and both of Louisiana's senators called her, trying to persuade her to support aid.[115] Boggs also faced pressure from her governor, who flew to the Capitol and spoke against the Nicaraguan government, and from her local paper, which lambasted her for a previous vote against aid.[116]

Boggs said the Central Americans' peace plan convinced her,[117] but reporters suggested another reason: Tip O'Neill and nuns. To aid Democratic efforts, Boggs's old friend O'Neill contacted her, even though the former Speaker had retired more than a year before.[118] O'Neill talked about her constituency, which he said was largely disinterested in the issue because it was predominantly black. (O'Neill was evidentially unaware that the city of New Orleans had the largest population of black Catholics in the country.[119]) As a Catholic, like O'Neill, she should consider the morality of Contra aid. Maryknollers had informed him about what was happening in Central America.[120] After her vote, Boggs left the House chamber. She noticed sisters who had been lobbying against aid, approached the women, and gave each a hug. As the congresswoman remarked, "The Sisters are very persuasive."[121] In highlighting Boggs's ties to O'Neill and nuns, reporters reiterated the O'Neill-Maryknoll connection in U.S.-Nicaragua policy debates.

Conservative Catholics were quick to blame Maryknollers, and other religious, for the latest House defeat.[122] The *Wanderer* cited "Paracommunists" who had taken over the Democratic Party. As examples, the paper noted NETWORK, the lobby of women religious, as well as "a coalition of Catholic Religious groups—Jesuits, Franciscans, Dominicans, and of course Maryknollers."[123] For Enrique Rueda, the problem was bigger: the U.S. church—Maryknoll in particular—had become "an integral part of this cancer that threatens our hemisphere." Rueda outlined the ways U.S. Catholics were to blame for facilitating communism's growth. These included U.S. trained priests (namely "renegade priest" Miguel d'Escoto) who worked with the Sandinistas, the "lunatic fringe of the Quixote Center" (which sponsored Quest for Peace), *Maryknoll* magazine ("pro-Sandinista propaganda"), and a "well-developed national network of pro-Sandinista organizations centered in the churches" that sent money to Nicaragua to support the popular church.[124]

Boggs's no vote was not the end. The House voted down an alternative proposal in March, ending Reagan's chances for military funding that spring. The same month, the Sandinistas and the Contras agreed to a sixty-day cease-fire as part of the Sapoá accord.[125] Though to some the Sandinistas' move came as a shock, Nicaragua's faltering economy left the government with few options. Since 1986, the country had spent 55 percent of its budget on the war, and in 1988, the economy entered a "severe recession." Ortega saw peace as the only way to improve things. In response to the agreement, Congress passed $35.4 million for nonlethal Contra aid, children harmed by the war, and a commission to verify the Sapoá accord.[126]

For its part, the Reagan administration again tried to destroy peace efforts behind the scenes. Elliott Abrams told the Contras they should not sign the

final accord. There was disagreement among their ranks, but military commander Enrique Bermúdez agreed. He sabotaged the talks with the Sandinistas
in June 1988, believing it would bring more U.S. military aid.[127] He was wrong.

Evangelicals and North

As Nicaraguans made efforts toward peace, the Iran-Contra prosecutions
moved forward. The same month the Sandinistas and Contras agreed to a cease-
fire, North and Poindexter entered not guilty pleas to conspiracy, theft, and
fraud charges.[128] With North's criminal charges, the promotion of him as hero
resurfaced. Catholics were not the only ones who enthusiastically defended
North as a man acting on Christian principles. In anticipation of his criminal
trial, several evangelical groups organized petition drives asking Reagan for a
pardon. For a twenty-dollar donation, Concerned Women for America sold
color photos of North being sworn in before his congressional testimony. For
twenty-five dollars, Jerry Falwell offered an audiotape of North delivering his
"Freedom Message" at Liberty University. Though the groups said their goal
was to secure North's pardon, the timing also suggested opportunism. As sex
scandals rocked the world of televangelism, evangelicals needed a way to boost
their members and their coffers.[129]

The conservative Catholic-Protestant support for North reflected the interfaith push behind Reagan's Central America policy. Both Beverly LaHaye,
president of Concerned Women of America, and Jerry Falwell were among
the "private sector supporters" who attended a meeting with Reagan ahead
of the March 1986 congressional vote on Contra aid, as discussed in chapter 6.
LaHaye and Falwell joined Catholics, such as Paul Weyrich and Phyllis Schlafly,
in mobilizing public support for U.S.-Nicaragua policy.[130] Meetings such as
these demonstrated how support for U.S.–Central America policy fostered interreligious cooperation.

North's backing among conservative Catholics and Protestants was unsurprising, as he solicited both groups' assistance. North recruited anticommunist evangelical groups, such as Pat Robertson's Christian Broadcasting
Network, Friends of the Americas, the Gospel Crusade, the Christian Emergency Relief Team, and Trans World Missions.[131] He also worked with priests
who sided with the Contras. North arranged for the congressional testimony
of Old Roman Catholic priest and Contra payee Thomas Dowling, and for
Father Frederico Arguello, who was close to Cardinal Obando, to receive
$31,000.[132] North also organized a photo-op with President Reagan for Dowl-
ing and Arguello in June 1986.[133]

North's appeal was not only that he pushed Contra aid in the name of fighting communism but also that his faith played a role. White House colleagues noted how North's faith influenced his work. As Robert McFarlane observed, "Ollie did often make clear to me in conversation, as well as to peers on the staff, that prayer, and confidence in the fact that he was being led by the Holy Spirit, was very matter-of-fact with him. He always felt that what he was doing was justified because he was accountable to a higher authority." Another NSC colleague remarked, "I don't think there's any question he thought he was doing God's work at the NSC."[134] After disclosure of the arms-for-hostages scheme, family and friends cited North's faith as helping him through the ordeal. As his sister Patricia remarked in 1987, "His faith in the Lord is his backbone right now."[135] A priest who knew North in Vietnam offered a similar view: "One of the things that keeps him going is his faith."[136]

North's religious background, which included both Catholic and Protestant practice, added to his popularity. North was raised Catholic. His mother was a "devout Catholic" and though his father was not, he "dutifully attended Mass with the family." Larry, as he was known in the family, served as an altar boy from age six until his senior year of high school.[137] While at the Naval Academy, he attended daily Mass. During the early 1980s, he and his family were members of St. Anthony's in Falls Church, Virginia. Ironically, one of the parish priests at the time was J. Bryan Hehir, who served as the USCC's associate general secretary for international justice and peace.[138] He drew the ire of conservative Catholics for his role in obtaining the bishops' support for the return of the Panama Canal.

North increasingly moved away from Catholicism after an experience in 1978. He suffered from back and leg pain caused by a 1964 car accident and later aggravated in war. After Lieutenant Colonel John S. Grinalds, North's commanding officer at Camp Lejeune, prayed over his legs, North reported no pain upon standing up. At Grinalds's urging, North began attending services at a charismatic Anglican church. North and his wife later joined the Church of the Apostles and became active in prayer groups and the Officers' Christian Fellowship for born-again military. According to a member of the fellowship, North requested prayers for his family and for work "so he could come up with a proper solution that would glorify God and be proper for the country."[139]

Although colleagues, family, and friends agreed that faith was important to North, reporters described it inconsistently, leading Catholics and Protestants to see what they wished. In the first months after disclosure of the Iran-Contra affair, reporters classified North as Catholic.[140] In the summer of 1987, *Time* implied North was Protestant by describing his 1978 born-again experience, but noted, North "still considers himself a Roman Catholic."[141]

Despite his popularity, North was convicted of destroying documents, obstructing Congress, and accepting illegal gratuity.[142] Congress then debated whether to restore his $23,000-a-year Navy pension. A 1974 federal law prohibited pensions for persons "holding office under the United States" convicted of destroying government documents. North's supporters proposed changing the interpretation that a Navy position constituted "holding office."[143] Though many senators pretended the bill was "generic," they knew if passed it would restore North's pension.[144] There was no fooling Senator Howard M. Metzenbaum (D-OH), who called it "the Ollie North Pension Bill."[145]

As they had done during the Iran-Contra hearings, senators invoked the Maryknoll Sisters and Tip O'Neill during their wrangling over North's pension. Senator Fritz Hollings (D-SC) blamed the sisters for North's actions. As Hollings (a Lutheran) noted, O'Neill and Edward Boland "got all mixed up with the Maryknoll nuns," leading them to place an obstacle—a "little restriction" on spending—with the Boland Amendments. Reagan should have vetoed the bill, but he did not. Instead, a game developed between the legislative and executive branches. When the illegal activity was exposed, Hollings argued, the president did not tell the truth about what he knew. North was not a renegade; he acted "officially."[146] North's supporters carried the day and they knew it. At the close of the debate, the bill's sponsor, Jesse Helms (R-NC), defiantly proclaimed while waving the bill, "Ollie, this one's for you."[147]

In the latter part of Reagan's second term, Catholics and non-Catholics employed similar themes to defend U.S.-Nicaragua policy. They pinned responsibility for Iran-Contra on the Maryknoll Sisters, just as Reagan officials and many conservative Catholics had argued the four churchwomen brought rape and murder upon themselves in El Salvador. Henry Hyde, in particular, blamed the Maryknoll Sisters for influencing O'Neill, or rather, O'Neill for falling under their spell. Hyde argued that liberation theology corrupted the Catholic Church and posed a national security threat, and that Maryknollers were the key movers. While the Contra funding battle initially pitted Reagan against O'Neill and the sisters, after the Iran-Contra revelations conservative rhetoric shifted to blame Maryknollers for the administration's illegal activity. Maryknollers forced patriots like North to make difficult, but necessary, choices to protect the country and the Catholic Church from communism. North, not the Maryknoll Sisters, was doing God's work.

The White House may have agreed, but it did not amplify this new round of conservative arguments because, by 1987, the context had changed. There were fewer voices like Hyde's. Democrats controlled Congress, and key Catholic allies in the White House were gone. Patrick Buchanan was no longer calling the speech-writing shots or crafting the White House's message. Buchanan still maintained the same take-no-prisoners approach, but from an outsider's perch. Consequently, Catholic debates over Central America policy and the church spilled into new settings, namely former CIA Director Casey's funeral. The Reagan administration was also less aggressive in dealing with its critics on Central America because of Iran-Contra. Wading into conversation about Nicaragua meant raising the specter of the scheme.

Others factors played a role. Central Americans signed the Esquipulas Accords, and the 1988 presidential candidates were not eager to push the issue. The Democrats nominated a split ticket. While Massachusetts governor Michael Dukakis opposed Contra aid, his running mate, Texas senator Lloyd Bentsen supported the Contras.[148] Vice President Bush avoided the topic because he had "extensive knowledge" of Iran-Contra.[149] His campaign manager James Baker also believed the Contra issue was an unpopular one.[150]

The White House wanted to use the Contra issue to divide Democrats, but it was also wary of hurting Bush's election chances. In the summer of 1988, the White House asked Senate minority leader Bob Dole to introduce military aid. The hope was that the vote would expose fissures in the Democratic ticket, given Dukakis's and Bentsen's differing views on Contra aid. By having Dole introduce the measure and Reagan follow with his support, the White House could maintain some distance and reduce any potential damage to the nominee. But the Democrats did not take the bait. They countered with a bill for nonlethal aid, and military aid for the Contras failed yet again.[151] In September, Congress approved nonlethal aid.[152] Two months later, Bush beat Dukakis 426 to 112 in the Electoral College.[153] But even a new man in the White House did not remove Maryknollers from Central America debates.

CHAPTER 8

Déjà Vu

Jesuits and Maryknollers

Shortly after 1:00 a.m. on November 16, 1989, soldiers left their vehicles and approached the UCA, San Salvador's Jesuit university. Colonel Guillermo Alfredo Benavides had ordered them to murder those he called the guerrillas' "intellectual leaders"—Father Ignacio Ellacuría and other Jesuits—and to leave no witnesses. As the soldiers walked the grounds, the lieutenants pointed to the living quarters of the "terrorist priests." The soldiers rounded up five Jesuits, took them outside, forced them to lie down on the grass, and shot them in the back of the head. They then shot Elba and Celina Ramos, the priests' cook and her daughter, as they clutched one another. Upon discovering a sixth priest in the hallway, they shot him as well. The Jesuits—Ignacio Ellacuría, Segundo Montes, Ignacio Martin-Baró, Armando López, Juan Ramón Moreno, and Joaquin López y López—were scholars at the UCA. Before leaving, the soldiers burned computers and documents. They shot a portrait of Archbishop Romero, aiming straight through the heart, and one carried the guerrillas' weapons of choice: an AK-47. To frame the FMLN, the soldiers placed a sign near the bodies: "The FMLN executed the enemy spies. Victory or death, FMLN." Members of the elite Atlacatl Battalion—the U.S.-trained unit behind the massacre at el Mozote—carried out the gruesome act. This particular unit within Atlacatl, described as the "best" by a U.S. military advisor stationed in El Salvador, received "intensive training by the Green Berets" forty-eight hours beforehand.[1]

Four days later, Senator Barbara Mikulski (D-MD) characterized the murders as a wake-up call for a reevaluation of "our whole military aid package to El Salvador." Aid facilitated state violence. As she remarked on the Senate floor, "Let us view this situation as if those Jesuits were martyrs and, as in the past, all martyrs focus our attention on a greater evil." The greater evil was violence, particularly by the state. "It is just not the priests that are dying, it is not just the Maryknoll nuns that were killed a number of years ago, it is not just Archbishop Romero who was killed while saying Mass in a hospital chapel; since 1980, 70,000 deaths have occurred in El Salvador, mostly civilians and mostly by the army—ordinary people, *campesinos* who wanted to talk about land reform, mothers and fathers, social workers, teachers, nurses, farmers, people who just wanted to be able to live in their own country in dignity." In recalling the churchwomen, Mikulski used the two sets of murders—the churchwomen and the Jesuits—as bookends to show how the United States not only stayed engaged in El Salvador since 1980 but also exponentially increased its aid to the tune of over $1 million a day. The senator was incensed that "after ten years of American involvement and American aid, nothing constructive has happened."[2]

Though for many Americans the UCA murders came as a surprise because El Salvador was not typically front-page news, for Mikulski the debate was personal. She condemned the churchwomen's murders in 1980 and first visited El Salvador in 1981.[3] Upon her return she cosponsored legislation to end U.S. military aid. As she wrote to the Maryknoll Fathers and Brothers, "I cannot tell you how deeply I was moved—and outraged—by what I saw in Central America, and especially by what I heard from the Salvadorean refugees and members of the religious community." She continued to stay in close contact with the religious community, especially Maryknollers.[4]

Mikulski's remarks about the UCA murders had a familiar ring. Just as they did after the churchwomen's murders, liberal Catholics said the United States should not support a government that persecuted Catholics, whereas some conservative Catholics dismissed charges of religious persecution. Liberal Catholics pushed for an end to U.S. aid; conservatives argued this was no time to abandon an ally. Despite the constant comparisons between the Jesuit and churchwomen murders, as this chapter argues, there were noticeable shifts in language. Unlike the attacks on the churchwomen's victimhood, only a minority of conservative Catholics suggested the murdered Jesuits were Marxist collaborators. Conservative Catholics' concerns about liberation theology, the church's direction, and Maryknoll were also muted. The ground beneath conservative U.S. Catholics had shifted. The domestic context differed. Unlike the Reagan White House, the George H. W. Bush administration did not reflect conservative Catholic views or seek to insert itself into intra-Catholic debates over U.S.–Central America relations. Reagan fought Congress over his proposed Central America policy; Bush strove to avoid congressional confrontation on the issue. The global context also changed. The Cold War was ending, which meant liberation theology seemed less menacing. Despite these changes, in El Salvador, the state still regarded liberation theology as a national security threat and levels of violence harkened back to the early 1980s.

A New President

Eleven months before the Jesuits' murders, Bush was inaugurated. Although as Bush's campaign manager James Baker encouraged Bush to avoid Central America as an issue, as Bush's secretary of state, Baker made Nicaragua the administration's top priority. He saw it as a way for the new president to repair damaged relations between the executive and legislative branches. Without a united front at home, Baker believed, the United States could not claim Soviet involvement in Central America "was the greatest stumbling block to improved relations." Baker also saw the conflicts in Nicaragua and El Salvador as obstructing democracy's growth in Latin America.[5]

Baker's task was not easy. As House Speaker Jim Wright wrote to Bush shortly after his election, "This has been the most incapable issue of the last eight years. Also the most politically polarizing and personally divisive question on the entire agenda." Similarly, Baker—Reagan's chief of staff during his first term—noted, "No other foreign policy issue was so visceral or so polarizing. For much of the decade, it had been the Holy Grail of both the political left and the right."[6] In nineteen major votes on Contra aid in the 1983–1988 congresses, 70 percent of members maintained the same record. There was little wiggle room. Only a "few dozen House members" remained in the undecided camp, mostly southern Democrats.[7] The situation was unlikely to change, given that Democrats maintained control of Congress after the 1988 election. And, Baker knew from his conversations with both Republicans and Democrats that military aid for the Contras would not pass. The issue was also time-sensitive, as nonlethal Contra aid would expire at the end of March—ten weeks after Bush's inauguration.[8]

In contrast to the Reagan White House, the Bush administration attempted to work with Congress and Central Americans. As a peace offering, Baker responded to Henry Hyde's advocacy by appointing a Democrat who supported Contra aid, Bernie Aronson, as assistant secretary of state for inter-American affairs. Baker also saw the Esquipulas Accords as an opening for repairing damaged relations with Congress because neither Democrats nor Contra supporters could oppose elections. In early 1989, the Central American presidents declared that by February 25, 1990, the Sandinistas would hold presidential elections, and within ninety days, the Central American presidents would devise a plan for Contra demobilization. Unlike the Reagan administration, which tried to torpedo the Central American presidents' efforts, the Bush White House supported the peace agreement. After twenty-two days of congressional negotiations brokered by Baker, Bush signed the bipartisan accord on March 24. It provided for $50 million in nonlethal Contra aid "through the Nicaraguan elections, subject to congressional review in eight months." The administration would drop Reagan's aim to overthrow the Sandinistas and, instead, honor the election outcome. By reaching an agreement with Congress, the administration could pressure the Soviets to accept the Esquipulas Accords and get its allies to as well.[9] Representative David Bonior (D-MI), head of the Democrats' Central America Task Force, called the bipartisan agreement "a radical departure from the policy of the previous Administration."[10]

El Salvador

Things seemed to be moving toward a peaceful resolution in Nicaragua, but in neighboring El Salvador, violence returned to levels unseen since the early 1980s. Guerrillas assassinated key leaders, while Rightist forces attacked church workers. In early 1988, Archbishop Rivera and Lutheran bishop Medrado Gómez received death threats.[11] In one week at the end of 1988, four new death squads, including the Anticommunist Revolutionary Action of Extermination, announced their formation. The same week, the Lutheran Church's main office was bombed. The Anticommunist Hand of Central America proclaimed it would kill "churchwomen doing the work of the devil." The church aided refugees.[12] And it was not just death squads claiming church workers aided communists. The National Guardsmen convicted of murdering the churchwomen argued they deserved amnesty because "the assassinated nuns belonged to a leftist religious order which participated in terrorist plans." Their appeal was denied.[13]

Few in the United States noticed. Beginning in 1984, El Salvador virtually receded from U.S. headlines. After Duarte's election as president, convictions in the churchwomen's case, and the defeat of key congressional opponents, such as Michael Barnes and Clarence Long, Congress did not challenge Reagan's El Salvador policy. Except when guerrillas killed four Marines and two civilians in June 1985, El Salvador was largely out of the spotlight, as the

Reagan administration wanted. After a July 1985 House vote to suspend aid was routed 375–47, no member proposed El Salvador as an issue for the next three years. In 1986 and 1987, Reagan's aid requests won approval with little change.[14] For fiscal year 1987, U.S. aid surpassed what the Salvadoran government raised in revenue, a first in U.S. aid history.[15]

El Salvador was off the U.S. public's radar, but the U.S. embassy and the Jesuits recognized a problem. In early January before Bush was inaugurated, Ambassador William Walker cabled that violence "questions seriously" the U.S. line that the "human rights situation in El Salvador continues to move in a positive direction."[16] The same month, Jesuits, fearing the worst, took precautionary measures. Central American Provincial José María Tojeira asked U.S. Jesuits to "set up an emergency response network to help them survive this repression and continue their work for the Church." U.S. pressure helped when the White Warriors threatened to kill all Jesuits who did not leave El Salvador by July 1977. Tojeira and other Jesuits worried "repressive violence would increase in the months ahead." In an emergency, each network person would call and write to "three key people," such as the Salvadoran embassy or president, chairs of congressional committees concerned with El Salvador, and their own representatives.[17] The Jesuits recognized the precarious situation months before the UCA murders.

Concern increased when the Rightist ARENA party, which already controlled the legislature, won the presidency. ARENA's Alfredo Cristiani, from one of El Salvador's most powerful families, defeated incumbent Christian Democrat Duarte five days before Bush signed the bipartisan Nicaragua agreement. The presidency shifted from a centrist Notre Dame graduate to a Rightist Georgetown University alum. As a CIA intelligence report recognized, ARENA "worked hard to promote a new, moderate image" and specifically appealed to the business community and the rural poor. ARENA stressed Christian Democrats' inability to improve the economy and used "its own resources to bring goods and services" to rural areas. ARENA portrayed itself as the party of law and order, in contrast to Christian Democrats who failed to address Leftist violence.[18]

ARENA packaged itself differently, but not everyone was buying it. Although Cristiani represented ARENA's technocratic wing, death squad leader D'Aubuisson still played a major role. Designated party "president for life" in 1985, D'Aubuisson campaigned with Cristiani.[19] The party's theme song still referenced its violent anticommunist origins with the line, "El Salvador will be the tomb where the reds are buried."[20] Archbishop Rivera was skeptical. As the prelate remarked shortly after the election, "The true president is Major Roberto D'Aubuisson." Cristiani, Rivera predicted, "will depend on him and above all on his militias."[21] Given ARENA's control of both the legislature and the presidency, Rivera was not optimistic. The public face might have changed, but Rivera worried the power behind the throne was still the same.

Just as in the 1970s, members of the armed forces and Rightists accused church workers of communist ties. Tutela Legal, the archdiocesan human rights office, reported that Atlacatl Battalion members attacked a field hospital, killed five wounded guerrilla fighters and three medical workers, and then raped and killed a doctor and fourteen-year-old nurse. In response, ARENA and the military said Tutela Legal supported the FMLN.[22] After guerrillas assassinated the attorney general, Colonel Juan Orlando Zepeda blamed UCA's Jesuits. The commander of the First Brigade, later defense vice minister, held the UCA responsible for "planning strategies of the FMLN, being a refuge and a haven for terrorist leaders, and being accomplices in the April 19th assassination of the Attorney General."[23] Some priests joined the chorus, as they had in the days of Archbishop Romero. Members of the armed forces and ARENA used Father Fredy Delgado's *The Popular Church Was Born in El Salvador* to argue that Marxists co-opted church groups and that Jesuits were behind the efforts.[24] In a *campo pagado*, the ARENA-affiliated Crusade for Peace and Work called on Cristiani to apply "summary justice" to the "terrorist hordes" directed by Fathers Ignacio Ellacuría and Segundo Montes, among others. The Jesuits' crime was practicing liberation theology.[25] ARENA's president was more moderate, but conservative Salvadorans' conversation remained the same: liberation theology was a security threat.

Despite the violence, U.S. news focused on events in Europe and Asia. During the spring of 1989, the call for democracy grew louder in Eastern Europe. In China, protesters confronted the government, which cracked down, killing hundreds and imprisoning thousands in early June. The world saw an unidentified person—known as "tank man"—repeatedly change his path to stay in front of tanks in Tiananmen Square.[26]

Two events in November 1989 thrust El Salvador onto the front pages and prompted reexamination of U.S. policy. First, on November 11, the FMLN launched an offensive based in the cities designed to inspire the population to rise up. Cubans aided the guerrillas' planning and the Sandinistas provided "key logistical support."[27] The Salvadoran army battled the estimated three thousand to five thousand FMLN fighters and then bombed poor civilian neighborhoods in an attempt to force the guerrillas out.[28] The offensive, which began two days after the Berlin Wall's initial dismantling, highlighted that after nearly a decade of war neither the government nor the guerrillas had the upper hand. The guerrillas could not muster sufficient public support for their efforts; the government could not defeat the rebels despite massive U.S. aid.

Five days into the offensive, members of the military murdered six Jesuits and two women at the UCA. As a CIA report concluded, the murders "marked a critical turning point in international perceptions of the offensive. Attention, particularly in Washington and other foreign capitals, shifted from the insurgent-initiated violence to the murders, which evoked memories of the rampant human rights abuses of the early 1980s and cast the government as ineffectual at best, and, at worst, openly repressive."[29] It was not just U.S. policy opponents that saw echoes of the early 1980s.

The murders were a culmination of threats and violence directed at Jesuits and the UCA for nearly two decades. In the 1970s, as discussed in chapter 3, El Salvador's powerful condemned Jesuits like Rutilio Grande, whose social activism they regarded as communism. Likewise, the Jesuit-run UCA drew elite Salvadorans' ire when it encouraged students, including elite youth, to engage with the country's social problems. After UCA Jesuits endorsed land reform in 1976, opponents bombed the university. Criticism increased once the war began, as members of the military and government, including President Duarte, described the Jesuits as its intellectual authors. UCA Rector Ignacio Ellacuría drew additional condemnation for being a founder of liberation theology, maintaining contacts with FMLN leadership, and advocating a negotiated settlement to end the war.[30] Conservative Salvadoran Catholics' accusations of heresy and treason against the Jesuits were similar to those conservative U.S. Catholics employed against Maryknoll.

Threats against the UCA Jesuits escalated in the days before the murders. At 11 p.m. on November 11, the government ordered all radio and television stations to connect to Radio Cadena Nacional, which the military and government now controlled.[31] The channel allowed people to share messages, such as their whereabouts and their views. Some announced, "The Jesuits are communists—kill them!" "Get Ellacuría—off with his head!" and "The Jesuits of the UCA are subversives and should be killed."[32] On November 12, a caller urged the removal of Jesuits, claiming they had hidden arms at the UCA for nearly ten years. For those that missed the charges via radio, *Prensa Gráfica* published them the next day.[33]

When the Jesuits were murdered four days later, it was about more than those six priests. As Rubén Zamora, secretary general of the center-Left Popular Christian Social Movement, insisted, "Such killings are part of a continuing campaign of intimidation against democratic forces—labor and peasant groups, Christian communities, human rights monitors, church workers and political parties—that have long argued for a negotiated solution and will be so important to its success."[34] Earlier in November, armed men, allegedly soldiers out of uniform, took two members of Zamora's party and another person. They were found at the morgue with a note, "For being traitors to the homeland."[35]

The UCA murders did not end attacks on religious, including Maryknollers. The congregation left El Salvador in 1981 after Roy Bourgeois went missing. The Fathers and Brothers returned in 1986, and the Sisters in 1988.[36] The day after the UCA murders, soldiers "ransacked and desecrated" the church Cristo Salvador, where a Maryknoller was pastor.[37] Salvadoran radio aired threats against Maryknollers and Jesuits.[38] Five days after the murders, thirty National Guardsmen raided an Episcopal church housing four hundred refugees. They "seized the lay workers and ransacked files." The move was not unusual. By that point of the offensive, the government had arrested forty church workers from a variety of denominations.[39]

The attacks were consistent with Salvadoran officials' rhetoric. Mauricio Eduardo Colorado, attorney general and known D'Aubuisson associate, wrote the pope two days after the murders. Because of his "tremendous concern first and foremost" for the bishops, Colorado explained, he requested the pope evacuate them from El Salvador because "large parts of the Salvadoran population" blamed liberationist bishops for the FMLN offensive. These unnamed bishops, Colorado wrote, "have persisted in keeping alive this questionable ideology of the church of the poor beyond the bounds of the general policy of the episcopal conference." Removal was necessary "for the security and well-being of all of the Salvadoran faithful."[40] The prelates were the danger, Colorado insisted.

The next day, Colorado held a press conference at the same time as the Jesuits' funerals and again insisted some bishops "had somewhat questionable political tendencies."[41] As he announced, "It is very difficult for me personally to protect these dignitaries from this Communist avalanche, because in a church or public place anything can happen." He then named specific clergy. "Monsignor Rosa Chávez has had a participation, and his brother is known by everyone to belong to the guerrillas. Monsignor Rivera y Damas has had very controversial opinions and that puts him in grave danger."[42] The man leading the UCA murder investigation openly justified them, and he threatened priests. It was like the 1970s when officials and the press condemned religious, and soon after, the same religious were attacked.

To many Congress members, the Jesuit murders underscored how little had changed since the churchwomen's murders. The year before the UCA murders, the United States sent $298 million in economic aid and $80 million in military aid to El Salvador. From 1982 to 1988, total U.S. aid was $3.2 billion, including $1 billion for military equipment. The United States also trained Salvadoran troops, whose involvement in the UCA murders challenged "the theory promoted by successive U.S. administrations that U.S. training brings about improved human rights behavior."[43] As the UCA murders prompted many to wonder, what was all that aid for?

Senators' responses recalled the churchwomen's murders. Patrick Leahy introduced a bill to cut aid by 30 percent until President Bush reported to Congress that the murders had been thoroughly investigated and those accused of ordering and carrying them out were brought to trial.[44] As Leahy explained, he "patterned" his bill on Senator Specter's 1983 proposal to withhold 30 percent of aid until those accused of murdering the churchwomen were brought to trial.[45] Subsequent Congresses held back aid to induce Salvadoran action. In 1986, Congress suspended $5 million to try to force progress in the case of two U.S. land reform advisors killed in 1981. In 1987, Congress withheld 10 percent of aid to prompt the arrest of those who killed U.S. Marines in 1985.[46] The small aid reservations mattered little. The U.S. aid spigot continued, and El Salvador's human rights record remained abysmal.

In supporting Leahy's bill, Congress members, especially Catholics, referenced the churchwomen as a yardstick to assess human rights in El Salvador and the U.S. role in the country. As Ted Kennedy contended, "The time has come to send a strong message to the military and the right wing death squads of El Salvador—no more United States aid without respect for fundamental human rights." He viewed President Cristiani's call for an investigation skeptically, given that no Salvadoran officer had been successfully prosecuted for a human rights infraction. Kennedy cited the murders of the "four" Maryknoll nuns—as he called them—revealing the extent of Maryknoll's association with the churchwomen's murders.[47] Similarly, Tom Harkin argued that unless the United States "put some tight controls on that money and what the military can do with it," there would be more human rights violations, just as in the past. As he contended, "We were outraged when the nuns were raped and killed and buried in a common grave in the dirt. That did not stop anything. We were outraged when Archbishop Oscar Romero . . . was assassinated. . . . Did that stop the military? Of course not. The outrage that we express at this brutality today is not going to stop the military of El Salvador. Quit kidding yourself. These are hardened killers." And, Harkin insisted, "they will go to any lengths to protect themselves and to protect whoever committed this heinous crime."[48]

House members also cited the churchwomen in supporting a similar proposal. Catholic David Obey (D-WI) proposed a 30 percent suspension in military aid. Bush called the measure an "absolutely unacceptable" reaction.[49] Like the senators, House members were exasperated. Conditions seemed to be no different from when the churchwomen were killed. Ohio's Rosemary Oaker, whose constituents once included churchwomen Kazel and Donovan, noted, "These kind of Gestapo-like executions are painfully reminiscent of the slaying of three American nuns and a lay worker who were brutalized and murdered in 1980."[50] Likewise, Jesuit-educated Edward Markey (D-MA) insisted the United States have some say about El Salvador's conditions, given that the "military-dominated government is wholly funded by the United States." Yet thousands, including U.S. citizens, had been murdered.[51]

Unlike the churchwomen, the Jesuits were not U.S. citizens, yet their murders elicited congressional calls for action. Several of the priests were well known to Congress because they spoke about El Salvador during their travels to the United States and they met with visiting congressional delegations.[52] As political scientist Timothy Byrnes points out, in murdering these men, "the Salvadoran army succeeded in drawing tremendous attention to the one group in all of El Salvador who probably had the closest, deepest, and longest relationship with politically significant people in the United States of any group in the country."[53]

The Catholic ties also did not hurt. There were more Catholics in Congress than any other denomination at the time.[54] Seventy-nine Catholics in Congress were Jesuit educated, including Senate Majority leader George Mitchell (D-ME) and his House counterpart Speaker Thomas Foley (WA). After the murders, Jesuit lobbying softened New York Republican Alfonse D'Amato's support for military aid.[55]

On the other hand, some Jesuit alums backed continued U.S. aid. The murders did not sway Henry Hyde.[56] Cristiani also wanted aid to continue. The day of the UCA murders, Georgetown University President Leo J. O'Donovan appealed to Cristiani as an alum. He wanted Cristiani "to effect an immediate cease-fire." O'Donovan also reminded Cristiani that Georgetown and the UCA had been sister schools since 1978.[57]

Neither Leahy's nor Obey's bills passed, but the Democratically led Congress did not let the issue go. Both chambers passed resolutions declaring the Salvadoran government's response to the murders would play a key role in determining future U.S. support.[58] In early December, Speaker Foley took unprecedented action by appointing the Speaker's Special Task Force on El Salvador to investigate the murders. It was the first special congressional group charged with investigating a human rights issue in another country.[59] The group, Foley explained, was to "gather all available information about the murders, those responsible and the process undertaken to bring them to justice."[60] He chose John Joseph "Joe" Moakley (D-MA), head of the Rules Committee, as chair, because of his reputation. As Moakley explained the decision, "He knew I was not looking for headlines." Michael Dukakis's former presidential campaign manager put in another way: Moakley is "so effective . . . because his efforts are not coming from the left but from Mr. Lunch Bucket Democrat."[61]

Moakley was not a big player in terms of foreign relations, but he was active regarding El Salvador. In late 1982, constituents from the Jamaica Plain Committee on Central America and representatives from Latinx and Catholic groups, including a priest and a nun, requested a meeting to discuss their opposition to U.S.–Central America policy.[62] After speaking with the group, Moakley volunteered—without prompting—to work for Extended Voluntary Departure (EVD) for Salvadorans. EVD allowed those who fled repression to be granted temporary status in the United States until circumstances improved in their home country. It was broader than refugee status, which required a person to show they had been individually targeted for persecution. Moakley achieved temporary protective status for Salvadorans with the Immigration Act of 1990.[63] Work on El Salvador, his biographer notes, came "to dominate Moakley's concerns," and it was as part of these efforts that he met two of the Jesuits murdered in 1989.[64]

El Salvador and the Cold War

Though Congress members referenced the churchwomen to stress the lack of human rights progress in El Salvador, circumstances were not the same as in 1980. Reagan was a Cold War president. Bush entered office when "the Cold War was all but won." He presided over "the dawn of America's unipolar moment," Andrew Preston points out.[65]

When the topic of Central America surfaced at an early December 1989 meeting between Bush and Mikhail Gorbachev, it revealed the two leaders' contrasting views of the region and of the Cold War. Bush was concerned about Nicaragua and its arms shipments to El Salvador. As he told Gorbachev, "the single most disruptive element" in the two countries' relations was Soviet support for Cuba and Nicaragua. Gorbachev insisted the Soviets had stopped sending military aid to Nicaragua. Soviet assistance mattered. According to the CIA, the Soviets sent $515 million in arms in 1988, the USSR's second highest since 1980.[66] But Gorbachev did not see Nicaragua's significance. He reminded Bush of the upcoming elections and stressed that if the United States and Soviet Union supported self-determination, Nicaragua should not concern them.[67] Both men agreed, however, on El Salvador. They would back "the UN secretary general's mediation in the Salvadoran negotiations."[68]

Bush's and Gorbachev's postmeeting comments revealed their disagreement over the world's state of affairs. Gorbachev told reporters they agreed "the characteristics of the cold war should be abandoned." He continued, "The arms race, mistrust, psychological and ideological struggle, all those should be things of the past."[69] Bush was cagey; he refused to echo Gorbachev's sentiments. Instead, he pointed to "areas where I think we have progress." Bush's response characterized his presidential approach: "prudent" and "reliable rather than revolutionary."[70]

Bush was reluctant to declare the Cold War's end, but the White House framed its action in Panama as part of the drug war, not anticommunist efforts. Weeks after the UCA murders, the United States invaded Panama and arrested its president, Manuel Noriega. After Noriega voiced support for the Sandinistas in 1987, the United States turned on the former CIA asset and Contra war ally. The United States obtained two grand jury indictments against him for drug trafficking and racketeering. Then, in May 1989, Noriega drew international condemnation when he voided the election his chosen successor lost. In October, he escaped an attempted coup. Noriega raised the stakes when he riled the Panamanian National Assembly to declare a state of war against the United States on December 15. The next day, Panamanian Defense Forces killed a U.S. Marine.[71] A U.S. Navy lieutenant was beaten, and his wife likely raped, Bush was informed.[72]

Without seeking congressional approval, Bush sent 10,000 additional U.S. troops and dropped 422 bombs on Panama in thirteen hours. Noriega hid in the papal nuncio's home and only surrendered to U.S. forces as a better alternative to the Panamanian mob he faced. The invasion left twenty-four U.S. service members and 139 Panamanian Defense Forces dead. Operation Just Cause was the largest U.S. military operation since Vietnam.[73]

Neither the U.S. invasion of Panama nor the Bush-Gorbachev meeting dampened U.S. religious leaders' advocacy regarding El Salvador. In meeting with Chief of Staff John H. Sununu and National Security Advisor Brent Scowcroft, Catholic bishops stressed the importance of the UCA murders. They argued the episode highlighted the need for "a thorough reconsideration of the extent, nature and appropriateness of U.S. military aid to El Salvador." Similarly, an interfaith coalition of high-level Episcopalians, Lutherans, Methodists, Baptists, and Catholics "warned Baker that U.S. aid to El Salvador must be connected to human rights improvements."[74]

To many, the U.S. rationale for intervening in Central America—to stop communism's spread—seemed questionable, if not outdated, as Bush and Gorbachev worked to improve superpower relations. Speaking at a New York memorial Mass for the slain Jesuits, Fordham University President Father Joseph A. O'Hare questioned what interest the United States could still have in Central America. "At a time when our Government leaders and our corporate executives hasten to socialize with the leaders of the Communist giants elsewhere in the world, why must we assemble our military might to deal with revolutionary movements in tiny Central American nations?" The same question remained as it had for the past decade: "Can we hand weapons to butchers and remain unstained by the blood of their innocent victims?"[75] Changed geopolitical circumstances and moral concerns demanded an end to military aid.

Whereas Catholic opponents stressed a Cold War–free future, supporters recalled a Cold War past to argue for continuity. If the United States gave into the FMLN, the *National Review* insisted, it would repeat the mistakes of Vietnam. "What we are now witnessing in El Salvador is an attempt to replay the Vietnam farce." The FMLN offensive "was Tet all over again" because it was a guerrilla military loss, but "a media success, shifting the political balance in the U.S. against the war." Similarly, the magazine alleged, religious figures were being used as communist propaganda. Just as "many, if not all, of the Buddhist monks who immolated themselves in flames were drugged and programmed" to protest Diem's regime, *National Review* wrote, "the six murdered Jesuits are the Buddhist bonzes" because FMLN fighters wearing army uniforms could have carried out the attacks.[76] *National Review* repeated one of its old lies. In 1983, it wrote in reference to the murdered churchwomen, "Buddhist monks have come back as Maryknollers."[77] Dead religious figures were communist propaganda ploys designed to tug on the heartstrings and change U.S. policy; the United States must stay the course.

Bush versus Reagan Administration Response

Bush officials' rhetorical response to the Jesuit murders contrasted with Reagan officials' remarks regarding the churchwomen. Bush's press secretary said the White House condemned the "outrageous" murders "in the strongest possible terms."[78] The message in El Salvador was the same. The day of the murders Ambassador Walker remarked, "I have difficulty in imagining what sort of animals would, in cold blood, execute priests and other innocents. This is a crime of such repugnance that to say I condemn or deplore it seems inadequate. It is a barbarous act that has not only brought shame to El Salvador, but will leave a gaping hole in this country's intellectual and academic community."[79] Bush officials defended the murder victims, whereas Alexander Haig and Jeane Kirkpatrick questioned the churchwomen's status as victims.

Administration officials and the president emphasized the need to prosecute the Jesuit murderers. In late November, Secretary of State Baker informed the U.S. embassy in San Salvador the case was "a crucial test for the Cristiani government and for democracy in El Salvador." Cristiani could only effectively go after those responsible—those on the Right—with a strong legal case. Baker continued, "Our principal objective should be to strengthen Cristiani's hand so that when the time comes to move against those responsible, it is well-coordinated and effective, while at the same time minimizing threats to his government's stability."[80] Cristiani's survival depended on a strong legal case, which the U.S. government needed to help him achieve. Bush similarly told an audience at the Catholic University of America in December, "We will do everything we can to bring to justice those who murdered those six Jesuit priests."[81] His remarks reflected the administration's "pragmatic" approach. As one official told the press, "We recognized that the continuation of U.S. aid would depend on El Salvador's response to this benchmark case."[82] A foreign service officer argued, "This Administration will do almost anything to prevent a confrontation with Congress over Central America."[83] Bush pressured Cristiani on the UCA case to avoid congressional conflict, whereas Reagan fought Congress's attempts to link aid to human rights. Although Bush administration language suggested a different goal, the motivation was the same: save U.S. policy without excessive concern for human rights.

The difference between Bush officials' response to the UCA murders and Reagan officials' remarks about the churchwomen's murders stemmed partly from the role of religion, especially Catholicism, in the two administrations. Bush, unlike Reagan, was not "ostentatiously religious."[84] As the regular Episcopalian church attender once remarked, "For me, prayer has always been important but quite personal."[85] Whereas devout conservative anticommunist Catholics like Haig, Casey, Walters, Allen, and Clark shaped Reagan's Central America policy, Bush did not surround himself with "especially religious" key foreign policy advisors.[86] The Bush White House also did not prioritize conservative Catholic support. The Reagan White House strategized ways to gain Catholic votes in 1984. Bush, by contrast, went after Protestants. He successfully wooed evangelicals in the 1988 election. Once in office, though, he "relegated Christian conservatives to the margins."[87]

U.S. intelligence also saw Maryknollers and Jesuits differently. A month after Bush won the presidency, a CIA report concluded Maryknollers and Jesuits were no longer a problem. "The Political Role of the Catholic Church in Central America" argued "radicalized Catholicism, often working in close cooperation with Marxist groups," played a role in fomenting the Sandinista revolution, the Salvadoran civil war, and the uprisings in Guatemala. Jesuits and Maryknollers had "largely borne" this "banner of radicalism," while "relative calm" persisted where the communities did not "gain a foothold." But, the report concluded, radicalized Catholicism's power waned in the 1980s because of the diminished presence of "radical foreign clergy," Pope John Paul II's focus on Central America, evangelical Protestantism's growth, and the "negative impact of the philosophy of the left in Nicaragua."[88] Quite simply, Jesuits and Maryknollers no longer threatened national security.

It was a far cry from the Reagan-era rhetoric targeting Maryknollers and the administration's surveillance efforts. Through a Salvadoran who became a U.S. citizen, the FBI and the Salvadoran National Guard worked together to watch Salvadorans and Americans. The FBI also spied on the Sanctuary movement and failed to investigate over two hundred cases of break-ins and arsons of churches, homes, and offices as well as death threats against activists from 1983 to 1990.[89] These covert operations received little attention when Congress first held hearings in February 1987 because developing Iran-Contra coverage distracted the public.

The FBI's investigation began in 1981 with CISPES, the Committee in Solidarity with the People of El Salvador, one of the first and largest groups focused on Central America. The five-year investigation expanded to include over one hundred organizations, such as the Maryknoll Sisters in Chicago and Oklahoma City, the Sisters of Mercy, the United Auto Workers, and a rape crisis center in Virginia. Fifty-two of the FBI's fifty-nine field offices were involved.[90] While in private the FBI was secretly working with the Salvadoran National Guard to spy on those who opposed U.S. policy, in public the bureau was assisting the investigation of the National Guardsmen accused of murdering the churchwomen.[91]

The key player in the FBI's efforts was a Salvadoran from a politically well connected family. Born in 1950, Franklin Agustín Martínez Varela changed his name to Frank Varelli upon becoming a naturalized U.S. citizen in 1982, as he testified before Congress. Varelli initially came to the United States in 1968 for college.[92] He returned to El Salvador at some point, and later served in the U.S. Army from 1978 to 1979. He then again returned to El Salvador.[93] An evangelical Baptist minister, Varelli held religious services denouncing liberation theology, including a three-night "crusade" at San Salvador's soccer stadium with more than one hundred thousand attendees.[94] His family sought political asylum after he and his father, former director of the national police and interior minister, escaped a 1980 assassination attempt.[95]

The FBI then recruited Varelli to develop ties with the Salvadoran National Guard. The bureau wanted to know whether U.S. opponents of Reagan's policies had ties to Salvadorans the National Guard "was seeking."[96] Varelli approached family friend General Carlos Eugenio Vides Casanova, National

Guard director, who at the time was obstructing the churchwomen murder investigation.[97] Vides Casanova saw Varelli's offer as a way to combat negative U.S. press coverage of El Salvador and the CIA's influence in his country. Vides Casanova, like many in the Salvadoran security forces and oligarchy, believed the CIA installed the 1979 junta that "had virtually delivered their country into the hands of the communists."[98]

Varelli served as a conduit between the FBI and the National Guard. He gave the National Guard names of Salvadorans being deported who were of concern to the Guard, while to the FBI he provided names of U.S. citizens who applied for visas to El Salvador and traveled there on cultural exchanges.[99] As Varelli later testified before Congress, he identified people "who were active or interested in Central American policies who might have terrorist tendencies," using information from the Salvadoran National Guard and both U.S. and Salvadoran Right-wing groups.[100]

Varelli infiltrated CISPES by posing as a refugee, and he maintained the FBI's "Terrorist Photograph Album."[101] The album, which contained nearly seven hundred profiles, included Maryknollers Peggy Healy, Tip O'Neill's information source on Central America, and Roy Bourgeois, who sparked media frenzy when he went missing in El Salvador. The entry for Maryknollers described them as "front runners in preaching the Marxist-Leninist 'Liberation Theology.'" In terms similar to those used to describe Maura Clarke at the Denton hearings, the album declared, "In El Salvador as well as Nicaragua, the Maryknoll priests and nuns are guilty of aiding, protecting and supporting the communist terrorists"[102] (see figure 4). To the FBI, liberation theology supporter equaled communist, which equaled terrorist. The album echoed conservative Catholics' accusations that Maryknollers were spreading communism through their support for liberation theology. In targeting liberation theology supporters, Varelli's FBI work was also a continuation of his anti-communist crusade.[103]

Despite the mutually beneficial relationship Varelli and the FBI enjoyed, the parties turned on one another. Varelli resigned when his identity was compromised. After the FBI refused him back pay, Varelli sued the bureau.[104] The FBI pointed a finger back at Varelli. FBI Director William Sessions argued the CISPES investigation was an anomaly led by bad apple Varelli.[105] Just like North and Iran-Contra, the FBI tried to isolate Varelli, while Varelli implicated White House higher-ups. According to Varelli, three FBI agents told him that the National Security Council relayed the White House's request for the investigation of U.S.–El Salvador policy opponents.[106] Varelli's work revealed Reagan White House rhetoric was part of a larger government aim of neutralizing the protest movement and of characterizing liberation theology supporters

PLAINTIFF'S EXHIBIT 8

Terrorist Photograph Album
D-432 (Rev. 2-8-83)

1. Name
SISTER PEGGY HEALY

2. Aliases
NONE

3. Date and Place of Birth
MASSAPEQUA, NEW YORK.

4. Citizenship: American
5. Sex:
6. Race: ☐ White ☐ Black ☐ Oriental ☐ Other
7. Height:
8. Weight:
9. Hair: Brown
10. Eyes: Blue

11. Scars, marks and identifying characteristics

12. ☒ Single ☐ Married ☐ Separated ☐ Divorced

13. Residence She travels between: Managua, Nicaragua. and Washington D.C.

14. Occupation/Employer (includes academic institutions)
Maryknoll Nun. Staff member of WOLA.
Pro-Sandinista. Pro-Castro Activist.

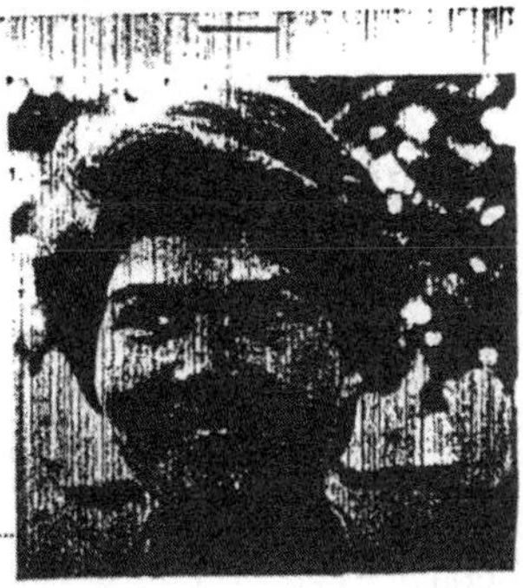

Date Taken March 1981

15. Identifying Information
Passport No. ______ Country of Issue ______ Date of Issue ______
Social Security No. ______ Alien Registration No. ______
U.S. Person ☒ Yes ☐ No Naturalized U.S. citizen ☐ Yes ☐ No

16. Terrorist affiliation Pro- Castro.Christian Socia-list. Official position Propaganda Agent

17. Narrative of activities
She is a nun with the Maryknoll Order.
Maryknoll is the popular title for "The Catholic Foreing Mission Society of America".It is a community of priests, brothers, sisters - and lay people that are suppose to be spreading the gospel all over the world. Instead they are the front runners in preaching the marxist-leninist "Liberation Theology". In El Salvador as well as Nicaragua, the Maryknoll priests and nuns are guilty of aiding, protecting and supporting the communist terrorists of the FDR-FMLN, FSLN. WOLA,is the Washington Office On Latin America. It is a powerful pro-Castro lobbying organization with staff members drawn from the National Lawyers Guild which seeks to influence the U.S. Congress and public on behalf of numerous leftist terrorist and Communist groups from Latin America. Operating under the banner of "human rights vio-

Office of Origin ______ File No. ______ Bufile No. ______ Date Prepared AUG 1 1 1983

EL SALVADOR'S TERRORISM
FBI DALLAS
BY: Franco

FBI/DOJ

FIGURE 4. Sister Peggy Healy entry, "The Terrorist Photograph Album," U.S. Congress. House. Committee on the Judiciary. *Break-Ins at Sanctuary Churches and Organizations Opposed to Administration Policy in Central America: Hearings before the Subcommittee on Civil and Constitutional Rights*. 100th Cong., 1st sess., February 19 and 20, 1987.

as a national security threat. The Bush administration, by contrast, did not share this priority.

Despite these differences from the Reagan approach, U.S. officials' actions in Miami and San Salvador regarding the UCA case suggested less of a break with the past. Lucia Barrera de Cerna, who lived next door to the UCA, saw five men with rifles, two of them in soldiers' camouflage uniforms, the

night of the murders. For her safety, she gave a sworn statement to a Salvadoran judge at the Spanish embassy and then flew to Miami with her family.
Faced with pressure from FBI officials and a Salvadoran colonel, she changed
her story. Officials asked Lucia and her husband who told them "to say these
lies" and how much money the Jesuits were giving them. Officials accused
Lucia of spying for the Jesuits. She denied her earlier account, she explained,
"out of fear." Likewise, her husband retracted after an FBI agent said,
"What you say here will decide whether you can stay here or go back to El
Salvador."[107]

Questionable behavior was not confined to the FBI. On January 2, U.S. military advisor Eric Buckland revealed that a Salvadoran officer told him that Colonel Benavides admitted his role in the murders. Embassy officials brought
Buckland and his contact before army officials. Unsurprisingly, the man denied Buckland's claims. In doing so, U.S. officials "burned" their source and
sent the message "to others in the armed forces that the United States was not
to be trusted."[108]

FBI behavior aside, Cristiani still feared Congress would cut aid. Just as
Duarte did when faced with certification, Cristiani announced developments in
the murder case. On January 7, the night before Moakley and his team arrived
in El Salvador,[109] Cristiani appeared on Salvadoran television and announced
"there was involvement of some elements of the armed forces" in the murders. It was the first time a conservative leader pointed a finger at the army.[110]
It also mattered that Cristiani's party was ARENA, founded by death squad
leader D'Aubuisson. Six days later, on January 13, Cristiani revealed the arrest
of eight men: Colonel Guillermo Alfredo Benavides Moreno, two lieutenants,
and five lower-ranked soldiers.[111] Another soldier had deserted in December.
Benavides was no ordinary officer. The former head of military intelligence
also led the military school and was part of "a small clique of officers that runs
the Army." Benavides was the highest-ranking officer indicted for human rights
crimes.[112]

The indictments were not enough for Congress. In February, Senator Christopher Dodd (D-CT), chair of the Foreign Relations Subcommittee on Western Hemisphere Affairs, proposed a bill calling for an immediate 50 percent
cut in aid. The bill included carrot-and-stick provisions for both sides. If the
Salvadoran government failed to pursue a negotiated settlement or investigate
the UCA murders, all aid would end. If, on the other hand, the FMLN refused
to negotiate or initiated a serious offensive, Bush could restore all aid.[113] As
with certification's requirement that Reagan vouch there was progress in the
churchwomen's case and on human rights issues, Dodd's bill left the executive branch with ultimate power.

Nicaragua

While Congress debated U.S.–El Salvador policy, Nicaraguans went to the polls. On February 25, 1990, Violeta Barrios de Chamorro, widow of murdered *La Prensa* editor and representative of a fourteen-party coalition, received 55 percent of the vote to Daniel Ortega's 41. The United States aggressively funded the Sandinista opposition and spent $500,000–$600,000 to help Contra leaders in Miami return to Nicaragua to vote.[114]

It was a referendum on the war. As Ortega's former vice president admitted, "there was practically no one left who was eligible for military service," there were desertions, and people no longer viewed death in war "as a necessary sacrifice." The people were tired. Ortega's aggressive image, accompanied by the theme song "El gallo ennavajado" ("The Fighting Gamecock"),[115] cemented the FSLN as the party of war, in contrast to Chamorro, sixteen years his senior and on crutches.[116]

To the White House, the election vindicated U.S. policy, and it changed its approach accordingly. Bush lifted the economic embargo in place since 1985. Secretary of State Baker proclaimed, "The war is over" in testifying before the Senate Budget Committee.[117] The Bush administration was all too happy to move on, as Nicaragua was far from the only matter on Bush's agenda. The major issue for European politics was German reunification, especially after East Germany fell apart in January.[118]

Conservative U.S. Catholics saw the electoral results as a victory for both U.S. foreign policy and conservative Catholicism. To them, the secret ballots revealed Nicaraguans' opposition to the Sandinistas, contrary to what "Jesuit activists, radical nuns, and liberation theologians" alleged.[119] Similarly, the *National Catholic Register*'s Joan Frawley Desmond reiterated the "prominent role played by Christian Church groups, including Catholic missionary orders like Maryknoll," in U.S. policy debates. As Sandinista and Reagan rhetoric confused Americans, Maryknollers and other missionaries had "played a crucial role as morally credible interpreters of the Nicaraguan scene." In doing so, Desmond argued, the missionaries became willing accomplices in promoting the Sandinista agenda and ignoring human rights abuses.[120]

Crisis magazine visualized the Catholic divide on its April 1990 cover. On the Right was the victorious Violeta Chamorro with Archbishop Obando by her side. Obando, standing piously with his hands folded, was the most prominent anti-Sandinista spokesperson and model of conservative Catholicism. On the Left was a habited nun. A peace necklace, a sign for Ortega at her side, and a tear streaming down her cheek, presumably for Ortega, compromised her status as a woman religious. She also wore sandals, suggesting she was a "sandalista," a derisive term Contra supporters used to describe North Americans who opposed U.S. policy and traveled to Nicaragua.[121] Behind her was a sulky priest, holding a book labeled "liberation theology." Near the two were other books. One was labeled "Marx" with a Soviet hammer and sickle. The other was labeled "Boff," for Brazilian priest Leonardo Boff, whom the Vatican disciplined for his writings on liberation theology. To *Crisis*, the election was about more than ousting the Sandinistas. Traditional Catholicism, U.S.-Nicaragua policy, and Sandinista opponents were collectively triumphant.

But to Maryknoller Rita Owzarek, the election was not a zero-sum game. Speaking about Maryknoll's role in Nicaragua she explained, "We worked with the poor when nothing was done for them during the Somoza dictatorships. We later collaborated with the revolutionary (Sandinista) government in projects that served the poor, and we will continue to cooperate with the new government where we can, especially by working with victims of the civil war." Maryknoll's commitment was to the poor, not any political leader or party. Maryknollers would also continue reverse mission to educate those in the United States about conditions in Nicaragua and how U.S. policy affected Nicaraguans.[122]

Chamorro's victory also impacted neighboring El Salvador. With the Sandinista defeat, the FMLN lost its key ally in the region.[123] At the same time, the FMLN saw less support from Cuba. As the Soviet Union unraveled, Cuba lost $4–$6 million in economic aid annually from the Soviets, which meant less Cuban aid for the Salvadoran rebels.[124] By the late spring of 1990, Gorbachev presided over a decrepit economy suffering from "inflation and scarcity," and he faced critics on both the Left and the Right.[125] On April 4, less than six weeks after Chamorro's election, the FMLN and Salvadoran government, under the UN secretary-general's watchful eye, signed the Geneva Accord, pledging to pursue negotiations to end the conflict.[126] The two sides had started talks before the Sandinista defeat at the polls.[127]

The UCA Case

The FMLN and Cristiani were working toward peace, but the UCA case was not progressing. The interim report of the Speaker's Special Task Force (or Moakley Commission), released April 30, 1990, said the murder investigation was at a "virtual standstill." The report lit a fire under both U.S. and Salvadoran officials. On Salvadoran television, Ambassador Walker called for more to be done, while the Salvadoran judge brought in new witnesses.[128]

Though the Moakley Commission shone a spotlight on authorities' handling of the UCA murders, the underlying conditions that targeted religious continued. Between January and June 1990, four church workers disappeared and thirty-five were arrested. The military often accused those arrested "of affiliation or collaboration with the FMLN." The Grupo Anticomunista Salvadoreña sent one parish in eastern El Salvador a list of twenty-one people it considered "responsible for death and destruction" in the country.[129] In the spring, Archbishop Rivera received new death threats.[130] Circumstances in El Salvador pointed to a larger problem than simply prosecuting one set of killers.

The U.S. debate also fell on familiar battle lines. The Maryknoll Fathers and Brothers, NETWORK, and the Jesuit Conference, among others, again implored Congress to end military aid in the face of "continued violence" and to push for negotiations.[131] Conservative U.S. Catholics' arguments about what was happening also sounded the same. Enrique Rueda argued, as he had at the 1983 Denton hearings, that "militant Marxists" were "actively" using the church "to help the guerrillas with the war against the people of El Salvador."[132] Rueda continued to allege some priests were communists, describing "several of the murdered Jesuits" as "generally considered collaborators with the enemies of democracies and freedom." In tricky word play recalling Reagan officials' and conservative Catholics' accusations about the churchwomen, Rueda blamed the men for their own deaths by noting they were "not so much innocent victims as victims of their own follies." Rueda also alleged Ignacio Ellacuría's "long collaboration with Marxist guerrillas."[133] The Cold War was ending, but Rueda's language was indistinguishable from his early 1980s arguments.

To stress that he was not alone, Rueda and the *Wanderer* cited conservative Catholics outside the United States who shared his views. Rueda repeated false claims made in *El Diario de hoy* by Edgar Chacón, leader of a Salvadoran Rightwing think tank, that Ellacuría was a terrorist with ties to ETA (Euskadi Ta Askatasuna) because he was from the Basque Country.[134] For its part, the *Wanderer* reprinted an article from Spain's *ABC* by historian Ricardo de la Cierva, who wrote several books critical of the Jesuits, including *The Jesuits, the Church and Marxism*.[135] Cierva claimed Ellacuría was connected to ETA, and he, like Rueda, cited Salvadoran Fredy Delgado's *The Popular Church Was Born in El Salvador*.[136] Rueda and the *Wanderer* laid bare the conservative Catholic echo chamber in which conservative U.S., Salvadoran, and Spanish Catholics cited one another.

Henry Hyde also sang the same song: liberation theology was the problem, especially when it influenced Congress. With O'Neill retired, Hyde targeted a different Massachusetts Democrat: Joe Moakley. Hyde argued that like O'Neill, Moakley followed the guidance of religious who did not recognize communism's danger. "I think Joe, as Tip, is a good man who is somewhat sentimental in his approach to the clergy," Hyde charged, recalling O'Neill's reliance on Maryknoll sisters. Hyde also chided fellow Catholic Moakley for "embracing" liberation theology. As Hyde explained, the problem existed long before Moakley. "The church has a myopic view of El Salvador. Ever since the murder of Archbishop Romero, they have not been friendly to the elected governments down there."[137] Hyde questioned priests' and nuns' ability to understand El Salvador just as he believed Maryknoll sisters were ignorant of Nicaragua.

Moakley did not dispute Hyde's charge "that religion drives his politics."[138] But unlike Hyde's, Moakley's was a quiet faith. The self-described "bread and butter politician from South Boston" attended Mass regularly. Moakley was "a sincere Catholic" who "never discussed his private beliefs in public."[139] His work on El Salvador profoundly affected him. Archbishop Romero's portrait hung in his office.[140] As Moakley remarked before his death in 2001, "Of all the things I've done, perhaps what remains closest to my heart is my work in El Salvador."[141]

Despite the déjà-vu-like quality to language like Rueda's and Hyde's, there were significant shifts in the conversation. The more Right-center Catholic *Crisis* focused on maintaining U.S. aid, not on criticizing the murdered Jesuits. *Crisis* opposed a "negotiated settlement," arguing the FMLN should not be invited to talks. But *Crisis* "support[ed] U.S. efforts to press the Salvadoran government to complete its investigation of the murder of the Jesuit priests." El Salvador, like other "fledging democracies of Latin America," needed "military aid to defeat the anti-democratic Marxists, economic aid to revive a failing economy, and political assistance to enable them to set up viable human rights institutions."[142] *Crisis*'s tone was a far cry from the early 1980s when the singular focus was defeating communism. Its arguments for continued U.S. aid and involvement were broader, perhaps in recognition of the shifting geopolitical circumstances.

The House changed its views, too, as it passed the Moakley-Murtha proposal in late May 1990 with more votes than any other Central America proposal in the preceding ten years. Moakley's bill mirrored Dodd's and he enlisted John Murtha's help. The Pennsylvania Democrat not only supported aid to El Salvador but also cosponsored the 1984 aid bill.[143] Moakley stressed the need for U.S. accountability. "Those who pulled the trigger and committed this heinous crime included men trained with American money, by American servicemen, on American soil. We all bear some responsibility for this crime—in much the same way we must all bear some responsibility for the war, which has claimed over 70,000 lives." He continued, "I am taking a stand today. Enough is enough. The time to act has come. They killed six priests in cold blood. I stood on the ground where my friends were blown away by men to whom the sanctity of human life bears no meaning—and men who will probably never be brought to justice."[144] His frustration was palpable and effective. The Senate passed Dodd's bill, and Bush signed the law in November 1990.

As in the 1980s, lawmakers credited Catholics, including Maryknollers, with the bill's passage. As a speechwriter for Senator Bill Bradley (D-NJ) remarked, "The Catholic Church played an extremely effective role in getting the cut. It wouldn't have happened otherwise." Missionary-witnesses were "extremely convincing," an aide to Mikulski insisted. Hyde's legislative assistant agreed. "The Catholic lobby is very effective on Central America," continuing, "especially [when they bring in] the Maryknoll nuns."[145] It was unclear if the Maryknoll Sisters played a larger role in lobbying efforts than others, or if the sisters loomed so large in Hyde's imagination that his staffer credited the women anyway.

But by the time the Dodd bill passed in November 1990, El Salvador was in the background. The main foreign policy issue was Iraq. On August 2, Iraqi forces invaded Kuwait, giving longtime Soviet ally Saddam Hussein 20 percent of the world's oil reserves. Bush threatened military intervention if Hussein did not withdraw by January 15, 1991. The president's call for war was contentious, "prompting one of the largest civil debates since before World War II."[146]

The Iraq discussion highlighted religious opposition to Bush's foreign policy and his distance from the religious community. Many churches, including the Roman Catholic Church, opposed military intervention. Notably, two groups of Reagan's ardent supporters on Central America—traditional Catholics and the Institute on Religion and Democracy—backed Bush's plan. To try to sway mainline and liberal Christians, Bush pitched the Iraq invasion as a call "for an international order based on peace, harmony, and unity." He tried to capitalize on both conservative and liberal Christians' understanding of the Cold War's end as an opportunity to reassess U.S. foreign policy. Bush's move backfired, however, as he "raised expectations of a genuinely idealistic, righteous new world order and a U.S. foreign policy that would enforce peace and justice, even at the expense of order." The episode also highlighted how despite soliciting Protestant votes in 1988, "the religious intensity of the campaign did not carry through into the administration."[147]

In the midst of the Iraq debates, both supporters and opponents of U.S.–El Salvador policy clamored for more attention. Jesuit *America* urged, "The American people, while concentrating upon Iraq and Kuwait, cannot afford to forget other chronic trouble spots where U.S. policy is engaged," namely

El Salvador.[148] Likewise, the *National Review* contended, "This cold-war battle continues, and winning the main event is no reason to lose the sideshow." The magazine insisted, "Restore military aid."[149] *National Review* got its wish. Bush reinstated aid on January 15, right before the combat phase of the war against Iraq began. Bush claimed the FMLN's treatment of civilians in late 1990 precipitated the change, not the FMLN's shooting down of a U.S. helicopter and killing of two U.S. military inside.[150]

Operation Desert Storm overshadowed Bush's decision on El Salvador. When Hussein did not comply with the January 15 deadline, U.S. commanders led troops from thirty countries into battle. The United Nations supported the undertaking, as did the Soviet Union, underscoring the end of Cold War hostilities.[151] As Cynthia Arnson argues, "State Department and Pentagon officials gambled that few in the Congress would mount a protest over El Salvador as tens of thousands of U.S. troops stood poised for combat against Iraq."[152] Bush delayed aid delivery for sixty days to encourage negotiation progress.[153]

Bush restored aid based on the FMLN's actions, but as the U.S. ambassador noted, El Salvador's military repeatedly ignored and undermined U.S. efforts regarding the UCA murder investigation, in violation of U.S. funding law. Weeks after Bush announced aid reinstatement, Ambassador Walker railed against their obstinacy. As Walker cabled DC, "The ESAF [El Salvador Armed Forces] remains committed to a hermetic conspiracy to protect its own at whatever cost." U.S. "pleas, threats, turning on and off the military assistance spigot, and appeals to institutional honor have all had the same results—zilch." The ESAF, according to Walker, neither appreciated the gravity of the situation nor seemed to care. Walker stressed the case's importance to the "Bush administration, the Congress on both sides of the aisle, and the American people," but the military did not get it. Instead, ESAF believes the problem is faulty "PR" by "the Salvadoran embassy in Washington" and "that CISPES is behind all the bad news." The attitude was the same, Walker cabled. "There is no acceptance of institutional responsibility, and a tacit belief that by offering up Benavides for trial the ESAF has done enough." The military did not fear any potential consequences. Because Bush restored the 50 percent cut, Walker warned, military leaders were "smug in the conviction that the USG [U.S. government] will never pull the plug." After all, since 1980, military aid was only suspended for six weeks after the churchwomen's murders. Carter resumed it after the January 1981 FMLN offensive. Walker stressed the need to "radically alter that perception." He complained specifically about Defense Minister Ponce and recommended "heavy conditioning of FY92 military assistance unless and until Ponce is removed and a new leadership solves the Jesuit affair."[154] Ponce, as it was later discovered, was protecting himself. He had ordered Ellacuría's murder and that there be no witnesses.

Walker's warning proved correct; only the nine men already charged stood trial in September 1991. The jury found commanding officer Colonel Benavides guilty of murdering the six priests, the housekeeper Elba Ramos, and her daughter Celina. Lieutenant Yusshy René Mendoza Vallecillos was found guilty of murdering fifteen-year-old Celina. Both were sentenced to thirty years. Despite the other men's confessions, the jury found no one specifically accused of carrying out the murders of the Jesuits or Elba Ramos guilty. Two lieutenants were sentenced to "instigation and conspiracy to commit acts of terrorism," while another was sentenced as an accessory. They "were released on bail and remained in the armed forces."[155] The crime's intellectual authors and those involved in the cover-up remained free, as in the murdered church-women's case.

Peace in El Salvador

Four months after the verdicts, in January 1992, Cristiani and the FMLN signed a peace agreement under UN auspices. In exchange for FMLN disarmament, the government agreed to political and military reforms.[156] Though the FMLN originally sought to abolish the military,[157] the parties consented to a smaller purged force and the creation of the National Civilian Police.[158] The parties also approved a UN-sponsored truth commission to examine human rights abuses during the war. One of the major reasons for the war—the unequal distribution of wealth—remained. As Erik Ching observes, "The people who held economic power before and during the war retained it afterward."[159]

Several factors played a role in bringing the two sides to the table. The FMLN underwent change during the 1980s. The organization "self-identified as Marxist-Leninists, but the insurgent leadership also included social democrats, radicalized Catholics, and eclectic intellectuals and activists." The FMLN "reshaped its negotiation policy" over time through FMLN-FDR leader contacts with Europeans, Canadians, and Latin Americans that opposed U.S.–Central America policy. At the same time, the process led to a shift away from "Marxist-Leninist ideology" to "democratic socialism between 1988 and 1991." The change was so profound that murdered Jesuit Ignacio Ellacuría likened it to Vatican II.[160]

ARENA also changed. Candidate Cristiani promoted talks with the FMLN, reversing the party's past strategy. The war hurt the country's chances of implementing "economic restructuring mandated by the Washington Consensus," and the 1989 offensive showed that the military could not defeat the guerrillas. The U.S. government also accepted negotiations that included the FMLN and pressured "military and elites to accept the process."[161]

Salvadoran business leaders were receptive to Cristiani's approach because they believed peace better served their goals. By the late 1980s, a new economic elite emerged, largely the result of U.S. aid. During the war, El Salvador's GDP and exports plummeted. Economic elites emigrated in response to kidnappings and extortion of business leaders. But the think tank Fundación Salvadoreña para el Desarrollo (FUSADES or Salvadoran Foundation for Economic and Social Development) altered the economic landscape. FUSADES, created in 1983, used U.S. funds to provide credit. It fueled opportunity and nurtured young economic elites, expanding the economic base beyond coffee. ARENA's ascension to power in the late 1980s provided an opening for the change these elites craved. They saw Cristiani as an ally, unlike Duarte, whom they regarded as a tool of the Left or as a communist.[162]

Just as with the Sandinistas' defeat, U.S. cold warriors were quick to assign Reagan credit for peace in El Salvador, even though Bush was president. Elliott Abrams argued the Salvadoran peace agreement was a "great victory for Salvadorans, and for U.S. foreign policy." He contended Reagan's two-prong policy—a "large military aid program" and a push for political reform—succeeded by preventing an FMLN victory and by encouraging Salvadorans to believe the system could redress their grievances. Though the end of the Cold War was a factor, Abrams insisted Reagan's efforts to fight communism played a larger role. As he asserted, "In this small corner of the cold war, American policy was right, and it was successful."[163]

El Salvador was the focus of U.S. attention, not Nicaragua. When Violeta Chamorro addressed Congress in April 1991, congressional aides were rounded up to fill the empty seats.[164] U.S. funds dried up too. As Maryknoller Dan Driscoll, whom reporter Jimmy Breslin contrasted with Oliver North in 1987, pointed out, U.S. funding for the Contra war in 1982 and 1983 translated into $416.67 for every Nicaraguan. By the spring of 1992, U.S. money for rebuilding was $5.76 for every Nicaraguan, "to cover the dirt streets and make up for the violations of the past decade."[165] Nicaragua quickly faded from view after the 1990 Sandinista defeat despite having been Baker's top priority for the incoming Bush administration.

The White House turned away from Nicaragua, but the Iran-Contra scandal still lurked in the background. The weekend before voters went to the polls in November 1992 to reelect Bush or choose his Democratic challenger Clinton, Special Prosecutor Lawrence Walsh indicted former secretary of defense

Caspar Weinberger on additional charges. After Bush's loss to Clinton, the outgoing president pardoned Abrams, Clarridge, Fiers, George, and McFarlane of perjury, making false statements to Congress, or withholding information from Congress. North's convictions for destroying documents, obstructing Congress, and accepting illegal gratuity were overturned. Only former CIA agent Thomas G. Clines was sentenced to jail time—sixteen months for tax evasion and other crimes—for helping North deliver illegal arms to the Contras.[166] In pardoning the former officials, Bush, like Henry Hyde, characterized Iran-Contra as a difference of political opinion, not criminal activity. The prosecutions were evidence of "the criminalization of policy differences" in the country, Bush said. The men acted during the Cold War, and patriotism motivated them. As Bush stressed, "It was time for the country to move on."[167] His Christmas Eve announcement was less than two weeks before Weinberger's trial was scheduled to begin.[168]

While Bush tried to turn the page on Iran-Contra, four months later a UN report forced a reckoning with El Salvador's past and the U.S. role in it. Released in March 1993, *From Madness to Hope: The 12-Year War in El Salvador* challenged the U.S. characterization of the conflict and named human rights abusers. The UN Commission on the Truth for El Salvador concluded that state forces and those closely aligned with them, such as death squads, were responsible for 85 percent of the cases the commission examined, while about 5 percent were attributable to the FMLN. The conclusion shattered the U.S. government's lie that the Salvadoran government was caught between the Right and the Left. The report also blamed those rumored to have been responsible for human rights abuses. It identified Roberto D'Aubuisson as architect of Archbishop Romero's assassination. It revealed that the guardsmen were ordered to murder the churchwomen and that Defense Minister García and National Guard Director Vides Casanova obstructed the investigation. The report also said that former defense minister Ponce ordered Ellacuría's murder and that the military covered up, concealed, and destroyed evidence.[169]

The responses of the Salvadoran and the U.S. governments to the UN report highlighted how much had not changed in El Salvador and how eager the United States was to distance itself from its role in the conflict. Five days after the report's release, the Salvadoran assembly voted for an amnesty bill.[170] Some identified in the report, such as Defense Minister Ponce, received not only full military honors upon their retirement but also praise. As President Cristiani noted at Ponce's and others' retirement ceremony, the men served with "merit, efficiency, and loyalty to the highest duties that the nation can demand."[171] For its part, the United States called for self-examination. Secretary of State Warren Christopher ordered a study of the State Department's handling of Salvadoran human rights issues during the same period covered in the report. President Clinton agreed to a congressional request to declassify documents related to thirty-two cases in the UN report.[172] But the public accounting focused only on the cases the UN examined, and papered over the fact that named human rights abusers, including Vides Casanova and García, had been living in the United States since 1989. Reagan gave the Legion of Merit Award to Vides Casanova in 1985.[173] The United States pointed a finger while ignoring its harboring of human rights abusers.

The war's end also did not stop intra-Catholic debates or prompt thorough self-examination, but Catholics did find common cause. By 1989, nearly one-third of Guatemalans were Protestants, up from 2 percent thirty years earlier and increasing by 10 percent a year.[174] As Pentecostalism exploded in Latin America, and nowhere more than in Guatemala, the Cold War's end revived Catholic-Protestant turf wars. Liberal and conservative Catholics, however, divided over the reason for conversions.

Instead of liberation-theology-supporting missionaries, conservative Catholics worried about Protestants challenging Catholicism's virtual monopoly. One priest serving in Latin America argued Protestantism was gaining converts because Catholicism was so much a part of Latin American life that it was taken for granted and because of "the spiritual vacancy of the city." U.S. Protestant missionaries took advantage of this vacuum. Latin American conversions, the priest argued, also strengthened Protestantism in the United States. Missionaries "from South Carolina" were "uniting what remains of Protestant America with an emergent Hispanic Protestantism."[175]

While conservative Catholics blamed a weakened church, liberal Catholics pointed to the U.S. government. Some Leftists and liberal Latin American Catholics saw evangelicalism's growth "as a U.S.-promoted conspiracy against liberation theology, and more generally against all social movements for the emancipation of the poor."[176] In a pastoral letter, one Guatemalan archbishop contended that U.S. Protestants aimed to further U.S. economic and political interests while countering the Catholic Church's work among the poor. To him, Protestantism's growth was another chapter in the long story of U.S interference.[177] Latin American intellectuals shared Catholic bishops' views of evangelicals as "captive to a foreign ideology and alienated from national culture."[178] The argument was an old one: in the 1920s, elite Nicaraguans objected to Baptist missionaries—the U.S. "spiritual vanguard"—as threatening Nicaragua's national culture by "de-Catholicizing it."[179] Such a conclusion ignored Catholicism's arrival with Spanish conquistadors (the original imperialists) and Protestants' presence in Latin America since the colonial period.[180]

Despite their disagreements, both conservative and liberal Catholics concluded manipulation caused conversions, as Latin Americans were incapable of making religious decisions on their own.[181] This perspective ignored factors that pushed and pulled Catholics toward Pentecostalism. In El Salvador, violence against liberationists convinced some that Protestantism was a "safer" alternative.[182] Others, especially women, were attracted to how Pentecostal churches provided a "spiritual cocoon" that protected and nurtured their members.[183]

Despite the constant comparisons between the Jesuit and churchwomen murders, the Bush administration's response revealed how the context changed between 1980 and 1989. Intra-Catholic debates no longer held the same political significance for U.S.–Central America relations because the Bush administration had nothing to gain by exploiting them. Whereas Reagan officials such as Kirkpatrick and Haig inserted themselves into intra-Catholic debates, the Bush White House steered clear. Conservative Catholics' warnings about liberation theology, and the Maryknollers and Jesuits who supported it, fell on deaf ears. With the Cold War ending, liberation theology seemed neutralized. Although conservative Catholics insisted the United States maintain its involvement in El Salvador, they were shouting at the rain. The influence and access to power that conservative Catholics had in the Reagan years were gone.

The Bush administration pushed the Jesuit case only to the point of a trial. It was not about larger human rights concerns or the relationship between the United States and El Salvador. The focus on the UCA case missed the larger point about U.S.–El Salvador relations, Jesuit Jon Sobrino alleged. The United States needed to fundamentally change its understanding of and approach to El Salvador. Sobrino, who lived and worked at the UCA but was abroad the night of the murders,[184] thanked Moakley for his work during a July 1991 forum. Like others before him, Sobrino stressed that communism did not cause the conflict in El Salvador. It was "institutionalized injustice and State repression." The U.S. government did not understand a problem that dated back to the 1930s. Instead, Sobrino charged, "successive U.S. governments have remained completely ignorant of fifty years of lies, injustice, fear and frustration here in El Salvador; they did not merely react with silence, but also with a complicit inactivity, tolerating and blessing everything that ran counter to the democracy they preach to us: electoral fraud, oppression and repression." The U.S. approach contradicted its own values. For there to be a change in El Salvador, Sobrino insisted, "there must also be a new beginning in the United States and in its relationship with us."[185]

Epilogue
Women, the Catholic Church, and U.S.–Central America Relations after the Cold War

"Paul Ryan has a nun problem," proclaimed a reporter in August 2017. During a town hall meeting broadcast live on CNN from Racine, Wisconsin, Sister Erica Jordan challenged the Republican House Speaker to explain his support for repealing the Affordable Care Act (ACA) and for the Republican tax plan. As she asked, "I know that you're Catholic, as am I, and it seems to me that most of the Republicans in the Congress are not willing to stand with the poor and working class as evidenced in the recent debates about health care and the anticipated tax reform." She continued, "So I'd like to ask you how you see yourself upholding the church's social teaching that has the idea that God is always on the side of the poor and dispossessed, as should we be." The crowd applauded.[1]

Ryan defended his position as acceptably Catholic: "Sister, you may—this may come as a surprise to you, but I completely agree with you. Where we may disagree is on how to achieve that goal." The government needed to change its approach, Ryan insisted. "The poor are being marginalized and misaligned in many ways because a lot of the programs that we have, well intended as they may be, are discouraging and disincentivizing work." Many booed.[2] There were echoes of the 1980s in the exchange, which featured nuns and a Catholic House Speaker in a major flashpoint debate. But unlike Maryknollers' alliance with Democrat Tip O'Neill on Contra policy, the Republican Ryan and the sisters were at odds over health care.

Jordan was not alone in her critiques. The month before, more than seven thousand sisters, organized by the lobby NETWORK, urged senators not to support the Republican health-care proposal.[3] Nor was this the first time nuns tangled with Ryan. Five years earlier, in 2012, sisters called Ryan's proposed budget "immoral," arguing it "undermined Catholic teachings to serve the poor and vulnerable." They also initiated "Nuns on the Bus," touring through nine swing states and lobbying in opposition.[4]

By contrast, President Barack Obama—a non-Catholic—embraced the women. "I just love nuns," he said in June 2015. That day, Obama spoke before the Catholic Health Association (CHA), the nation's largest group of non-profit health-care providers. It was no accident. Obama credited CHA Chief Executive Sister Carol Keehan with the ACA's passage. While Keehan and others, including NETWORK, eventually supported the act after the administration made changes, the U.S. Catholic Conference of Bishops (USCC) and other Catholics opposed the requirement that employers cover preventative care, which Health and Human Services (HHS) interpreted to include contraception. As Obama said, "had it not been for" Keehan, there would have been no ACA.[5] In recognition of her role, Obama gave Keehan one of the pens he used to sign the act.[6]

The women had their share of Catholic critics. The far Right traditionalist website Churchmilitant said "dissident" and "activist nuns" led Nuns on the Bus. One reader, "Alphonso—Pre-Vatican 2," proposed a solution: "Those 'short haired, pant-wearing' nuns need to get off the bus, walk to a Catholic Church, cover their heads, sign themselves with holy water and engage in Eucharistic Adoration for 40 days and 40 nights."[7] Similarly, a *Washington Post* reader argued "so many Sisters support the ACA because they are not Catholic, but dissident and have set themselves as above the doctrines of the Church. They have led many into apostasy."[8] To these Catholics, the women were leading other Catholics astray, as supporters of Reagan's Central America policy charged in the 1980s. The language had slightly changed—there were no more accusations of "Marxist nuns"—but the meaning was the same: the women were not real nuns.

In discussing sisters' role in the health-care debate, one reporter's words were eerily similar to those she used in the Reagan era. The *National Catholic Register*'s Joan Frawley Desmond—the same reporter who critiqued Maryknollers for opposing Reagan's Central America policy—critiqued Keehan. As Desmond contended, Keehan's "support has helped to provide moral credibility for the administration during tough moments." Keehan assuaged Catholic lawmakers' concerns regarding "the use of tax-payer funds to subsidize direct abortion," and in the process, contradicted the claims of the USCC and "many other pro-life organizations," Desmond charged.[9] What the reporter did not mention was that the Catholic Health Association and the USCC independently analyzed the ACA language regarding abortion and arrived at different conclusions.[10]

Desmond's critiques were nearly identical to those she raised against women religious who opposed Reagan's Central America policy. Desmond charged Keehan with guiding Catholic lawmakers away from church teachings through her "moral credibility," just as Desmond argued Maryknollers and other missionaries "played a crucial role as morally credible interpreters of the Nicaraguan scene" during the 1980s.[11] The battle lines were familiar: nuns' power came from their moral authority. This time, though, their experiential expertise came from running health systems, not living in Central America. Desmond also noted the sisters opposed the USCC in the health-care battle, just as Henry Hyde and others argued Maryknollers opposed members of the male church hierarchy that supported Reagan's Nicaragua policy. Finally, Desmond questioned sisters' motives. She contended the hospital industry saw a "financial windfall" after passage of the ACA, with Catholic hospitals "outperforming their secular counterparts in some regions of the country."[12] (In reality, with more insured people, all hospitals earned greater profits, and in some areas, Catholic hospitals had outperformed secular ones before the ACA.) To Desmond, greed now motivated the sisters to act against U.S. and church interests, whereas in the 1980s it was Marxism. To the sisters, however, their inspiration was the same: to serve the poor.

Maryknoll and the School of the Americas

Health-care disagreements revealed the continuing debates over women's role in the church, but the focus on Maryknoll was absent. This was partly because Maryknollers were not the primary movers in the health-care debate. Instead, Maryknoll critiques shifted to another arena: protests over the School of the Americas (SOA). After the Moakley Commission discovered five of the nine soldiers arrested for the UCA murders were SOA graduates, Maryknoller Roy Bourgeois started a new kind of protest focused on the school.

SOA descended from the Latin American Ground School (LAGS), founded in 1946 to centralize U.S. military training in the Panama Canal Zone that began in 1939. Anthropologist Lesley Gill contends LAGS not only trained Latin Americans in military techniques; it also sought to instill an appreciation for the "American way of life" and, ultimately, a shared "vision" of U.S. empire. The Cuban Revolution prompted the school's restructuring and a focus on fighting communism; it became known as the School of the Americas in 1963. In 1984, it moved to Fort Benning, Georgia, as part of the preparatory canal-transfer efforts.[13] SOA provided the U.S. government with a way to pursue its political goals without putting boots on the ground. To avoid exceeding the limit of fifty-five U.S. military advisors in El Salvador Congress imposed in the early 1980s, Salvadorans were sent to the SOA.[14] The SOA had trained more than sixty thousand Latin Americans by the year 2000.[15]

Roy Bourgeois did not initiate protests against U.S. training of Salvadoran soldiers. After the churchwomen's murders in 1980, protesters demonstrated and fasted to object to U.S. training of the Salvadoran military.[16] CISPES organized protests at Fort Bragg, where Salvadoran officers were training.[17] But Bourgeois found a new target after the Moakley Commission's revelations. In September 1990, he, along with nine Salvadorans and Americans, embarked on a thirty-five-day water only fast outside the SOA. Then, in November, Bourgeois and two others placed photos of the eight murdered at the UCA and a white cross at the SOA entrance. They also poured blood in an SOA hallway to remind Americans, as Bourgeois later wrote from prison, that "we cannot wash our hands of the blood of innocent people killed in El Salvador by soldiers trained in the U.S." The three were arrested and convicted of damaging government property.[18]

Bourgeois's SOA protests stemmed from activism inspired by the murders of Archbishop Romero and the churchwomen, especially his friends and fellow Maryknollers Maura Clarke and Ita Ford.[19] The Louisianan volunteered for Vietnam and was ordained in 1972; his time in mission included five years in Bolivia.[20] Bourgeois saw his activism as a moral imperative. He toured the United States speaking out against U.S. policy.[21] In response to the charge that priests should stay out of politics, he argued, "The sending of guns to soldiers who kill innocent people, including priests and Sisters and an archbishop who spoke out for the poor, is not politics but a moral issue . . . [therefore] . . . I as a priest, as a missioner, as a Christian must address them."[22]

Protests mushroomed as more information about the school and its graduates became public. In 1993 SOA Watch, which grew out of the 1990 protest, obtained a list of graduates through a Freedom of Information Act request and published them on its website.[23] The group included men involved with the murders of the churchwomen and of the Jesuits as well as Panama's Noriega and Guatemala's Efrain Ríos Montt.[24] In 1995, the school's profile increased after thirteen protesters, including a nun, were arrested and served jail time for crossing the line into Fort Benning. The next year, SOA training manuals became public as part of Congress's investigation into CIA activities in Guatemala. The manuals detailed methods designed to–as they said—

"neutralize" opponents, and they failed to differentiate between "armed guerrilla insurgents and unarmed, peaceful protestors." The disclosure led to bipartisan opposition and more people at the annual Fort Benning protests. In response, the SOA changed its approach to protesters. In 1998 it began moving those engaged in civil disobedience offsite rather than arresting them. The school also altered its curriculum and sent representatives to debate its opponents on college campuses.[25] Protests led the SOA to close in 2000, but it reopened the next year with a new name, the Western Hemisphere Institute for Security Cooperation (WHINSEC).[26]

By the late 1990s, those associated with the SOA and its congressional supporters saw Maryknoll as the ringleader of efforts to disband the school, recalling charges made during the Reagan years. In 1998, Mac Collins (R-GA) proclaimed on the House floor, "There is an ongoing movement led by the Maryknoll Order of the Catholic Church to attack American foreign policy and her right to defend her interests through closure of the U.S. Army School of the Americas." While opponents claimed graduates committed human rights abuses, Collins asserted there were "very few" of these incidents. The school promoted human rights by instructing Latin American military and police on how to address the illegal drug trade. These graduates protected Latin Americans from "wayward military officials and drug death squads" and protected U.S. citizens, especially children, from the drug trade's scourge. Without the SOA, Collins contended, Latin Americans would not receive training "in democracy and human rights."[27]

Military men also railed against liberation-theology-inspired Maryknollers. In 1999 Colonel Glen Weidner, SOA's public relations head, blamed "leftist missionaries linked to liberation theology" for promoting a "Black Legend" about the SOA. He singled out Bourgeois.[28] Russell W. Ramsey, former army lieutenant colonel and WHINSEC visiting professor, held a similar view. Ramsey claimed the FMLN rebranded the SOA the "School of Assassins" and promoted this idea "through useful front organizations under the guise of Catholic social activism." As an example, Ramsey cited a "splinter element" within Maryknoll.[29] Ramsey also connected Maryknollers' SOA activism to their opposition to Reagan's Nicaragua policy. He charged that Maryknollers corrupted Christianity by supporting the Sandinista government and threatened U.S. security interests by promoting a "fictitious history of the School of the Americas." As Ramsey alleged, the Sandinistas pushed a "heretical" version of liberation theology that "elements of the Maryknoll order" in the United States "expounded" on.[30] Ramsey noted liberation theology was not problematic, only the "heretical" version associated with the Sandinistas and Maryknoll. Though an evangelical Protestant minister, Ramsey recycled decades-old conservative

Catholic criticisms of Maryknoll. At the same time, Ramsey narrowed his censure. It was a renegade part of Maryknoll that followed an unorthodox version of liberation theology. As Ramsey's words revealed, conservative Catholics' 1970s and 1980s charges against Maryknollers still lingered, even outside the Catholic community.

Pope Francis's Response

Just as U.S. domestic debates focused less on Maryknoll, the Vatican's response to Central America and liberation theology also showed a marked changed from the 1980s. With the ascendancy of Argentine Jorge Mario Bergoglio—Pope Francis—to the papacy in 2013, liberation theology was no longer the third rail.

Francis's move to canonize Óscar Romero showed a Vatican eager to move on from past church battles. For defending the poor against the government, Romero was a polarizing figure in life and in death. Concern about his possible Marxism blocked his canonization process; three Salvadoran ambassadors to the Vatican worked to obstruct it as well.[31] In 2015, Pope Francis beatified San Salvador's archbishop, a key step on the road to official sainthood. In a note read at the beatification ceremony, Francis wrote that Romero "guided, defended and protected his flock, remaining loyal to the Gospel, in communion with the Church." The pope also described the beatification as "the moment for favorable and proper national reconciliation."[32] This was not just a vindication of Romero's actions but also an attempt to heal past wounds.

In 2014, Miguel d'Escoto successfully petitioned Pope Francis to reinstate him as an active priest. The Vatican suspended the Maryknoller in 1985 after he refused to give up his post as Nicaragua's foreign minister. As a *National Catholic Reporter* writer declared, "Many see in Francis' gesture of mercy a signal that the theology of liberation espoused by D'Escoto and other Latin American clergy was not a Marxist-motivated ideology so much as it was an interpretation of Catholic social teaching in the context of Latin American life in the second half of the 20th century."[33] Liberation theology had been declawed.

Defense of the poor and liberation theology was one thing; women in the church was another. While Pope Francis reinstated d'Escoto, Roy Bourgeois remained excommunicated. The Maryknoller had committed an infraction far worse than serving in government as a priest. His repeated challenges to U.S. foreign policy, specifically the SOA, were also not the issue. Under Pope Benedict in 2008, the Vatican excommunicated Bourgeois after he participated in a ceremony in which a woman was ordained.[34] In writing to the Vatican, Bourgeois defended his refusal to recant his participation or his statements supporting women's ordination, which he linked to his SOA protest. In recalling a 2000 Vatican Radio interview, Bourgeois explained: "I stated that I could not address the injustice of the SOA and remain silent about injustice in my Church." He concluded, "There will never be justice in the Catholic Church until women can be ordained."[35] In March 2011, Maryknoll asked Bourgeois to "publicly recant" his position or face expulsion.[36] The next year, the Vatican officially dismissed Bourgeois from the priesthood but did not specify his infraction. The letter indicated he had no right "to any appeal," as the decision came from Pope Benedict.[37] In November 2016, Pope Francis reaffirmed Benedict's decision, citing John Paul II's 1994 declaration that women could not be priests.[38]

The discipline of Bourgeois versus the welcoming of d'Escoto and the celebration of Romero revealed that women's role in the church was far more controversial than liberation theology. In outlasting the Cold War, the debate over the role of women, and especially sisters, in the church underscores the degree to which Catholics' fights over U.S.–Central America policy were never solely or entirely about the Cold War.

U.S. Reconsideration of El Salvador

Debates over the U.S. role in El Salvador also outlasted the 1980s. Under Barack Obama, the United States repudiated the human rights abuses of the Salvadoran civil war. In 2009, the Department of Homeland Security (DHS) initiated deportation proceedings against General Vides Casanova.[39] DHS's Human Rights Violators and War Crimes Center, charged with identifying, investigating, and prosecuting people living in the United States suspected of war crimes and human rights abuses, acted under a 2004 war criminal statute.[40] In the first case of its kind, DHS obtained a deportation order for Vides Casanova in 2012.[41] The immigration judge held that the general "assisted or otherwise participated in" the rape and murder of the churchwomen and the torture of two Salvadorans because he neither supervised his subordinates nor properly investigated after the crimes.[42]

The judge's decision revealed the extent to which the U.S. government abandoned Cold War thinking and a former ally, and downplayed its role. Vides Casanova argued the United States could not deport him for behavior it was aware of and presumably condoned during the 1980s. As his lawyer argued in court filings, Vides Casanova followed "the advice, military and financial assistance of the U.S. government."[43] For its part, the U.S. government classified the former general as a war criminal and, in doing so, sought to distance itself from his crimes. But as Maryknoll President Janice McLaughlin recognized, the United States furthered the violence in El Salvador not only by supporting the government but also by granting asylum to people like Vides Casanova.[44]

Despite U.S. government efforts to turn the page on its role in the Salvadoran civil war, its legacy continues. The economic ties between El Salvador and the United States are stronger than before the war. On January 1, 2001, the country adopted the U.S. dollar as its legal currency. I have heard Salvadorans half heartedly joke that the country's number one export is people. By 2009, an estimated 25 percent of Salvadorans lived in the United States.[45] As they did in the 1980s, remittances keep the Salvadoran economy afloat; they outpace U.S. aid. In 2017, remittances made up 20.4 percent of El Salvador's GDP, an increase from a little over 1 percent in 1980.[46] Salvadorans often call the United States *"departmento quince,"* the unofficial addition to the fourteen units that compose El Salvador.[47]

Salvadoran migration to the United States is another link with the 1980s, and a continuing source of tension. Many Salvadorans, as in the 1980s, flee not only poor economic conditions but also violence, especially from gangs. Many current gang members fled to the United States with their families as children during the civil war. They later joined gangs (*las maras*) that developed in Los Angeles—the Mara Salvatrucha (MS-13) and Barrio Dieciocho (18th Street Gang) for various reasons, including for self-protection. Many of these gang members were later deported, though some had never been to El Salvador and some did not speak Spanish.[48] In 2016, twenty-four years after the peace accords were signed, El Salvador had the world's highest homicide rate. The World Health Organization (WHO) classifies a murder rate above 10 for every 100,000 people as an epidemic. El Salvador's murder rate in 2016 was eight times the WHO level.[49]

Daniel Ortega and Nicaragua

In neighboring Nicaragua, there are also links to the past through Daniel Ortega, not the U.S. government. Ortega won his first five-year term as president in 2006. He then changed the constitution, allowing him to run for a consecutive term, and was elected again in 2011 and 2016. To gain and hold power, Ortega surrounded himself with new and old allies.

Ortega reconciled with Cardinal Obando y Bravo, one of the Sandinistas' most outspoken critics. The two made peace when Ortega ran in 2006 and supported a ban on therapeutic abortions.[50] There were also rumors, as the U.S. ambassador to Nicaragua cabled, that Ortega was "blackmailing Obando y Bravo with information proving that the Cardinal fathered children with his secretary and that he has engaged in corrupt practices in his management of the private Catholic University."[51] In 2016, Ortega issued an official proclamation that recognized Obando "as a dedicated man who has demonstrated great love for his nation, always at the service of the nation's poorest people, and who has always fought for the right causes."[52] Obando died in 2018.

Ortega could have been relegated to the political wilderness for sexual abuse; instead, his wife and Maryknoller Miguel d'Escoto defended him. Ortega's stepdaughter Zoilamérica Narváez Murillo accused him of abusing her from when she was eleven in 1978 until 1990, when she married.[53] In 1998, Narváez filed suit, but the judge dismissed the case on statute of limitations grounds.[54] She also pursued a complaint with the Inter-American Human Rights Council but withdrew it after her mother publicly pressured her.[55] For his part, Ortega blocked investigations "using his power in the National Assembly." He also made an agreement—el Pacto—with then president Arnoldo Alemán. Each man granted the "other immunity from criminal prosecution while lowering the percentage of the vote necessary to win a presidential election in the first round from 45 percent to 35 percent."[56] Narváez also told d'Escoto about the abuse. He advised her to bear the cross she was given and consider Ortega's image.[57] D'Escoto also publicly minimized her claims by saying "they never took hold." Years later, in a letter published in Nicaragua and abroad, Narváez accused d'Escoto of being part of the "conspiracy of silence" surrounding her abuse.[58] The former United Nations General Assembly president died in 2017. In Nicaragua, as elsewhere, sexual abuse by the powerful was disregarded.

Critics saw a replay with the Somoza dictatorship, not of the Sandinista revolution. When Ortega ran for a third term in 2016, former Sandinista Gioconda Belli charged him with re-creating a dynasty, like the one the Sandinistas overthrew. She noted Ortega's control of "state institutions such as the electoral council, the supreme court, the national assembly, the army and the police," and his removal of presidential term limits. Ortega's wife ran as vice president, making it a family affair, just as the Somozas had done.[59]

The parallels to Somoza intensified. After the government announced reform to social security and pensions in April 2018, protests erupted. State forces killed forty people, intensifying the opposition, and over the next few months, the number killed totaled over three hundred. In May 2019, the Catholic bishops called for dialogue, respect for human rights, and "a Nicaragua where the freedom of expression is exercised without restrictions." They noted "political prisoners, the lack of respect for constitutional rights" as well as the large numbers of Nicaraguans fleeing the country, which the UN estimated at over sixty-two thousand.[60] The bishops condemned the same deprivations that occurred under Somoza.

Maryknoll's Significance

During the 1980s, the Maryknoll order took on the significance it did because of a particular moment in U.S. domestic and foreign relations. Maryknoll mattered because of its place within U.S. Catholicism. U.S. Catholics viewed Maryknoll as the premier U.S. contribution to Catholic missionary work. Generations of Catholics learned of foreign lands and their place as Catholics within the larger world through Maryknollers who visited parochial schools and through *Maryknoll* magazine. Maryknoll was a source of vicarious pride. Martyrdoms in 1950s communist China only solidified Maryknoll's reputation as the model of Catholic anticommunism and U.S. patriotism.

The marriage of Catholic and U.S. anticommunist aims unraveled in the 1960s and 1970s. Some Maryknollers in Latin America began to question U.S. Cold War policy because of their exposure to liberation theology, and because of their experiences witnessing the Alliance for Progress's impact in the 1960s and U.S. involvement in Salvador Allende's overthrow in 1973. Many Maryknollers became the missionized; they, not the Latin Americans the church sent them to *Romanize*, were converted. Maryknollers' reassessment of U.S. foreign policy and adoption of liberation theology outraged conservative U.S. Catholics. To them, Maryknollers were no longer true Catholics but Marxist dupes. They felt betrayed by the former paragon of Catholic Cold War ideals. Maryknoll's shift caused an identity crisis among U.S. Catholics. What should the missionary's role be? What was, and who was, the Catholic Church? What was the relationship between political activism and social justice efforts? Was the church's role to feed the hungry and clothe the naked, or to address institutional inequalities that caused poverty?

Conservative Nicaraguan and Salvadoran Catholics engaged in similar debates. Their object of scorn, however, tended to be Jesuits. And violence often followed talk. Especially in El Salvador, involvement in Christian base communities led campesinos to question social inequalities, threatening to upend society. The critiques of Central American conservative Catholics sounded similar to those of U.S. conservative Catholics because at their heart, they were both expressing unease over the church's post–Vatican II direction. In the late 1970s, conservative Catholics' condemnations of Maryknoll expanded outside of Catholic circles, primarily because of Maryknollers' opposition–led by Miguel d'Escoto–to Somoza's dictatorship.

But this intra-Catholic debate would not have impacted U.S. foreign policy if Ronald Reagan had not won the presidency. There were Catholics in Carter's administration, and his White House also regarded church people, including Archbishop Romero, as inappropriately involved in politics. But Reagan's approach differed in significant respects. Reagan surrounded himself with conservative, fervently anticommunist Catholics who played key roles in shaping U.S.–Central America policy. They saw liberation theology as a threat to both Catholicism and U.S. national security. Reagan and his advisors prioritized Central America among his foreign policy concerns.

Neither intra-Catholic debates nor U.S.–Central America policy would have been as volatile if Catholics had not also been key opponents of Reagan's Central America policy. Reagan's conservative Catholic advisors faced off against liberal Catholic opponents. Besides reflecting advisors' religious-political views, the White House adopted conservative Catholic rhetoric for political gain. Maryknoll became the focal point for these arguments. First, it was the murdered churchwomen in El Salvador debates, then the missionaries in Nicaragua in Contra debates. The order became the stand-in for what was wrong with the church and U.S.–Central America policy.

By undercutting Maryknoll, in one fell swoop Reagan officials could critique Central America opponents and promote the conservative Catholic viewpoint. The White House successfully wedged itself between the two competing Catholic camps and won more Catholic votes in 1984. Conservative Catholic criticisms of Maryknoll developed so that by 1985–1986, non-Catholics contended they were defending the church more than Catholics, like Tip O'Neill, who opposed U.S. Contra policy. The contentious intra-Catholic debates began to disappear from U.S. political discussions with the Iran-Contra scandal and key conservative Catholics' departure from the White House. The Bush administration had little interest and seemingly nothing to gain by involving itself in these debates, especially as the Cold War unraveled and anticommunism lost some of its salience.

The Reagan White House, its Catholic supporters, and non-Catholic allies bestowed larger-than-life status on the Maryknoll Sisters: "Reagan's Gun-Toting Nuns." While in the United States this was a divisive, political, and religious debate, in Central America, Nicaraguans and Salvadorans paid with their lives. The Contra war left more than 30,000 dead.[61] Seventy-five thousand Salvadorans died, 350,00 were wounded, and about 1 million were displaced.[62] The preoccupation with the women revealed the extent to which intra-Catholic debates overlapped with and influenced debates over U.S.–Central America policy.

Notes on Research Methods

Reagan's Gun-Toting Nuns incorporates sources in English and Spanish from state and nonstate actors, secular and religious individuals, and conservative and liberal perspectives. I conducted research at eighteen U.S. and Central American archives. The "Primary Sources" section includes archives, newspapers, organizational newsletters, U.S. congressional hearings, and memoirs, among other sources.

I have often been asked how I "looked for religion" in the archives and how I analyzed the connection between religious and political views, especially when people do not often credit their faith with influencing their views or their actions. I began my primary source exploration by scanning every available issue of the *Wanderer*, the *National Catholic Register*, the *National Catholic Reporter*, the *National Review*, *Crisis*, *America*, *Maryknoll*, and *Revista Maryknoll* from 1975 to 1992. In some cases, I started in 1970. My goal was to understand both liberal and conservative political and religious views as well as how discussions of U.S.–Central America relations fit into broader Catholic conversations. Besides articles, I paid close attention to letters to the editor to get a sense of readers' opinions. I also read every issue of *Latinamerica Press*, published in Peru, beginning in 1976, and NACLA's *Report on the Americas* from 1967 to 1992. I scanned other periodicals during selected years, such as the Vatican City State's *L'Osservatore Romano* in the 1980s, San Salvador's *Diario de hoy* in the early 1980s, Managua's *Novedades* in the late 1970s, and *Revista Envío* in the 1980s.

In other periodicals, I searched for particular topics, such as Maryknoll. I used newspapers throughout the United States to compare discussions of U.S.–Central America policy geographically, and to notice any differences between religious and secular press coverage and among more Left-, center-, and Right-leaning publications. I read organizational publications, such as those by the Cardinal Mindszenty Foundation and the Institute on Religion and Democracy. I also searched in foreign newspapers for coverage of Catholicism, U.S. foreign relations, Central America, and Maryknoll. Ultimately, I used this primary source research to identify key players from conservative and liberal perspectives, and then to locate initial archives.

My approach to government sources was similar. I read through the descriptions of all individual documents in the Declassified National Security Archives' collections on El Salvador, Nicaragua, and Iran-Contra to identify anything potentially useful because I discovered early that key terms did not flag topics of interest to my research questions. I scanned the Department of State *Bulletin* from 1977 to 1987 for the same reason. I searched for useful documents in the *Foreign Relations of the United States*, presidential remarks, and congressional publications. I compared government documents with government actors' first-person accounts and with sources from nonstate and more religiously focused individuals. I noted the public packaging of policy versus private conversations about it. I also spent considerable time reading letters to members of Congress and the president as well as their replies to constituents. I hoped to gain a sense of the public's priorities and whether they placed Central America together with other concerns.

Finally, I spoke to many people with firsthand experience. In March 2008, I used the Maryknoll archives and stayed with the sisters at their retirement home. During meals, I spoke informally with the women about their decisions to join the order, their experiences as missioners, and their opinions about the churchwomen's murders and the Reagan administration's response. I formally interviewed Sisters Teresa Alexander and Madeline Dorsey, who served in El Salvador with the murdered churchwomen. I spoke to many others, but I did not cite them, either because I did not use any direct quotations from them or because some asked me not to. These include a former Maryknoll sister who served in Nicaragua, a former senator, a former congressional chief of staff who advocated for the churchwomen, a former U.S. ambassador to El Salvador, a family member of the murdered churchwomen, U.S. women religious who served in Central America, U.S., Irish, and Australian women religious who protested against U.S. policy, and activists in the United States, El Salvador, and Nicaragua. My research trips to El Salvador included visits to key historical sites, including memorials and the Military Museum. I also acted as a participant-observer at the thirtieth anniversary commemorations of the churchwomen's murders held in El Salvador and Washington, DC, and during a U.S. delegation to Nicaragua in 2016 that focused on women's postrevolutionary status.

For secondary sources, please refer to the endnotes. I read broadly in Catholic and religious history, U.S. foreign relations, Latin America history, and human rights.

Notes

Introduction

1. William A. Wilson to Ronald Reagan, February 20, 1987, RM475001-555000, WHORM-Religious Matters, Ronald Reagan Presidential Library (RRPL), Simi Valley, CA.

2. Ronald Reagan to Bill Wilson, March 5, 1987, RM475001-555000, WHORM-Religious Matters, RRPL.

3. Mark R. Day, "Reagan's Man at the Vatican," *National Catholic Reporter*, October 2, 1981.

4. Penny Lernoux, "Latin America: Crisis in the Shadow of the Cross," *Los Angeles Times*, May 31, 1981.

5. Report of the Secretary of State's Panel on El Salvador, July 1993, Department of State (DOS) Documents on El Salvador: Human Rights, 1980–1993, box 37, National Archives (NARA), College Park, MD.

6. Amy L. Koehlinger, *The New Nuns: Racial Justice and Religious Reform in the 1960s* (Cambridge, MA: Harvard University Press, 2007); Mary J. Henold, *Catholic and Feminist: The Surprising History of the American Catholic Feminist Movement* (Chapel Hill: University of North Carolina Press, 2008).

7. Emily S. Rosenberg, "Gender," *Journal of American History* 77, no. 1 (1990): 119.

8. For examples, see Kristin L. Hoganson, *Fighting for American Manhood: How Gender Politics Provoked the Spanish-American and Philippine-American Wars* (New Haven, CT: Yale University Press, 1998); Robert D. Dean, *Imperial Brotherhood: Gender and the Making of Cold War Foreign Policy* (Amherst: University of Massachusetts Press, 2001); Andrew J. Rotter, *Comrades at Odds: The United States and India, 1947–1964* (Ithaca, NY: Cornell University Press, 2000); Seth Jacobs, *America's Miracle Man in Vietnam: Ngo Dinh Diem, Religion, Race, and U.S. Intervention in Southeast Asia, 1950–1957* (Durham, NC: Duke University Press, 2004); Frank Costigliola, "'Unceasing Pressure for Penetration': Gender, Pathology, and Emotion in George Kennan's Formation of the Cold War," *Journal of American History* 83, no. 4 (1997): 1309–1339.

9. Penny Lernoux, Arthur Jones, and Robert Ellsberg, *Hearts on Fire: The Story of the Maryknoll Sisters* (Maryknoll, NY: Orbis, 1993), 25.

10. Maryknoll Fathers and Brothers, "A Brief History," accessed April 26, 2013, http://www.maryknollsociety.org/index.php/articles/2-articles/397.

11. Lernoux, Jones, and Ellsberg, *Hearts on Fire*, 25.

12. Lernoux, Jones, and Ellsberg, *Hearts on Fire*, xxviii–xxix, 37, 40.

13. Lernoux, Jones, and Ellsberg, *Hearts on Fire*, 35–36, 132.

14. Susan Fitzpatrick-Behrens, *The Maryknoll Catholic Mission in Peru, 1943–1989: Transnational Faith and Transformation* (Notre Dame, IN: University of Notre Dame Press, 2012), 22–23, 26, 30.

15. John W. O'Malley, *What Happened at Vatican II* (Cambridge, MA: Belknap, 2008), 5.

16. Mark S. Massa, *The American Catholic Revolution: How the '60s Changed the Church Forever* (New York: Oxford University Press, 2010), 2–3.

17. "Turmoil in the Dutch Church," *National Catholic Register*, December 4, 1977; Federico Alessandrini, "Vatican Methodical on Lefebvre," *National Catholic Register*, July 24, 1977.

18. Massa, *American Catholic Revolution*, 7.

19. O'Malley, *What Happened*, 114.

20. See Patrick Allitt, *Catholic Intellectuals and Conservative Politics in America, 1950–1985* (Ithaca, NY: Cornell University Press, 1993); John T. McGreevy, *Parish Boundaries: The Catholic Encounter with Race in the Twentieth-Century Urban North* (Chicago: University of Chicago Press, 1996); Matthew J. Cressler, *Authentically Black and Truly Catholic: The Rise of Black Catholicism in the Great Migration* (New York: New York University Press, 2017).

21. Edward T. Brett, *The U.S. Catholic Press on Central America: From Cold War Anticommunism to Social Justice* (Notre Dame, IN: University of Notre Dame Press, 2003), 123; Penny Lernoux, *People of God: The Struggle for World Catholicism* (New York: Viking, 1989), 11.

22. Brett, *Catholic Press*, 210.

23. Rotter, *Comrades at Odds*; Jacobs, *America's Miracle Man*; William Inboden, *Religion and American Foreign Policy, 1945–1960: The Soul of Containment* (New York: Cambridge University Press, 2008); Dianne Kirby, "Divinely Sanctioned: The Anglo-American Cold War Alliance and the Defence of Western Civilization and Christianity, 1945–48," *Journal of Contemporary History* 35, no. 3 (2000): 385–412.

24. See, for example, Philip E. Muehlenbeck, ed., *Religion and the Cold War: A Global Perspective* (Nashville: Vanderbilt University Press, 2012).

25. Sara Diamond, *Spiritual Warfare: The Politics of the Christian Right* (Boston: South End Press, 1989); Michael Löwy, *The War of the Gods: Religion and Politics in Latin America* (London: Verso, 1996), 114; Greg Grandin, *Empire's Workshop: Latin America, the United States, and the Rise of the New Imperialism* (New York: Owl Books, 2007), 143–145; Virginia Garrard-Burnett, *Terror in the Land of the Holy Spirit: Guatemala Under General Efraín Ríos Montt 1982–1983* (New York: Oxford University Press, 2010); Martin Durham and Margaret Power, "Transnational Conservatism: The New Right, Neoconservatism, and Cold War Anti-Communism," in *New Perspectives on the Transnational Right* (New York: Palgrave Macmillan, 2010), 133–148; Lauren Frances Turek, "To Support a 'Brother in Christ': Evangelical Groups and U.S.-Guatemalan Relations During the Ríos Montt Regime," *Diplomatic History* 39, no. 4 (2015): 689–719; Aaron T. Bell, "A Matter of Western Civilisation: Transnational Support for the Salvadoran Counterrevolution, 1979–1982," *Cold War History* 15, no. 4 (2015): 511–531; Kyle Burke, *Revolutionaries for the Right: Anticommunist Internationalism and Paramilitary Warfare in the Cold War* (Chapel Hill: University of North Carolina Press, 2018).

26. Van Gosse, "'The North American Front': Central American Solidarity in the Reagan Era," in *Reshaping the U.S. Left: Popular Struggles in the 1980s*, ed. Mike Davis and Michael Sprinker (New York: Verso, 1988), 11–50; Edward T. Brett, "The Attempts

of Grassroots Religious Groups to Change U.S. Policy Towards Central America: Their Methods, Successes, and Failures," *Journal of Church & State* 36, no. 4 (1994): 773–794; Christian Smith, *Resisting Reagan: The U.S. Central America Peace Movement* (Chicago: University of Chicago Press, 1996); Van Gosse, "'El Salvador Is Spanish for Vietnam': The New Immigrant Left and the Politics of Solidarity," in *The Immigrant Left in the United States*, ed. Paul Buhle and Dan Georgakas (Albany: State University of New York Press, 1996), 302–329; Dana L. Robert, "The Influence of American Missionary Women on the World Back Home," *Religion and American Culture* 12, no. 1 (2002): 59–89; Svenja Blanke, "Civic Foreign Policy: Human Rights, Faith-Based Groups and U.S.-Salvadoran Relations in the 1970s," *The Americas* 61, no. 2 (2004): 217–244; Sharon Erickson Nepstad, *Convictions of the Soul: Religion, Culture, and Agency in the Central America Solidarity Movement* (Oxford: Oxford University Press, 2004); María Cristina García, *Seeking Refuge: Central American Migration to Mexico, the United States, and Canada* (Berkeley: University of California Press, 2006); Timothy A. Byrnes, *Reverse Mission: Transnational Religious Communities and the Making of US Foreign Policy* (Washington, DC: Georgetown University Press, 2011); Roger Peace, *A Call to Conscience: The Anti-Contra War Campaign* (Amherst: University of Massachusetts Press, 2012).

27. Charles T. Strauss, "Quest for the Holy Grail: Central American War, Catholic Internationalism, and United States Public Diplomacy in Reagan's America," *U.S. Catholic Historian* 33, no. 1 (2015): 163–197; Theresa Keeley, "Reagan's Real Catholics vs. Tip O'Neill's Maryknoll Nuns: Gender, Intra-Catholic Conflict, and the Contras," *Diplomatic History* 40, no. 3 (2016): 530–558; Lauren Frances Turek, "Ambassador for the Kingdom of God or for America? Christian Nationalism, the Christian Right, and the Contra War," *Religions* 7, no. 12 (2016): 1–16.

28. Robert Wuthnow, *The Restructuring of American Religion: Society and Faith Since World War Two* (Princeton, NJ: Princeton University Press, 1988).

29. Andrew Preston, "Introduction: The Religious Cold War," in *Religion and the Cold War*, xi (emphasis in original).

30. I follow Peter R. D'Agostino's approach of seeing the U.S. church in an international context. Peter R. D'Agostino, *Rome in America: Transnational Catholic Ideology from the Risorgimento to Fascism* (Chapel Hill: University of North Carolina Press, 2004). Other scholars stress transnational connections among conservative Catholics. See Margaret Power, "Transnational Connections Among Right-Wing Women: Brazil, Chile, and the United States," in *Women of the Right: Comparisons and Interplay Across Borders*, ed. Kathleen M. Blee and Sandra McGee Deutsch (University Park: Pennsylvania State University Press, 2012), 21–35; Margaret Power, "Traditional, Conservative, Catholic, and Anti-Communist: Tradition, Family, and Property (TFP)," in *New Perspectives*, 85–106.

31. Jeffrey L. Klaiber, "Prophets and Populists: Liberation Theology, 1968–1988," *The Americas* 46, no. 1 (1989): 1–2, 5.

32. Thomas Niehaus, "Liberation Theology," in *Encyclopedia of Latin American History and Culture*, ed. Jay Kinsbruner and Erick D. Langer, 2nd ed. (Detroit: Gale, 2008), 192–193.

33. Allen Goebl, "U.S. Policy Needs Juan and María," *Maryknoll*, July 1984, 22.

34. Gustavo Gutiérrez, *Teología de la liberación: Perspectivas* (Lima: Centro de Estudios y Publicaciones, 1971).

35. Virginia Garrard-Burnett, "Church Responses to Political Violence in Central America: From Liberation Theology to Human Rights," in *Religious Responses to*

Violence: Human Rights in Latin America and the Present, ed. Alexander White (Notre Dame, IN: University of Notre Dame, 2016), 125.

36. See selections in *Human Rights and Transnational Solidarity in Cold War Latin America,* ed. Jessica Stites Mor (Madison: University of Wisconsin Press, 2013); Tehila Sasson, "Milking the Third World? Humanitarianism, Capitalism, and the Moral Economy of the Nestlé Boycott," *American Historical Review* 121, no. 4 (2016): 1196–1224; Patrick William Kelly, *Sovereign Emergencies: Latin America and the Making of Global Human Rights Politics* (Cambridge: Cambridge University Press, 2018); and *Religious Responses to Violence.*

37. Madeline Dorsey to Penny Lernoux, April 18, 1988, folder SMES1969–1993, box 1, El Salvador: Martyrs (ESM), Maryknoll Sisters Archives (MSA), Maryknoll Mission Archives (MMA), Maryknoll, NY.

38. R. Scott Appleby, "The Triumph of Americanism: Common Ground for U.S. Catholics in the Twentieth Century," in *Being Right: Conservative Catholics in America,* ed. Mary Jo Weaver and R. Scott Appleby (Bloomington: University of Indiana Press, 1995), 56–57.

39. Joseph A. Komonchak, "Interpreting the Council: Catholic Attitudes toward Vatican II," *Being Right,* 19–20, 25, 28.

40. George Weigel, "The Neoconservative Difference: A Proposal for the Renewal of Church and Society," *Being Right,* 138, 143–145.

41. Komonchak, "Interpreting the Council," *Being Right,* 19.

42. R. Scott Appleby, "The Triumph of Americanism: Common Ground for U.S. Catholics in the Twentieth Century," *Being Right,* 39.

43. David J. Molineaux, "Traditionalists, Modernizers, and Prophets," *Latinamerica Press,* September 1, 1983.

44. The scholarship of "lived religion" highlights religion as more than theological or as experienced within church walls. For a foundational text, see Robert A. Orsi, *The Madonna of 115th Street: Faith and Community in Italian Harlem, 1880–1950* (New Haven, CT: Yale University Press, 1985).

45. John A. Farrell, *Tip O'Neill and the Democratic Century* (Boston: Little Brown, 2001), 519–520.

46. Strauss, "Quest for the Holy Grail."

47. Brett, *Catholic Press,* 160, 207.

48. Donna Whitson Brett and Edward T. Brett, *Martyrs of Hope: Seven Missioners in Central America* (Maryknoll, NY: Orbis, 2018), 32–34.

49. Smith, *Resisting Reagan,* 51.

1. From Senator McCarthy's Darlings to Marxist Maryknollers

1. Gerald R. Ford, "The President's News Conference," September 16, 1974, Gerhard Peters and John T. Woolley, The American Presidency Project (APP), University of California, Santa Barbara, https://www.presidency.ucsb.edu/node/256615.

2. Central Governing Board to Gerald Ford, October 2, 1974, folder 1, box 2, Office of Social Concerns (OSC), MSA.

3. Barbara Hendricks, "Maryknoll Is Our Home," *Channel,* Winter/Spring 1978, 9, folder 1, box 16, Same Fate as the Poor (SFP), MSA.

4. John F. McConnell, "The Whole Way: Frs. Walsh and Price and the Mystique of Martyrdom," *Channel*, Fall 1977, 6, folder 1, box 16, SFP, MSA; Hendricks, "Maryknoll Is Our Home," 9.

5. Angelyn Dries, *The Missionary Movement in American Catholic History* (Maryknoll, NY: Orbis, 1998), 79.

6. Penny Lernoux, Arthur Jones, and Robert Ellsberg, *Hearts on Fire: The Story of the Maryknoll Sisters* (Maryknoll, NY: Orbis, 1993), 3, 92–93, 100, 108, 225.

7. Talk, Mother Mary Joseph to Senior Novices, May 7, 1951, folder 1, box 16, SFP, MSA.

8. Lernoux, Jones, and Ellsberg, *Hearts on Fire*, 11.

9. Penny Lernoux, *Cry of the People: The Struggle for Human Rights in Latin America— The Catholic Church in Conflict with U.S. Policy* (New York: Penguin, 1982), 283.

10. Lernoux, Jones, and Ellsberg, *Hearts on Fire*, 10–11, 16, 234.

11. Lernoux, Jones, and Ellsberg, *Hearts on Fire*, 124.

12. See Robert D. Dean, *Imperial Brotherhood: Gender and the Making of Cold War Foreign Policy* (Amherst: University of Massachusetts Press, 2001).

13. Lernoux, Jones, and Ellsberg, *Hearts on Fire*, 124.

14. Patrick Allitt, *Catholic Intellectuals and Conservative Politics in America, 1950–1985* (Ithaca, NY: Cornell University Press, 1993), 16.

15. Pope Pius XI, Encyclical, *Divini Redemptoris* (On Atheistic Communism), March 19, 1937, https://w2.vatican.va/content/pius-xi/en/encyclicals/documents/hf_p-xi_enc_19370319_divini-redemptoris.html. Pius XI quoted the earlier encyclicals.

16. John W. O'Malley, *What Happened at Vatican II* (Cambridge, MA: Belknap Press of Harvard University Press, 2008), 91.

17. Seth Jacobs, *America's Miracle Man in Vietnam: Ngo Dinh Diem, Religion, Race, and U.S. Intervention in Southeast Asia, 1950–1957* (Durham, NC: Duke University Press, 2004), 61, 67–68, 78–79.

18. Dries, *Missionary Movement*, 161; Maria del Rey, *Nun in Red China* (New York: McGraw-Hill, 1953).

19. Lernoux, Jones, and Ellsberg, *Hearts on Fire*, 126; Sister Maria del Rey, *Bernie Becomes a Nun* (New York: Farrar, Straus & Cudahy, 1956); Sister Maria del Rey, *Her Name Is Mercy* (New York: Scribner, 1957).

20. "Laborare Est Orare," *Time*, April 11, 1955, 78–85.

21. Lernoux, Jones, and Ellsberg, *Hearts on Fire*, 14.

22. Allitt, *Catholic Intellectuals*, 16.

23. Lernoux, Jones, and Ellsberg, *Hearts on Fire*, 14.

24. Susan Fitzpatrick-Behrens, *The Maryknoll Catholic Mission in Peru, 1943–1989: Transnational Faith and Transformation* (Notre Dame, IN: University of Notre Dame Press, 2012), 6, 19.

25. Dries, *Missionary Movement*, 180.

26. Fitzpatrick-Behrens, *Maryknoll Catholic Mission*, 8.

27. Walter LaFeber, *Inevitable Revolutions: The United States in Central America* 2nd ed. (New York: Norton, 1993), 150.

28. Dries, *Missionary Movement*, 181.

29. Quoted in John T. McGreevy, *Parish Boundaries: The Catholic Encounter with Race in the Twentieth-Century Urban North* (Chicago: University of Chicago Press, 1996), 171.

30. Mark S. Massa, *The American Catholic Revolution: How the '60s Changed the Church Forever* (New York: Oxford University Press, 2010), xii.

31. Fitzpatrick-Behrens, *Maryknoll Catholic Mission*, 29.

32. Lernoux, Jones, and Ellsberg, *Hearts on Fire*, 147, 167.

33. Judith M. Noone, *The Same Fate as the Poor*, rev. ed. (Maryknoll, NY: Orbis, 1995), 45–47.

34. Fitzpatrick-Behrens, *Maryknoll Catholic Mission*, 20, 253n4.

35. Noone, *Same Fate*, 48.

36. Jeanne Evans, ed., *"Here I Am, Lord": The Letters and Writings of Ita Ford* (Maryknoll, NY: Orbis, 2005), x, 8–9, 20, 23, 39, 44, 46.

37. Lernoux, Jones, and Ellsberg, *Hearts on Fire*, 143–144, 166–167.

38. Lernoux, Jones, and Ellsberg, *Hearts on Fire*, 144, 148, 166–169.

39. Lernoux, Jones, and Ellsberg, *Hearts on Fire*, 168, 174–175.

40. Ivan Illich, "The Seamy Side of Charity," *America*, January 21, 1967, https://www.americamagazine.org/issue/100/seamy-side-charity.

41. Christian Smith, *The Emergence of Liberation Theology: Radical Religion and Social Movement Theory* (Chicago: University of Chicago Press, 1991), 118–119.

42. Illich, "Seamy Side."

43. Lernoux, *Cry of the People*, 284.

44. Quoted in Gary MacEoin, "U.S. Mission Efforts Threatened by CIA 'Dirty Tricks,'" *St. Anthony Messenger*, 1975, 34, folder CIA 1974–76 (CIA), box 98, U.S. Catholic Mission Association (USCMA), MMA.

45. Report, John M. Breen to John J. McCormack, folder 1, box 7, Maryknoll Fathers and Brothers Archives (MFBA), MMA. There is no typed date, but "9 enero 1969" is handwritten, indicating a mistake or that the account was written years after the episode.

46. Lernoux, Jones, and Ellsberg, *Hearts on Fire*, 158.

47. Shawn Francis Peters, *The Catonsville Nine: A Story of Faith and Resistance in the Vietnam Era* (New York: Oxford University Press, 2012), 59.

48. Thomas Melville and Marjorie Melville, *Whose Heaven, Whose Earth?* (New York: Alfred A. Knopf, 1970), 8, 11–12, 24, 39.

49. Peters, *Catonsville Nine*, 61.

50. Melville and Melville, *Whose Heaven*, 153.

51. Lernoux, Jones, and Ellsberg, *Hearts on Fire*, 156.

52. Melville and Melville, *Whose Heaven*, 216.

53. Peters, *Catonsville Nine*, 62.

54. Melville and Melville, *Whose Heaven*, 212, 214.

55. Peters, *Catonsville Nine*, 63; Lernoux, Jones, and Ellsberg, *Hearts on Fire*, 158.

56. Melville and Melville, *Whose Heaven*, 261.

57. Lernoux, *Cry of the People*, 29; Rick Edwards, "Religion in the Revolution? . . . A Look at Golconda," *NACLA Report on the Americas*, February 1970, 2.

58. Lernoux, Jones, and Ellsberg, *Hearts on Fire*, 158.

59. Thomas R. Melville, "Revolution is Guatemala's Only Solution," *National Catholic Reporter*, January 31, 1968; William R. MacKaye, "Guatemala Revolt Defended," *Washington Post*, January 27, 1968.

60. "Former Nun Explains Stand in Letter," *Washington Post*, February 18, 1968.

61. Melville and Melville, *Whose Heaven*, 283–284; "102 Maryknollers Score Ex-Members," *New York Times*, February 28, 1968. According to Tom Melville, "Few

Maryknollers had actually signed the statement or agreed with it." Melville and Melville, *Whose Heaven*, 284.

62. Melville and Melville, *Whose Heaven*, 284.

63. Report, Breen to McCormack.

64. Report, Breen to McCormack; Edward T. Brett, *The U.S. Catholic Press on Central America: From Cold War Anticommunism to Social Justice* (Notre Dame, IN: University of Notre Dame Press, 2003), 50.

65. Report, Breen to McCormack; Arnold R. Isaacs, "Guatemala Calls a State of Siege," *Baltimore Sun*, March 19, 1968.

66. Melville and Melville, *Whose Heaven*, 283.

67. See "Two Priests Are Silenced by Superior," *Baltimore Sun*, January 19, 1968; "3 in Maryknoll Order Suspended for Aiding Guatemala Guerrillas," *Washington Post*, January 19, 1968; "Suspended US Priests Linked to Guerrillas," *Chicago Tribune*, January 19, 1968; George Dugan, "Maryknoll Suspends 2 Priests as Guatemala Guerrilla Aides," *New York Times*, January 19, 1968; Editorial, "Why the Alliance Falters," *New York Times*, January 27, 1968.

68. Report, Breen to McCormack.

69. Murray Polner and Jim O'Grady, *Disarmed & Dangerous: The Radical Life and Times of Daniel and Philip Berrigan, Brothers in Religious Faith and Civil Disobedience* (New York: Basic Books, 1997), 196–198. Press photos featured the Berrigans, suggesting only they were involved.

70. Myra MacPherson, "The Thomas Melvilles: Church Dissenters," *Washington Post*, September 26, 1968.

71. Quoted in Polner and O'Grady, *Disarmed & Dangerous*, 200.

72. Patricia McNeal, *Harder Than War: Catholic Peacemaking in Twentieth-Century America* (New Brunswick, NJ: Rutgers University Press, 1992), 174.

73. Peters, *Catonsville Nine*, 108.

74. Peters, *Catonsville Nine*, 122–123, 125, 128 (emphasis in original).

75. Massa, *American Catholic Revolution*, 113–114.

76. Pope Paul VI, Encyclical, *Populorum Progressio* (On the Development of Peoples), March 26, 1967, http://www.vatican.va/holy_father/paul_vi/encyclicals/documents/hf_p-vi_enc_26031967_populorum_en.html.

77. Teresa Whitfield, *Paying the Price: Ignacio Ellacuría and the Murdered Jesuits of El Salvador* (Philadelphia: Temple University Press, 1994), 37.

78. Gerald M. Costello, *Mission to Latin America: The Successes and Failures of a Twentieth-Century Crusade* (Maryknoll, NY: Orbis, 1979), 149, 153.

79. Lernoux, *Cry of the People*, 38.

80. Paul E. Pierson, "The Rise of Christian Mission and Relief Agencies," in *The Influence of Faith: Religious Groups and U.S. Foreign Policy*, ed. Elliott Abrams (Lanham, MD: Rowman & Littlefield, 2001), 166; Lernoux, *Cry of the People*, 40–42.

81. LaFeber, *Inevitable Revolutions*, 16–17.

82. Fernando Cardenal, *Faith & Joy: Memoirs of a Revolutionary Priest*, trans and ed. Kathleen McBride and Mark Lester (Maryknoll, NY: Orbis, 2015), 6.

83. David J. Molineaux and Mary Judith Ress, *Maryknoll in Chile: The First Fifty Years* (Santiago: Mosquito Editores, 1993), 129.

84. James Goff, "The Golconda Statement by Colombian Priests," *NACLA Report on the Americas*, December 1968, 13–14.

85. "Subversion of the Church in Latin America," n.d., folder 100, box 12, Subseries 2, Series 7, James Cannon Files, 1968–1971 (JC), Record Group (RG) 15, Nelson A. Rockefeller Papers (NAR), Rockefeller Archive Center, Sleepy Hollow, NY.

86. Malcolm W. Browne, "Liberal Catholic Priests in Argentina Are Nearing Open Revolt Against the Traditionalist Hierarchy," *New York Times*, April 21, 1968.

87. Margaret Power, "Traditional, Conservative, Catholic, and Anti-Communist: Tradition, Family, and Property (TFP)," in *New Perspectives on the Transnational Right* (New York: Palgrave Macmillan, 2010), 85, 87, 94.

88. Malcolm W. Browne, "Church in Latin America Develops a Leftward Trend," *New York Times*, July 7, 1969, 1, folder 1721, box 196, Series O, RG 4, NAR; James N. Green, *We Cannot Remain Silent: Opposition to the Brazilian Military Dictatorship in the United States* (Durham, NC: Duke University Press, 2010), 108.

89. *Arriba Muchachos*, box 2, Entry-A1-53: 1953–1983, Press & Publication Service / Publications Divisions, RG 0306, United States Information Agency (USIA), NARA.

90. Barry Bishop, "Report from Latin America: Religion's Role Is Big in Drama of Latin Nations," *Chicago Tribune*, March 24, 1968.

91. John Gordon Mien to Covey Oliver, February 27, 1968, *Foreign Relations of the United States (FRUS), 1964–1968*, vol. XXXI, https://history.state.gov/historicaldocuments/frus1964-68v31/d100.

92. Memorandum, Viron P. Vaky to Covey Oliver, March 29, 1968, *FRUS, 1964–1968*, vol. XXXI, https://history.state.gov/historicaldocuments/frus1964-68v31/d102 (emphasis in original).

93. See Stephen G. Rabe, *The Killing Zone: The United States Wages Cold War in Latin America* (New York: Oxford University Press, 2012), xxxi; Daniel Wilkinson, *Silence on the Mountain: Stories of Terror, Betrayal, and Forgetting in Guatemala* (Boston: Houghton Mifflin, 2002), 324–325; Gilbert M. Joseph, "What We Know and Should Know: Bringing Latin America More Meaningfully into Cold War Studies," in *In from the Cold: Latin America's New Encounter with the Cold War*, ed. Gilbert M. Joseph and Daniela Spenser (Durham, NC: Duke University Press, 2008), 25.

94. Memorandum of Meeting, June 12, 1969, *FRUS, 1969–1976*, vol. E–10, https://history.state.gov/historicaldocuments/frus1969-76ve10/d150.

95. Memorandum of Meeting, June 13, 1969, *FRUS, 1969–1976*, vol. E–10, https://history.state.gov/historicaldocuments/frus1969-76ve10/d154.

96. Molineaux and Ress, *Maryknoll in Chile*, 127.

97. Browne, "Liberal Catholic Priests."

98. Browne, "Church in Latin America Develops a Leftward Trend."

99. Memorandum of Meeting, June 13, 1969.

100. Editorial Note, Document 6, DOS, *FRUS, 1969–1976*, vol. E–10, https://history.state.gov/historicaldocuments/frus1969-76ve10/d6.

101. National Security Study Memorandum 68, July 12, 1969, *FRUS, 1969–1976*, vol. E–10, https://history.state.gov/historicaldocuments/frus1969-76ve10/d7.

102. Memorandum of Meeting, June 13, 1969.

103. Nelson A. Rockefeller, *Rockefeller Report on the Americas: The Official Report of a United States Presidential Mission for the Western Hemisphere* (Chicago: Quadrangle, 1969), 5.

104. Luigi Einuadi, Richard Maulin, Alfred Stepan, and Michael Fleet, *Latin American Institutional Development: The Changing Catholic Church* (Santa Monica, CA: RAND Corporation, 1969), 67–69, 73.

105. Intelligence Memorandum 2609/69, October 9, 1969, *FRUS, 1969–1976*, vol. E–10, https://history.state.gov/historicaldocuments/frus1969-76ve10/d13.

106. Rockefeller, *Rockefeller Report*, 31. For discussion of Rockefeller's positive assessment of changes in the church, see Theresa Keeley, "Medellín Is 'Fantastic': Drafts of the 1969 Rockefeller Report on the Catholic Church," *Catholic Historical Review* 101, no. 4 (2015): 809–834.

107. Rabe, *Killing Zone*, 119; Conversation, Richard Nixon, Henry Kissinger, H. R. Halderman, Alexander Haig, and Richard Helms, March 5, 1971, *FRUS, 1969–1976*, vol. E–10, https://history.state.gov/historicaldocuments/frus1969-76ve10/d36.

108. McNeal, *Harder Than War*, 202–203; *Time*, January 25, 1971.

109. Memorandum, Conversation CIA Director and Imelda Marcos, September 22, 1970, *FRUS, 1969–1976*, vol. XX, https://history.state.gov/historicaldocuments/frus1969-76v20/d227.

110. Margaret Power, "The Engendering of Anticommunism and Fear in Chile's 1964 Presidential Election," *Diplomatic History* 32, no. 5 (2008): 931, 934, 938, 943–945, 952.

111. Rabe, *Killing Zone*, 126.

112. Julio Huasi, "Arroyo on Chile's Christians for Socialism," *NACLA Report on the Americas*, March 1972, 16–17.

113. Smith, *Emergence of Liberation Theology*, 20; Molineaux and Ress, *Maryknoll in Chile*, 232–233.

114. Molineaux and Ress, *Maryknoll in Chile*, 235, 237.

115. Molineaux and Ress, *Maryknoll in Chile*, 232–233, 242.

116. Betty Medsger, "Missionaries Rap ITT 'Plot' in Chile," *Washington Post*, May 6, 1972.

117. Juan de Onis, "American Colony in Chile Declines," *New York Times*, July 5, 1972.

118. Molineaux and Ress, *Maryknoll in Chile*, 243.

119. Rabe, *Killing Zone*, 126–127, 129.

120. Rabe, *Killing Zone*, 138.

121. Evans, *"Here I Am,"* 57–58, 60, 88–90.

122. Quoted in Evans, *"Here I Am,"* 86–87.

123. Dries, *Missionary Movement*, 230.

124. MacEoin, U.S. Mission Efforts."

125. "Misioneros de EU se quejan de las actividades de la CIA," *Excélsior*, March 15, 1975, and "U.S. Activities in Chile Assailed," *Target*, December 1, 1974, folder CIA, box 98, USCMA.

126. Minutes, "Meeting to Further Consider Action of Missionary-CIA Issue—July 10, 1975," folder CIA, box 98, USCMA.

127. Dries, *Missionary Movement*, 230.

128. Philip Agee, *Inside the Company: CIA Diary*, American ed. (New York: Stonehill, 1975).

129. Victor Marchetti and John D. Marks, *The CIA and the Cult of Intelligence* (New York: Knopf, 1974).

130. Dries, *Missionary Movement*, 230.

131. Kenneth A. Briggs, "Churches Angered by Disclosures, Seek to Bar Further C.I.A. Use of Missionaries in Intelligence Work," *New York Times*, January 29, 1976.

132. Lernoux, *Cry of the People*, 144.

133. Quoted in Hugh Amico, "Banzer Plan," *National Catholic Reporter*, August 26, 1977.

134. "Bolivian Government Plan"; "Plan modelo de estrategia Contra la iglesia católica latinoamericana," *Orientación*, May 29, 1977, box 38, Brockman-Romero Papers (B-RP), Special Collections and Archives, DePaul University, Chicago, IL; Amico, "Banzer Plan."

135. Hal Brands, *Latin America's Cold War* (Cambridge, MA: Harvard University Press, 2010), 90.

136. "Anticommunist Congress Focuses on the Church," *Latinamerica Press*, August 25, 1977.

137. "U.S. Ambassador to Bolivia Cancels Talk to Missioners," *Latinamerica Press*, May 29, 1975.

138. Charles Curry to Frank Church, June 9, 1975, folder CIA, box 98, USCMA.

139. Barbara Hendricks to William Colby, July 28, 1975, folder CIA, box 98, US-CMA.

140. William Colby to Barbara Hendricks, August 21, 1975, folder CIA, box 98, US-CMA.

141. Minutes, "Meeting to Further Consider Action of Missionary-CIA Issue."

142. Charles Curry, "Various Reflections on CIA-Missionary Issues," January 30, 1976, folder CIA, box 98, USCMA.

143. "Anti-U.S. Terrorist Acts in Greece: 1975–October 1999," October 1999, Terrorism and U.S. Policy, 1968–2002, Digital National Security Archives (DNSA), The George Washington University.

144. "11 CIA Agents Named," *Los Angeles Times*, August 16, 1976.

145. "Magazine Names 'CIA Agents' Based in Madrid," *Times* (London), January 14, 1976; Gerard Kemp, "60 CIA Agents in London Named by Marxist Paper," *Daily Telegraph*, March 4, 1976; "CIA Agent in Africa Exposed," *Black Panther*, March 27, 1976, all in folder 30, box 14, Series VI, Philip Agee Papers (AP), Tamiment Library and Robert F. Wagner Labor Archive, New York University, New York, NY; Peter Costigan, "Uproar Over Naming CIA Agents Greets U.S. Envoy to Australia," *Washington Post*, May 20, 1977, folder Espionage and Operations, 1975–1981, box 17, Series VIII, AP.

146. The *Los Angeles Times* carried the story on its front page, but there appears to have been no other U.S. coverage despite the story originating with Reuters. "11 CIA Agents."

147. Barbara L. Worth, letter to the editor, *Maryknoll*, August 1973, 34–35.

148. Robert Ellsberg, "Through Eyes of the Poor," *Maryknoll*, July 1988, 24.

149. David J. Bosch, "Contextual Missionary Theology from Orbis," *Missionalia* 13, no. 3 (November 1985): 121.

150. George C. Higgins, "Orbis Leads Its Chosen Field," *Maryknoll*, April 1981, 57.

151. Gustavo Gutiérrez, *A Theology of Liberation: History, Politics, and Salvation* (Maryknoll, NY: Orbis, 1973).

152. Ellsberg, "Through Eyes," 24. It was still Orbis's best-selling work in 1988.

153. Dries, *Missionary Movement*, 214.

154. Joyce Hollyday, "No Oil Wells, No Pizza—Just Books," *Sojourners*, December 1991, 38–39.

155. Frank Morriss, "A Full Diet of Insult," *Wanderer*, September 9, 1976.

156. Edward Berbusse, "Liberation Theology's Shadow Falls on Church," *Wanderer*, September 9, 1976.

157. "Journal Supports Opposition to Marxism by Italy's Bishops," *Wanderer*, January 29, 1976; "French Bishops Launch Drive Against Communist Party," *Wanderer*, January 29, 1976; "Marxist Priests Challenge Bishop," *Wanderer*, February 5, 1976; "Portugal's Bishops Warn Against Supporting Communists and Radical Left," *Wanderer*, December 2, 1976; Robert J. Fox, "The Communist Plot to Destroy the Church," *National Catholic Register*, January 2, 1977, referencing a 1976 report from Italy.

2. Religious or Political Activists for Nicaragua?

1. 123 Cong. Rec. 20188 (1977).

2. Diane C. Lore, "Former Rep. Jack Murphy Dead at 88, Was 'Epitome of Public Service,'" *Staten Island Live.com*, May 27, 2015, 6:22 a.m. EST, http://www.silive.com/obituaries/index.ssf/2015/05/former_staten_island_congressm.html.

3. Robert A. Pastor, *Not Condemned to Repetition: The United States and Nicaragua*, 2nd ed. (Boulder, CO: Westview, 2002), 45.

4. Michel Gobat, *Confronting the American Dream: Nicaragua Under U.S. Imperial Rule* (Durham, NC: Duke University Press, 2005), 21–22, 29–30, 34, 40, 69–70, 103, 141.

5. Gobat, *Confronting the American Dream*, 143, 205, 215, 218, 236, 246, 264. Salvadorans gave money and fought for Sandino's forces. Jeffrey L. Gould and Aldo A. Lauria-Santiago, *To Rise in Darkness: Revolution, Repression, and Memory in El Salvador, 1920–1932* (Durham, NC: Duke University Press, 2008), 49.

6. Andrew J. Kirkendall, *Paulo Freire and the Cold War Politics of Literacy* (Chapel Hill: University of North Carolina Press, 2010), 119, 121.

7. Tim Merrill, ed., *Nicaragua: A Country Study* (Washington, DC: GPO for the Library of Congress, 1993), http://countrystudies.us/nicaragua/25.htm.

8. Merrill, *Nicaragua*, 267, 273; Pastor, *Not Condemned*, 29.

9. Lawrence Pezzullo and Ralph Pezzullo, *At the Fall of Somoza* (Pittsburgh: University of Pittsburgh Press, 1993), 13, 17.

10. Judith M. Noone, *The Same Fate as the Poor*, rev. ed. (Maryknoll, NY: Orbis, 1995), 51–56.

11. Virginia Garrard-Burnett, "Church Responses to Political Violence in Central America: From Liberation Theology to Human Rights," in *Religious Responses to Violence: Human Rights in Latin America and the Present*, ed. Alexander White (Notre Dame, IN: University of Notre Dame, 2016), 127.

12. Tommie Sue Montgomery, "The Church in the Salvadoran Revolution," *Latin American Perspectives* 10, no. 1 (1983): 72.

13. Anna L. Peterson and Manuel A. Vásquez, eds., *Latin American Religions: Histories and Documents in Context* (New York: New York University Press, 2008), 208.

14. Montgomery, "The Church in the Salvadoran Revolution," 67.

15. Peterson and Vásquez, *Latin American Religions*, 209–210.

16. Garrard-Burnett, "Church Responses," 129.

17. Edward T. Brett, *The U.S. Catholic Press on Central America: From Cold War Anticommunism to Social Justice* (Notre Dame, IN: University of Notre Dame Press, 2003), 86; Eileen Markey, *A Radical Faith: The Assassination of Sister Maura* (New York: Nation Books, 2016), 108–109.

18. Garrard-Burnett, "Church Responses," 129; Ernesto Cardenal, *El Evangelio en Solentiname* (Salamanca: Ediciones Sígueme, 1976).

19. Philip J. Williams, *The Catholic Church and Politics in Nicaragua and Costa Rica* (Pittsburgh: University of Pittsburgh Press, 1989), 48.

20. See Jeremi Suri, *Power and Protest: Global Revolution and the Rise of Détente* (Cambridge, MA: Harvard University Press, 2003).

21. Brett, *Catholic Press*, 87; Markey, *Radical Faith*, 130–131.

22. Markey, *Radical Faith*, 131.

23. Brett, *Catholic Press*, 87.

24. Brett, *Catholic Press*, 87.

25. Memorandum of Conversation, October 22, 1970, Lawson Moyer, Bio Files, box 5, entry A1 5734, DOS, RG 59, NARA.

26. Memorandum of Conversation, March 13, 1970, box 5, entry A1 5734, DOS, RG 59, NARA.

27. Quoted in Noone, *Same Fate*, 62.

28. Markey, *Radical Faith*, 76, 92–94, 111.

29. Markey, *Radical Faith*, 116–117, 119–121, 133, 138.

30. Williams, *Church and Politics*, 29.

31. Williams, *Church and Politics*, 29.

32. Margaret Randall, *Sandino's Daughters: Testimonies of Nicaraguan Women in Struggle* (New Brunswick, NJ: Rutgers University Press, 1995), 86–88; Markey, *Radical Faith*, 165–166.

33. Williams, *Church and Politics*, 30, 32.

34. Markey, *Radical Faith*, 150, 162–163.

35. Maura John Clarke, 1972, folder 1, box 1, Middle/Central America History (M/CA), MSA.

36. Markey, *Radical Faith*, 173–175.

37. Michael Dodson and Laura Nuzzi O'Shaughnessy, *Nicaragua's Other Revolution: Religious Faith and Political Struggle* (Chapel Hill: University of North Carolina Press, 1990), 134.

38. Markey, *Radical Faith*, 175.

39. "Missionary Priests List Violations of Human Rights in Nicaragua," *Latinamerica Press*, July 22, 1976; Phillip Berryman, *Stubborn Hope: Religion, Politics, and Revolution in Central America* (Maryknoll, NY: Orbis, 1994), 21.

40. Phillip Berryman, *The Religious Roots of Rebellion: Christians in Central American Revolutions* (Eugene, OR: Wipf & Stock, 1984), 70–71.

41. Bernardo Wagner and Daniel Kabat to Manual Salazar, June 13, 1976, reprinted in U.S. Congress, House, Committee on International Relations, *Human Rights in Nicaragua, Guatemala, and El Salvador: Implications for U.S. Policy, Before the Subcommittee on International Organizations*, 94th Cong., 2nd sess., 1976, 239.

42. "Clergy Defend U.S. Priest Charged with Subversion," *Latinamerica Press*, August 5, 1976.

43. *Human Rights in Nicaragua*, 11–15.

44. Cynthia J. Arnson, *Crossroads: Congress, the President, and Central America, 1976–1993*, 2nd ed. (University Park: Pennsylvania State University Press, 1993), 12.

45. "Why Nicaraguan Priest Testified to Congressional Committee," *Latinamerica Press*, July 22, 1976.

46. Quoted in Fernando Cardenal, *Faith & Joy: Memoirs of a Revolutionary Priest*, trans and ed. Kathleen McBride and Mark Lester (Maryknoll, NY: Orbis, 2015), 69.

47. James Theberge, Telegram 3490, July 22, 1976, *FRUS, 1969–1976*, vol. E–11, https://history.state.gov/historicaldocuments/frus1969-76ve11p1/d265.

48. James Theberge, Telegram 3798, August 12, 1976, *FRUS, 1969–1976*, vol. E–11, https://history.state.gov/historicaldocuments/frus1969-76ve11p1/d266.

49. Arnson, *Crossroads*, 24–25.

50. Quoted in Arnson, *Crossroads*, 27.

51. "Hierarchy Condemns Repression in Nicaragua," *Latinamerica Press*, February 25, 1977; "Nicaragua Pastoral Printed," *National Catholic Reporter*, April 15, 1977.

52. Brett, *Catholic Press*, 89–90.

53. "Sacred Heart Priest Joins Ranks of F.S.L.N. in Nicaragua," *Latinamerica Press*, January 19, 1978. Sergio Ramírez says García intended to write "a public letter . . . explaining his allegiance to the armed struggle," but Ramírez wrote "it in religious language because it had to sound like a letter from a real priest." Sergio Ramírez, *Adiós Muchachos: A Memoir of the Sandinista Revolution*, trans. Stacey Alba D. Skar (Durham, NC: Duke University Press, 2012), 127.

54. Ramírez, *Adiós Muchachos*, 128.

55. Pezzullo and Pezzullo, *At the Fall*, 260.

56. William M. LeoGrande, *Our Own Backyard: The United States in Central America, 1977–1992* (Chapel Hill: University of North Carolina Press, 1998), 19.

57. Arnson, *Crossroads*, 28.

58. Lars Schoultz, *Human Rights and United States Policy toward Latin America* (Princeton, NJ: Princeton University Press, 1981), 59.

59. Anastasio Somoza and Jack Cox, *Nicaragua Betrayed* (Belmont, MA: Western Islands, 1980), 24–25, 55, 67.

60. J. H. Elliott, *Empire of the Atlantic World: Britain and Spain in America 1492–1830* (New Haven, CT: Yale University Press, 2006), 309.

61. Dale K. Van Kley, "Plots and Rumors of Plots: The Role of Conspiracy in the International Campaign Against the Society of Jesus, 1758–1768," in *The Jesuit Suppression in Global Context: Causes, Events, & Consequences*, ed. Jeffrey D. Burson and Jonathan Wright (New York: Cambridge University Press, 2015), 13.

62. Jeffrey D. Burson and Jonathan Wright, "Introduction: Towards a New History of Eighteenth-Century Jesuit Suppression in Global Context," in Burson and Wright, *Jesuit Suppression*, 8.

63. Elliott, *Empire of the Atlantic*, 205.

64. Charles J. Beirne, "Jesuit Education for Justice: The Colegio in El Salvador, 1968–1984," in *Education and War*, ed. Elizabeth E. Blair, Rebecca B. Miller, and Mara Casey Tieken (Cambridge, MA: Harvard University Press, 2009), 12–14.

65. Roger Peace, *A Call to Conscience: The Anti-Contra War Campaign* (Amherst: University of Massachusetts Press, 2012), 149.

66. United Nations, Press kit for H. E. Father Miguel d'Escoto Brockman, M. M., accessed February 12, 2012, http://www.un.org/ga/president/63/presskit/president.shtml.

67. Gary MacEoin, "Nicaraguan Foreign Minister Fears 'Vietnamization' of Central America," *Latinamerica Press*, May 22, 1980. For an example of his earlier views, see Miguel d'Escoto, "A Look at the Chilean Coup," *Maryknoll*, April 1974, 55–56.

68. Miguel d'Escoto to Jimmy Carter, April 19, 1977, folder Nicaragua IV, box 2, James Theberge Papers (JTP), Georgetown University Special Collections (GUSC), Washington, DC.

69. U.S. Congress, House, *Foreign Assistance and Related Agencies Appropriations for 1978, Part 3, Before the Committee on Appropriations*, 95th Cong. 1st sess., 1977, 560–563.

70. *Appropriations for 1978*, 542–543.

71. Richard Millett, *Guardians of the Dynasty: A History of the U.S. Created Guardia Nacional de Nicaragua and the Somoza Family* (Maryknoll, NY: Orbis, 1977).

72. Thomas W. Walker, Review of *Guardians of the Dynasty: A History of the U. S. Created Guardia Nacional de Nicaragua and the Somoza Family*, by Richard Millett, *The Americas* 34, no. 4 (April 1978): 578.

73. Miguel d'Escoto, introduction to *Guardians of the Dynasty*, 6, 9, 11.

74. Professors of the Baptist Seminary, "Americans, Look Serious [sic] at What Your Government Is Doing in Nicaragua," in Goffs to Friend, October 25,1978, folder 818, box 45, James and Margaret Goff Papers (GP), Yale Divinity School Library, Yale University, New Haven, CT.

75. Patricia McNeal, *Harder Than War: Catholic Peacemaking in Twentieth-Century America* (New Brunswick, NJ: Rutgers University Press, 1992), 239.

76. Miguel d'Escoto to Fellow Christian, May 1, 1977, folder MFAB, box 25, Conference of Major Superiors of Men Papers (CMSM), University of Notre Dame Archives (UNDA), South Bend, IN.

77. Memorandum, Thomas J. Marti to Thomas More, May 5, 1977, with d'Escoto's letter, folder MFAB, box 25, CMSM, UNDA.

78. Arnson, *Crossroads*, 27.

79. 123 Cong. Rec. 20187–20188 (1977).

80. 123 Cong. Rec. 20190 (1977). Murphy inserted "Statement by Catholic Priests in Nicaragua," in *Appropriations for 1978*, 590.

81. Albin Krebs, "Rep. L.P. McDonald of Georgia among the Americans Lost on Jet," *New York Times*, September 2, 1983.

82. 123 Cong. Rec. 20696–20697 (1977).

83. 123 Cong. Rec. 20579 (1977).

84. Arnson, *Crossroads*, 28.

85. "Congresista Norteamericana deja mal parado al Cura Miguel Escoto [sic]," *Las Novedades*, April 27, 1977.

86. *Appropriations for 1978*, 566, 568.

87. Press release, NGIS, "Church Accused of Marxist Infiltration: Father of Girl-Terrorist Charges Priests of Inciting Youth to Subversion," May 20, 1977, folder Nicaragua-July 1977 (N77), box 3, JTP.

88. Edgard Barberena S., "Luchó por servir, la muerte la rondó y sigue sirviendo," *El Nuevo Diario*, December 5, 2010.

89. "Priests Respond to Threats in Nicaragua," *Latinamerica Press*, July 7, 1977.

90. "Priests Respond."

91. George H. Nash, *The Conservative Intellectual Movement in America since 1945*, 30th ed. (Wilmington, DE: ISI Books, 2006), 16, 533.

92. "Media Notes," *Human Events*, April 2, 1977.

93. Press release, "Maryknoller Deported from Philippines," n.d. [November 1976], folder 42, box 25, CMSM, UNDA.

94. U.S. Congress, Senate, *Rhodesia, Before the Committee on Foreign Relations*, 96th Cong., 1st sess., 1979, 51.

95. *Rhodesia*, 51–87; "Ousted Nun 'Will Return,'" *National Catholic Reporter*, September 30, 1977; Trudy Howard, "Amnesty Group Comes to Marymount," *New York Times*, November 27, 1977; U.S. Congress, House, Committee on Foreign Affairs, *Political Developments in Southern Rhodesia, Before the Subcommittees on International Organizations and on Africa*, 95th Cong., 1st sess., 1977, 1–12; U.S. Congress, House, Committee on Foreign Affairs, *Economic Sanctions Against Rhodesia, Before the Subcommittees on International Organizations and on Africa*, 96th Cong., 1st sess., 1979, 2–14.

96. J. Bryan Hehir, "Struggle in Central America: A View from the Church," *Foreign Affairs* 43 (Summer 1981): 86.

97. Gary MacEoin, "U.S. Mission Efforts Threatened by CIA 'Dirty Tricks," *St. Anthony Messenger*, 1975, 37, folder CIA, box 98, USCMA, MMA.

98. "World Awareness Program W.A.P.," *Maryknoll News Notes*, May / June 1978, folder 5, box 15, Office of Justice and Peace (OJP) 1974–1977, MMA.

99. Barbara J. Keys, *Reclaiming American Virtue: The Human Rights Revolution of the 1970s* (Cambridge, MA: Harvard University Press, 2014), 178–213.

100. Patrick William Kelly, "Human Rights and Christian Responsibility: Transnational Christian Activism, Human Rights, and State Violence in Brazil and Chile in the 1970s," in *Religious Responses*, 95–122.

101. U.S. Congress, House, Committee on Appropriations, *Foreign Assistance and Related Programs Appropriations for 1980, Before the Subcommittee on Foreign Operations and Related Programs*, 96th Cong., 2nd sess., 1979, 153.

102. Carol Coston, "Network's New Image," *NETWORK Newsletter*, October 1978, folder 40, box 28, Leadership Conference of Women Religious Papers (LCWR), UNDA.

103. For examples, see U.S. Congress, House, Committee on Foreign Affairs, *Human Rights in South Korea: Implications for U.S. Policy, Before the Subcommittees on Asian and Pacific Affairs and on International Organizations and Movements*, 93rd Cong., 2nd. sess., 1974, 99–101; U.S. Congress, Senate, Committee on Human Resources, *Marketing and Promotion of Infant Formula in the Developing Nations, Before the Subcommittee on Health and Scientific Research*, 95th Cong., 2nd. sess., 1978, 13–16.

104. Keys, *Reclaiming American Virtue*, 139–140.

105. James Abourezk to Raymond A. Hill, July 22, 1975, folder 5, box 31, OJP, MMA.

106. Keys, *Reclaiming American Virtue*, 271.

107. Donald Fraser to Thomas J. Marti, November 6, 1978, folder 5, box 31, OJP, MMA.

108. Pastor, *Not Condemned*, 46.

109. "Prominent Nicaraguans Support F.S.L.N. Action," *Latinamerica Press*, November 10, 1977.

110. Cardenal, *Faith & Joy*, 83.

111. "Nicaraguan Priest Acclaims 'Sandinist [*sic*] Patriots'—Miguel d'Escoto," *Latinamerica Press*, November 10, 1977.

112. Pastor, *Not Condemned*, 48.

113. LeoGrande, *Our Own Backyard*, 17–18.

114. June Carolyn Erlick, "Nicaragua's Los Doce: 'They Might Try to Kill One of Us,'" *National Catholic Reporter*, August 18, 1978.

115. Ian R. MacKenzie, "A 'Distorted' Media View of Somoza's Nicaragua," *Washington Post*, November 22, 1977.

116. H. W. Brands, *Reagan: The Life* (New York: Doubleday, 2015), 186–187.

117. Press release, NGIS, "Ronald Reagan Comments on Campaign to Discredit Nicaragua," December 19, 1977, folder N77, box 3, JTP.

118. Penny Lernoux, *Cry of the People: The Struggle for Human Rights in Latin America—The Catholic Church in Conflict with U.S. Policy* (New York: Penguin, 1982), 93; "Two U.S. Nuns Beaten," *National Catholic Register*, January 22, 1978.

119. "Happenings in Open 3, Managua, Nicaragua per phone call of Peg Healy 12/19/77," folder Nicaragua Revolution-SJC (NR-SJC), box 3, Nicaragua, MSA.

120. "Account of the Happenings in Open 3 in Managua, Nicaragua, on the 20th of December 1977," folder NR-SJC, box 3, Nicaragua, MSA.

121. LeoGrande, *Our Own Backyard*, 18.

122. Williams, *Church and Politics*, 45, 47, 49.

123. Pastor, *Not Condemned*, 44.

124. Cyrus Vance, *Hard Choices: Critical Years in America's Foreign Policy* (New York: Simon & Schuster, 1983), 156.

125. Zbigniew Brzezinski, *Power and Principle: Memoirs of the National Security Adviser, 1977–1981*, rev. ed. (New York: Farrar, Straus and Giroux, 1985), 51.

126. Vance, *Hard Choices*, 140–141.

127. Sean Wilentz, *The Age of Reagan: A History, 1974–2008* (New York: HarperCollins, 2008), 101; David Skidmore, "Foreign Policy Interest Groups and Presidential Power: Jimmy Carter and the Battle Over Ratification of the Panama Canal Treaties," *Presidential Studies Quarterly* 23, no. 3 (1993): 482.

128. Wilentz, *Age of Reagan*, 67.

129. "Panama Canal Implementation Bill Clears," *Congressional Quarterly Almanac*, 1979, 142–156, accessed December 19, 2016, http://library.cqpress.com/cqalmanac/cqal79-1184561.

130. David F. Schmitz and Vanessa Walker, "Jimmy Carter and the Foreign Policy of Human Rights: The Development of a Post-Cold War Foreign Policy," *Diplomatic History* 28, no. 1 (2004): 138.

131. Arnson, *Crossroads*, 30.

132. Schmitz and Walker, "Jimmy Carter," 138.

133. Somoza and Cox, *Nicaragua Betrayed*, 143; LeoGrande, *Our Own Backyard*, 20.

134. Erlick, "Nicaragua's Los Doce."

135. Moises Sandoval, "10 Re-enter Nicaragua Despite Risks," *National Catholic Reporter*, July 14, 1978.

136. LeoGrande, *Our Own Backyard*, 20.

137. Amnesty International, *Report 1979* (London: Amnesty International Publications, 1979), 69; Gioconda Belli, *The Country Under My Skin: A Memoir of Love and War*, trans. Kristina Cordero and Gioconda Belli (New York: Anchor Books, 2003), 194–195.

138. John Huey, "Human Rights and Nicaragua," *Wall Street Journal*, September 19, 1978.

139. "In Nicaragua You Can't Be in the Middle," *National Catholic Reporter*, August 18, 1978.

140. Peg Dillon to Mark Schneider, September 1978 (no day), folder NR-SJC, box 3, Nicaragua, MSA.

141. "Priests Demand Nicaragua Aid," *Catholic Standard*, September 21, 1987, reprinted in 124 Cong. Rec. 30874 (1978).

142. James E. Goff, "Latin American Churches Want Somoza to Resign," *Washington Post*, October 13, 1978.

143. Arnson, *Crossroads*, 31.

144. 124 Cong. Rec. 30874 (1978).

145. 124 Cong. Rec. 30876 (1978).

146. Larry McDonald inserted the letter into the *Congressional Record*. 124 Cong. Record 31777–31778 (1978).

147. "Report of Congressman Charles Wilson's Press Conference of December 4, 1978," folder 7, box 19, Kirk O'Donnell Files (KOD), Thomas P. O'Neill Papers (OP), John J. Burns Library, Boston College, Chestnut Hill, MA.

148. Alan Riding, "Taking Aim," *New York Times*, November 19, 1978.

149. Karen DeYoung, "Congressman Denounces U.S. Nicaraguan Efforts," *Washington Post*, December 7, 1978.

150. "Panama Canal Implementation."

151. Arnson, *Crossroads*, 34.

152. DeYoung, "Congressman Denounces."

153. "Panama Canal Implementation."

154. LeoGrande, *Our Own Backyard*, 23.

155. Williams, *Church and Politics*, 37.

156. LeoGrande, *Our Own Backyard*, 23.

157. Pastor, *Not Condemned*, 110.

158. Advertisement, Committee for Justice and Freedom in the Americas, "Congress Asks: Please, Mr. President, Not Another Cuba!," *New York Times*, June 18, 1979.

159. "Panama Canal Implementation."

160. Arnson, *Crossroads*, 33.

161. Pastor, *Not Condemned*, 111.

162. LeoGrande, *Our Own Backyard*, 24.

163. "Panama Canal Implementation."

164. Pastor, *Not Condemned*, 118–119.

165. Pezzullo and Pezzullo, *At the Fall*, 11–12; Arnson, *Crossroads*, 34.

166. Pastor, *Not Condemned*, 45.

167. Pezzullo and Pezzullo, *At the Fall*, 44–45.

168. Graham Hovey, "U.S. Proposals on Nicaragua Crisis Meet Sharp Criticism from O.A.S.," *New York Times*, June 23, 1979.

169. Quoted in Pezzullo and Pezzullo, *At the Fall*, 78.

170. Warren Hoge, "Sandinist [*sic*] Chiefs Express Anger at U.S. for Not Making Contact: Hopes for Good Relations," *New York Times*, June 28, 1979.

171. Quoted in Pezzullo and Pezzullo, *At the Fall*, 171.

172. Markey, *Radical Faith*, 179, 184–185.

173. Joe Cullen, "Maryknoll Nun: Nicaraguans Back Struggle," *Ossining Citizen Register* (Ossining, NY), June 13, 1979, folder 13, box 1, OSC, MSA.

174. Nicaraguan Group to Other Sisters, June 18, 1979, folder Nicaragua Insurrection (NI), unknown box, OSC, MSA.

175. Press release, "Statement of the Maryknoll Sisters Regarding Nicaragua," July 12, 1979. Their statement was featured in "Maryknoll Sisters Support Opponents

of Gen Somoza," *Catholic News*, July 19, 1979. Both documents are in folder NI, unknown box, OSC, MSA.

176. Berryman, *Stubborn Hope*, 21–22.

177. Pastor, *Not Condemned*, 161.

178. "Priests Preach Pro-Marxist Gospel to Third World," *Human Events*, July 28, 1979.

179. "Communists Poised to Take Over Nicaragua," *Human Events*, July 28, 1979.

180. "Priests Preach Pro-Marxist Gospel to Third World," *Wanderer*, August 16, 1979.

3. Subversives in El Salvador

1. William J. Grimm, "Battle-Tested Scholar," *Maryknoll*, March 1991, 19.

2. Bernard Survil, "Relief Aid 'Pacifies,'" *National Catholic Reporter*, March 18, 1977; Gerald M. Costello, *Mission to Latin America: The Successes and Failures of a Twentieth-Century Crusade* (Maryknoll, NY: Orbis, 1979), 207.

3. Penny Lernoux, Arthur Jones, and Robert Ellsberg, *Hearts on Fire: The Story of the Maryknoll Sisters* (Maryknoll, NY: Orbis, 1993), 231.

4. Erik Ching, *Stories of Civil War in El Salvador: A Battle over Memory* (Chapel Hill: University of North Carolina Press, 2016), 28.

5. Walter LaFeber, *Inevitable Revolutions: The United States in Central America*, 2nd ed. (New York: Norton, 1993), 72.

6. Ching, *Stories of Civil War*, 29.

7. Erik Ching, "In Search of the Party: The Communist Party, the Comintern, and the Peasant Rebellion of 1932 in El Salvador," *The Americas* 55, no. 2 (1988): 205–206.

8. Ching, "In Search of the Party," 222; Jeffrey L. Gould and Aldo A. Lauria-Santiago, *To Rise in Darkness: Revolution, Repression, and Memory in El Salvador, 1920–1932* (Durham, NC: Duke University Press, 2008), xxiv, 161.

9. Gould and Lauria-Santiago, *To Rise in Darkness*, xxiii.

10. Ching, "In Search of the Party," 206.

11. Ching, *Stories of Civil War*, 113, 141.

12. Philip Berryman, *The Religious Roots of Rebellion: Christians in Central American Revolutions* (Eugene, OR: Wipf & Stock, 1984), 92, 94–95.

13. Joaquín M. Chávez, *Poets and Prophets of the Resistance: Intellectuals and the Origins of El Salvador's Civil War* (New York: Oxford University Press, 2017), 22, 29.

14. Chávez, *Poets and Prophets*, 17–18, 22, 41–42.

15. Ching, *Stories of Civil War*, 25–26.

16. Berryman, *Religious Roots*, 98.

17. LaFeber, *Inevitable Revolutions*, 177.

18. Peter M. Sánchez, *Priest Under Fire: Padre David Rodríguez, the Catholic Church, and El Salvador's Revolutionary Movement* (Gainesville: University Press of Florida, 2015), 53.

19. LaFeber, *Inevitable Revolutions*, 242.

20. William M. LeoGrande, *Our Own Backyard: The United States in Central America, 1977–1992* (Chapel Hill: University of North Carolina Press, 1998), 35.

21. LaFeber, *Inevitable Revolutions*, 175–176.

22. Chávez, *Poets and Prophets*, 58–59, 72.

23. Leigh Binford, "Peasants, Catechists, Revolutionaries: Organic Intellectuals in El Salvador's Revolution, 1980–1992," in *Landscapes of Struggle: Politics, Society, and Community in El Salvador*, ed. Aldo Lauria-Santiago and Leigh Binford (Pittsburgh: University of Pittsburgh Press, 2004), 106, 109, 113–114, 116.

24. Binford, "Peasants, Catechists," 119.

25. Luis Armando González, "Iglesia, organizaciones populares y violencia sociopolítica," in *El Salvador: La transición y sus problemas*, ed. Rodolfo Cardenal and Luis Armando González (San Salvador: UCA Editores, 2007), 245–247.

26. Binford, "Peasants, Catechists," 120.

27. Chávez, *Poets and Prophets*, 75.

28. Sánchez, *Priest Under Fire*, 56.

29. U.S. Congress, House, Committee on International Relations, *Religious Persecution in El Salvador, Before the Committee on International Relations, Subcommittee on International Organizations*, 95th Cong., 1st sess., 1977, 7.

30. Chávez, *Poets and Prophets*, 95.

31. Sánchez, *Priest Under Fire*, 65.

32. Berryman, *Religious Roots*, 104.

33. Sánchez, *Priest Under Fire*, 68.

34. Binford, "Peasants, Catechists," 105–106.

35. Berryman, *Religious Roots*, 30.

36. Binford, "Peasants, Catechists," 106.

37. Louise Ahrens, "A Special Communication from the Central Governing Board Regarding El Salvador," February 23, 1988, folder SMES 1969–1993, box 6, ESM, MSA.

38. Donald L. Bank, "Are They Real Sisters?," *Maryknoll*, April 1973, 51–52.

39. Maryknoll Mission Archives, Biographies, "Sister Joan Petrik, MM," accessed November 23, 2019, http://maryknollmissionarchives.org/?deceased-sisters=sister -joan-petrik-mm.

40. Tommie Sue Montgomery, *Revolution in El Salvador: From Civil Strife to Civil Peace*, 2nd ed. (Boulder, CO: Westview Press, 1995), 88.

41. Gustavo Gutiérrez, "Praxis of Liberation and the Christian Faith," trans. by Goffs, Jesuit Project for Third World Awareness, Resource Service I: 9 (July, 1974), folder 12, box 19, B-RP.

42. Montgomery, *Revolution in El Salvador*, 89–90; Berryman, *Religious Roots*, 107.

43. Montgomery, *Revolution in El Salvador*, 90–91.

44. Binford, "Peasants, Catechists," 121–122.

45. Ching, *Stories of Civil War*, 38.

46. Sánchez, *Priest Under Fire*, 98, 107–111.

47. Ching, *Stories of Civil War*, 37–39.

48. Sánchez, *Priest Under Fire*, 107, 111–113.

49. Sánchez, *Priest Under Fire*, 118–120.

50. *Religious Persecution in El Salvador*, 9.

51. Sánchez, *Priest Under Fire*, 124.

52. Montgomery, *Revolution in El Salvador*, 92.

53. "Salvadoran Landowners Inflamed over Clergy Support of Campesinos," *Latinamerica Press*, February 3, 1977.

54. Ching, *Stories of Civil War*, 85.

55. "FARO denuncia a los jesuitas," *El Mundo*, January 15, 1977, folder *El Mundo* 1973–1979, box 39, B-RP (capitalization in original).

56. "Salvadoran Upper-Class Catholics Question Church's Role," *Latinamerica Press*, February 3, 1977.

57. "Dossier sobre la persecución de la iglesia en El Salvador," 18, folder 1, box 1, B-RP.

58. Teresa Whitfield, *Paying the Price: Ignacio Ellacuría and the Murdered Jesuits of El Salvador* (Philadelphia: Temple University Press, 1994), 100.

59. John Spain, Information Submitted to Bishop Chávez y González on February 21, 1977, folder 3, box 25, OJP, MFBA.

60. Government Report, Bernard Survil, Sumario de actividades, folder 3, box 25, OJP, MFBA.

61. Spain, Information Submitted.

62. Government Report, Lawrence McCulloch, Sumario de actividades, folder 3, box 25, OJP, MFBA.

63. *Religious Persecution in El Salvador*, 82–83.

64. Berryman, *Religious Roots*, 121.

65. Kempton B. Jenkins to Donald Fraser, March 8, 1977, in U.S. Congress, House, Committee on International Relations, *The Recent Presidential Elections in El Salvador: Implications for U.S. Foreign Policy, Before the Subcommittee on International Organizations and Subcommittee on Inter-American Affairs*, 95th Cong., 1st sess., 1977, 89–90.

66. *Recent Presidential Elections*, 39, 54.

67. Cf. Berryman, *Religious Roots*, 122, with *Recent Presidential Elections*, 2.

68. Reprinted in *Recent Presidential Elections*, 82.

69. *Recent Presidential Elections*, 5.

70. *Recent Presidential Elections*, 1, 8.

71. Douglas J. Bennett to Donald Fraser, April 22, 1977, in *Recent Presidential Elections*, 92.

72. *Recent Presidential Elections*, 4, 6.

73. Reprinted in *Recent Presidential Elections*, 56–57.

74. Svenja Blanke, "Civic Foreign Policy: Human Rights, Faith-Based Groups and U.S.-Salvadoran Relations in the 1970s," *The Americas* 61, no. 2 (2004): 229.

75. Ronald Hennessey, Report of Interview with Bishop Emmanuel Gerarda, February 25, 1977, folder 3, box 25, OJP, MFBA.

76. John Spain to Ronald Hennessey, March 7, 1977, folder 3, box 25, OJP, MFBA.

77. Raymond Bonner, *Weakness and Deceit: U.S. Policy and El Salvador* (New York: Times Books, 1984), 39.

78. See David F. Schmitz and Vanessa Walker, "Jimmy Carter and the Foreign Policy of Human Rights: The Development of a Post-Cold War Foreign Policy," *Diplomatic History* 28, no. 1 (2004): 113–143.

79. Alan Riding, "Salvador Confused by American Moves," *New York Times*, July 25, 1977.

80. "U.S., Salvador at Odds in Case of Missing Man," *Los Angeles Times*, March 27, 1977.

81. "U.S.-Salvador Strain," *Washington Post*, March 26, 1977.

82. Bonner, *Weakness and Deceit*, 39–40.

83. Memorandum, William Luers to Philip Habib, March 18, 1977, ES00007, El Salvador, 1977–1984 (ES1977–1984), DNSA.

84. Memorandum, Luers to Habib.

85. Cable, Cyrus Vance to Embassy, April 2, 1977, ES00012, ES1977–1984, DNSA.

86. Cable, Ignacio Lozano to DOS, April 20, 1977, ES00017, ES1977–1984, DNSA.

87. Cable, Warren Christopher to Embassy, April 30, 1977, ES00018, ES1977–1984, DNSA.

88. Cable, Ignacio Lozano to DOS, May 3, 1977, ES00021, ES1977–1984, DNSA.

89. Berryman, *Religious Roots*, 123–124.

90. Montgomery, *Revolution in El Salvador*, 95.

91. Montgomery, *Revolution in El Salvador*, 93; June Carolyn Erlick, "Vance-Carter Lukewarm to Romero's Aid Pleas," *National Catholic Reporter*, April 11, 1980.

92. Montgomery, *Revolution in El Salvador*, 85.

93. Montgomery, *Revolution in El Salvador*, 94–95; Berryman, *Religious Roots*, 124.

94. Russell Crandall, *The Salvador Option: The United States in El Salvador, 1977–1992* (New York: Cambridge University Press, 2016), 141; Max Echegaray, "Romero: Homilies for 'the Voiceless,'" *National Catholic Reporter*, April 4, 1980.

95. Berryman, *Religious Roots*, 124–125.

96. Montgomery, *Revolution in El Salvador*, 95.

97. Ricardo Fuentes Castellanos, "De Medellín a Riobamba y San Salvador," *El Mundo*, March 25, 1977, folder *El Mundo* 1973–1979, box 39, B-RP (capitalization in original).

98. Ricardo Fuentes Castellanos, "En apoyo de la fuerza armada," *El Mundo*, May 6, 1977, folder *El Mundo* 1973–1979, box 39, B-RP (capitalization in original).

99. Charles J. Beirne, "Jesuit Education for Justice: The Colegio in El Salvador, 1968–1984," in *Education and War*, ed. Elizabeth E. Blair, Rebecca B. Miller, and Mara Casey Tieken (Cambridge, MA: Harvard University Press, 2009), 18.

100. Berryman, *Religious Roots*, 125.

101. Penny Lernoux, *Cry of the People: The Struggle for Human Rights in Latin America—The Catholic Church in Conflict with U.S. Policy* (New York: Penguin, 1982), 75.

102. Aaron T. Bell, "A Matter of Western Civilisation: Transnational Support for the Salvadoran Counterrevolution, 1979–1982," *Cold War History* 15, no. 4 (2015): 517.

103. "Extraña situacion [*sic*] de la iglesia 'no perseguida' de El Salvador," *Orientación*, May 29, 1977, box 38, B-RP.

104. Hildebrando Recinos Cordova, "No hay iglesia perseguida," *El Mundo*, May 9, 1977, folder *El Mundo* 1973–1979, box 39, B-RP.

105. Lernoux, *Cry of the People*, 75–76; "Jesuits Defy Salvadoran Terrorists," *Latinamerica Press*, June 30, 1977.

106. Reprinted in *Religious Persecution in El Salvador*, 71.

107. Sánchez, *Priest Under Fire*. 132.

108. See Mother Ervin Rademacher to Walter Mondale, July 20, 1977, folder CO46, Countries, White House Central Files (WHCF), Jimmy Carter Presidential Library (JCPL), Atlanta, GA; Peter J. Henroit to Cyrus Vance, July 1, 1977, folder ES-General Henroit, box 39, Center of Concern Papers (COC), UNDA.

109. Memorandum, Robert Pastor to Zbigniew Brzezinski, telegram from William Guste, July 22, 1977, folder CO46, Countries, WHCF, JCPL.

110. William J. Guste Jr. to Jimmy Carter, July 20, 1977, folder CO46, Countries, WHCF, JCPL.

111. "Widening Gyre," *National Review*, August 6, 1977. Though founder William F. Buckley argued *National Review* "is no more a Catholic magazine because its editor is a Catholic," *National Review* often focused on Catholic issues absent in secular conservative periodicals. John B. Judis, *William F. Buckley, Jr.: Patron Saint of the Conservatives* (New York: Simon & Schuster, 1988), 187.

112. "Churchmen Urge U.S. El Salvador Protest," *National Catholic Reporter*, July 29, 1977.

113. Memorandum, Cyrus Vance to Jimmy Carter, July 9, 1977 (NLC-7-18-5-3-7), JCPL.

114. Jimmy Carter to William J. Guste, July 25, 1977, folder RM 3, box Religious Matters; Memorandum, Christine Dodson to Denis Clift, August 8, 1977, folder CO46, WHCF, Countries, Executive, CO45–47, JCPL.

115. Lernoux, *Cry of the People*, 80.

116. *Religious Persecution in El Salvador*.

117. Lernoux, *Cry of the People*, 80.

118. Robert F. Drinan, John J. McAward, and Thomas P. Anderson, *Human Rights in El Salvador—1978*, Report of Findings of an Investigatory Mission (Boston: Unitarian Universalist Committee, 1978), 84, folder 10, box 10, B-RP.

119. Berryman, *Religious Roots*, 129–130.

120. LeoGrande, *Our Own Backyard*, 39.

121. Drinan, McAward, and Anderson, *Human Rights in El Salvador*, 84, 87.

122. Drinan, McAward, and Anderson, *Human Rights in El Salvador*, 24, 67–69.

123. LeoGrande, *Our Own Backyard*, 37.

124. Georgie Ann Geyer, "From Here to Eternity," *Washington Post Magazine*, September 10, 1978.

125. Jo Siedlecka, "Reception at Houses of Parliament Celebrates Oscar Romero," *Independent Catholic News*, July 12, 2015, http://www.indcatholicnews.com/news.php?viewStory=27909.

126. Organization of American States, Inter-American Commission on Human Rights, *Report on the Situation of Human Rights in El Salvador*, 1978, http://www.cidh.org/countryrep/ElSalvador78eng/TOC.htm; Berryman, *Religious Roots*, 136–137.

127. Berryman, *Religious Roots*, 135–137.

128. "En el Salvador hay iglesia perseguida," *La Crónica del Pueblo*, January 23, 1979; "Los comités de solidaridad con el pueblo salvadoreño en los E.E.U.U. denuncian la persecución de la iglesia y la violación de los derechos humanos," *La Crónica del Pueblo*, February 5, 1979, El Museo de la Palabra y la Imagen, San Salvador (MUPI), El Salvador.

129. Fausto Fernandez-Ponte, "Pide Carter espiar a religiosos liberales," *Excélsior*, February 3, 1979, folder 2, box 20, B-RP.

130. Penny Lernoux, "CIA Ordered to Survey Latin American Church," *National Catholic Reporter*, February 16, 1979. *Temp e Presenca* story discussed in Ann Gormly to Katherine Popwich, October 5, 1979, folder CIA 1979–80, box 98, USCMA, MMA.

131. Quotations taken from Lernoux, "CIA Ordered to Survey." For reference to Sunday school, see Jimmy Carter, *White House Diary* (New York: Farrar, Straus and Giroux, 2010), 35.

132. Carter, *White House Diary*, 346.

133. Chávez, *Poets and Prophets*, 13.

134. Berryman, *Religious Roots*, 140.

135. Cynthia J. Arnson, *Crossroads: Congress, the President, and Central America, 1976–1993*, 2nd ed. (University Park: Pennsylvania State University Press, 1993), 36–38.

136. Ching, *Stories of Civil War*, 102, 104.

137. Cable, Frank Devine to DOS, October 24, 1979, ES00262, ES1977–1984, DNSA.

138. LaFeber, *Inevitable Revolutions*, 248.

139. José Napoleón Duarte and Diana Page, *Duarte: My Story* (New York: G. P. Putnam, 1986), 105; LeoGrande, *Our Own Backyard*, 48; Berryman, *Religious Roots*, 99.

140. Duarte and Page, *Duarte*, 105.

141. June Carolyn Erlick, "Martyr Bishop Becomes 'St. Oscar' for Many," *National Catholic Reporter*, March 20, 1981.

142. June Carolyn Erlick, "Military Aid Not Helpful, Says Bishop," *National Catholic Reporter*, November 23, 1979.

143. Madeline Dorsey, "A Brief History of El Salvador Mission: June '76 to May '81," May 1992, folder SMES 1969–1993, box 6 ESM, MSA.

144. Joan Petrik to Sisters, December 29, 1979, folder 5, box 7, SFP, MSA.

145. Jeanne Evans, ed., *"Here I Am, Lord": The Letters and Writings of Ita Ford* (Maryknoll, NY: Orbis, 2005), 140.

146. Melinda Roper and Cecilia Ruggiero, General Assembly Documents, October 15–December 1978, folder 4, box 16, SFP, MSA (emphasis in original).

147. Roper and Ruggiero, General Assembly Documents.

148. Minutes, Meeting to Explore a Proposal of Hildegard Goss-Myar for a Solidarity Campaign for the Liberation of Central America, July 30, 1979, folder 1 and International Fellowship of Reconciliation, "World Peace Day 1980," folder 2, box 40, Catholic Peace Fellowship Papers (CPF), UNDA.

149. Parish Bulletin, St. Mary's, January 6, 1980, folder 7, box 40, CPF, UNDA.

150. See Van Gosse, "'The North American Front': Central American Solidarity in the Reagan Era," in *Reshaping the U.S. Left: Popular Struggles in the 1980s*, ed. Mike Davis and Michael Sprinker (New York: Verso, 1988), 19–22.

151. U.S. Policy to El Salvador and Central America—minutes, January 28, 1980, folder SCC-2/15/80, box 32, Meetings SCC 251–299, Zbigniew Brzezinski Collection (ZBC), JCPL.

152. Memorandum, Zbigniew Brzezinski to Jimmy Carter, January 29, 1980, U.S. Policy to El Salvador, folder SCC-2/15/80, box 32, Meetings SCC 251–299, ZBC, JCPL.

153. Memorandum, Robert Pastor to Zbigniew Brzezinski et al., SCC Meeting on El Salvador, February 15, 1980, JCPL.

154. U.S. Policy, January 28, 1980.

155. Memorandum, Peter Tarnoff to Zbigniew Brzezinski, February 15, 1980, EL00657, El Salvador, 1980–1994 (ES1980–1994), DNSA.

156. Special Coordination Committee Meeting (SCCM), January 28, 1980, folder SCC-2/15/80, box 32, Meetings SCC 251–299, ZBC, JCPL.

157. Betty Glad, *An Outsider in the White House: Jimmy Carter, His Advisors, and the Making of American Foreign Policy* (Ithaca, NY: Cornell University Press, 2009), 252.

158. SCCM, February 15, 1980, minutes, folder SCC-2/15/80, box 32, Meetings SCC 251–299, ZBC, JCPL.

159. Glad, *Outsider in the White House*, 257.

160. Alan Riding, "Latin Church in Siege: Priests," *New York Times*, May 6, 1979.

161. June Carolyn Erlick, "El Salvador's Five Catholic Bishops," *National Catholic Reporter*, February 12, 1982.

162. Sánchez, *Priest Under Fire*, 96.

163. Glad, *Outsider in the White House*, 257.

164. Sánchez, *Priest Under Fire*, 137.

165. George Weigel, *Witness to Hope: The Biography of Pope John Paul II* (New York: Cliff Street Books, 1999), 284–285.

166. Riding, "Latin Church in Siege."

167. Glad, *Outsider in the White House*, 252–253.

168. Boutros Boutros-Ghali, *From Madness to Hope: The 12-Year War in El Salvador* (New York: United Nations, 1993), https://www.usip.org/sites/default/files/file/ElSalvador-Report.pdf; Quoted in June Carolyn Erlick, "Right Wing Bombs El Salvador Catholic Center, Library," *National Catholic Reporter*, February 29, 1980.

169. Óscar Romero to Jimmy Carter, February 17, 1980 (Spanish), folder 6, box 25, OJP, MFBA.

170. Erlick, "Right Wing Bombs."

171. Duarte and Page, *Duarte*, 19, 66; Chávez, *Poets and Prophets*, 84, 200–202.

172. For examples, see Anthony Bellagamba to Jimmy Carter, February 21, 1980, folder Catholics-USCMC 1974–78, box Ethnic Affairs, JCPL; Mailgram, Walter F. Sullivan to Cyrus Vance, February 21, 1980, El Salvador II, Part 21C, box 42, DOS, RG 59, NARA.

173. Thomas J. Marti to Jimmy Carter, February 27, 1980, El Salvador II, Part 1, box 38, DOS, RG 59, NARA.

174. "Archbishop Romero Plays Critical Role," *Maryknoll News Notes*, January/February 1980, folder 5, box 15, OJP, MMA.

175. "'Military Not the Answer,'" *National Catholic Reporter*, March 21, 1980.

176. "Ecumenical Visit to El Salvador," March 22–25, 1980, folder 41, box 8, National Assembly of Women Religious Papers (CARW), UNDA.

177. LeoGrande, *Our Own Backyard*, 43.

178. Robert E. White, "Romero Remembered: Close Encounter with a Martyr," *Commonweal*, March 22, 2010, 7.

179. Office of Central American Affairs to Thomas J. Marti, March 12, 1980, El Salvador II, Part 4, DOS, RG 59, NARA.

180. John H. Coatsworth, *Central America and the United States: The Clients and the Colossus* (New York: Twayne, 1994), 153.

181. Judith Noone, *The Same Fate as the Poor*, rev. ed. (Maryknoll, NY: Orbis, 1995), 93.

182. Stephanie Russell, "Millions Mourn Slain Romero," *National Catholic Reporter*, April 4, 1980.

183. LeoGrande, *Our Own Backyard*, 48–49.

184. LeoGrande, *Our Own Backyard*, 46; Noone, *Same Fate*, 94.

185. LeoGrande, *Our Own Backyard*, 46; Noone, *Same Fate*, 96.

186. Noone, *Same Fate*, 96.

187. Evans, "Here I Am," 140.

188. Roger Peace, *A Call to Conscience: The Anti-Contra War Campaign* (Amherst: University of Massachusetts Press, 2012), 70.

189. For examples, see James Rasuch to Jimmy Carter, April 1, 1980, and Governing Board, Conference of Netherlands Religious to Cyrus Vance, April 9, 1980, El Salvador II, Part 21D, DOS, RG 59, NARA.

190. Cable, Cyrus Vance to Embassy, March 26, 1980, ES00552, ES1977–1984, DNSA.

191. James W. Michaels Jr., "House Unit Approves Aid to El Salvador," *National Catholic Reporter*, April 11, 1980.

192. James L. Connor, "El Salvador's Agony and U.S. Policies," *America*, April 26, 1980, 360–361.

193. Connor, "El Salvador's Agony," 360, 362.

194. James W. Michaels Jr., "Religious, Government Differ on Aid," *National Catholic Reporter*, April 25, 1980.

195. Joan Petrik to sisters, friends, and relatives, May 15, 1980, in Pat Haggerty to Tom and Dan [no last names provided], June 8, 1980, folder 6, box 25, OJP, MFBA.

196. Petrik to sisters, friends, and relatives.

197. Henry E. Catto Jr., "Send El Salvador U.S. Aid Quickly," *New York Times*, May 4, 1980, in Steering Committee of the Religious Task for El Salvador to Member, June 1980, folder 41, box 8, CARW, UNDA.

198. Proposal, "Emergency Committee of Vicariate of Chalatenango Archdiocese of San Salvador," June 25, 1980, folder SMES1969–1993, box 6, ESM, MSA.

199. Eileen Markey, *A Radical Faith: The Assassination of Sister Maura* (New York: Nation Books, 2016), 222.

200. Donna Whitson Brett and Edward T. Brett, *Martyrs of Hope: Seven Missioners in Central America* (Maryknoll, NY: Orbis, 2018), 224.

201. Proposal, "Emergency Committee."

202. J. Bryan Hehir to Bishop Kelly, July 1, 1980, folder 6, box 8, SFP, MSA.

203. Noone, *Same Fate*, 104.

204. Evans, *"Here I Am,"* 142.

205. Noone, *Same Fate*, 105.

206. Noone, *Same Fate*, 107–108.

207. Noone, *Same Fate*, 124–125.

208. "Sisters Who Served in El Salvador and Their Ministries 1969–1986," unnumbered folder, box 1, M/CA, MSA.

209. Markey, *Radical Faith*, 220.

210. Halina King, "Maddie," Plough, *Trailblazers in Habits*, accessed November 23, 2019, http://www.plough.com/en/topics/justice/social-justice/madeline-dorsey-maryknoll-sister; Maryknoll Sisters, "Madeline Dorsey," accessed November 23, 2019, https://maryknollsisters.org/mk-sister/sister-madeline-marie-dorsey/.

211. Markey, *Radical Faith*, 224.

212. Markey, *Radical Faith*, 225.

213. Markey, *Radical Faith*, 225–226.

214. Markey, *Radical Faith*, 226, 232.

215. Editorial, *Plain Dealer* (Cleveland), December 6, 1980.

216. Stephanie Russell, "Four Heroic Lives End in Martyrdom: Kazel," *National Catholic Reporter*, December 19, 1980.

217. Brett and Brett, *Martyrs of Hope*, 102, 111.

218. Tom Quigley, letter to the editor, *National Catholic Reporter*, November 28, 1980.

219. June Carolyn Erlick, "Violence from Right, Left Drives Refugees from El Salvador," *National Catholic Reporter*, September 19, 1980.

220. Maura Clarke to Mary Manning, August 11, 1980, folder 2, box 10-SFP, MSA.

221. Maura Clarke to Mom, Dad, et al., October 1980, folder 4, box 10-SFP, MSA.

222. Coatsworth, *Central America and the United States*, 154.

223. LaFeber, *Inevitable Revolutions*, 253.

224. Peace, *Call to Conscience*, 70–72.

225. Evans, *"Here I Am,"* 229.

226. Brian Atwood to Matthew F. McHugh, October 22, 1980, ES00822, ES1977–1984, DNSA.

4. U.S. Guns Kill U.S. Nuns

1. Ana Carrigan and Bernard Stone, *Roses in December: The Story of Jean Donovan* (New York: First-Run Features Home Video, 1982).

2. Penny Lernoux, "Latin America: Crisis in the Shadow of the Cross," *Los Angeles Times*, May 31, 1981.

3. U.S. Congress, Senate, *Foreign Assistance Legislation for Fiscal Year 1982, Before the Committee on Foreign Affairs*, 97th Cong. 1st sess., 1981, 163.

4. William M. LeoGrande, *Our Own Backyard: The United States in Central America, 1977–1992* (Chapel Hill: University of North Carolina Press, 1998), 64; Donna Whitson Brett and Edward T. Brett, *Murdered in Central America: The Stories of Eleven U.S. Missionaries* (Maryknoll, NY: Orbis, 1988), 195; Ana Carrigan, *Salvador Witness: The Life and Calling of Jean Donovan*, anniv. ed. (Maryknoll, NY: Orbis, 2005), 271; Raymond Bonner, *Weakness and Deceit: U.S. Policy and El Salvador* (New York: Times Books, 1984), 80.

5. J. Michael Hogan, *The Panama Canal in American Politics: Domestic Advocacy and the Evolution of Policy* (Carbondale: Southern Illinois University Press, 1986), 101, 105–106.

6. Patricia McNeal, *Harder Than War: Catholic Peacemaking in Twentieth-Century America* (New Brunswick, NJ: Rutgers University Press, 1992), 157.

7. Hogan, *Panama Canal*, 105.

8. Stanley J. Blujus, letter to the editor, *National Catholic Register*, September 25, 1977.

9. Alf Tomas Tønnessen, *How Two Political Entrepreneurs Helped Create the American Conservative Movement, 1973–1981: The Ideas of Richard Viguerie and Paul Weyrich* (Lewistown, NY: Edwin Mellen, 2009), 15, 23, 122, 125.

10. Sean Wilentz, *The Age of Reagan: A History, 1974–2008* (New York: HarperCollins, 2008), 67, 102.

11. David Skidmore, "Foreign Policy Interest Groups and Presidential Power: Jimmy Carter and the Battle over Ratification of the Panama Canal Treaties," *Presidential Studies Quarterly* 23, no. 3 (1993): 490–491.

12. Hogan, *Panama Canal*, 119.

13. Mary Hanna, "Catholics and the Moral Majority," *Crisis*, November 1982, 10.

14. Andrew Preston, *Sword of the Spirit, Shield of Faith: Religion in American War and Diplomacy* (New York: Alfred A. Knopf, 2012), 545–547.

15. George Weigel, *Witness to Hope: The Biography of Pope John Paul II* (New York: Cliff Street Books, 1999), 252, 266.

16. "Pope John Paul II," *National Review*, November 10, 1978.

17. Weigel, *Witness to Hope*, 346, 351–352.

18. *Time*, October 15, 1979.

19. David Sanford, "The Pope's Groupies," *Harper's*, December 1979, 86.

20. Raymond A. Schroth, *Bob Drinan: The Controversial Life of the First Catholic Priest Elected to Congress* (New York: Fordham University Press, 2010), 308.

21. James V. Schall, "Priests as Politicians," *National Catholic Register*, September 16, 1979.

22. Editorial, "Priests in Politics," *America*, May 17, 1980, 413.

23. Memorandum, Albion W. Knight to Bill Richardson et al., "'To Recover a Strong America! Concept," n.d., folder 19, box Conservative Movement, Paul Weyrich Papers (WP), American Heritage Center, University of Wyoming, Laramie, WY.

24. Charles Rooney, "Revolutionary Gives Credit to Catholics," *National Catholic Reporter*, December 7, 1979.

25. June Carolyn Erlick, "CELAM-Hosted Bishops' Conference 'Suspect,'" *National Catholic Reporter*, June 6, 1980.

26. June Carolyn Erlick, "Central Problem: Reconstruction: Nicaragua Today 'Is Laboratory for All of Latin America,'" *National Catholic Reporter*, February 22, 1980.

27. "Republican Party Platform of 1980," July 15, 1980, APP, https://www.presidency.ucsb.edu/node/273420.

28. Penny Lernoux, "Latin Reaction on Election Shows Split," *National Catholic Reporter*, November 21, 1980.

29. LeoGrande, *Our Own Backyard*, 57.

30. Cable, Robert E. White to DOS, October 19, 1980, EL00679, ES1980–1994, DNSA.

31. Eileen Markey, *A Radical Faith: The Assassination of Sister Maura* (New York: Nation Books, 2016), 240.

32. Carrigan, *Salvador Witness*, 231–232.

33. Markey, *Radical Faith,* 240–241.

34. Doug Rossinow, *The Reagan Era: A History of the 1980s* (New York: Columbia University Press, 2015), 28.

35. Cable, Robert E. White to DOS, November 9, 1980, ES00846, ES1977–1984, DNSA.

36. Markey, *Radical Faith*, 245.

37. Bonner, *Weakness and Deceit*, 75.

38. June Carolyn Erlick, "Funeral Becomes Unity Rally," *National Catholic Reporter*, December 12, 1980.

39. Cable, Robert E. White to DOS, November 28, 1980, ES00878, ES1977–1984, DNSA.

40. Anthony Lewis, "Another Noble Cause," *New York Times*, December 1, 1980.

41. Memorandum, Pedro Sanjuan to Robert Neumann, December 1, 1980, ES00893, ES1977–1984, DNSA; Juan de Onis, "Reagan's State Dept. Latin Team Asks Curbs on 'Social Reformers,'" *New York Times*, December 4, 1980.

42. Markey, *Radical Faith*, 250.

43. Judith Noone, *The Same Fate as the Poor*, rev. ed. (Maryknoll, NY: Orbis, 1995), 1; Bonner, *Weakness and Deceit*, 74–75; Cable, Jerrold Mark Dion to DOS, December 11, 1980, ES00963, ES1977–1984, DNSA.

44. "Report to the President of Special Mission to El Salvador," December 12, 1980, ES00982, ES1977–1984, DNSA.

45. Bonner, *Weakness and Deceit*, 74.

46. Christopher Dickey, "4 U.S. Catholics Killed in El Salvador," *Washington Post*, December 5, 1980; Carrigan, *Salvador Witness*, 248.

47. Cable, Robert E. White to DOS, December 5, 1980, ES00909, ES1977–1984, DNSA.

48. See, for example, Gary MacEoin, "Christian Groups Set Priority on El Salvador," *National Catholic Reporter*, December 19, 1980 and editorial, *Des Moines Register*, December 9, 1980 for eight thousand dead. The State Department listed nine thousand. Peter Tarnoff to Zbigniew Brzezinski, December 11, 1980, EL00688, ES1980–1994, DNSA. San Salvador archdiocese's legal aid office reported eleven thousand. June Carolyn Erlick, "Salvadorean Troops Responsible for Deaths," *National Catholic Reporter*, November 14, 1980. The Senate Foreign Relations Committee reported twelve thousand. U.S. Congress, Senate, *Situation in El Salvador, Before the Committee on Foreign Relations*, 97th Cong., 1st sess., 1981, 29.

49. DOS, Daily Press Briefing, December 5, 1980, ES00923, ES1977–1984, DNSA.

50. Cable, Embassy to DOS, November 30, 1980, EL00684, ES1980–1994, DNSA.

51. Memorandum, NSC, SCC Meeting on El Salvador, December 11, 1980, EL01360, ES1980–1994, DNSA.

52. "Kennedy Condemns the Violence," *New York Times*, December 5, 1980.

53. Editorial, *Cincinnati Post*, December 11, 1980. Other papers expressed the same sentiment. Editorial, *Honolulu Advertiser*, December 6, 1980; Editorial, *Syracuse Herald American*, December 7, 1980.

54. James W. Michaels Jr., "Leaders Urge Human Rights Stand," *National Catholic Reporter*, December 26, 1980.

55. Marjorie Hyer, "Four Murders Trigger U.S. Catholic Protests," *Washington Post*, December 10, 1980.

56. Hyer, "Four Murders Trigger."

57. Maryknoll Sisters to Friends, December 10, 1980, Sr. Betty Ann's Files (SBAF).

58. Stephanie Russell, "Catholics Protest Salvadorean Arms," *National Catholic Reporter*, March 6, 1981.

59. Homily, Melinda Roper, December 14, 1980, SBAF.

60. "Statement from the Bishop, Apostolic Administrator, Priests and Women Religious of the Archdiocese of San Salvador," December 5, 1980, folder 3, box 33, Religious Task Force on Central America and Mexico (RTFCAM), MMA.

61. DOS, Statement, December 17, 1980, ES00984.

62. "Ambassador Kirkpatrick: Reagan-Appointed Democrat Speaks Her Mind on World, Politics," *Tampa Tribune*, December 25, 1980.

63. Jeane Kirkpatrick, "Dictatorships and Double Standards," *Commentary*, November 1979, 35.

64. LeoGrande, *Our Own Backyard*, 69.

65. Erik Ching, *Stories of Civil War in El Salvador: A Battle Over Memory* (Chapel Hill: University of North Carolina Press, 2016), 41.

66. LeoGrande, *Our Own Backyard*, 70.

67. *Situation in El Salvador*, 6.

68. "Sudden Death over Dinner," *Time*, January 19, 1981.

69. Cable, Lawrence Pezzullo to DOS, January 16, 1981, NI01254, Nicaragua (NC), DNSA.

70. June Carolyn Erlick, "'U.S. Guns Kill U.S. Nuns'—Embassy Rally," *National Catholic Reporter*, January 30, 1981.

71. Pezzullo to DOS, January 16, 1981.

72. H. W. Brands, *Reagan: The Life* (New York: Doubleday, 2015), 278.

73. "U.S. Ecumenical Group in Mexico Alerts President Reagan to Salvadoran Reality," *Latinamerica Press*, February 5, 1981.

74. LeoGrande, *Our Own Backyard*, 54.

75. Lewis A. Tambs, ed., *A New Inter-American Policy for the Eighties* (Washington, DC: Council for Inter-American Security, 1980), 3, 9.

76. *New Inter-American Policy*, 17, 19–20.

77. "Anticommunist Congress Focuses on the Church," *Latinamerica Press*, August 25, 1977.

78. Frank Morriss, "Liberationist Theologian Gets Warm Welcome in Denver," *Wanderer*, September 23, 1976.

79. "The Week," *National Review*, April 3, 1981, 330.

80. Stephen Kinzer, "Military Regimes in Latin America," *Boston Globe*, November 7, 1980; Greg Grandin, *Empire's Workshop: Latin America, the United States, and the Rise of the New Imperialism* (New York: Owl Books, 2007), 70.

81. "Catholic Church Is a Major Influence . . . on U.S. Policies toward El Salvador," *Congressional Quarterly*, April 24, 1982, 899, folder USCC-OA 12420, box OA12420, Robert Reilly Files (RRF), RRPL.

82. "Terri Shaw, "Mimeographs Roar in Propaganda War: Handout-to-Handout Warfare on Central America Policy," *Washington Post*, March 7, 1982.

83. Grandin, *Empire's Workshop*, 70.

84. Gary Scott Smith, *Faith and the Presidency: From George Washington to George W. Bush* (Oxford: Oxford University Press, 2006), 340–341; J. L. Sullivan, "Catholics 'In,' and Social Teachings 'Out' with Reagan," *National Catholic Reporter*, April 30, 1982.

85. Deal W. Hudson, *Onward, Christian Soldiers: The Growing Political Power of Catholics and Evangelicals in the United States* (New York: Threshold Editions, 2008), 237n20.

86. Sullivan, "Catholics 'In,' and Social Teachings 'Out.'"

87. Carl Bernstein and Marco Politi, *His Holiness: John Paul II and the History of Our Time* (New York: Doubleday, 1996), 261 (emphasis in original).

88. Bernstein and Politi, *His Holiness*, 262.

89. "Cauldron in Central America: What Keeps the Fire Burning?," *New York Times*, December 7, 1980.

90. Alexander M. Haig, *Caveat: Realism, Reagan, and Foreign Policy* (New York: Macmillan, 1984), 77.

91. Quoted in Brands, *Reagan*, 329–330.

92. Cynthia J. Arnson, *Crossroads: Congress, the President, and Central America, 1976–1993*, 2nd ed. (University Park: Pennsylvania State University Press, 1993), 55.

93. "Alexander Haig," *The Economist*, February 25, 2010, http://www.economist.com/node/15577297.

94. Tim Weiner, "Alexander M. Haig Dies at 85," *New York Times*, February 20, 2010.

95. LeoGrande, *Our Own Backyard*, 174.

96. Bob Woodward, *Veil: The Secret Wars of the CIA, 1981–1987* (New York: Simon and Schuster, 1987), 117.

97. Brands, *Reagan*, 263.

98. LeoGrande, *Our Own Backyard*, 100.

99. Ronald Reagan, "Address to the Nation about Christmas and the Situation in Poland," December 23, 1981, APP, https://www.presidency.ucsb.edu/node/246384.

100. Lou Cannon, *President Reagan: The Role of a Lifetime* (New York: Simon & Schuster, 1991), 196.

101. CIA National Foreign Assessment Center, West European Attitudes Toward El Salvador, January 13, 1981, folder ES 12/80-1/81, box 21, ZBC, JCPL.

102. Christian Smith, *Resisting Reagan: The U.S. Central America Peace Movement* (Chicago: University of Chicago Press, 1996), 163–164.

103. "U.K. Catholics Attack U.S.," *National Catholic Reporter*, May 1, 1981.

104. "Irish Catholics Denounce Violence of Salvadoran Junta," *Latinamerica Press*, December 10, 1981.

105. Cable, DOS to ARA Diplomatic Posts, February 4, 1981, ES01301, ES1977–1984, DNSA.

106. Haig, *Caveat*, 95, 118.

107. LeoGrande, *Our Own Backyard*, 104.

108. LeoGrande, *Our Own Backyard*, 107–108.

109. Arnson, *Crossroads*, 56.

110. LeoGrande, *Our Own Backyard*, 88–89.

111. Arnson, *Crossroads*, 76.

112. Raymond Bonner, "The Agony of El Salvador," *New York Times*, February 22, 1981.

113. DOS, Daily Press Briefing, February 11, 1981, ES01332, ES1977–1984, DNSA.

114. A. J. Matt Jr., "Bishops at the Precipice," *Wanderer*, February 12, 1981.

115. Robert Parry, "Lefever: Junta Deserves U.S. Military Backing," Associated Press, February 23, 1981.

116. CIS, Press Release, "Murdered Nuns in El Salvador Suspected of Aiding Guerrillas," March 3, 1981, ES01426, ES1977–1984, DNSA.

117. CIS, Press Release.

118. Ricardo Fuentes Castellanos, "La Orden Maryknoll y el comunismo II," *La Prensa Gráfica*, January 30, 1981.

119. Paul A. Fisher, "USCC Continues Saturation Bombing of Reagan's Salvadoran Policy," *Wanderer*, March 19, 1981.

120. J. Paul Wyatt, "Jean Marie Donovan, the Lay Missionary," United Press International, December 23, 1980.

121. *Foreign Assistance Legislation for Fiscal Year 1982*, 163. Though dated a day after Haig's remarks, the *Wanderer* published before the issue's indicated date. Although it is unclear if Haig read that issue of the *Wanderer*, he did have knowledge of the paper. On July 9, 1981, the *Wanderer* published his letter thanking the paper for sending him an interview with a Salvadoran bishop. Alexander Haig, letter to the editor, *Wanderer*, July 9, 1981.

122. Fuentes, "Maryknoll y el comunismo II"; Ricardo Fuentes Castellanos, "La Orden Maryknoll y el comunismo I," *La Prensa Gráfica*, January 29, 1981.

123. "Far from the Field Afar," *Wanderer*, January 29, 1981.

124. The Cardinal Mindszenty Foundation, "Far From the Field Afar," *The Mindszenty Report*, September 1980.

125. Donald T. Critchlow, *Phyllis Schlafly and Grassroots Conservatism: A Woman's Crusade* (Princeton, NJ: Princeton University Press, 2005), 80–81.

126. For a conservative Catholic response, see Paul A. Fisher, "The Wanderer Asks Gen. Daniel Graham," *Wanderer*, March 26, 1981. For sisters objecting to Reagan's failure to mention the rapes, see Mary O'Keefe and Merle Nolde to Ronald Reagan, December 18, 1980, SBAF.

127. Melinda Roper to Alexander Haig, March 20, 1981, folder 6, box 6, ESM, MSA.

128. Bruce Buursma, "Where Are the Nuns?," *Chicago Tribune*, April 19, 1981.

129. Cynthia Glavac, *In the Fullness of Life: A Biography of Dorothy Kazel, O.S.U.* (Denville, NJ: Dimension Books, 1996), 24.

130. Reprinted in *Situation in El Salvador*, 235–236.

131. Anthony Lewis, "Showing His Colors," *New York Times*, March 29, 1981.

132. *Foreign Assistance Authorization for Fiscal Year 1982*, 36.

133. Elaine Markoutsas, "New Habits: Nuns Shed Tradition and with It Their Comfortable, Self-Assured Identities," *Chicago Tribune*, November 6, 1977.

134. Mary Bader Papa, "Mother Teresa's Example," *National Catholic Reporter*, January 25, 1980.

135. Editorial, "Nobel Prize and the Faith Factor," *National Catholic Reporter*, November 21, 1980.

136. Bruce Buursma, "Internationally, the Fervor Is Political," *Chicago Tribune*, April 19, 1981.

137. "Activist Nun at Papal Mass," *New York Times*, November 15, 1979.

138. John Dart, "Socialist Banner Carried by Nun," *Los Angeles Times*, July 19, 1980.

139. "Stinging Nuns: An Order in the Courts," *Time*, October 1, 1979, 78.

140. *Situation in El Salvador*, 230.

141. Carl Bernstein, "The Holy Alliance," *Time*, February 24, 1992.

142. Gregory F. Domber, *Empowering Revolution: America, Poland, and the End of the Cold War* (Chapel Hill: University of North Carolina Press, 2014), 17.

143. Claiborne Pell, Edward Zorinsky, and Joseph R. Biden to Ronald Reagan, March 13, 1981, in *Situation in El Salvador*, 3.

144. *Situation in El Salvador*, 2.

145. Margaret Swedish, *A Message Too Precious to Be Silenced: The Four US Church Women and the Meaning of Martyrdom* (Washington, DC: Religious Task Force on Central America, September 1992), 1, 21–23.

146. Karen Kaminsky, "Traveling Light," *Maryknoll*, October 1983, 16; Margaret Swedish, "Epilogue," in *Salvador Witness*, 265.

147. Laurie Becklund, "400 in L.A. Denounce Aid to El Salvador," *Los Angeles Times*, March 5, 1981; "Tucson Protest Group Links Bible to El Salvador," *New York Times*, April 27, 1981; "Echoes of '60s Heard in Protest on Salvador," *Chicago Tribune*, May 4, 1981; Timothy M. Phelps, "U.S. Role in El Salvador Protested," *New York Times*, April 19, 1981.

148. "Thousands Pray, March, Petition," *National Catholic Reporter*, April 3, 1981.

149. "Sister's Speech Banned," *National Catholic Reporter*, April 3, 1981.

150. "Thousands Pray, March, Petition."

151. Russell, "Catholics Protest Salvadorean Arms."

152. Dana L. Robert, "The Influence of American Missionary Women on the World Back Home," *Religion and American Culture* 12, no.1 (2002): 74.

153. Sharon Erickson Nepstad, *Convictions of the Soul: Religion, Culture, and Agency in the Central America Solidarity Movement* (Oxford: Oxford University Press, 2004), 77, 103.

154. Nepstad, *Convictions of the Soul*, 84.

155. Penny Lernoux, Arthur Jones, and Robert Ellsberg, *Hearts on Fire: The Story of the Maryknoll Sisters* (Maryknoll, NY: Orbis, 1993), 254.

156. Ethel Marie to Joseph P. Moakley, February 15, 1982, folder 8, box 1, James McGovern Files (McGovern), MS 100.03.04, John Joseph Moakley Archive (MA), Suffolk University, Boston, MA.

157. Arnson, *Crossroads*, 65, 68.

158. LeoGrande, *Our Own Backyard*, 89.

159. Cannon, *President Reagan*, 198–199.

160. Brands, *Reagan*, 300.

161. Cable, FBI Legal Attaché to FBI Director, April 1981 (day unclear), *FBI File on the American Churchwomen Killed in El Salvador, December 2, 1980* (Wilmington, DE: Scholarly Resources, 1990).

162. Christopher P. Winner, "Congress' View of El Salvador Shifting," *National Catholic Reporter*, May 15, 1981.

163. In May 1981, twenty-nine Congress members sued Reagan, alleging he violated the War Powers Resolution. Crockett v. Reagan, 720 F.2d. 1355 (D.C. Cir. 1983).

164. "General Plan to Appeal to Catholics," n.d., folder Catholic Strategy-1 (CS-1), box OA12418, RRF, RRPL. The memo said another U.S. visit by the pope "should be kept in mind for 1982 or later," suggesting the memo was written in 1981.

165. "Haig Asserts Soviet Wanes Spiritually, but Rises as Threat," *New York Times*, May 10, 1981.

166. William M. LeoGrande, *Central America and the Polls: A Study of U.S. Public Opinion Polls on U.S. Foreign Policy toward El Salvador and Nicaragua under the Reagan Administration* (Washington, DC: WOLA, 1984), 4.

167. Memorandum, Elizabeth Dole to Edwin Meese, James A. Baker, and Michael Deaver, "Ethnic/Catholic Strategy," n.d., folder CS-1, box OA12418, RRF, RRPL.

168. Paul Scott, "Signs of Our Troubled Times," *Wanderer*, April 9, 1981.

169. James Theberge to Edwin Meese, April 15, 1981, folder ES/Domestic, box 90502, Jacqueline Tillman Files (JTF), RRPL.

170. Joseph E. Persico, *Casey: From the OSS to the CIA* (New York: Viking, 1990), 262–263.

171. Memorandum, William Casey to Alexander Haig, Foreign Policy in Central America, May 12, 1981, folder ES/Domestic, box 90502, JTF, RRPL.

172. Persico, *Casey*, 6, 574.

173. James Noonan to Ronald Reagan, May 13, 1981; Press Statement, James P. Noonan and Roy Bourgeois, May 8, 1981 023000–027999, box 1, Co046 El Salvador, RRPL.

174. Richard T. Reed, "Praise the Left and Pass the Ammunition," *National Review*, September 4, 1981.

175. Alan McCoy to James Noonan, May 1, 1981, folder 42, box 25, CMSM, UNDA.

176. Noonan to Reagan, May 13, 1981.

177. Christopher P. Winner, "Priest's Act 'Hurt Work in Missions,'" *National Catholic Reporter*, May 22, 1981.

178. Noonan to Reagan, May 13, 1981; Press Statement, Noonan and Bourgeois, May 8, 1981.

179. Reed, "Praise the Left."

180. Juan de Onis, "Capital Rally Assails Arms to Salvador," *New York Times*, May 4, 1981.

181. Winner, "Priest's Act."

182. "Maryknolls May Leave El Salvador," *National Catholic Register*, May 24, 1981.

183. "Honduras niega ingreso religiosos de Maryknoll," *La Prensa Gráfica*, May 18, 1981, folder 5, box 16, B-RP.

184. "Honduras Bars Priests," *National Catholic Register*, May 31, 1981.

185. Thomas O. Enders to James Noonan, June 9, 1981, 023000–027999, box 1, Co046 El Salvador, RRPL.

186. Memorandum, James Noonan to General Council, July 13, 1981, folder G/ES correspondence, 1980–1981, box 25, OJP, MMA.

187. "Maryknollers to Stay Away from El Salvador," *National Catholic Reporter*, August 28, 1981.

188. Flora Lewis, "Showing the Difference," *New York Times*, January 11, 1982.

189. Arnson, *Crossroads*, 71, 84, 88, 101.

190. I. M. Destler, "The Elusive Consensus: Congress and Central America," in *Central America: Anatomy of Conflict*, ed. Robert S. Leiken and Carnegie Endowment for International Peace (New York: Pergamon, 1984), 325–326.

191. Bonner, *Weakness and Deceit*, 76.

192. LeoGrande, *Our Own Backyard*, 154.

193. Mark Danner, *Massacre at el Mozote* (New York: Vintage: 1994), 131.

194. Danner, *Massacre at el Mozote*, 128.

195. María Cristina García, *Seeking Refuge: Central American Migration to Mexico, the United States, and Canada* (Berkeley: University of California Press, 2006), 24.

196. "House Joint Resolution 399: Declaring the President's Certification with Respect to El Salvador Null and Void," February 2, 1982, ES02530, ES1977–1984, DNSA.

197. Fermán Cienfuegos to Thomas P. O'Neill, February 20, 1982, folder 4, box 17, KOD, OP.

198. Phillip Berryman, *Stubborn Hope: Religion, Politics, and Revolution in Central America* (Maryknoll, NY: Orbis, 1994), 70.

199. "La Verdad sobre las misionares asesinadas," *Cartas a las iglesias*, February 1–14, 1982, 4–5, no folder, box 25, B-RP.

200. José Napoleón Duarte and Diana Page, *Duarte: My Story* (New York: G. P. Putnam, 1986), 172.

201. LeoGrande, *Our Own Backyard*, 150.

202. Steven V. Roberts, "Rift on El Salvador Grows in Congress," *New York Times*, February 4, 1982.

203. LeoGrande, *Our Own Backyard*, 157.

204. Kenneth A. Briggs, "U.S. Catholic Bishops Firmly Opposing Salvador Policy," *New York Times*, February 21, 1982, folder 6, box 16, B-RP.

205. Shaw, "Mimeographs Roar."

206. García, *Seeking Refuge*, 32, 87, 99.

207. Smith, *Resisting Reagan*, 69; Van Gosse, "'The North American Front': Central American Solidarity in the Reagan Era," in *Reshaping the U.S. Left: Popular Struggles in the 1980s*, ed. Mike Davis and Michael Sprinker (New York: Verso, 1988), 34.

208. García, *Seeking Refuge*, 100.

209. Alexander M. Haig, *Inner Circles: How America Changed the World* (New York: Warner Books, 1992), 547.

210. LeoGrande, *Our Own Backyard*, 174–175.

211. LeoGrande, *Our Own Backyard*, 89.

212. Woodward, *Veil*, 113.

213. Arnson, *Crossroads*, 79–80, 108.

214. Roger Peace, *A Call to Conscience: The Anti-Contra War Campaign* (Amherst: University of Massachusetts Press, 2012), 1.

215. Peace, *Call to Conscience*, 20.

216. LeoGrande, *Our Own Backyard*, 115.

217. Peace, *Call to Conscience*, 21–22.

218. Arnson, *Crossroads*, 106, 110; John Brecher, John Walcott, David Martin, and Beth Nissen, "A Secret War for Nicaragua," *Newsweek*, November 8, 1982.

219. Walter LaFeber, *Inevitable Revolutions: The United States in Central America*, 2nd ed. (New York: Norton, 1993), 296.

5. Reagan and the White House's Maryknoll Nun

1. Ronald Reagan, "Remarks at the St. Ann's Festival in Hoboken, New Jersey," July 26, 1984, APP, https://www.presidency.ucsb.edu/node/261626.

2. William Gribbin, *The Churches Militant: The War of 1812 and American Religion* (New Haven, CT: Yale University Press, 1973), 2. Gribbin describes Protestants' response to the war as "ecclesiastical guerrilla warfare."

3. Greg Grandin, *Empire's Workshop: Latin America, the United States, and the Rise of the New Imperialism* (New York: Owl Books, 2007), 121–134; Christian Smith, *Resisting Reagan: The U.S. Central America Peace Movement* (Chicago: University of Chicago Press, 1996), 288–295.

4. Sergio Ramírez, *Adiós Muchachos: A Memoir of the Sandinista Revolution*, trans. Stacey Alba D. Skar (Durham, NC: Duke University Press, 2012), 129.

5. Fernando Cardenal, *Faith & Joy: Memoirs of a Revolutionary Priest*, trans and ed. Kathleen McBride and Mark Lester (Maryknoll, NY: Orbis, 2015), 178–180, 185.

6. Andrew Kirkendall, *Paulo Freire and the Cold War Politics of Literacy* (Chapel Hill: University of North Carolina Press, 2010), 124, 127.

7. Kirkendall, *Paulo Freire*, 124, 140.

8. Quoted in Ramírez, *Adiós Muchachos*, 214.

9. Kirkendall, *Paulo Freire*, 140, 150.

10. Ramírez, *Adiós Muchachos*, 213–215.

11. William M. LeoGrande, *Our Own Backyard: The United States in Central America, 1977–1992* (Chapel Hill: University of North Carolina Press, 1998), 317.

12. Cynthia J. Arnson, *Crossroads: Congress, the President, and Central America, 1976–1993*, 2nd ed. (University Park: Pennsylvania State University Press, 1993), 124.

13. "Frente a guerra no declarada de Reagan: FSLN llama a la defensa de la Patria," *Barricada*, April 9, 1983, trans. with Goffs to Friend, July 1983, folder 826, box 45, GP.

14. Paul Weyrich, "Reframing the Issue and Organizing the Grass Roots: Keys to Victory in Central America," folder 9, box 17, WP.

15. Paul A. Fisher, "The Wanderer Asks Paul Weyrich," *Wanderer*, December 18, 1980.

16. Memorandum, A. J. Matt Jr. to Paul Weyrich, July 25, 1979, and Weyrich to Matt, August 4, 1979, folder 18, box 3, WP.

17. Mary Hanna, "Catholics and the Moral Majority," *Crisis*, November 1982, 10.

18. Memorandum, John Grecco to Morton Blackwell, June 1, 1983, folder OWG 6/1/83-2, box OA12422, RRF, RRPL.

19. Memorandum, Morton Blackwell to Elizabeth Dole, March 31, 1981, folder C for A-1, box 7, Morton Blackwell Files (MBF), RRPL.

20. Memorandum, Elizabeth Dole to Edwin Meese, James Baker III, and Michael Deaver, n.d., folder CS-1, box OA12418, RRF, RRPL.

21. Memorandum, Peter [no last name given] to Paul Weyrich, August 12, 1983, folder 11, box 15, Catholics 1970–1983, WP; Memorandum, Morton Blackwell to Linas Kojelis, August 26, 1983, folder CS-1, box OA12418, RRF, RRPL.

22. Memorandum, Blackwell to Kojelis (emphasis in original).

23. "General Plan to Appeal to Catholics," n.d., folder CS-1, box OA12418, RRF, RRPL.

24. Memorandum, Ronald Reagan to William Casey et al., c. July 12, 1983, NI01761, NC, DNSA.

25. National Security Decision Directive 77, January 14, 1983, IC00068, Iran-Contra (I-C), DNSA.

26. Memorandum, William Clark to George Shultz, c. May 19, 1983, IC00103, I-C, DNSA; Memorandum, Walter Raymond to William Clark, May 21, 1983, IC00105, I-C, DNSA. "Immediately" in Raymond to Clark memo.

27. Memorandum, George Shultz to Ronald Reagan, May 25, 1983, IC00106, I-C, DNSA.

28. Memorandum, James Baker to Faith Ryan Whittlesey, Establishment of OWG, May 4, 1983, folder OWG-Memos-4, box 35, Faith Ryan Whittlesey Files (FRWF), RRPL.

29. Memorandum, Morton Blackwell to Faith Ryan Whittlesey, OWG Agenda, May 17, 1983, folder OWGMtg-5/16/83, box OA12422, RRF, RRPL.

30. Memorandum, Faith Ryan Whittlesey to George Shultz, May 12, 1983, IC00100, I-C, DNSA.

31. Summary of Working Group Activity, August 8, 1983, folder OWGMtg-8/8/83-1, box OA12422, RRF, RRPL.

32. "Central America Speakers Bureau Activity Report Past/Present/Future," folder 1984 Spkrs-1, box OA12422, RRF, RRPL.

33. Briefing Paper, August 3, 1983, folder OWGMtg-8/3/83, box OA12422, RRF, RRPL (emphasis in original); Memorandum, Morton Blackwell to Faith Ryan Whittlesey, June 21, 1983, folder OWG–Participants-2, OA12422, RRF, RRPL.

34. Whittlesey to Shultz, May 12, 1983.

35. Memorandum, Walter Raymond to William Clark, May 20, 1983, IC00104, I-C, DNSA. Raymond explaining Whittlesey's views.

36. Smith, *Resisting Reagan*, 274.

37. Action Items, n.d., folder OWGMtg-5/25/1983, box OA12422, RRF, RRPL.

38. Tim Golden, "Reagan Countering Critics of Policies in Central America," *Los Angeles Times*, December 21, 1983, folder OWGMtg-1/9/84, box OA13515, RRF, RRPL.

39. Robert Parry and Peter Kornbluh, "Iran Contra's Untold Story," *Foreign Policy* 72 (Autumn 1988): 5; Executive Order 12333, December 4, 1981, IC00042, I-C, DNSA.

40. Grandin, *Empire's Workshop*, 124, 126–129, 132–133.

41. U.S. Comptroller General to Jack Brooks and Dante Fascell, Op. Comp. Gen. No. B-229069, September 30, 1987, IC04287, I-C, DNSA.

42. Philip J. Williams, *The Catholic Church and Politics in Nicaragua and Costa Rica* (Pittsburgh: University of Pittsburgh Press, 1989), 53.

43. "Problems within the Church in Nicaragua," *Revista Envío*, September 1981, http://www.envio.org.ni/articulo/3106.

44. Patricia Hynds, "Religious Reflections on Nicaragua Today," in *Nicaragua: A Look at Reality*, May 1983, folder CATT mailing-July 1983, box 6, Quixote Center Papers (QCP), Marquette University Special Collections and Archives, Milwaukee, WI. Hynds may have drawn on the work of Mexican political scientist Ana Maria Ezcurra. "Church Role in Anti-Sandinista Campaign Examined," *Latinamerica Press*, May 5, 1983.

45. "'Church Unity Grounded in Option for the Poor,'" *Latinamerica Press*, August 4, 1983.

46. "Political Conflict Tests Church," *Latinamerica Press*, August 25, 1983.

47. "Church Role in Anti-Sandinista."

48. Ramírez, *Adiós Muchachos*, 131.

49. "Political Conflict Tests."

50. "Subversion of the Church in Latin America," n.d., folder 100, box 12, Subseries 2, Latin American Mission, 1968–1972, Series 7, JC, RG 15, NAR.

51. Phillip Berryman, *Stubborn Hope: Religion, Politics, and Revolution in Central America* (Maryknoll, NY: Orbis, 1994), 33; "Religious News in Nicaragua," *Revista Envío*, October 1981, http://www.envio.org.ni/articulo/3120. Although some progressive Salvadoran Catholics positively used "popular church" to describe themselves, conservative Nicaraguans used the phrase to critique liberal Nicaraguan Catholics. Anna Lisa Peterson, *Martyrdom and the Politics of Religion: Progressive Catholicism in El Salvador's Civil War* (Albany, NY: State University Press, 1997), xxiv.

52. Marie-Dominique Chenu, "Attacks on 'Popular Church' Contradict Vatican II Teachings," *Latinamerica Press*, July 7, 1983.

53. Juan Gutiérrez, *The New Libertarian Gospel: Pitfalls of the Theology of Liberation* (Chicago: Franciscan Herald, 1977); Bonaventure Kloppenburg, *The People's Church* (Chicago: Franciscan Herald, 1978); "Catholics Warned against 'Liberation Theology,'" *Wanderer*, July 26, 1979.

54. Ramírez, *Adiós Muchachos*, 138.

55. Berryman, *Stubborn Hope*, 36–37.

56. Ramírez, *Adiós Muchachos*, 136.

57. Ronald Reagan, "Address Before a Joint Session of the Congress on Central America," April 27, 1983, APP, https://www.presidency.ucsb.edu/node/262883.

58. Andrew Preston, "Introduction: The Religious Cold War," in *Religion and the Cold War: A Global Perspective*, ed. Philip E. Muehlenbeck (Nashville: Vanderbilt University Press, 2012), xiv.

59. Joan Frawley, "Purifying the Faithful," *National Catholic Register*, May 8, 1983.

60. "Description of Some of the Invitees," Catholic Briefing on Foreign Policy, folder 11/10/1983-4, box 5, OA12421, RRF, RRPL; Arthur E. Carpenter, "Social Origins of Anti-Communism: The Information Council of the Americas," *Louisiana History* 30, no. 2 (1989): 130.

61. Myrna Oliver, "Obituaries, Patrick J. Frawley, Jr.," *Los Angeles Times*, November 5, 1998; "Firing on the Right," *Time*, November 11, 1974.

62. Charlotte Hays, "Hehir, Neuhaus Dispute Human Liberty Agenda," *National Catholic Register*, July 31, 1984.

63. "Statement by U.S. Religious in Nicaragua in Response to Address by Reagan to Joint Session of Congress," April 29, 1983, enc. Marie Augusta Neal to Tip O'Neill, May 16, 1983, folder 9, box 9, KOD, OP.

64. Kevin McKiernan, "Shrines and Slogans: The Divided Church in Nicaragua," *Mother Jones*, April 1984, 29, folder Nicaragua 2, box 2201-165, UNDA.

65. "El Punto de vista de Monseñor Vega," *Amanecer*, January–February 1984, 9–10, folder ES Churchwomen, box 36, COC, UNDA.

66. "Al pueblo de Nicaragua y al mundo," *El Nuevo Diario*, September 13, 1983, trans. with Goffs to Friend, September 1983, folder 827, box 45, GP.

67. Ramírez, *Adiós Muchachos*, 132.

68. George Weigel, *Witness to Hope: The Biography of Pope John Paul II* (New York: Cliff Street Books, 1999), 272, 281, 289, 348.

69. "General Plan to Appeal to Catholics" (emphasis added).

70. J. William Middendorf to Morton Blackwell, May 17, 1983, folder OWG-Mtg-5/18/83-2, box OA12422, RRF, RRPL; Memorandum, Morton Blackwell to Faith Ryan Whittlesey, May 16, 1983, folder OWGMtg-5/16/83, box OA12422, RRF, RRPL.

71. Remarks, J. William Middendorf to the Graduating Class of Christian Broadcasting University, May 14, 1983, folder OWGMtg-5/18/83-2, box OA12422, RRF, RRPL. Middendorf seems to have referenced Foreign Service officer Richard C. Brown's master's thesis, "The Challenge to the U.S. of Liberation Theology in Latin America," which circulated in the administration. Peter Dailey to William Clark, December 15, 1982, folder LibTheo LA-1, RAC box 006, Alfonso Sapia-Bosch Files (ASBF), RRPL.

72. Memorandum, Fred Fielding to Richard Darman, June 8, 1983, folder OWG-Memos-2, box 35, Correspondence, FRWF, RRPL.

73. Michael Dodson and Laura Nuzzi O'Shaughnessy, *Nicaragua's Other Revolution: Religious Faith and Political Struggle* (Chapel Hill: University of North Carolina, 1990), 19; Betsy Cohn and Patricia Hynds, "The Manipulation of the Religious Issue," in *Reagan versus the Sandinistas: The Undeclared War on Nicaragua*, ed. Thomas W. Walker (Boulder, CO: Westview, 1987), 97–122.

74. Jeane J. Kirkpatrick and Charles M. Lichenstein, "Marxist Totalitarianism in Our Hemisphere: Nicaragua," *World Affairs* 145, no. 4 (1983): 352, reprinting Kirkpatrick's statement, U.N. Security Council, On the Complaint of Nicaragua, March 23, 1983; Remarks, Faith Whittlesey to Council for National Policy, August 18, 1984, folder CNP Remarks CA-1985, box 20F, FRWF, RRPL. Kirkpatrick used the term "puppet popular church," while Whittlesey used "fake popular church."

75. Arturo J. Cruz, "Nicaragua's Imperiled Revolution," *Foreign Affairs* 61, no. 5 (1983): 1038.

76. LeoGrande, *Our Own Backyard*, 371–372, 489.

77. "Thugs on the Left, Thugs on the Right: Central American Churches Face New Threats," *Religion & Democracy* (Fall 1983), folder 1, box 25, David M. Jessup Papers (DJP), Manuscript, Archives, and Rare Book Library, Emory University, Atlanta, GA.

78. Draft Outline, "Proposal for Institute of [sic] Religion and Democracy," [no date, no author], folder 4, box 25, DJP.

79. See, for example, Steve Askin, "Institute Says It Reveals Threat—Others Say It Is a Threat—to U.S. Church," *National Catholic Reporter*, February 4, 1983; Draft Outline, "Proposal."

80. Ecumenical Committee of U.S. Church Personnel in Nicaragua, "Is There Religious Persecution in Nicaragua?," September 21, 1984, with Goffs to Friend, July 1984, folder 836, box 45, GP.

81. Robert Wuthnow, *The Restructuring of American Religion: Society and Faith Since World War Two* (Princeton, NJ: Princeton University Press, 1988).

82. Lou Cannon, *President Reagan: The Role of a Lifetime* (New York: Simon & Schuster, 1991), 384.

83. LeoGrande, *Our Own Backyard*, 317–318.

84. "Conferencia Episcopal sugiere 'Objeción de Conciencia': Nadie puede ser obligado a tomar armas por un partido," *La Prensa*, September 1, 1983, trans. with Goffs to Friend, folder 827, box 45, GP.

85. "Varias organizaciones Cristianas se pronuncian: Documento Obando se inscribe en campo político," *El Nuevo Diario*, September 8, 1983, trans. with Goffs to Friend, September 1983, folder 827, box 45, GP.

86. "Al pueblo de Nicaragua y al mundo."

87. Philip Taubman, "U.S. Officials Say C.I.A. Helped Nicaraguan Rebels Plan Attacks," *New York Times*, October 16, 1983.

88. Richard J. Meislin, "Nicaragua Reports an Attack by Insurgents on Major Port," *New York Times*, October 15, 1983.

89. Richard J. Meislin, "3 on Kissinger Panel Meet Anti-Sandinista Chief," *New York Times*, October 12, 1983.

90. Taubman, "U.S. Officials Say."

91. "Exxon Stops Supplying Nicaraguans with Oil," *New York Times*, October 16, 1983.

92. Meislin, "Nicaragua Reports."

93. Dominicans Call for Solidarity with Nicaragua, October 15, 1983, trans. with Goffs to Friend, November 1983, folder 829, box 45, GP.

94. Taubman, "U.S. Officials Say."

95. Arnson, *Crossroads*, 115.

96. "Ante invasión a Granada: Grupos Católicos y evangélicos opinan," *El Nuevo Diario*, November 2, 1983, trans. with Goffs to Friend, November 1983, folder 829, box 45, GP.

97. CONFER to Our Brother and Sisters Religious of the United States, October 30, 1983, folder CMSM Projections-CA, box 3, CMSM, UNDA.

98. "The History of Quest for Peace: November 1983–June 1986," folder Quest history, box 5, QCP.

99. Smith, *Resisting Reagan*, 79.

100. Sharon Erickson Nepstad, *Convictions of the Soul: Religion, Culture, and Agency in the Central America Solidarity Movement* (Oxford: Oxford University Press, 2004), 137.

101. Gioconda Belli, *The Country Under My Skin: A Memoir of Love and War*, trans. Kristina Cordero and Gioconda Belli (New York: Anchor Books, 2003), 303–304, 311.

102. Belli, *Country Under My Skin*, 311–312.

103. Arlen Specter to George Shultz, August 26, 1983, ES04216, ES1977–1984, DNSA.

104. Joan Frawley, "Revolutionists Win Converts Among Catholic Missionaries," *Wall Street Journal*, October 7, 1983.

105. Paul Newpower, "Critique of WSJ Article," folder 10, box 20, RTFCAM, MMA.

106. Patrick J. Frawley Jr., to Our Friends, November 1983, folder 16, box 13 Communications, MSA.

107. Newpower, "Critique of WSJ Article."

108. U.S. Congress, Senate, Committee on the Judiciary, *Marxism and Christianity in Revolutionary Central America, Before the Subcommittee on Security and Terrorism*, 98th Cong., 1st sess., 1984.

109. Paul A. Fisher, "Jeremiah A Denton . . . The Senate's Warrior for God and Country," *Wanderer*, July 9, 1981.

110. Alf Tomas Tønnessen, *How Two Political Entrepreneurs Helped Create the American Conservative Movement, 1973–1981: The Ideas of Richard Viguerie and Paul Weyrich* (Lewistown, NY: Edwin Mellen, 2009), 244.

111. Cable, Anthony Quainton to DOS, December 8, 1983, NI01904, NC, DNSA; Memorandum, M. Charles Hill to Robert McFarlane, May 8, 1984, ES05136, ES1977–1984, DNSA.

112. Paul A. Fisher, "The Wanderer Asks Sen. Jeremiah Denton," *Wanderer*, July 9, 1981.

113. *Marxism and Christianity*, 2–3.

114. Patrick J. Leahy, "The Church We Love Is Being Used," *Washington Post*, March 8, 1981, folder 2, box 25, WP.

115. A. J. Matt, "Welcome Aboard, Fr. Rueda," *Wanderer*, July 18, 1985.

116. *Marxism and Christianity*, 8, 13.

117. For example, see Enrique T. Rueda, "A Catholic Priest Looks at El Salvador," *Wanderer*, April 30, 1981.

118. CIS, Press Release.

119. Casey Crandall, "Talented Priest Challenges Leftist Bishops," *Conservative Digest*, August 1982, 8, folder 1, box 24, RTFCAM.

120. Free Congress Research and Education Foundation, *Annual Report 1984*, 38, folder 17, box 17, WP.

121. Memorandum, John Scafe to Jonathan Miller et al., March 12, 1984, IC00359, I-C, DNSA.

122. *Marxism and Christianity*, 95, 282.

123. Colman McCarthy, "In Flight from the Sandinistas," *Washington Post*, August 21, 1982; Chronology of Events Related to Central America/Maryknoll's Presence, folder 10, box 20, RTFCAM. For article alleging the couple's CIA ties, see David Armstrong, "En Nicaragua: La CIA financia 'la oposición,'" *Soberanía*, June 1982, 45.

124. *Marxism and Christianity*, 115.

125. Budget Document, S/LPD, August 27, 1984, IC00548, I-C, DNSA.

126. *Marxism and Christianity*, 116–117.

127. *Marxism and Christianity*, 118, 120–121.

128. Joanne Omang, "Catholic Groups Differ with Pope over Nicaragua," *Washington Post*, July 23, 1984.

129. Theresa Keeley, "Not Above the Fray: Religious and Political Divides' Impact on U.S. Missionary Sisters in Nicaragua," *U.S. Catholic Historian* 37, no. 1 (2019): 147–166.

130. *Marxism and Christianity*, 122–123.

131. Chronology of Events Related to Central America/Maryknoll's Presence.

132. Melinda Roper to Geraldine Macías, October 26, 1983, folder 7, box 13 Communications, MSA.

133. Agenda, "Briefing on Foreign Policy Issues for Members of the Religious Community," November 10, 1983, folder CB-11/10/1983-1, box 5, OA12421, RRF, RRPL.

134. Mark Schapiro and Eric Burnard, "Keeping Faith," *Nation*, January 17, 1987, folder 17, box 18, RTFCAM; Robert R. Reilly, "The Source of Human Rights," *Wanderer*, August 20, 1981.

135. Grant proposal, Philip F. Lawler to Leslie Lenkowsky, February 22, 1983, folder ACC, box 1, DJP.

136. Description of Some of the Invitees, n.d., folder CB-11/10/1983-1, box 5, OA12421, RRF, RRPL.

137. James Schall to Faith Ryan Whittlesey, November 11, 1983, folder CB-11/10/1983-5, box OA12421, RRF, RRPL.

138. Jane Blewett to Faith Ryan Whittlesey, November 15, 1983, folder CB-11/10/1983-5, box OA12421, RRF, RRPL.

139. "El Comunismo domina la iglesia popular de Nicaragua," *La Religión*, November 8, 1983 and Daniel P. Driscoll to Helene O'Sullivan and Paul Newpower, December 13, 1983, with Helene O'Sullivan to Thomas P. O'Neill, December 20, 1983, folder 14, box 8, KOD, OP.

140. O'Sullivan to O'Neill.

141. Translation of Leo Shea and James Sweeney to Director of *La Religión*, November 19, 1983; James Sweeney to Tip O'Neill, February 2, 1984, folder 14, box 8, KOD, OP.

142. Sweeney to O'Neill.

143. Sweeney to O'Neill.

144. Margaret Goff and Venezuelan Correspondent, "Venezuelan Grassroots Christians Protest Government Backing of Salvadoran Junta," *Latinamerica Press*, October 8, 1981.

145. Arnson, *Crossroads*, 83.

146. LeoGrande, *Our Own Backyard*, 151.

147. Arnson, *Crossroads*, 147.

148. LeoGrande, *Our Own Backyard*, 240.

149. Arnson, *Crossroads*, 141, 143.

150. LeoGrande, *Our Own Backyard*, 228; Joseph A. O'Hare, "Of Many Things," *America*, December 17, 1983, 380.

151. Bill Carter, "'Choices' Deserves to Rank with Best Movies Made for TV," *Baltimore Sun*, December 5, 1983; John J. O'Connor, "TV: Drama of Churchwomen Slain in El Salvador," *New York Times*, December 5, 1983.

152. Roger Peace, *A Call to Conscience: The Anti-Contra War Campaign* (Amherst: University of Massachusetts Press, 2012), 105.

153. Smith, *Resisting Reagan*, 78.

154. Gerald F. Seib, "Voices of Dissent: Catholic and Other U.S. Church Groups Oppose Reagan's Hard-Line Policy on Central America," *Wall Street Journal*, December 8, 1983, folder 4, box 22, RTFCAM.

155. Marie Gayte, "'I Told the White House If They Give One to the Pope, I May Ask for One': The American Reception to the Establishment of Diplomatic Relations between the United States and the Vatican in 1984," *Journal of Church and State* 54, no. 1 (2012): 7, 22–23.

156. Andrew Preston, *Sword of the Spirit, Shield of Faith: Religion in American War and Diplomacy* (New York: Alfred A. Knopf, 2012), 591.

157. Dinesh D'Souza, "Nukes, Central America Spark New Lay Committee," *National Catholic Register*, May 9, 1982, folder ACC, box 1, DJP.

158. Edward T. Brett, *The U.S. Catholic Press on Central America: From Cold War Anticommunism to Social Justice* (Notre Dame, IN: University of Notre Dame Press, 2003), 123, 157; Penny Lernoux, *People of God: The Struggle for World Catholicism* (New York: Viking, 1989), 11. Both emphasize conservative Catholics' shared views with Reagan.

159. Geraldine O'Leary de Macías, *Only Another Tyranny: Testimonies on Nicaragua* (Washington, DC: Editions MUSAWAS, 1984), 1–20.

160. For examples, see "1983 Speakers for OWG," folder 1984 Spkrs-1; Agenda, Roundtable with Hispanic Leaders, February 14, 1985, folder RHL-2/14/85, box OA12422, RRF, RRPL; Agenda, Special Briefing for the Friends of the Nicaraguan Refugee Fund, January 22, 1985, folder NRF-1/22/85-1, box OA12421, RRF, RRPL.

161. "Central America Speakers Bureau Activity Report Past/Present/Future," folder 1984 Spkrs-1, box OA12422, RRF, RRPL.

162. Contract, S/LPD, April 16, 1984, IC00398, I-C, DNSA; S/LPD, Contract, S/LPD, March 1, 1985, IC00898, I-C, DNSA; Memorandum, Frank Gardner to George F. Twohie, February 25, 1985, IC00871, I-C, DNSA.

163. See, for example, Special OWG Briefing for White House Fellows, July 10, 1984, folder WHF, box OA12421, RRF, RRPL.

164. Paul A. Fisher, "The Wanderer Asks Geraldine Macías," *Wanderer*, May 10, 1984.

165. Richard Bodurtha, "Dialogue—Geraldine O'Leary," *National Catholic Register*, October 9, 1983.

166. Oliver North was popular, but he asked attendees not to photograph or record him, or to reveal his identity. Thomas J. Carty, *Backwards in High Heels: Faith Whittlesey, Reagan's Madam Ambassador in Switzerland and the West Wing* (Havertown, PA: Casemate, 2012), 133–134.

167. Attendees at the February 15, 1984 OWG meeting received a copy of Geraldine Macías, "A Revolution Stolen," *Retired Officer*, February 1984, 20–23, folder OWGMtg-2/15/84, box OA13515, RRF, RRPL.

168. John DiStaso, "Nicaragua Warning Voiced," *Union Leader* (New Hampshire), August 20, 1983, folder 10, box 20, RTFCAM; Stanley Interrante, "Dornan Conference Held to Counter Leftist Propaganda," *Wanderer*, November 1, 1984.

169. See Roger Fontaine, "Accuracy, Balance of WOLA Found Lacking by Its Critics," *Washington Times*, April 10, 1985, folder 45, box 22, DJP; "A Church Divided," *Wanderer*, February 6, 1986; Philip Lawler, "Selective Sources," *Crisis*, September 1984, 49.

170. Geraldine O'Leary-Macías, *Lighting My Fire: Memoirs* (Bloomington, IN: Trafford, 2013), 260.

171. LeoGrande, *Our Own Backyard*, 140–141.

172. Memorandum, Richard Allen to George Bush, March 31, 1981, folder 023999, box 94, Country Files–Ireland, RRPL.

173. Paul Kengor and Patricia Clark Doerner, *The Judge: William P. Clark, Ronald Reagan's Top Hand* (San Francisco: Ignatius, 2007), 40.

174. Dailey to Clark, December 15, 1982.

175. Memorandum, Alfonso Sapia-Bosch to William Clark, RE: Liberation Theology, January 3, 1983, folder LibTheo LA-1, RAC box 006, ASBF, RRPL.

176. Proinsias De Rossa, Dáil Éireann Debate, "Visit of the President of the United States: Motion," vol. 350, no. 4, May 15, 1984, http://oireachtasdebates.oireachtas.ie/debates%20authoring/debateswebpack.nsf/takes/dail1984051500014?opendocument.

177. Mary N. Harris, "Irish Historical Writing on Latin America, and on Irish Links with Latin America," in *Europe and the World in European Historiography*, ed. Csaba Lévai (Pisa: Pisa University Press, 2006), 252.

178. Greg Daly, "The Irish Connection," *Irish Catholic* (Dublin), May 21, 2015, http://www.irishcatholic.ie/article/irish-connection.

179. Latin American Solidarity Centre, "Irish El Salvador Support Committee," accessed June 16, 2016, http://latinamericasolidarity.freeservers.com/irishelsalvadorsupportctte.htm.

180. Mary McGrory, "Reagan Has to Go Abroad to Hit Potholes in Campaign Trail," *Washington Post*, May 1, 1984; "Ireland Remembers Salvador Martyr," *Tablet* (London), February 27, 1993.

181. Tim Pat Coogan, *Wherever Green Is Worn: The Story of the Irish Diaspora* (New York: Palgrave, 2002), 608.

182. Harris, "Irish Historical Writing," 252.

183. Embassy Dublin to Secretary of State, October 1983, folder 130295–189999, box 94, Country Files-Ireland, RRPL.

184. Report of Private Briefing Given by Geraldine O'Leary de Macías, January 23, 1983, folder 11, box 8, OSC, MSA. The report incorrectly lists the year as 1983.

185. Sally O'Neill to Helene O'Sullivan, February 6, 1984, folder 11, box 8, OSC, MSA.

186. O'Neill to O'Sullivan.

187. Report of Private Briefing.

188. Memorandum, Charles Sylvester to Mr. Haass, May 21, 1984, folder 227000–229999, box 94, Country Files-Ireland, RRPL. For Dailey's campaign work, see "Envoy to Ireland Rejoins Interpublic," *New York Times*, November 17, 1983. Quotations from Sylvester to Haass.

189. O'Neill to O'Sullivan, February 6, 1984; Eamonn Casey to Helene O'Sullivan, January 17, 1984; George Gelber to Helene O'Sullivan, January 26, 1984, folder 11, box 8, OSC, MSA.

190. AnneMarie to Pat [no last names provided], January 29, 1984, folder 11, box 8, OSC, MSA.

191. Memorandum, Scafe to Miller et al.

192. AnneMarie to Pat.

193. Timothy Byrnes, *Catholic Bishops in American Politics* (Princeton, NJ: Princeton University Press, 1991), 119–121.

194. Stanley Interrante, "Ferraro—The Personification of Modernist Hypocrisy," *Wanderer*, October 4, 1984.

195. Suzanne Garment, "We Conventioneers Leave Our Brains in San Francisco," *Wall Street Journal*, July 20, 1984.

196. Jon Margolis, "Democrats a Hit—Oratorically Speaking," *Chicago Tribune*, July 20, 1984.

197. Tommie Sue Montgomery, *Revolution in El Salvador: From Civil Strife to Civil Peace*, 2nd ed. (Boulder, CO: Westview Press, 1995), 1–2, 133–134.

198. "In View," *Crisis*, July 1984, 6.

199. LeoGrande, *Our Own Backyard*, 257.

200. Terence Hunt, "Says Mondale-Ferraro from 'Most Liberal Wing,'" Associated Press, July 24, 1984.

201. "Bush Continues Attack on Democratic Ticket," *New York Times*, July 25, 1984; Lou Cannon, "Reagan & Co.: Aides Can't Change Theme Song of Show That's Run 40 Years," *Washington Post*, July 30, 1984.

202. Hunt, "Says Mondale-Ferraro."

203. Omang, "Catholic Groups Differ."

204. Ronald Reagan, "Remarks at a Reagan-Bush Rally in Glen Ellyn, Illinois," October 16, 1984, APP, https://www.presidency.ucsb.edu/node/260837; in Portland, Oregon, October 23, 1984, APP, https://www.presidency.ucsb.edu/node/261028; in Seattle, Washington, October 23, 1984, APP, https://www.presidency.ucsb.edu/node/261035; in Columbus, Ohio, October 24, 1984, APP, https://www.presidency.ucsb.edu/node/261055; in Millersville, Pennsylvania, October 29, 1984, APP, https://www.presidency.ucsb.edu/node/260448; in Parkersburg, West Virginia, October 29, 1984, APP, https://www.presidency.ucsb.edu/node/260477.

205. Charles T. Strauss, "Quest for the Holy Grail: Central American War, Catholic Internationalism, and United States Public Diplomacy in Reagan's America," *U.S. Catholic Historian* 33, no. 1 (2015): 195.

206. Memorandum, Faith Ryan Whittlesey to George Bush, "Blunting Allegations of Inordinant [*sic*] Influence of Far Right Religious Groups upon WH Policy," October 10, 1984, folder Religion/Politics, box 14f, FRWF, RRPL.

6. Real Catholics versus Maryknollers

1. Timothy A. Byrnes, *Reverse Mission: Transnational Religious Communities and the Making of US Foreign Policy* (Washington, DC: Georgetown University Press, 2011), 100. I have heard other versions.

2. See David Gergen, "Where the Top Figures Turn for Advice," *U.S. News & World Report*, May 20, 1985; Michael White, "US Backs 'Non-Lethal' Private Aid for Contras," *Guardian* (London), May 2, 1986; Joshua Muravchik, "Why the Democrats Lost," *Commentary*, January 1985, 24; David Rogers and David Ignatius, "The Contra Fight: How CIA-Aided Raids in Nicaragua in '84 Led Congress to End Funds," *Wall Street Journal*, March 6, 1985; Editorial, "In Praise of Tip O'Neill," *Wall Street Journal*, May 10, 1985; Editorial, "The O'Neill Doctrine," *Wall Street Journal*, June 11, 1985; Jeffery L. Sheler et al., "Out of the Pulpit, into the Streets; Church Activists Are on the March," *U.S.*

News & World Report, April 21, 1986; Richard E. Cohen, "Getting Religion," *National Journal*, September 14, 1985.

3. See Patrick Reilly, "House Speaker O'Neill Is Under Close Scrutiny," *National Catholic Register*, October 29, 1978, criticizing O'Neill for doing "nothing to help this country's unborn children" despite his position as Speaker.

4. Many mention the O'Neill-Maryknoll connection but do not explore it. See William M. LeoGrande, *Our Own Backyard: The United States in Central America, 1977–1992* (Chapel Hill: University of North Carolina Press, 1998), 454–455; Roger Peace, *Call to Conscience: The Anti-Contra War Campaign* (Amherst: University of Massachusetts Press, 2012), 82–83; Robert Surbrug Jr., *Beyond Vietnam: The Politics of Protest in Massachusetts, 1974–1990* (Boston: University of Massachusetts Press, 2009), 229; Christian Smith, *Resisting Reagan: The U.S. Central America Peace Movement* (Chicago: University of Chicago Press, 1996), 381; Bob Woodward, *Veil: The Secret Wars of the CIA, 1981–1987* (New York: Simon and Schuster, 1987), 225; Dana L. Robert, "The Influence of American Missionary Women on the World Back Home," *Religion and American Culture* 12, no. 1 (2002): 74; Byrnes, *Reverse Mission*, 98–100. Byrnes discusses how Maryknollers' information impacted O'Neill's views.

5. I borrow from Robert Dean's claim that a shared culture of manhood—"imperial brotherhood"—influenced the Kennedy and Johnson administrations' decision to escalate U.S. involvement in Vietnam. Robert D. Dean, *Imperial Brotherhood: Gender and the Making of Cold War Foreign Policy* (Amherst: University of Massachusetts Press, 2001).

6. LeoGrande, *Our Own Backyard*, 345.

7. Cynthia J. Arnson, *Crossroads: Congress, the President, and Central America, 1976–1993*, 2nd ed. (University Park: Pennsylvania State University Press, 1993), 178–179.

8. CIA, "Freedom Fighters' Manual," ca. October 1983, NI01838, NC, DNSA.

9. LeoGrande, *Our Own Backyard*, 276.

10. John A. Farrell, *Tip O'Neill and the Democratic Century* (Boston: Little Brown, 2001), 609.

11. Rowland Evans and Robert Novak, "A New Role for the Speaker," *Washington Post*, April 13, 1983, folder 6, box 19, KOD, OP.

12. Philip Taubman, "The Speaker and His Sources on Latin America," *New York Times*, September 12, 1984.

13. Taubman, "Speaker."

14. Taubman, "Speaker."

15. Tip O'Neill and William Novak, *Man of the House: The Life and Political Memoirs of Speaker Tip O'Neill* (New York: Random House, 1987), 370.

16. Farrell, *O'Neill*, 612.

17. O'Neill and Novak, *Man of the House*, 370.

18. "Who Fooled Tip," *Crisis*, June 1989, 41.

19. Byrnes, *Reverse Mission*, 99.

20. U.S. Congress, House, Committee on Appropriations, *Foreign Assistance and Related Programs Appropriations for 1980, Before the Subcommittee on Foreign Operations and Related Programs*, 96th Cong., 1st sess., 1979, 153, 164.

21. Roger Fontaine, "Accuracy, Balance of WOLA Found Lacking by Its Critics," *Washington Times*, April 10, 1985, folder 45, box 22, DJP.

22. WOLA, "You are cordially invited to hear Sister Peggy Healy MM talk about Current Events in Nicaragua," folder 2, box 19, KOD, OP.

23. *Appropriations for 1980*, 153–154, 157.

24. Margaret Healy, "A Lost Opportunity for Nicaragua—and for Us," *Newsday*, March 19, 1980, folder MSC/OSC/N, box unknown, OSC, MSA. O'Neill's files contain two examples of their correspondence. The Maryknoll archives do not contain Healy's correspondence because she left the community. Peggy Healy to Tip O'Neill, December 1981, folder 7, box 19, KOD, OP; Tip O'Neill to Peggy Healy, December 10, 1984, folder 1, box 10, KOD, OP.

25. Byrnes, *Reverse Mission*, 104–105.

26. O'Neill and Novak, *Man of the House*, 11, 20–21.

27. O'Neill and Novak, *Man of the House*, 23, 170.

28. Farrell, *O'Neill*, 431.

29. Mary McGrory, "Two Democrats: One Lost, One Found," *Washington Post*, February 7, 1988.

30. Farrell, *O'Neill*, 613.

31. Report, Gray Orfila International to Adolfo Calero, August 9, 1984, IC00530, I-C, DNSA.

32. Cynthia Glavac, *In the Fullness of Life: A Biography of Dorothy Kazel, O.S.U.* (Denville, NJ: Dimension Books, 1996), 24.

33. Bruce Buursma, "Where Are the Nuns?," *Chicago Tribune*, April 19, 1981.

34. See Dean, *Imperial Brotherhood*; David K. Johnson, *The Lavender Scare: The Cold War Persecution of Gays and Lesbians in the Federal Government* (Chicago: University of Chicago Press, 2004); Naoko Shibusawa, "The Lavender Scare and Empire: Rethinking Cold War Antigay Politics," *Diplomatic History* 36, no. 4 (2012): 723–752.

35. Farrell, *O'Neill*, 644–645.

36. Sydney H. Schanberg, "George the Gender Bender," *New York Times*, October 20, 1984.

37. Bill Peterson, "Ferraro Candidacy Highlights Debate Over Women's Role," *Washington Post*, September 18, 1984.

38. Editorial, "One-Sided Advice," *News-Sun* (Waukegan, IL), October 1, 1984, folder 24, box 13, communications, MSA.

39. Michael Novak, "The Case Against Liberation Theology," *New York Times*, October 21, 1984.

40. James L. Oberstar, letter to the editor, *Maryknoll*, June 1986, 57.

41. Steven Dozinger, "Kidnapped American Nun Blames U.S. Government," United Press International, January 11, 1985.

42. Press statement, Nancy Donovan, January 11, 1985, in Helene O'Sullivan to Tip O'Neill, January 18, 1985, folder 7, box 19, KOD, OP.

43. Suzanne DeChillo, "Maryknoll Pursues Its Vision of Mission: Maryknoll Pursues Activist Mission," *New York Times*, March 31, 1985.

44. Dozinger, "Kidnapped American Nun."

45. LeoGrande, *Our Own Backyard*, 117, 306–307.

46. Peter Kornbluh, "The Selling of the F.D.N.," *Nation*, January 17, 1987, 40–41.

47. "A los congresistas de los Estados Unidos de América," February 11, 1985, trans. with Goffs to Friend, March 1985, folder 838, box 45, GP.

48. LeoGrande, *Our Own Backyard*, 414.

49. Peace, *Call to Conscience*, 178.

50. "Nicaraguan Refugee Fund," December 1984, folder NRF-2, box OA1242, RRF, RRPL.

51. LeoGrande, *Our Own Backyard*, 419.

52. U.S. Congress, House, Committee on Foreign Affairs, *U.S. Support for the Contras, Before the Subcommittee on Western Hemisphere Affairs*, 99th Cong., 1st sess., 1985, 269–270.

53. Henry Hyde, "Ruminations of a Conservative Congressman," *Crisis*, September 1983, 46–47.

54. Angela Grimm, "Henry Hyde—Conscience of the Congress," *Crisis*, March 1988, 16.

55. *Support for the Contras*, 311–312.

56. Robert Parry and Peter Kornbluh, "Iran Contra's Untold Story," *Foreign Policy* 72 (Autumn 1988): 15. The Old Catholics formed in the late nineteenth century over disputes related to Vatican I. *New Catholic Encyclopedia*, s.v. "Old Catholics," 2nd ed. (Detroit: Gale, 2003).

57. *Support for the Contras*, 304–305.

58. Ronald Reagan, "Remarks at a Conference on Religious Liberty," April 16, 1985, APP, https://www.presidency.ucsb.edu/node/260076.

59. "Conference Denounces Religious Persecution in the World," *Wanderer*, May 2, 1985.

60. Sari Gilbert, "Vatican Disputes Reagan Statements," *Washington Post*, April 19, 1985, folder 9, box 53, RTFCAM, MMA.

61. "'Winning Strategy': Say Foes, 'Don't Follow Pope,'" *National Catholic Reporter*, August 3, 1984.

62. Perhaps no post–World War II work articulated this fear more than Paul Blanshard's *American Freedom and Catholic Power* (Boston: Beacon Press, 1949).

63. Marie Gayte, "'I Told the White House If They Give One to the Pope, I May Ask for One': The American Reception to the Establishment of Diplomatic Relations between the United States and the Vatican in 1984," *Journal of Church and State* 54, no. 1 (2012): 9–13.

64. Michael Novak to Henry Hyde, April 18, 1985, folder 9, box 53, RTFCAM.

65. Quoted in Woodward, *Veil*, 402.

66. Arnson, *Crossroads*, 198–199, 202–204.

67. Dan T. Carter, *The Politics of Rage: George Wallace, the Origins of the New Conservatism, and the Transformation of American Politics*, 2nd ed. (Baton Rouge: Louisiana State University Press, 2000), 301, 433.

68. Tom Turnipseed, "Reagan Whistles Dixie's Tune," *New York Times*, July 17, 1985.

69. Memorandum, William Hamilton to Congressman Coehlo, Survey of Southern Voters, June 4, 1985, folder 3, box 19, KOD, OP.

70. Cal Thomas, "O'Neill Listens to Wrong Voices on Nicaraguans," *St. Paul Pioneer Press*, June 17, 1985; "Why Tip Opposes Contra Aid," *Daily News* (Philadelphia, PA), June 14, 1985; "O'Neill's Stance on Nicaragua Shows a Shallow Understanding," *Democrat and Chronicle* (Rochester, NY), June 13, 1985; "O'Neill's Stance on Nicaragua Shows a Shallow Understanding," *Journal Star* (Peoria, IL), June 13, 1985, in folder 24, box 13 communications, MSA.

71. Ronald Reagan, Remarks of the President at Presentation of Medal of Freedom to Mother Teresa, June 20, 1985, APP, https://www.presidency.ucsb.edu/node/260458; Memorandum, Linda Chavez, Photo-Op with Mother Teresa, December 13, 1985, folder MTFilm 12/16/85-1, box OA15074, Carl Anderson Files (CAF), RRPL.

72. Ronald Reagan, *The Reagan Diaries*, ed. Douglas Brinkley (New York: Harper-Collins, 2007), 339.

73. "Reagan: A Reel Glimpse of the Man Behind President," *New York Times*, June 1, 2007.

74. Ronald Reagan, "Remarks at the Santa-Cali-Gon Days Celebration in Independence, Missouri," September 2, 1985, APP, https://www.presidency.ucsb.edu/node/260619.

75. For a discussion of how Rambo reflected the "hard body" images of the Reagan years versus the "soft bodies" of the Carter years, see Susan Jeffords, *Hard Bodies: Hollywood Masculinity in the Reagan Era* (New Brunswick, NJ: Rutgers University Press, 1994), 13.

76. Robert S. Greenberger, "Reagan Promise on Rebel Aid Has Signs of Rambo Rhetoric," *Wall Street Journal*, February 3, 1986; "Rambo Rides High in Washington," *Observer* (London), March 30, 1986.

77. See Dudley Clendinen, "Friends and Foes of Contras Rally at Florida Base," *New York Times*, December 14, 1986; Emergency Committee to End Contra Funding, advertisement, *New York Times*, March 17, 1986; Marianne Means, "Will Reagan Change in 1986?," *Tri-State Defender* (Memphis, TN), March 5, 1986.

78. Vladimir Posner, "'USA Acted Like a Bully' Against Libya," BBC Summary of World Broadcasts, April 21, 1986.

79. "Who Shapes U.S. Foreign Policy? Rambo and That 'Other War,'" *Phyllis Schlafly Report*, May 1986, Northwestern University, Special Collections, Evanston, IL (NUSC).

80. Paul Weyrich to Sylvester Stallone, May 1, 1986, Bob Dole to Sylvester Stallone, May 2, 1986, Pete Wilson to Sylvester Stallone, April 30, 1986, in memorandum, Eric Licht to Paul Weyrich, Freedom Fighters, May 2, 1986, folder 12, box 4, WP.

81. Debbie Sontag, "A Revolt Over 'Ramba' Contra Poster: A Symbol or Sinful?," *Miami Herald*, January 30, 1986.

82. LeoGrande, *Our Own Backyard*, 428.

83. Goffs to Friends, July 1985, folder 839, box 45, GP.

84. Press Release, Embassy of Nicaragua, July 8, 1985, folder NER, box 36, COC, UNDA.

85. "'Fast for Peace,'" *National Catholic Register*, July 21, 1985.

86. Editorial, "Nicaraguan Minister's Religious Fast to Head Off War with U.S. Merits Support," *National Catholic Reporter*, August 2, 1985.

87. Conor Cruise O'Brien, "God and Man in Nicaragua," *Atlantic Monthly*, August 1986, 63.

88. "D'Escoto Ends Fast, Attacks U.S. Church Leaders," *National Catholic Register*, August 18, 1985; Kathleen Kelly, "Fasting with Miguel D'Escoto," *National Catholic Reporter*, August 30, 1985; "D'Escoto's Fast Underscores Different Models in Nicaraguan Church," CAHI *Updates*, August 12, 1985, folder 10, box 5, RTFCAM; "Maryknoll Backs d'Escoto in Open Fast for Peace," *National Catholic Reporter*, July 19, 1985.

89. "D'Escoto to My Brothers and Sisters of the Armed Forces," July 12, 1985, folder 3, box 26, OJP, MMA.

90. Press Release, Embassy of Nicaragua, July 8, 1985.

91. Peace, *Call to Conscience*, 166.

92. Kelly, "Fasting with Miguel."

93. "D'Escoto Ends Fast."

94. O'Brien, "God and Man," 64.

95. Michael Dodson and Laura Nuzzi O'Shaughnessy, *Nicaragua's Other Revolution: Religious Faith and Political Struggle* (Chapel Hill: University of North Carolina Press, 1990), 220.

96. William M. Boteler to Maryknoller, April 30, 1985, folder 3, box 26, JP, MMA.

97. Boteler to Maryknoller.

98. Dodson and O'Shaughnessy, *Nicaragua's Other Revolution*, 221–222; CIA Directorate of Intelligence, "Nicaragua: Prospects for the Opposition," March 1986, 6, in CIA Freedom of Information Act Electronic Reading Room.

99. Dodson and O'Shaughnessy, *Nicaragua's Other Revolution*, 222–223.

100. "Crece rechazo a la campaña de Obando; Se pronuncian cristianos de todo el país," in *El Nuevo Diario*, January 30, 1986, trans. with Goffs to Friend, January–February 1986, folder 842, box 45, GP.

101. "D'Escoto's Fast Underscores."

102. Dodson and O'Shaughnessy, *Nicaragua's Other Revolution*, 225.

103. "D'Escoto's Fast Underscores."

104. "D'Escoto's Fast Underscores."

105. "D'Escoto Fast 'Not Christian,'" *National Catholic Register*, August 25, 1985.

106. Peace, *Call to Conscience*, 166.

107. Dodson and O'Shaughnessy, *Nicaragua's Other Revolution*, 226.

108. "D'Escoto Ends Fast, Attacks U.S. Church Leaders," *National Catholic Register*, August 18, 1985.

109. Michael Novak, "Maryknoll's Miguel D'Escoto," *Crisis*, September 1985, 6.

110. Enrique T. Rueda, "The Faithful in Nicaragua Need Our Support," *Wanderer*, August 29, 1985.

111. Ronald Reagan, "Radio Address to the Nation on Tax Reform and the Situation in Nicaragua," December 14, 1985, APP, https://www.presidency.ucsb.edu/node/259445.

112. "Mensaje del Padre Miguel d'Escoto al iniciarse el Vía Crucis," Jalapa, February 14, 1986, trans. with Goffs to Friend, March 1986, folder 842, box 45, GP.

113. Dodson and O'Shaughnessy, *Nicaragua's Other Revolution*, 228–229.

114. Joseph Mulligan, "Nicaraguan Bishops Continue Opposition Role; Other Catholics Support Sandinista Government," March 1986, folder 9, box 53, RTFCAM.

115. "The Church of the Poor in Nicaragua," *Revista Envío*, April 1986, http://www.envio.org.ni/articulo/3501.

116. Mulligan, "Bishops Continue."

117. Dodson and O'Shaughnessy, *Nicaragua's Other Revolution*, 229.

118. Mulligan, "Bishops Continue"; Dodson and O'Shaughnessy, *Nicaragua's Other Revolution*, 229.

119. "Comments by Fr. Miguel D'Escoto on Finishing the Vía Crucis of Peace and Life," February 28, 1986, in Goffs to Friend, March 1986, folder 842, box 45, GP.

120. "Church of the Poor."

121. CIA Directorate of Intelligence, "Nicaragua," 5.

122. CIA, Directorate of Intelligence, "Nicaragua," 13.

123. Patrick J. Buchanan, "The Contras Need Our Help," *Washington Post*, March 5, 1986, folder 4, box 13, Communications, MSA.

124. LeoGrande, *Our Own Backyard*, 447–448.

125. "Dialogue with Patrick J. Buchanan," *National Catholic Register*, March 1, 1987.

126. Patrick J. Buchanan, "Tales from 'Blessed Sacrament': The Church I Knew, That Is No More," *Crisis*, April 1988, 22–23.

127. Buchanan, "Tales," 23 (capitalization in original).

128. John Geitner to Patrick Buchanan, March 5, 1986, and John Geitner to Patrick Buchanan, March 10, 1986, folder 394000–394999, box 240, Nicaragua, WHORM, RRPL.

129. See Robert Royal, "Maryknoll's Failed Revolution," *Crisis*, March 1985, 20–22.

130. LeoGrande, *Our Own Backyard*, 411–413.

131. Bill DeOre, cartoon, *Dallas Morning News*, August 19, 1985.

132. Enrique T. Rueda, "Some Positive Steps to Help Rescue the Church in Nicaragua," *Wanderer*, February 27, 1986.

133. Enrique T. Rueda, "Catholics Are Suffering for the Faith in Nicaragua," *Wanderer*, January 30, 1986.

134. Enrique T. Rueda, "'What Ever Happened to Your Commitment to God's Church?,'" *Wanderer*, March 27, 1986.

135. Enrique T. Rueda, "Open Letter to Maryknoll Created a Stir," *Wanderer*, June 5, 1986.

136. Editorial, St. Augustin Bulletin, March 9, 1986, folder 9, box 13, Communications, MSA.

137. Memorandum, Linas Kojelis to Ronald Reagan, March 1, 1986, IC02428, I-C, DNSA.

138. Paul A. Fisher, "The Wanderer Asks Lew Lehrman," *Wanderer*, May 30, 1985.

139. LeoGrande, *Our Own Backyard*, 448, 454.

140. Kathryn Sikkink, *Mixed Signals: U.S. Human Rights Policy and Latin America* (Ithaca, NY: Cornell University Press, 2004), 149.

141. Ronald Reagan, "Address to the Nation on the Situation in Nicaragua," March 16, 1986, APP, https://www.presidency.ucsb.edu/node/258535.

142. Ben Wattenberg, "Tip Is Sincere, but He's Wrong," *Philadelphia Inquirer*, March 27, 1986, folder 24, box 13, Communications, MSA. The op-ed also ran as "Tip Following the Wrong Orders on Nicaragua," *Star Ledger* (Newark, NJ), March 28, 1986, and "When Maryknoll Talks, Tip Listens," *Washington Times*, March 27, 1986.

143. Farrell, *O'Neill*, 671.

144. Dear Colleague Letter, April 10, 1986, folder 7, box 19, KOD, OP.

145. "Why Would the USCC Deny It?," *catholic eye*, 1986, folder 1, box 22, RTF-CAM.

146. Miguel Obando y Bravo, "Nicaragua: The Sandinistas Have 'Gagged and Bound' Us," *Washington Post*, May 22, 1986.

147. 132 Cong. Rec. 15281–15282 (1986).

148. Henry J. Hyde, "Maryknoll Memories and Managua," *Wall Street Journal*, June 25, 1986.

149. "Contras and Democrats," *Wall Street Journal*, June 25, 1986.

150. Jimmy Breslin, "There's No Protection against Moral Fatigue," *Toronto Star*, July 6, 1986.

151. LeoGrande, *Our Own Backyard*, 473.

152. Memorandum, Robert Kagan to Walter Raymond, September 18, 1986, NI02880, NC, DNSA.

7. Maryknoll and Iran-Contra

1. U.S. Congress, *Iran-Contra Investigation: Testimony of Dewey R. Clarridge, C/CATF, and Clair George, Before the Senate Select Committee on Secret Military Assistance to Iran and the Nicaraguan Opposition and House Select Committee to Investigate Covert Arms Transactions with Iran*, 100th Cong., 1st sess., 1987, 164.

2. William M. LeoGrande, *Our Own Backyard: The United States in Central America, 1977–1992* (Chapel Hill: University of North Carolina Press, 1998), 477–478.

3. Gaddis Smith, *The Last Years of the Monroe Doctrine 1945–1993* (New York: Hill and Wang, 1994), 204.

4. LeoGrande, *Our Own Backyard*, 479.

5. LeoGrande, *Our Own Backyard*, 481.

6. Lawrence E. Walsh, *Firewall: The Iran-Contra Conspiracy and Cover-Up* (New York: W. W. Norton, 1997), xiv, 19–20.

7. Doug Rossinow, *The Reagan Era: A History of the 1980s* (New York: Columbia University Press, 2015), 186.

8. Walsh, *Firewall*, xiv; 6–7; H. W. Brands, *Reagan: The Life* (New York: Doubleday, 2015), 547–548, 559.

9. Andrea Mitchell, *Talking Back: . . . To Presidents, Dictators, and Assorted Scoundrels* (New York: Penguin, 2006), 112.

10. Ronald Reagan, "Address to the Nation on the Iran Arms and Contra Aid Controversy," November 13, 1986, APP, https://www.presidency.ucsb.edu/node/258119.

11. Peter Kornbluh and Malcolm Byrne, eds., *The Iran-Contra Scandal: The Declassified History* (New York: New Press, 1993), 405–406.

12. LeoGrande, *Our Own Backyard*, 481.

13. Ronald Reagan, "Remarks Announcing the Review of the National Security Council's Role in the Iran Arms and Contra Aid Controversy," November 25, 1986, APP, https://www.presidency.ucsb.edu/node/258235.

14. Brands, *Reagan*, 635.

15. Walsh, *Firewall*, 14–15.

16. Kornbluh and Byrne, *Iran-Contra Scandal*, 328, 330–331.

17. James Gerstenzang, "Bishop Questions Casey's Ethical Outlook at Funeral," *Los Angeles Times*, May 10, 1987.

18. Memorandum, William Casey to Robert McFarlane, Supplemental Assistance to Nicaragua Program, March 27, 1984, in Kornbluh and Byrne, *Iran-Contra Scandal*, 383.

19. Walsh, *Firewall*, 19.

20. LeoGrande, *Our Own Backyard*, 542–543.

21. Sophia Casey to Ronald Reagan, November 28, 1987, folder 534000–540246, box 143, WHORM-Nicaragua, RRPL.

22. "Bishop Criticizes U.S. Policy during Services for Former CIA Chief," *Wanderer*, May 21, 1987; Steven V. Roberts, "Contra Controversy Raised at Casey Funeral," *New York Times*, May 10, 1987.

23. Colman McCarthy, "A Bishop's Refreshing Candor," *Washington Post*, May 16, 1987.

24. William F. Buckley, "Casey Eulogy Bishop's Comments Out of Line," *Philadelphia Inquirer*, May 13, 1987.

25. Phyllis Zagano, "Observations: A Mass of Contradictions," *Crisis*, June 1987, 55.

26. Roberts, "Contra Controversy Raised at Casey Funeral."

27. Gerstenzang, "Bishop Questions."

28. John R. McGann, "Pastoral Letter on El Salvador," July 18, 1983, folder 7, box 16, B-RP.

29. "William J. Casey, RIP," *National Review*, June 5, 1987.

30. Gerstenzang, "Bishop Questions."

31. Buckley, "Casey Eulogy."

32. "William J. Casey, RIP."

33. McCarthy, "Bishop's Refreshing Candor."

34. Zagano, "Mass of Contradictions."

35. Kim Chatelain, "Catholic Church Ignored 1985 Report Warning of Child Sex Abuse Crisis," Nola.com, February 20, 2019, https://expo.nola.com/news/g66l-2019/02/e571fda9184994/vatican-summit-on-sexual-abuse-has-its-roots-in-cajun-country-.html.

36. Laurie Goodstein and David M. Halbfinger, "Church Office Failed to Act on Abuse Scandal," *New York Times*, July 1, 2010.

37. Tracey Kaplan, "Beverly Hills Church Cuts Eulogies for CIA's Casey," *Los Angeles Times*, July 12, 1987.

38. Stanley Interrante, "Memorial Service for William Casey 'Edited,'" *Wanderer*, July 30, 1987.

39. Kaplan, "Beverly Hills."

40. Mark Bryce to Ronald Reagan, May 11, 1987, folder 502000–503999, box 142, WHORM-Nicaragua, RRPL.

41. Alison Mitchell, "Contras to Get $140,000 Raised by Casey Fund," *Newsday*, December 1, 1987.

42. Robert Fresco, "Peace Plan Dries Up Casey Contra Fund," *Newsday*, April 5, 1989.

43. LeoGrande, *Our Own Backyard*, 496.

44. Kornbluh and Byrne, *Iran-Contra Scandal*, 329–330.

45. LeoGrande, *Our Own Backyard*, 497.

46. Ben Bradlee Jr., *Guts and Glory: The Rise and Fall of Oliver North* (London: Grafton, 1998), photo between 308–309, 519–520.

47. LeoGrande, *Our Own Backyard*, 497.

48. "Aid to the Contras," *Eagle Forum Newsletter*, August 1987, NUSC.

49. Schlafly to Eagle, *Eagle Forum Newsletter*, September 1987, NUSC (emphasis in original removed).

50. Select Comm. on Iran-Contra Affair, at 667–668 (Hyde, Supplemental Views).

51. LeoGrande, *Our Own Backyard*, 496.

52. "Buchanan Leaves Reagan Fold," *Chicago Tribune*, February 4, 1987.

53. Patrick J. Buchanan, "You've Won, Mr. President; Now Pardon Ollie and John," *Washington Post*, July 19, 1987.

54. Buchanan, "You've Won."

55. Select Comm. on Iran-Contra Affair, at 667 (Hyde, Supplemental Views).

56. Buchanan, "You've Won."

57. Enrique Rueda, "There Is Hope for Us Yet," *Wanderer*, August 6, 1987 (emphasis in original).

58. "A Prophetic Pastoral Letter and Massive Support for the Literacy Crusade," *Revista Envío*, December 1983, https://www.envio.org.ni/articulo/3544.

59. James Brockman, "Local Opinion Divided on Apparition Reports by Nicaraguan Peasant," Religious News Service, May 15, 1981, folder 15, box 17, B-RP.

60. Brockman, "Local Opinion."

61. "The Contras: New Bottles, Old Wine," *Revista Envío*, June 1987, https://www.envio.org.ni/articulo/3772.

62. "A Prophetic Pastoral Letter and Massive Support for the Literacy."

63. Brockman, "Local Opinion."

64. "Church-State Relations A Chronology-Part II," *Revista Envío*, December 1987, http://www.envio.org.ni/articulo/3184.

65. Michael Dodson and Laura Nuzzi O'Shaughnessy, *Nicaragua's Other Revolution: Religious Faith and Political Struggle* (Chapel Hill: University of North Carolina Press, 1990), 230–231, 234.

66. Advertisement, "Apparition of Our Lady in Nicaragua," *Wanderer*, October 22, 1987. An imprimatur is an episcopal seal of approval. Before Vatican II all Catholic books required one; since the 1960s, increasingly only conservative authors have sought them out.

67. "Church-State Relations." In 1995, Martínez said Mary criticized the Chamorro government. Aldo Díaz Lacayo, "Nicaragua Briefs," *Revista Envío*, June 1995, http://www.envio.org.ni/articulo/1868.

68. For examples, see "Putting Iran-Contra in Perspective," *Phyllis Schlafly Report*, August 1987, NUSC; "The Pro-American Activities Committee," *National Review*, July 3, 1987.

69. Buchanan, "You've Won." By contrast, Buckley and *National Review* defended Reagan but did not support North and Poindexter. Buckley pushed for the men to testify so they could expose the insubordination Buckley believed led to Iran-Contra. John B. Judis, *William F. Buckley, Jr., Patron Saint of the Conservatives* (New York: Simon & Schuster, 1988), 467–468.

70. "Aid to the Contras," *Eagle Forum Newsletter*.

71. Quoted in Sean Wilentz, *The Age of Reagan: A History, 1974–2008* (New York: HarperCollins, 2008), 235.

72. David G. Savage, "Hyde View on Lying Is Back Haunting Him," *Los Angeles Times*, December 4, 1998.

73. "Putting Iran-Contra."

74. *Iran-Contra Investigation*, 164.

75. Henry Hyde, "Liberation Theology and American Foreign Policy," *Crisis*, January 1987, in 133 Cong. Rec. 4429-4430 (1987).

76. Rose Kennedy Lane, letter to the editor, *Pilot*, August 14, 1987, folder 12, box 13, MSA.

77. Select Comm. on Iran-Contra Affair, H.R. Rep. No. 100–433 and S. Rep. No. 100–216, at 21, 22 (1987).

78. Select Comm. on Iran-Contra Affair, 437 (minority report).

79. Wilentz, *Age of Reagan*, 240.

80. William Bole, "Religious Activists Display 'Reparations Shipment' to Nicaragua," *Washington Post*, July 18, 1987, folder Quest for Peace 1980s, box 5, QCP; Roger Peace, *A Call to Conscience: The Anti-Contra War Campaign* (Amherst: University of Massachusetts Press, 2012), 200.

81. Colman McCarthy, "Against Ollie North: Quiet Commitment," *Washington Post*, July 18, 1987.

82. 133 Cong. Rec. 19580–19581 (1987).

83. Celes Stancin, letter to the editor, *Maryknoll*, May 1987, 57.

84. Emmett P. O'Neill, letter to the editor, *Maryknoll*, May 1987, 57.

85. Bea Waltz, letter to the editor, *Maryknoll*, June 1988, 38.

86. Mike Chew, letter to the editor, *Maryknoll*, June 1987, 57; John Tirpak, letter to the editor, *Maryknoll*, July 1987, 57.

87. Dolores Morin, letter to the editor, *Maryknoll*, February 1988, 56.

88. Frank Partee, letter to the editor, *Maryknoll*, February 1987, 57.

89. James J. McDevitt, letter to the editor, *Maryknoll*, May 1987, 57; James M. Finley, letter to the editor, *Maryknoll*, June 1987, 56.

90. Alberto Nuñez, letter to the editor, *Maryknoll*, June 1987, 57.

91. Dennis Novak, letter to the editor, *Maryknoll*, July 1988, 38.

92. Charlotte Stephen, letter to the editor, *Maryknoll*, October 1988, 45.

93. Catherine A. O'Brian, letter to the editor, *New York Times*, September 23, 1987.

94. "U.S. Priest in Jail Gets a Lift: He's in the News in Managua," *New York Times*, September 8, 1987.

95. "U.S. Priest in Jail."

96. Peace, *Call to Conscience*, 196.

97. "U.S. Priest in Jail."

98. "U.S. Priest in Jail."

99. O'Brian, letter to the editor.

100. Lindsey Gruson, "Talks with Cubans in Louisiana Go on as Siege Is Said to Stabilize," *New York Times*, November 26, 1987.

101. Elaine Sciolino, "Nicaragua's U.N. Voice," *New York Times*, September 28, 1986.

102. Bob Woodward and Lou Cannon, "CIA Document Based on Lobby Techniques," *Washington Post*, March 1, 1986; Sciolino, "Nicaragua's U.N. Voice."

103. Joanne Omang, "Nicaraguan Leader Makes U.S. Tour," *Washington Post*, October 9, 1984.

104. Woodward and Cannon, "CIA Document."

105. LeoGrande, *Our Own Backyard*, 510–512.

106. LeoGrande, *Our Own Backyard*, 513–514, 516.

107. Brands, *Reagan*, 558.

108. LeoGrande, *Our Own Backyard*, 513, 515.

109. Christian Smith, *Resisting Reagan: The U.S. Central America Peace Movement* (Chicago: University of Chicago Press, 1996), 352.

110. LeoGrande, *Our Own Backyard*, 507, 509.

111. LeoGrande, *Our Own Backyard*, 517–518, 528.

112. Cynthia J. Arnson, *Crossroads: Congress, the President, and Central America, 1976–1993*, 2nd ed. (University Park: Pennsylvania State University Press, 1993), 221–222.

113. LeoGrande, *Our Own Backyard*, 523–524.

114. Arnson, *Crossroads*, 223.

115. David Lauter, "War to Continue Despite Aid Cutoff, Officials Say," *Los Angeles Times*, February 4, 1988.

116. Mary McGrory, "Two Democrats: One Lost, One Found," *Washington Post*, February 7, 1988.

117. McGrory, "Two Democrats."

118. Lauter, "War to Continue."

119. Philip Hannon, Nancy Collins, and Peter Finney Jr., *The Archbishop Wore Combat Boots: From Combat to Camelot to Katrina—A Memoir of an Extraordinary Life* (Huntingdon, IN: Our Sunday Visitor, 2010), 356.

120. McGrory, "Two Democrats."

121. Lauter, "War to Continue."

122. Gary Potter, "Anti-Communist Aid Defeated in House Vote," *Wanderer*, February 11, 1988.

123. "The Paracommunists," *Wanderer*, February 11, 1988.

124. Enrique Rueda, "This Nation Has Become a Toothless Tiger," *Wanderer*, April 7, 1988.

125. Arnson, *Crossroads*, 224.

126. LeoGrande, *Our Own Backyard*, 538–539.

127. LeoGrande, *Our Own Backyard*, 539–41.

128. Philip Shenon, "North and 3 Co-Defendants Plead Not Guilty in Iran-Contra Affair," *New York Times*, March 25, 1988.

129. "Religious Right Drums Up Support for North," *Los Angeles Times*, September 3, 1988.

130. Memorandum, Linas Kojelis to Ronald Reagan, March 1, 1986, IC02428, I-C, DNSA.

131. Michael Löwy, *The War of the Gods: Religion and Politics in Latin America* (London: Verso, 1996), 114.

132. Robert Parry and Tamar Jacoby, "Covert Aid and the Church," *Newsweek*, June 15, 1987; Jim McManus, "Reports Say Clergy in Managua Tapped North's War Chest," *National Catholic Reporter*, June 19, 1987; Jim McManus, "Reagan Crew, Contra Foes Square Off for New Round," *National Catholic Reporter*, July 3, 1987.

133. McManus, "Reports Say Clergy."

134. Bradlee, *Guts and Glory*, 421–422.

135. Richard Stengel, Jeanne McDowell, and Alessandra Stanley, "True Belief Unhampered by Doubt: From Small-Town Boy to Shadow Secretary of State, Oliver North Did Not Know When to Stop," *Time*, July 13, 1987.

136. Peter Grier, "Col. Oliver North: Beyond the Cartoon to a Complex Man," *Christian Science Monitor*, December 26, 1986.

137. Stengel, McDowell, and Stanley, "True Belief."

138. "Religious Right Drums Up."

139. Bradlee, *Guts and Glory*, 416.

140. For examples see Shirley Christian, "The White House Crisis: Profile of the Colonel; Friends Say Oliver North Is Taking It Like a Soldier," *New York Times*, November 30, 1986; Grier, "Col. Oliver North."

141. Stengel, McDowell, and Stanley, "True Belief."

142. Arnson, *Crossroads*, 298.

143. Susan F. Rasky, "After Sharp Debate, Senate Votes to Let North Collect His Pension," *New York Times*, November 3, 1989.

144. Mary McGrory, "A Senate Protection Measure?," *Washington Post*, November 7, 1989.

145. Rasky, "After Sharp Debate."

146. 135 Cong. Rec. 27017 (1989).

147. Rasky, "After Sharp Debate."

148. Arnson, *Crossroads*, 225.

149. Rossinow, *Reagan Era*, 184.

150. Arnson, *Crossroads*, 225.

151. LeoGrande, *Our Own Backyard*, 547–548.

152. Arnson, *Crossroads*, 225.

153. Wilentz, *Age of Reagan*, 272.

8. Déjà Vu

1. Teresa Whitfield, *Paying the Price: Ignacio Ellacuría and the Murdered Jesuits of El Salvador* (Philadelphia: Temple University Press, 1994), 9–11, 13–14, 169, 171.

2. 135 Cong. Rec. 30493-30494 (1989).

3. Cynthia J. Arnson, *Crossroads: Congress, the President, and Central America, 1976–1993*, 2nd ed. (University Park: Pennsylvania State University Press, 1993), 59.

4. Barbara Mikulski to Joe Healy, February 11, 1981, folder 65, box 2, William A. Wilson Collection (WAWC), GUSC.

5. James A. Baker III, *The Politics of Diplomacy: Revolution, War and Peace, 1989–1992* (New York: G. P. Putnam, 1995), 42, 49.

6. Baker, *Politics of Diplomacy*, 47–48.

7. William M. LeoGrande, *Our Own Backyard: The United States in Central America, 1977–1992* (Chapel Hill: University of North Carolina Press, 1998), 526–527.

8. Baker, *Politics of Diplomacy*, 49–50.

9. Baker, *Politics of Diplomacy*, 51–52, 54–55, 58–59, 151.

10. Robert Pear, "Baker Plan: A New Deal," *New York Times*, March 25, 1989.

11. "Salvadoran Bishops Condemn Intensified Violence as They Are Targeted," *Maryknoll News Notes*, March/April 1988.

12. "El Salvador's Death Squads Return—Pastoral Letter to Congress," *Maryknoll News Notes*, March/April 1989.

13. Tommie Sue Montgomery, *Revolution in El Salvador: From Civil Strife to Civil Peace*, 2nd ed. (Boulder, CO: Westview Press, 1995), 204–205.

14. LeoGrande, *Our Own Backyard*, 269, 274–275.

15. Mark O. Hatfield, Jim Leach, and George Miller, *Bankrolling Failure: United States Policy in El Salvador and the Urgent Need for Reform*, Report to the Arms Control and Foreign Policy Caucus (Washington, DC: The Caucus,1987), 1.

16. Cable, William Walker to DOS, January 7, 1989, EL00986, ES1980–1994, DNSA.

17. William H. Millers to Brother/Member of Central America Advocacy Network, May 26, 1989, folder 3, box 17, B-RP.

18. CIA Intelligence Report, March 14, 1989, EL00257, ES1980–1994, DNSA.

19. Montgomery, *Revolution in El Salvador*, 197, 213.

20. Whitfield, *Paying the Price*, 326.

21. "Rivera y Damas Raps Right-Wing Victory," *National Catholic Register*, April 16, 1989.

22. "Church Agency Says Salvador Army Massacred Civilians," *National Catholic Register*, March 12, 1989; "Salvador Prelate Challenges Military," *National Catholic Register*, May 7, 1989.

23. Quoted in Pax Americas, "Threats and Crackdown against Churches, Unions, Press and Political Opposition in El Salvador," December 6, 1989, in U.S. Congress, House, Committee on Foreign Affairs, *El Salvador at the Crossroads: Peace or Another Decade of War, Before the Subcommittees on Human Rights and International Organizations, and on Western Hemisphere Affairs*, 101 Cong., 2nd sess., 1990, 216.

24. Ana Arana, "Salvador Church Relations with Military Grow Tense," *Miami Herald*, May 21, 1989, in Millers to Brother/Member of Central America Advocacy Network.

25. Quoted in Pax Americas, "Threats and Crackdown," 216.

26. Jeffrey A. Engel, *When the World Seemed New: George H.W. Bush and the End of the Cold War* (Boston: Houghton Mifflin Harcourt, 2017), 123, 168, 180.

27. Russell Crandall, *The Salvador Option: The United States in El Salvador, 1977–1992* (New York: Cambridge, 2016), 432.

28. Erik Ching, *Stories of Civil War in El Salvador: A Battle Over Memory* (Chapel Hill: University of North Carolina Press, 2016), 186–187.

29. Directorate of Intelligence, "El Salvador: The FMLN after the November 1989 Offensive," January 26, 1990, https://www.cia.gov/library/readingroom/docs/DOC_0000677227.pdf.

30. Whitfield, *Paying the Price*, 204, 222, 299.

31. Pax Americas, "Threats and Crackdown," 219.

32. Whitfield, *Paying the Price*, 5.

33. Pax Americas, "Threats and Crackdown," 217.

34. Rubén Zamora, "For Salvador, Democracy before Peace," *New York Times*, January 24, 1990.

35. Kenneth E. Sharpe, "Salvadoran Events Disprove Assurances of US 'Experts,'" *Baltimore Sun*, November 19, 1989.

36. Stephen T. De Mott, "Where Violence Reigns," *Maryknoll*, January 1987, 26; Joseph R. Veneroso, "Ten Years, Four Women . . . and Counting," *Maryknoll*, December 1990, 38.

37. Press Release, Maryknoll Justice and Peace Office, November 20, 1989, folder 6, box 19, RTFCAM.

38. Press Release, LCWR/CMSM, c. November 19–21, 1989, folder 6, box 19, RTFCAM.

39. Mark A. Uhlig, "Salvadoran Security Forces Raid Episcopal Church, Arresting 17," *New York Times*, November 21, 1989.

40. Mark A. Uhlig, "Salvadoran Asks Pope to Remove 'Some Bishops,'" *New York Times*, November 19, 1989.

41. Quoted in 135 Cong. Rec. 30436 (1989).

42. Quoted in Pax Americas, "Threats and Crackdown," 218.

43. Robert Pear, "With Deaths Tied to Salvador Army, Aid Fight Is Likely," *New York Times*, January 9, 1990.

44. 135 Cong. Rec. 30500 (1989).

45. 135 Cong. Rec. 30510 (1989).

46. Robert Pear, "Congress Is as Skeptical as Ever on Salvador Aid," *New York Times*, January 14, 1990.

47. 135 Cong. Rec. 30445 (1989). Senator Frank Lautenberg made nearly identical remarks. 135 Cong. Rec. 30514 (1989).

48. 135 Cong. Rec. 30501–30502 (1989).

49. Robert Pear, "House Rejects Curb on Salvador Aid," *New York Times*, November 21, 1989.

50. 135 Cong. Rec. 30231 (1989).

51. 135 Cong. Rec. 30228 (1989).

52. Arnson, *Crossroads*, 247.

53. Timothy A. Byrnes, *Reverse Mission: Transnational Religious Communities and the Making of US Foreign Policy* (Washington, DC: Georgetown University Press, 2011), 29.

54. Byrnes, *Reverse Mission*, 59.

55. Sheila Kaplan, "Grief Begets Activism: In Wake of El Salvador Murders, Jesuits Step Up Efforts to Influence U.S. Policy," *Legal Times*, December 4, 1989, unnumbered folder, box 18, Central America Historical Institute Records (CAHIR), Swarthmore College Peace Collection, Swarthmore, PA (SCPC).

56. Kaplan, "Grief Begets."

57. Leo J. O'Donovan to Alfredo Cristiani, November 16, 1989, in *America*, December 16, 1989, 445.

58. Pear, "House Rejects Curb"; Robert Pear, "How Outrage in U.S. Spurred Action in Jesuit Case," *New York Times*, January 21, 1990.

59. Arnson, *Crossroads*, 251.

60. Whitfield, *Paying the Price*, 85.

61. Clifford Krauss, "Religion and Politics Become Fused in Congressman's District, and Heart," *New York Times*, August 23, 1990.

62. Jamaica Plain Committee on Central America member to John Joseph Moakley, December 13, 1982, folder 13, box 1, Series 03.04, McGovern, MA.

63. Mark Robert Schneider, *Joe Moakley's Journey: From South Boston to El Salvador* (Boston: Northeastern University, 2013), 125–126, 181–182.

64. Schneider, *Moakley's Journey*, 126; Krauss, "Religion and Politics."

65. Andrew Preston, "The Politics of Realism and Religion: Christian Responses to Bush's New World Order," *Diplomatic History* 34, no. 1 (2010): 103.

66. Crandall, *Salvador Option*, 419, 457.

67. Engel, *When the World*, 300.

68. Joaquín Chávez, "How Did the Civil War in El Salvador End?," *American Historical Review* 120, no. 5 (2015): 1791.

69. Andrew Rosenthal, "The Malta Summit," *New York Times*, December 4, 1989.

70. Engel, *When the World*, 9, 25, 306.

71. Douglas G. Brinkley, "The Bush Administration and Panama," in *From Cold War to New World Order: The Foreign Policy of George H.W. Bush*, ed. Meena Bose and Rosanna Perotti (Westport, CT: Greenwood, 2002), 176–179.

72. Engel, *When the World*, 306.

73. Brinkley, "Bush Administration and Panama," 180–181.

74. Quoted in Pear, "How Outrage."

75. Joseph A. O'Hare, "In Solidarity with the Slain Jesuits of El Salvador," *America*, December 16, 1989, 446.

76. "El Salvador: Keep Your Eye on the Ball," *National Review*, December 22, 1989, 13–14.

77. "Suicide in Central America," *National Review*, May 13, 1983, 539.

78. "Statement by Press Secretary Fitzwater on the Murders at the University of Central America in El Salvador," November 16, 1989, APP, https://www.presidency.ucsb.edu/node/263551.

79. Whitfield, *Paying the Price*, 79.

80. Cable, James Baker to William Walker, November 22, 1989, EL01050, ES1980–1994, DNSA.

81. George Bush, "Remarks at the Catholic University of America Anniversary Dinner," December 12, 1989, APP, https://www.presidency.ucsb.edu/node/264229.

82. Pear, "How Outrage."

83. Pear, "Congress Is as Skeptical."

84. Preston, "Politics of Realism," 96.

85. Engel, *When the World*, 30.

86. Preston, "Politics of Realism," 103.

87. Preston, "Politics of Realism," 98–99, 101.

88. CIA Directorate of Intelligence, "The Political Role of the Catholic Church in Central America," December 1988, EL00240, ES1980–1994, DNSA.

89. Christian Smith, *Resisting Reagan: The U.S. Central America Peace Movement* (Chicago: University of Chicago Press, 1996), 298–300; Ross Gelbspan, *Break-Ins, Death Threats and the FBI: The Covert War against the Central America Movement* (Boston: South End Press, 1991), x, 219.

90. Philip Shenon, "F.B.I. Papers Show Wide Surveillance of Reagan Critics," *New York Times*, January 28, 1988.

91. Paul Weingarten, "FBI Broke Into Group's Office, Informant Tells Subcommittee," *Chicago Tribune*, February 22, 1987.

92. U.S. Congress, House, Committee on the Judiciary, *Break-Ins at Sanctuary Churches and Organizations Opposed to Administration Policy in Central America, Before the Subcommittee on Civil and Constitutional Rights*, 100th Cong., 1st sess., 1987, 427, 435, 524.

93. *Break-Ins at Sanctuary Churches*, 524. In his congressional testimony, Varelli did not mention a return to El Salvador or his work as a Baptist preacher, yet a Salvadoran newspaper covered Varelli's religious work in 1977. Gelbspan, *Break-Ins, Death Threats*, 234.

94. Gelbspan, *Break-Ins, Death Threats*, 35.

95. *Break-Ins at Sanctuary Churches*, 427, 430.

96. *Break-Ins at Sanctuary Churches*, 436, 572.

97. Boutros Boutros-Ghali, *From Madness to Hope: The 12-Year War in El Salvador* (New York: United Nations, 1993), https://www.usip.org/sites/default/files/file/ElSalvador-Report.pdf.

98. Gelbspan, *Break-Ins, Death Threats*, 49–50.

99. Gelbspan, *Break-Ins, Death Threats*, 55, 58.

100. *Break-Ins at Sanctuary Churches*, 432–433.

101. Gelbspan, *Break-Ins, Death Threats*, 61, 97–98.

102. *Break-Ins at Sanctuary Churches*, 432–433, 464–469.

103. Gelbspan, *Break-Ins, Death Threats*, 35.

104. Weingarten, "FBI Broke Into."

105. Gelbspan, *Break-Ins, Death Threats*, 8.

106. Smith, *Resisting Reagan*, 317.

107. Elaine Sciolino, "Witnesses in Jesuit Slayings Charge Harassment in U.S.," *New York Times*, December 18, 1989.

108. Arnson, *Crossroads*, 251.

109. Pear, "How Outrage."

110. Lindsey Gruson, "Salvador Leader Links the Military to Priests' Killing," *New York Times*, January 8, 1990.

111. Lindsey Gruson, "Salvadoran President Announces Arrests of 8 in Killing of 6 Jesuits," *New York Times*, January 14, 1990.

112. Lindsey Gruson, "Court in El Salvador Indicts 8 Soldiers in Jesuit Slayings," *New York Times*, January 20, 1990.

113. LeoGrande, *Our Own Backyard*, 573.

114. Arnson, *Crossroads*, 237–238.

115. Sergio Ramírez, *Adiós Muchachos: A Memoir of the Sandinista Revolution*, trans. Stacey Alba D. Skar (Durham, NC: Duke University Press, 2012), 191–192, 196–197.

116. Fernando Cardenal, *Faith & Joy: Memoirs of a Revolutionary Priest*, trans and ed. Kathleen McBride and Mark Lester (Maryknoll, NY: Orbis, 2015), 229–230.

117. Arnson, *Crossroads*, 239.

118. Engel, *When the World*, 313, 318.

119. Dinesh D'Souza, "Cry of the People: Nicaragua's Poor Reject Socialism," *Crisis*, April 1990, 19.

120. Joan Frawley Desmond, "Adiós, Danny," *National Catholic Register*, March 11, 1990.

121. *Crisis*, April 1990; James K. Fitzpatrick, "Domestic Sandalistas," *Wanderer*, April 12, 1990.

122. John Spain, "Healing Process Goes On," *Maryknoll*, October 1990, 46–48.

123. LeoGrande, *Our Own Backyard*, 573.

124. Crandall, *Salvador Option*, 462.

125. Engel, *When the World*, 359.

126. Whitfield, *Paying the Price*, 174.

127. Chávez, "How Did the Civil," 1791.

128. Whitfield, *Paying the Price*, 171, 175.

129. "Update on the Status of the Churches in El Salvador," January 1–June 6, 1990, folder 2, box 55, GP.

130. "New Threats against El Salvador's Archbishop," *National Catholic Register*, April 22, 1990.

131. "Salvadoran Blues," *Crisis*, September 1990, 3.

132. Enrique T. Rueda, "'This Is Not the El Salvador You Usually Read About," *Wanderer*, March 15, 1990.

133. Enrique T. Rueda, "Leftist Clergy and the Revolution in El Salvador," *Wanderer*, May 3, 1990.

134. Rueda, "Leftist Clergy."

135. Ricardo de la Cierva, *Jesuitas, iglesia, y marxismo 1965–1985: La teología de la liberación desenmascarada* (Barcelona: Plaza & Janes, 1986).

136. Ricardo de la Cierva, "Misinformation Distorts Truth about El Salvador Conflict," *Wanderer*, May 31, 1990.

137. Krauss, "Religion and Politics." Though Hyde did not mention it, O'Neill continued to lobby his colleagues regarding El Salvador.

138. Krauss, "Religion and Politics."

139. Schneider, *Moakley's Journey*, 15, 102; Remarks by Congressman Moakley, May 22, 1990, folder 309, box 19, Series 03.04, McGovern, MA.

140. Krauss, "Religion and Politics."

141. Schneider, *Moakley's Journey*, 2.

142. "Salvadoran Blues," *Crisis*, 3–4.

143. Whitfield, *Paying the Price*, 177–179.

144. 136 Cong. Rec. 11551 (1990).

145. Susan Moran, "Which Comes First? Confused Priorities at the U.S. Catholic Conference," *Crisis*, November 1, 1991.

146. Engel, *When the World*, 376, 388, 402, 431.

147. Preston, "Politics of Realism," 101, 105–106, 108–109, 111, 114.

148. Editorial, "El Salvador: Will the Senate Bite the Bullet?," *America*, September 29, 1990, 171.

149. "The Week," *National Review*, January 28, 1991, 13.

150. Arnson, *Crossroads*, 257.

151. Engel, *When the World*, 395.

152. Arnson, *Crossroads*, 257.

153. "U.S. Aid to El Salvador Slashed, Restored," *Congressional Quarterly Almanac 1990*, http://library.cqpress.com/cqalmanac/cqal90-1118707.

154. Cable, William G. Walker to Bernard Aronson and Robert M. Kimmitt, February 19, 1991, EL01260, ES1980–1994, DNSA.

155. Boutros-Ghali, *From Madness to Hope*.

156. Chávez, "How Did the Civil," 1792.

157. Ching, *Stories of Civil War*, 191.

158. Chávez, "How Did the Civil," 1792.

159. Ching, *Stories of Civil War*, 50, 191.

160. Chávez, "How Did the Civil," 1786–1788.

161. Chávez, "How Did the Civil," 1785, 1788.

162. Angelika Rettberg, "The Private Sector and Peace in El Salvador, Guatemala, and Colombia," *Journal of Latin American Studies* 39, no. 3 (2007): 468–473.

163. Elliott Abrams, "An American Victory," *National Review*, February 3, 1992, 39–40.

164. Schneider, *Moakley's Journey*, 177.

165. Daniel P. Driscoll, "Jesus Carries Cross Again," *Maryknoll*, March 1992, 54.

166. Arnson, *Crossroads*, 297–300.

167. George H. W. Bush, "Proclamation 6518—Grant of Executive Clemency," December 24, 1992, APP, https://www.presidency.ucsb.edu/node/268672.

168. Arnson, *Crossroads*, 300.

169. Boutros-Ghali, *From Madness to Hope*.

170. Whitfield, *Paying the Price*, 389.

171. Quoted in Priscilla B. Hayner, *Unspeakable Truths: Confronting State Terror and Atrocity* (New York: Routledge, 2002), 40.

172. Arnson, *Crossroads*, 290–291.

173. Advertisement, *La Prensa Gráfica*, January 27, 1985, folder 9, box 16, B-RP.

174. Susan Benesch, "Religions Slugging It Out to Win Over Guatemalans," *St. Petersburg Times*, December 18, 1989.

175. Richard Rodriguez, "Losing Ground: As Catholicism Fails to Respond to Spiritual Needs, Latin Americans Are Embracing Evangelical Protestantism," *Crisis*, November 1989, 42.

176. Michael Löwy, *The War of the Gods: Religion and Politics in Latin America* (London: Verso, 1996), 113.

177. Benesch, "Religions Slugging."

178. David Stoll, "Introduction," in *Rethinking Protestantism in Latin America*, ed. Virginia Garrard-Burnett and David Stoll (Philadelphia: Temple University Press, 1993), 6.

179. Michel Gobat, *Confronting the American Dream: Nicaragua Under U.S. Imperial Rule* (Durham, NC: Duke University Press, 2005), 180–181.

180. Ondina E. González and Justo L. González, *Christianity in Latin America: A History* (New York: Cambridge University Press, 2008), 184–188.

181. Virginia Garrard-Burnett, "Conclusion: Is This Latin America's Reformation?," in *Rethinking Protestantism*, 199.

182. Frances Hagopian, "Social Justice, Moral Values, or Institutional Interests? Church Responses to the Democratic Challenge in Latin America," in *Religious Pluralism, Democracy, and the Catholic Church in Latin America*, ed. Frances Hagopian (Notre Dame, IN: University of Notre Dame, 2009), 270.

183. Anne Motley Hallum, "Taking Stock and Building Bridges: Feminism, Women's Movements, and Pentecostalism in Latin America," *Latin American Research Review* 38, no. 1 (2003): 169–186; David Martin, *Tongues of Fire: The Explosion of Protestantism in Latin America* (Oxford: Blackwell, 1990). Virginia Garrard-Burnett describes Martin's work with the term "spiritual cocoon." Garrard-Burnett, "Conclusion," in *Rethinking Protestantism*, 202.

184. Whitfield, *Paying the Price*, 3.

185. "Speeches from a UCA Forum on Contemporary Issues by Reverend Miguel Francisco Estrada, Rector, John Joseph Moakley, and Father Jon Sobrino, 1 July 1991," folder 272, box 16, Series 03.04, McGovern, MA.

Epilogue

1. Michael J. O'Loughlin, "Paul Ryan Defends Poverty Reform Efforts to Catholic Nun," *America*, August 22, 2017, https://www.americamagazine.org/politics-society/2017/08/22/paul-ryan-defends-poverty-reform-efforts-catholic-nun.

2. O'Loughlin, "Ryan Defends."

3. Amanda Duberman, "Thousands of Nuns Sign a Blistering Letter to Senate Republicans on Health Care," *Huffpost*, July 24, 2017, https://www.huffpost.com/entry/nuns-on-the-bus-health-care_n_597616a6e4b00e4363e11315.

4. Suzy Khimm, "Budget Smackdown! Paul Ryan vs. Catholic Nuns on a Bus," *Washington Post*, July 2, 2012.

5. Michelle Boorstein, "'I Love Nuns': Obama Appeals to Religious Allies as His Landmark Health Care Law Awaits Supreme Court Decision," *Washington Post*, June 9, 2015.

6. Joan Desmond, "Sister Carol Keehan: 'It Has Been My Privilege to Work with the President,'" *National Catholic Register*, June 9, 2015.

7. Richard Ducayne, "Nuns on the Bus Go Round Again," Churchmilitant.com, July 7, 2016, https://www.churchmilitant.com/news/article/nuns-on-the-bus-back-on-the-road.

8. Reader's post in response to Boorstein, "'I Love Nuns.'"

9. Desmond, "Sister Carol Keehan."

10. Pamela Schaeffer, "Health Reform: Refining Strategies and Vision," *Health Progress*, March-April 2015, 62.

11. Joan Frawley Desmond, "Adiós, Danny," *National Catholic Register*, March 11, 1990.

12. Desmond, "Sister Carol Keehan."

13. Lesley Gill, *The School of the Americas: Military Training and Political Violence in the Americas* (Durham, NC: Duke University Press, 2004), 26, 65, 73–74.

14. Teresa Whitfield, *Paying the Price: Ignacio Ellacuría and the Murdered Jesuits of El Salvador* (Philadelphia: Temple University Press, 1994), 153.

15. Stephen G. Rabe, *The Killing Zone: The United States Wages Cold War in Latin America* (New York: Oxford University Press, 2012), 188.

16. Gene Palumbro, "Fast Begins to Protest Salvadoreans' Ouster," *National Catholic Reporter*, February 12, 1982. They also pushed for extended voluntary departure status for Salvadorans and they protested the Reagan administration's detention of Haitian refugees.

17. Van Gosse, "'The North American Front': Central American Solidarity in the Reagan Era," in *Reshaping the U.S. Left: Popular Struggles in the 1980s*, ed. Mike Davis and Michael Sprinker (New York: Verso, 1988), 25.

18. Roy Bourgeois, "Serving Time, to Heal," *Maryknoll*, November 1991, 44; Roy Bourgeois, "Bearing Witness," *Progressive*, April 1992, 31. Quotation from "Bearing Witness."

19. Bourgeois, "Serving Time," 42–43.

20. Gill, *School of the Americas*, 203–204; Sharon Erickson Nepstad, *Convictions of the Soul: Religion, Culture, and Agency in the Central America Solidarity Movement* (New York: Oxford University Press, 2004), 143–144.

21. Bourgeois, "Serving Time," 43.

22. Roy Bourgeois, "Self Profiles of Priesthood," *Maryknoll*, July 1990, 15.

23. Gill, *School of the Americas*, 137, 211.

24. Gill, *School of the Americas*, 12, 198; Rabe, *Killing Zone*, 188, 191.

25. Gill, *School of the Americas*, 208–209, 211–213, 220–221.

26. Rabe, *Killing Zone*, 189.

27. 105 Cong. Rec. 8584–8585 (1998).

28. Gill, *School of the Americas*, 50–51.

29. Russell W. Ramsey and Antonio Raimondo, "Human Rights Instruction at the U.S. School of the Americas," *Human Rights Review* 2 (April–June 2001): 92 (editor's note), 106.

30. Russell W. Ramsey, "Latin America," in *Ashgate Research Companion to U.S. Foreign Policy*, ed. Robert J. Pauly Jr. (Surrey, England: Ashgate, 2010), 217.

31. Carlos Dada, "The Beatification of Óscar Romero," *New Yorker*, May 19, 2015, http://www.newyorker.com/news/news-desk/the-beatification-of-oscar-romero.

32. Catholic News Service, "Francis: Beatification of Oscar Romero Is a Cause for Great Joy," *Catholic Herald*, May 25, 2015, http://www.catholicherald.co.uk/news/2015/05/25/francis-beatification-of-oscar-romero-is-a-cause-for-great-joy/.

33. Patricia Lefevere, "Fr. Miguel D'Escoto Put His Priestly Life at the Service of the Poor," *National Catholic Reporter*, June 13, 2017.

34. Laurie Goodstein, "Catholic Priest Faces Excommunication," *New York Times*, November 13, 2008.

35. School of Americas Watch, Roy Bourgeois to the Congregation for the Doctrine of the Faith, November 7, 2008, http://www.soaw.org/presente/index.php?option=com_content&task=view&id=191&Itemid=74.

36. Joshua J. McElwee, "Maryknoll Gives Bourgeois Notice of Removal from Order," *National Catholic Reporter*, March 29, 2011.

37. Joshua J. McElwee, "Letter Officially Dismisses Bourgeois," *National Catholic Reporter*, February 1, 2013.

38. Philip Pullella, "Pope Says He Believes Ban on Female Priests Is Forever," Religious News Service, November 1, 2016, http://religionnews.com/2016/11/01/pope-says-he-believes-ban-on-female-priests-isforever/.

39. Center for Justice and Accountability (CJA), "U.S. Removal Proceedings: General Vides Casanova," accessed April 30, 2013, http://cja.org/article.php?list=type&type=548.

40. CJA, "U.S. Removal Proceedings"; U.S. Department of Homeland Security, "Human Rights Violators & War Crimes Unit," Overview, accessed April 30, 2013, http://www.ice.gov/human-rights-violators.

41. Julia Preston, "Salvadoran May Face Deportation for Murders," *New York Times*, February 24, 2012.

42. Julia Preston and Randal C. Archibold, "U.S. Justice Dept. Releases Judge's Ruling on Ex-Salvadoran General," *New York Times*, April 12, 2013.

43. Preston and Archibold, "Dept. Releases."

44. Press Release, Maryknoll Sisters, "Salvadoran General Vides Casanova Ordered Deported," April 11, 2013, http://www.maryknollsisters.org/catholic-mission/index.php/resources/news/1054-salvadoran-general-vides-casanova-ordered-deported-for-role-in-1980-murders-of-missioners-maryknoll-sisters-gratified-by-us-justice-departments-ruling.

45. Rabe, *Killing Zone*, 191.

46. World Bank, "Personal Remittances, Received (% of GDP)," accessed May 4, 2019, https://data.worldbank.org/indicator/BX.TRF.PWKR.DT.GD.ZS?locations=SV.

47. Erik, *Stories of Civil War in El Salvador: A Battle Over Memory* (Chapel Hill: University of North Carolina Press, 2016), 58.

48. WOLA, *Central American Gang-Related Asylum: A Resource Guide*, May 2008.

49. Óscar Martínez, "How Not to Assemble a Country," *NACLA Report on the Americas* 49, no. 2 (2017): 139.

50. Max Blumenthal, "The Kinder, Gentler Daniel Ortega," *The Nation*, January 19, 2007.

51. Stephen Kinzer, "Daniel Ortega Is Sandinista in Name Only," *Al-Jazeera-America*, April 6, 2015, http://america.aljazeera.com/opinions/2015/4/daniel-ortega-is-a-sandinista-in-name-only.html.

52. Arlen Cerda, "Miguel y Obando y Bravo: The Nicaraguan Comandante's National Hero," *Havana Times*, March 10, 2016, https://havanatimes.org/nicaragua/miguel-obando-y-bravo-the-nicaraguan-comandantes-national-hero/.

53. Mirta Ojitomarch, "A Victim of Sexual Abuse in a Prison of Political Ideals," *New York Times*, March 29, 1998.

54. "Abuse Charges Dropped against Ortega," *Los Angeles Times*, December 20, 2001.

55. Mac Margolis, "Nicaragua's President Accused of Sex Abuse by His Stepdaughter," *Daily Beast*, May 20, 2013, https://www.thedailybeast.com/nicaraguas-president-accused-of-sex-abuse-by-his-stepdaughter.

56. Blumenthal, "Kinder, Gentler."

57. José Adán Silva, "La tormenta de Miguel D'Escoto," *La Prensa*, August 17, 2014, http://www.laprensa.com.ni/2014/08/17/reportajes-especiales/207879-la-tormenta-de-descoto.

58. Also Díaz Lacayo, "Zoilamérica Again Spotlighted through No Doing of Her Own," *Revista Envío*, August 2001, http://www.envio.org.ni/articulo/1527August 2001.

59. Gioconda Belli, "Nicaragua Is Drifting towards Dictatorship Once Again," *Guardian*, August 24, 2016, https://www.theguardian.com/commentisfree/2016/aug/24/nicaragua-dictatorship-sandinista-ortega-murillo.

60. "Nicaraguan Bishops Lament Continued Suffering under Ortega," *Catholic News Agency*, May 1, 2019, https://www.catholicnewsagency.com/news/nicaraguan-bishops-lament-continued-suffering-under-ortega-91144; UN News, "Nicaragua Crisis: One Year In, More Than 60,000 Have Fled, Seeking Refuge," April 16, 2019, https://news.un.org/en/story/2019/04/1036711.

61. Roger Peace, *A Call to Conscience: The Anti-Contra War Campaign* (Amherst: University of Massachusetts Press, 2012), 24.

62. Ching, *Stories of Civil War*, 3.

Primary Sources

Cited Archives and Other Repositories

Brockman-Romero Papers (B-RP), Special Collections and Archives, DePaul
    University, Chicago, IL
Central America Historical Institute Records (CAHIR), Swarthmore College Peace
    Collection, Swarthmore, PA (SCPC)
David M. Jessup Papers (DJP), Manuscript, Archives, and Rare Book Library, Emory
    University, Atlanta, GA
Georgetown University Special Collections (GUSC), Washington, DC
    James Theberge Papers (JTP)
    William A. Wilson Papers (WAWP)
James and Margaret Goff Papers (GP), Yale Divinity School Library, Yale University,
    New Haven, CT
Jimmy Carter Presidential Library (JCPL), Atlanta, GA
    Special Coordination Committee Meeting (SCCM)
    White House Central Files (WHCF)
    Zbigniew Brzezinski Collection (ZBC)
John Joseph Moakley Archive (MA), Suffolk University, Boston, MA
    James McGovern Files (McGovern)
Maryknoll Mission Archives (MMA), Maryknoll, NY
    El Salvador: Martyrs (ESM)
    Maryknoll Fathers and Brothers Archives (MFBA)
    Maryknoll Sisters Archives (MSA)
    Middle / Central America History (M / CA)
    Office of Justice and Peace (OJP)
    Office of Social Concerns (OSC)
    Religious Task Force on Central America and Mexico (RTFCAM)
    Same Fate as the Poor (SFP)
    Sr. Betty Ann's Files (SBAF)
    U.S. Catholic Mission Association (USCMA)
El Museo de la Palabra y la Imagen, San Salvador (MUPI), El Salvador
    La Crónica del Pueblo (San Salvador)
National Archives, College Park (NARA), MD
    Department of State (DOS)
    United States Information Agency (USIA)

Nelson A. Rockefeller Papers (NAR), Rockefeller Archive Center, Sleepy Hollow, NY
James Cannon Files, 1968–1971 (JC)
Northwestern University, Special Collections, Evanston, IL (NUSC)
Eagle Forum Newsletter
Phyllis Schlafly Report
Paul Weyrich Papers (WP), American Heritage Center, University of Wyoming,
Laramie, WY
Philip Agee Papers (AP), Tamiment Library and Robert F. Wagner Labor Archive,
New York University, New York, NY
Quixote Center Papers (QCP), Marquette University Special Collections and
Archives, Milwaukee, WI
Ronald Reagan Presidential Library (RRPL), Simi Valley, CA
Alfonso Sapia-Bosch Files (ASBF)
Carl Anderson Files (CAF)
Faith Ryan Whittlesey Files (FRWF)
Jacqueline Tillman Files (JTF)
Juanita Duggan Files (JDF)
Morton Blackwell Files (MBF)
Robert Reilly Files (RRF)
White House Office of Records Management (WHORM)
Thomas P. O'Neill Papers (OP), John J. Burns Library, Boston College, Chestnut
Hill, MA
Kirk O'Donnell Files (KOD)
University of Notre Dame Archives (UNDA), South Bend, IN
Catholic Peace Fellowship Papers (CPF)
Center of Concern Papers (COC)
Conference of Major Superiors of Men Papers (CMSM)
Leadership Conference of Women Religious Papers (LCWR)
National Assembly of Women Religious Papers (CARW)

U.S. Periodicals and News Sources

Al-Jazeera-America (New York)
America (New York)
Associated Press
Atlantic Monthly
Baltimore Sun
Black Panther (Oakland)
Boston Globe
Catholic News Agency (Denver)
Central America Historical Institute *Updates* (Washington, DC)
Chicago Tribune
Christian Science Monitor
Cincinnati Post
Commentary (New York)
Commonweal (New York)

Congressional Quarterly (Washington, DC)
Congressional Quarterly Almanac (Washington, DC)
Conservative Digest (Washington, DC)
Crisis (South Bend, IN, during my research)
Daily News (Philadelphia)
Dallas Morning News
Democrat and Chronicle (Rochester, NY)
Des Moines Register
Foreign Affairs (New York)
Foreign Policy (Washington, DC)
Harper's (New York)
Honolulu Advertiser
Huffpost (web-based)
Human Events (Washington, DC)
Journal Star (Peoria, IL)
Latin American Documentation Service
Legal Times (Washington, DC)
Los Angeles Times
Maryknoll (Maryknoll, NY)
Maryknoll News Notes
Miami Herald
The Mindszenty Report (St. Louis)
NACLA Report on the Americas (New York)
Nation (New York)
National Catholic Register (Los Angeles, during my research)
National Catholic Reporter (Kansas City, MO)
National Review (New York)
New York Times
News-Sun (Waukegan, IL)
Newsday (Long Island, NY)
Newsweek (New York)
Nola.com (Louisiana)
Philadelphia Inquirer
The Pilot (Boston)
Plain Dealer (Cleveland)
Politico (Arlington County, VA)
Religion & Democracy (Washington, DC)
Religious News Service (Columbia, MO)
Retired Officer (Alexandria, VA)
St. Paul Pioneer Press
St. Petersburg Times
Syracuse Herald American
Tampa Tribune
Time (New York)
Tri-State Defender (Memphis, TN)
Union Leader (Union, New Hampshire)

United Press International (Washington, DC)
U.S. News & World Report (Washington, DC)
Wall Street Journal
Wanderer (St. Paul, Minnesota)
Washington Post
Washington Times (Washington, DC)

Foreign Periodicals and News Sources

Amanecer (Managua)
Barricada (Managua)
BBC Summary of World Broadcasts (London)
Cartas a las iglesias (San Salvador)
Catholic Herald (London)
Daily Telegraph (London)
Economist (London)
Excélsior (Mexico City)
Guardian (London)
Havana Times
Independent (London)
Independent Catholic News (web-based UK)
Irish Catholic (Dublin)
Latinamerica Press (Lima)
El Mundo (San Salvador)
Las Novedades (Managua)
El Nuevo Diario (Managua)
Observer (London)
Orientación (San Salvador)
La Prensa (Managua)
La Prensa Gráfica (San Salvador)
La Religión (Caracas)
Revista Envío (Managua)
Soberanía (Managua)
Target (Nairobi)
Times (London)
Toronto Star

Document Collections

The American Presidency Project (APP), John Woolley and Gerhard Peters,
    University of California, Santa Barbara
Central Intelligence Agency Freedom of Information Act Electronic Reading Room
Congressional Record
Digital National Security Archives (DNSA), The George Washington University
   El Salvador, 1977–1984 (ES1977–1984)
   El Salvador, 1980–1994 (ES1980–1994)

Iran-Contra (I-C)
Nicaragua (NC)
Terrorism and U.S. Policy, 1968–2002
FBI File on the American Churchwomen Killed in El Salvador, December 2, 1980 (Wilmington, DE: Scholarly Resources, 1990)
Foreign Relations of the United States (FRUS)
   1964–1968, Volume XXXI, South and Central America; Mexico
   1969–1976, Volume E–10, Documents on American Republics, 1969–1972
   *1969–1976, Volume E–11, Documents on Mexico, Central America, and the Caribbean,
   1973–1976*
   1969–1976, Vol. XX, Southeast Asia, 1969–1972

Congressional Hearings

U.S. Congress. House. *Foreign Assistance Legislation for Fiscal Year 1982: Hearings before the Committee on Foreign Affairs.* 97th Cong., 1st sess., March 13,18, 19, and 23, 1981.

U.S. Congress. House. Committee on Appropriations. *Foreign Assistance and Related Agencies Appropriations for 1978: Hearings before the Subcommittee on Foreign Operations and Related Agencies.* 95th Cong., 1st sess., April 5, 1977.

——. *Foreign Assistance and Related Programs Appropriations for 1980: Hearings before the Subcommittee on Foreign Operations and Related Programs.* 96th Cong., 1st sess., July 25, 1979.

U.S. Congress. House. Committee on Foreign Affairs. *Economic Sanctions Against Rhodesia: Hearings before the Subcommittees on Africa and on International Organizations.* 96th Cong., 1st sess., April 2, May 14, 16, and 21, 1979.

——. *El Salvador at the Crossroads: Peace or Another Decade of War: Hearings before the Subcommittees on Human Rights and International Organizations, and on Western Hemisphere Affairs.* 101st Cong., 2nd sess., January 24, 31, and February 6, 1990.

——. *Human Rights in South Korea: Implications for U.S. Policy: Hearings before the Subcommittees on Asian and Pacific Affairs and on International Organizations and Movements.* 93rd Cong., 2nd sess., July 30, August 5, and December 20, 1974.

——. *Political Developments in Southern Rhodesia: Hearings before the Subcommittee on Africa.* 95th Cong., 1st sess., October 4, 1977.

——. *U.S. Support for the Contras: Hearings before the Subcommittee on Western Hemisphere Affairs.* 99th Cong., 1st sess., April 16, 17, and 18, 1985.

U.S. Congress. House. Committee on International Relations. *Human Rights in Nicaragua, Guatemala, and El Salvador: Implications for U.S. Policy: Hearings before the Subcommittee on International Organizations.* 94th Cong., 2nd sess., June 8 and 9, 1976.

——. *The Recent Presidential Elections in El Salvador: Implications for U.S. Policy: Hearings before the Subcommittees on International Organizations and on Inter-American Affairs.* 95th Cong., 1st sess., March 9 and 17, 1977.

——. *Religious Persecution in El Salvador: Hearings before the Subcommittee on International Organizations.* 95th Cong., 1st sess., July 21 and 29, 1977.

U.S. Congress. House. Committee on the Judiciary. *Break-Ins at Sanctuary Churches and Organizations Opposed to Administration Policy in Central America: Hearings before the Subcommittee on Civil and Constitutional Rights.* 100th Cong., 1st sess., February 19 and 20, 1987.

U.S. Congress. Joint Hearings. *Iran-Contra Investigation: Testimony of Dewey R. Clarridge, C/CATF, and Clair George: Hearings before the Senate Select Committee on Secret Military Assistance to Iran and the Nicaraguan Opposition and House Select Committee to Investigate Covert Arms Transactions with Iran.* 100th Cong., 1st sess., August 4, 5, and 6, 1987.

U.S. Congress. Senate. *Foreign Assistance Authorization for Fiscal Year 1982: Hearings before the Committee on Foreign Relations.* 97th Cong., 1st sess., March 19, 24, 26, April 3, 10, 22, and May 4, 1981.

——. *Rhodesia: Hearings before the Committee on Foreign Relations.* 96th Cong., 1st sess., November 27, 29, 30, and December 3, 1979.

——. *The Situation in El Salvador: Hearings before the Committee on Foreign Relations.* 97th Cong., 1st sess., March 18 and April 9, 1981.

U.S. Congress. Senate. Committee on Human Resources. *Marketing and Promotion of Infant Formula in the Developing Nations, 1978: Hearings before the Subcommittee on Health and Scientific Research.* 95th Cong., 2nd sess., May 23, 1978.

U.S. Congress. Senate. Committee on the Judiciary. *Marxism and Christianity in Revolutionary Central America: Hearings before the Subcommittee on Security and Terrorism.* 98th Cong., 1st sess., October 18 and 19, 1983.

Other Published Primary Sources and Collections of Primary Sources

Agee, Philip. *Inside the Company: CIA Diary.* American ed. New York: Stonehill, 1975.

Baker, James A. *The Politics of Diplomacy: Revolution, War and Peace, 1989–1992.* New York: G. P. Putnam's Sons, 1995.

Belli, Gioconda. *The Country Under My Skin: A Memoir of Love and War.* Translated by Kristina Cordero and Gioconda Belli. New York: Anchor Books, 2003.

Boutros-Ghali, Boutros. *From Madness to Hope: The 12-Year War in El Salvador.* New York: United Nations, 1993.

Brzezinski, Zbigniew. *Power and Principle: Memoirs of the National Security Adviser, 1977–1981.* Rev. ed. New York: Farrar, Straus and Giroux, 1985.

Cardenal, Fernando. *Faith & Joy: Memoirs of a Revolutionary Priest.* Translated and edited by Kathleen McBride and Mark Lester. Maryknoll, NY: Orbis, 2015.

Carter, Jimmy. *White House Diary.* New York: Farrar, Straus and Giroux, 2010.

Duarte, José Napoleón, and Diana Page. *Duarte: My Story.* New York: G. P. Putnam, 1986.

Einuadi, Luigi, Richard Maulin, Alfred Stepan, and Michael Fleet. *Latin American Institutional Development: The Changing Catholic Church.* Santa Monica, CA: RAND Corporation, 1969.

Evans, Jeanne, ed. *"Here I Am, Lord": The Letters and Writings of Ita Ford.* Maryknoll, NY: Orbis, 2005.

Haig, Alexander M. *Caveat: Realism, Reagan, and Foreign Policy.* New York: Macmillan, 1984.

——. *Inner Circles: How America Changed the World.* New York: Warner Books, 1992.

Kornbluh, Peter, and Malcolm Byrne, eds. *The Iran-Contra Scandal: The Declassified History*. New York: New Press, 1993.

Melville, Thomas, and Marjorie Melville. *Whose Heaven, Whose Earth?* New York: Alfred A. Knopf, 1970.

O'Leary-Macías, Geraldine. *Lighting My Fire: Memoirs*. Bloomington, IN: Trafford, 2013.

O'Neill, Tip, and William Novak. *Man of the House: The Life and Political Memoirs of Speaker Tip O'Neill*. New York: Random House, 1987.

Pastor, Robert A. *Not Condemned to Repetition: The United States and Nicaragua*. 2nd ed. Boulder, CO: Westview, 2002.

Pezzullo, Lawrence, and Ralph Pezzullo. *At the Fall of Somoza*. Pittsburgh: University of Pittsburgh Press, 1993.

Ramírez, Sergio. *Adiós Muchachos: A Memoir of the Sandinista Revolution*. Translated by Stacey Alba D. Skar. Durham, NC: Duke University Press, 2012.

Randall, Margaret. *Sandino's Daughters: Testimonies of Nicaraguan Women in Struggle*. New Brunswick, NJ: Rutgers University Press, 1995.

Reagan, Ronald. *The Reagan Diaries*. Edited by Douglas Brinkley. New York: HarperCollins, 2007.

Rockefeller, Nelson A. *Rockefeller Report on the Americas: The Official Report of a United States Presidential Mission for the Western Hemisphere*. Chicago: Quadrangle, 1969.

Somoza, Anastasio, and Jack Cox. *Nicaragua Betrayed*. Belmont, MA: Western Islands, 1980.

Tambs Lewis A., ed. *A New Inter-American Policy for the Eighties*. Washington, DC: Council for Inter-American Security, 1980.

Vance, Cyrus. *Hard Choices: Critical Years in America's Foreign Policy*. New York: Simon & Schuster, 1983.

Walsh, Lawrence E. *Firewall: The Iran-Contra Conspiracy and Cover-Up*. New York: W. W. Norton, 1997.

INDEX

abortion, 5, 104, 108, 131, 158, 196–97, 241–42, 248

Abrams, Elliott, 126, 166, 195, 204, 206, 236–37

ACC (American Catholic Committee), 154

Affordable Care Act, 240–42

Agee, Philip, 35, 37

AIM (Accuracy in Media), 117, 125

Alas, José Inocencio, 73, 86

Alexander, Teresa, 98, 107

Allen, Richard, 5, 112, 133, 156, 224

Allende, Salvador, 14, 32–34, 52, 89, 249

Alliance for Progress, 18, 20, 24, 26–28, 72, 249

America, 20, 95, 105, 233

Americas Watch, 170

Amnesty International, 58

ANEP (National Free Enterprise Association/Asociacíon Nacional de la Empresa Privada), 77, 79, 84

anticommunism: of Catholics, 2, 5–6, 9–10, 11, 16, 26, 103, 105, 112–13, 121, 123–24, 135, 138, 140, 159, 171, 178, 191, 196, 224, 250; of evangelicals, 6, 207; of Maryknoll, 2, 15–18, 20–21, 52, 117, 249; of U.S. government, 2, 6–7, 18, 20, 27, 54, 62, 64, 79, 105–6, 111–115, 120, 128–29, 133, 167, 179, 181–82, 184, 193–94, 208–9, 222, 224, 236, 242–43, 250. *See also* Communism

Anticommunist League of Nicaragua, 57

Aparicio y Quintanilla, Pedro Arnoldo, 73–74, 76, 91

Araujo, Arturo, 71

Arbenz, Jacobo, 18, 21, 44

ARDE (Democratic Revolutionary Alliance Democratic Revolutionary Alliance/Alianza Revolucionaria Democrática), 129, 149

ARENA (National Republican Alliance/Alianza Republicana Nacionalista), 215–16, 228, 235–36

Argentina, 26–27, 30, 36, 129, 245

Arguello, José, 136–37

Argueta, Fabio, 73

Arias Sánchez, Óscar, 205

Arms Export Control Act, 190

Atlacatl battalion, 126, 211, 216

Atwood, Brian, 99–100

Baker, James, 113, 123, 134, 182, 210, 213–14, 222–24, 229, 236

Banzer Plan, 36–37, 88

Baptists, 54, 88, 104, 133, 173, 176, 222, 238

Barnes, Michael, 128, 214

Barrera de Cerna, Lucia, 227–28

Bay of Pigs, 44, 148

Belli, Gioconda, 145, 248

Belli, Humberto, 133

Benavides, Guillermo Alfredo, 211, 228, 234–35

Benedict XVI (pope), 194, 245–46

Berrigan brothers, 24–25, 31

Big Pine I and II, 132, 143

bishops: Central American, 90; Latin American, 25–26, 88, 92–93, 105, 137, 238; Mexican, 178; Nicaraguan, 45–46, 50–51, 138–40, 143–44, 177–80, 248–49; Salvadoran, 73, 79, 91, 218; U.S., 116, 123, 133, 154, 157, 169, 177, 182, 184, 194–95, 222. *See also* USCC

Boggs, Lindy, 205–6

Boland Amendments, 129–30, 133–34, 162–63, 188, 190, 196, 209. *See also* Contras

Bolaños Hunter, Miguel, 148–49, 151, 170

Bolivia, 35–37, 243

bombing, 27, 63, 77, 93–95, 108, 214, 216–17

Bonpane, Blase, 22, 55

Borgnovo, Mauricio, 84

Bouchey, L. Francis, 112, 116

Bourgeois, Roy, 124–25, 203, 218, 226, 242–46

BPR (Revolutionary Popular Block/Bloque Popular Revolucionario), 76

Bradford, Marjorie. *See* Melville, Marjorie

Brazil, 27, 36, 45, 59, 87, 112, 137

Breslin, Jimmy, 186, 201, 236

Brody, Reed, 170

Brzezinski, Zbigniew, 62, 87, 90–91

Buchanan, Patrick, 112, 133, 162, 181–82, 184, 191, 196–97, 199, 209–10

Bush, George H.W., 12–13, 122, 153, 156, 159, 210, 212–15, 219, 221–24, 227–29, 234–37, 239, 250

Calero, Adolfo, 169–70, 192, 205

campesinos, 90; in Guatemala, 22–23; in Nicaragua, 47–48, 53, 55, 132, 145, 197–98, 202; in El Salvador, 70–77, 80, 86, 95, 98, 100, 107, 212, 217, 249

capitalism, 8, 10, 29, 36, 38, 52, 146

Capuchin Fathers, 45, 48–50, 57

Cardenal, Ernesto, 45–46, 50–51, 57, 132, 197–99

Cardenal, Fernando, 26, 45, 49, 54–55, 57, 59–60, 64, 67

Cardinal Mindszenty Foundation, 117–18

Carter, Jimmy: and 1980 election, 106, 167, 174; and El Salvador, 2, 12, 70, 81–82, 85, 87–89, 91–92, 95, 100, 108–11, 113, 127, 130, 159, 234; and human rights policy, 12, 61–63, 70, 81–82, 93, 100, 108, 110; and Iran, 87, 167; and Maryknoll, 52–54, 66; and Nicaragua, 52–54, 61–66, 100, 115, 129; and Panama, 61–62, 64–66, 103, 134

Casey, Sophia, 195

Casey, William, 5, 12, 112–13, 124, 129–30, 173, 182, 189, 191–95, 210, 224

Castro, Fidel, 32, 46, 62, 72, 184, 200

catechists, 73–74, 76, 98–99. *See also* DPs

Catholic Center (Catholic Center for Free Enterprise, Strong Defense, and Traditional Values), 148, 172, 178

Catonsville Nine, 24–25, 30, 197

Catto, Henry E., Jr., 96–97

CBI (Caribbean Base Initiative), 153

CEBs (Christian base communities/comunidades eclesiales de base), 44–46, 48, 50, 57, 61, 69, 73–75, 83, 89, 127, 143

CELAM (Episcopal Conference of Latin America), 25, 74

Center for Intercultural Formation, 20

certification (El Salvador), 125–27, 134, 146, 153, 193, 228. *See also* churchwomen; Sheraton murders

Chalatenango, 73, 97, 106–7

Chamorro, Pedro Joaquín, 54, 61, 67, 94, 229

Chamorro, Violeta Barrios de, 67, 229–30, 236

Chávez y González, Luis, 70, 72–73

Cheney, Richard, 201

Chile, 14, 27, 32–35, 52, 59, 89, 93, 97, 182

China, 4, 15–17, 121, 164, 181, 216, 249

Christopher, Warren, 82, 237

Church, Frank, 37, 64

churchwomen, 250; activism inspired by, 3, 108–9, 120–22, 153–54, 156, 158, 193, 212, 243; conservative accusations against, 13, 109–10, 115–19, 131, 146, 148–49, 170, 209, 223; and Jesuit murders, 218–21, 223–24, 231, 239; murder, 2, 11, 101–2, 106–8, 114, 234, 237; murder investigation, 7, 122, 125–27, 130, 145, 153, 159, 163, 214, 225–26, 228, 246

CIA (Central Intelligence Agency): and Catholics, 30–31, 36, 87–88, 114, 180, 192; coup and Contra support, 17, 32–35, 129–31, 135, 142, 144, 150, 163, 170, 188–89, 222, 226, 237, 243; and Maryknoll, 2, 15, 20, 32–35, 37–38, 224; reports, 145, 161, 215, 217, 221, 224. *See also* Casey, William

Cienfuegos, Fermán, 126–27

CIS (Council for Inter-American Security), 112, 116–17, 148–49

CISPES (Committee in Solidarity with the People of El Salvador), 99, 225–26, 234, 243

Claramount, Ernesto Antonio, 78

Clark, William, 5, 112, 156, 224

Clarke, Maura: allegations against, 116, 118–19, 148, 151, 170, 226; murder of, 2, 101–2, 106–7, 193, 243; work of, 18–19, 44, 46–48, 66, 74, 98–99, 153. *See also* churchwomen

Clarridge, Duane R., 129, 192, 237

Clinton, William J., 199, 236–38

coffee, 70–71, 89, 144, 236

Colby, William, 37

Cold War: and Catholics, 4, 6–7, 14–16, 27, 37, 138, 151, 186, 246; end and aftermath of, 213, 221–23, 231, 233–34, 236, 238–39, 240–50; and gender, 155, 162, 167; Maryknoll support for U.S. policy, 14–15, 39, 52, 60, 68; Maryknoll questioning of U.S. policy, 3, 12, 34–35, 52, 249; U.S. foreign policy, 6, 15, 100, 130, 138, 236–37

Colorado, Mauricio, 218

Communism: godless, 3, 6, 16–17, 52, 123, 129, 137–38, 172; leftist Catholics accused of, 3–4, 18, 22–23, 26–27, 29–33, 36, 38–39, 46, 51, 55, 61, 67, 77, 80, 84–85, 99, 105–7, 111–12, 116–17, 136–37, 141, 146–48, 152, 167–68, 178, 183–85, 200, 202, 206, 214, 216–17, 226, 231; Maryknoll rethinking of, 15, 21–23, 34, 165, 249; and Latin American revolutionaries, 71–72, 76, 173. *See also* anticommunism; Cuba; guerrillas; liberation theology; Soviet Union

CONFER (Conference of Religious of Nicaragua), 46–47, 63, 143

congressional hearings: on El Salvador, 49, 79, 82, 85, 120; on the FBI, 225, 227; on human rights, 49; on Iran-Contra, 191, 195, 199, 201, 203–4, 209; on liberation theology, 7, 87–88, 146–50, 153, 226, 231; on Nicaragua, 49, 55, 65, 172–73

Connor, James, 95–96

conscientization, 25–26, 45

conscription: United States, 24, 197; Nicaragua, 143–44

Contras: and Marian devotion, 198–99; Maryknoll views on, 11–12, 169–73, 182, 189, 200–2, 206; Sandinista struggle with, 132–33, 138, 143–45, 153, 177–79, 250; U.S. debates over, 7, 11, 143, 161, 171, 175, 180–87, 193, 199–202, 210, 213, 250; U.S. support for, 6, 129, 144, 149–50, 162–63, 166–67, 170, 172–76, 192, 194–96, 203–5, 207, 213–14, 229–30. *See also* ARDE; Boland Amendments; FDN; Iran-Contra scandal

CpS (Christians for Socialism/Cristianos por el Socialismo), 32–33

Cranshaw, Robert, 57, 84

Cranshaw, William, 56–57, 84

Cristiani, Alfredo, 215–16, 219–20, 224, 228, 230, 235–37

Crónica, La, 78

Cruz, Arturo J., 142

Cuba, 114; revolution in, 18, 25, 71–72, 110, 242; support for guerrillas, 50, 64–65, 88, 113, 115, 216; Soviet support of, 221, 230; U.S. fear of, 64, 88, 124, 148, 165, 184, 205

Cuomo, Mario, 158–59

Curry, Charles, 33–34, 37, 41

cursillos, 21, 46

D'Aubuisson, Roberto, 94, 159, 215, 218, 228, 237

d'Escoto, Miguel, 245–46; conservative criticism of, 41, 55–56, 60–61, 64, 67, 117, 150, 172, 185, 200, 206; as Nicaraguan

foreign minister, 12, 67, 116, 148, 176, 186, 203; and Orbis, 38; political activity of, 51–54, 60, 62–63, 64, 66, 176–80, 248, 250

Dailey, Peter H., 156–57

death squads, in Brazil, 27; in El Salvador, 6, 84, 94, 96, 99, 106, 153, 159, 214–15, 219, 228, 237; in Guatemala, 22

Deaver, Michael, 113–14, 182

Delgado, Fredy, 216, 231

Denton, Jeremiah, 5, 146–49, 153, 199, 226, 231

Desmond, Joan F. *See* Frawley, Joan

development: community: 46, 48, 52, 73–74; debates about, 21, 25–26, 66; of democracy, 142; economic, 10, 18, 20–21, 31. *See also* USAID

Devine, Frank, 88–89

Diario de Hoy, El, 125, 231

Dillon, Peg, 61, 63

Los Doce, 59–60, 63, 66, 67, 142

Dodd, Christopher, 228, 232–33

Dole, Elizabeth, 123, 134

Dole, Robert, 175, 203, 210

Donovan, Jean, 2, 98, 101, 107, 117, 153, 157, 220. *See also* churchwomen

Donovan, Nancy, 169–72, 186

Dorsey, Madeline, 8, 89, 98, 107

Dowling, Thomas, 172, 207

DPs (Delegates of the Word/Delegados de la Palabra), 45, 48–49, 57, 61, 86. *See also* catechists

draft. *See* conscription

Drinan, Robert F., 86–87, 104–5

Driscoll, Dan, 201–2, 236

Duarte, José Napoleón, 93, 108–9, 115, 124–25, 127, 158–59, 163, 214–15, 217, 228, 236

Dukakis, Michael, 210, 220

Ecumenical Committee of U.S. Church Personnel in Nicaragua, 142

Eisenhower, Dwight, 16, 104

elections: Chile, 32–33; El Salvador, 71, 76–79, 82, 125, 147, 215; Nicaragua, 42, 214, 221, 229–30, 247–48; Panama, 222; Philippines, 32; United States, 59, 105–6, 108, 130–31, 134, 143, 158–60, 162–63, 182, 189, 210, 213, 224, 236

Ellacuría, Ignacio, 76–77, 211, 216–17, 231, 235, 237

Ellsberg, Robert, 38–39

Enders, Thomas O., 112, 125

Episcopal Conference of El Salvador, 49, 79, 91, 218

ERP (People's Revolutionary Army/El Ejército Revolucionario del Pueblo), 75–76

Esquipulas accords, 204–5, 210, 213–14

evangelical Protestants, 6, 138, 141, 147, 173–74, 189, 207, 224–25, 238, 244. *See also* Moral Majority; New Right

evangelization, 1, 3, 15, 19–20, 38, 103

Excélsior, 49, 87

FAL (Armed Liberation Forces/Fuerza Armadas de Liberación), 76

Falwell, Jerry, 104, 133, 207. *See also* Moral Majority; New Right

Farabundo Martí, Augustín, 71

FARO (Agricultural Front of the Eastern Region/Frente Agrario de la Región Oriental), 77, 79, 84

fasting, 90, 121, 176–79, 243

FBI (Federal Bureau of Investigation), 34, 122, 225–26, 228

FDN (Nicaraguan Democratic Force/Fuerza Democrática Nicaragüense), 129, 169–70, 176

FDR (Democratic Revolutionary Front/Frente Democrático Revolucionario), 99, 107–8, 114, 235

FECCAS (Christian Federation of Salvadoran Campesinos/Federación Cristiana de Campesinos Salvadoreños), 75, 78

feminism, 3, 9, 119, 194

Ferraro, Geraldine, 158, 167–68

Field Afar, A, 4, 15. *See also Maryknoll*

Fiers, Alan, 188, 195, 199, 237

FMLN (Farabundo Martí National Liberation Front/Frente Farabundo Martí para la Liberación Nacional): accusations against, 211, 223, 231, 234, 237, 244; association with churchwomen and Jesuit martyrs, 110, 118, 148, 216–18; final offensive of, 110, 127, 223; formation of, 99; and peace talks, 228, 230, 232, 235–36

Fontaine, Roger, 112, 116, 133

Fourteen families (las catorce), 70

Ford, Francis X., 15–16

Ford, Gerald, 14, 35, 62, 81, 104, 157

Ford, Ita, 2, 18–19, 34, 89, 95, 97–99, 101, 106–7, 118–19, 193, 243. *See also* churchwomen

FPL (Popular Liberation Forces/Fuerzas Populares de Liberación), 75–76, 84

Francis (pope), 245–46

Fraser, Donald, 49, 59, 79–80, 82

Frawley, Joan, 139, 146, 151, 181, 229, 241–42

Frawley, Patrick J., Jr., 139, 146

Freedom Fighters' Manual, 163

Frei, Eduardo, 32

Freire, Paulo, 45

FSLN. *See* Sandinistas

FUAR (United Front of Revolutionary Action/Frente Unido de Acción Revolucionaria), 72

Fuentes Castellanos, Ricardo, 83–84, 116–18

FUSADES (Salvadoran Foundation for Economic and Social Development/Fundación Salvadoreña para el Desarrollo), 236

García, José Guillermo, 106–7, 237–38

Gaudium et Spes, 19

Geitner, John, 181–82

Georgetown University, 85, 87, 215, 220

Gerlock, Ed, 58

God: invoked by conservatives, 16, 179, 192–93, 196, 198, 208–9; kingdom of, 97; in liberation theology, 9, 23, 34, 45–46, 69, 74, 90, 120, 240; opposition to violence of, 92, 94

Golconda group, 26, 30

Gorbachev, Mikhail, 221–22, 230

Grande, Rutilio, 75, 80, 82–83, 217

Grenada, 144–45, 151

Guardia Nacional (Nicaragua), 42, 44, 47–50, 52–54, 56–57, 61, 64–65

guerrillas: and liberation theology, 8; Colombia, 22, 30; El Salvador, 71, 75–76, 84–86, 89, 93, 97, 107, 110, 115–17, 143, 148, 211, 214, 216, 218, 223, 231, 236; Guatemala, 21, 23–24, 29; Nicaragua, 47, 50, 57, 128, 144, 171. *See also* Contras; FMLN; Sandinistas

Gutiérrez, Gustavo, 8, 38–39, 75

Haig, Alexander, 123–24, 128–29, 186; as churchwomen critic, 2, 13, 101, 117–19, 146, 151, 181, 223; as conservative Catholic, 2, 5, 103, 112–13, 224, 239; as controversial figure, 114, 122, 138

Halbert, John, 69–70

Harkin, Thomas, 201, 219

Hasenfus, Eugene, 189

Hassan, Moisés, 67, 105

Healy, Peggy, 48, 61, 164–66, 169, 186, 226–27

Helms, Jesse, 62, 119, 209

Hendricks, Barbara, 20, 37

Heritage Foundation, 9, 104–5, 133, 151, 183, 192, 198

Hernández Martínez, Maximiliano, 71, 107

Hogan, James, 24

hostages: in Central America, 47, 63; in Iran, 2, 90, 111, 113, 167; in Lebanon, 175, 188–90, 208

Human Events, 57–59, 67

human rights, 140, 154, 164; and Bush policy, 224, 239; and Carter policy, 12, 61–63, 70, 81–82, 93, 100, 108, 110; in El Salvador, 2, 12, 69, 80–82, 85, 90, 99–100, 125–27, 145, 169, 215–17, 219–22, 228, 232, 235, 237–38, 246; in Guatemala, 11; Maryknoll advocacy for, 3, 8–9, 11, 35, 37, 42, 46–48, 53, 58–59, 69, 80–81, 90, 189, 229; in Nicaragua, 42, 49–51, 53–55, 61–63, 65, 155, 159, 170–72, 189, 229, 248; and Reagan policy, 107, 111, 113–15, 131, 138, 152, 159; and SOA, 219, 244. *See also* religious freedom

Hyde, Henry: as conservative Catholic, 162, 171, 173, 184–85, 189, 196–97, 200–1, 209; and El Salvador, 220, 231–33; and Iran-Contra, 189, 191, 196–97, 199, 237; support for Contras, 5, 184–85, 188, 213, 242

Illich, Ivan, 20, 31

imperialism, 16, 24, 27, 29, 31, 42, 143, 162, 238

inequality, 3, 8, 25, 44, 46, 53, 70–71, 100, 249

injustice: denunciation of, 49, 53, 90, 120, 246; structures of, 8, 25–26, 80, 140, 239. *See also* justice

Inter-Religious Task Force on El Salvador/ Central America, 95

IRD (Institute on Religion and Democracy), 142

Iran-Contra scandal, 2, 13, 187, 189–91, 195–97, 199–202, 204, 207–10, 225–26, 236–37, 250. *See also* Contras

Iran, 2, 87, 101, 111, 113, 141, 167, 188–90, 195. *See also* Iran-Contra scandal

Ireland, 114, 156–58

Jamias, Margarita, 66

Jesuit Fathers and Brothers, 104–5, 151, 225; conservative criticism of, 51, 57, 68, 77, 84–85, 125, 206, 229, 231, 249; and

Colombia, 30, 74; and education, 52, 76, 84, 86, 112, 220; and El Salvador, 75–77, 79, 83–86, 91, 95, 98, 107, 125, 127; and liberation theology, 39, 44, 52, 74–75, 85, 137, 239; and Nicaragua, 45, 49, 51, 57, 60–61, 64, 68, 136. *See also* Jesuit martyrs

Jesuit martyrs, 12, 211–13, 215–18, 220–24, 228, 231–32, 235, 239, 243

John Paul II (pope), 1, 91–92, 104–5, 112, 131, 137–38, 140–42, 151, 162, 172–73, 177, 185, 225, 246

John XXIII (pope), 18

Johnson, Lyndon B., 32, 62

Jordan, Erica, 240–41

just war doctrine, 66, 76

justice: as church aim, 15, 20, 24, 49, 52–53, 67, 90, 97, 127, 157, 249; linked with peace, 8, 36, 54, 58, 114, 149, 208. *See also* injustice

Kane, Theresa, 119

Kazel, Dorothy, 2, 98, 101, 102, 107, 117, 220. *See also* churchwomen

Keehan, Carol, 241–42

Kennedy, John F., 18, 162, 166

Kennedy, Edward, 34–35, 64, 108, 200, 219

Kirkpatrick, Jeane, 109–11, 113, 116–19, 142, 193, 223, 239

Kissinger, Henry, 31, 62, 117, 153

Knights of Columbus, 24, 183

Koch, Edward, 51

Korea, 15, 17, 58–59, 146

LaMazza, John, 36–37

land reform, 22, 69–73, 76–77, 86, 89, 92, 94, 110, 125, 212, 217, 219

Lawyers Committee for International Human Rights, 170

Leahy, Patrick, 147–48, 219–20

Lebanon, 151, 175, 189–90

Lefever, Ernest, 116–18

Lemus López, José María, 71

liberation theology, 7–8; conservative critiques of, 12, 38–39, 74, 84, 111–13, 137, 141, 171, 199, 212, 231–32, 239; and El Salvador, 75, 83, 139, 213, 216–17, 225, 239; and Maryknoll, 8, 38–39, 55, 116, 146, 148, 167–68, 172, 191, 199–200, 202, 244, 249; and Nicaragua, 132, 148, 244; Reagan administration opposition to, 112–13, 116–17, 120, 156–57, 186; as security threat, 69, 77, 87, 111, 147–48, 199–200, 209, 213, 216, 226–27, 250; and the Vatican, 92, 194, 230, 245–46

Lleras Restrepo, Carlos, 29–30
Long, Clarence, 163, 214
López Trujillo, Alfonso, 74
Lozano, Ignacio, 81–82

Macías, Edgard, 149–52, 167
Macías, Geraldine O'Leary de, 132, 149–51, 154–58, 160, 167, 174, 181
MacKenzie, Ian R., 60. *See also* NGIS
Managua earthquake, 47. *See also* OPEN 3
Marcos, Imelda, 32
Marian apparition, 189, 197–99
martial law: in El Salvador, 72; in Nicaragua 48, 59, 61, 63; in Poland, 114
Martínez, Bernardo, 197–98
martyrdom, 3, 15–16, 39, 90, 120–21, 138, 193, 212, 249
Maryknoll, 3–4, 249–50; anticommunism of, 14–18; in Asia, 15–17, 19; in Bolivia, 36–37; and Bush administration, 224–25; and Carter administration, 52–54, 66; and Chile, 14, 33–35; and the CIA, 15, 32–35, 37–38, 224; and the Cold War, 3, 12, 14–18, 34–35, 39, 52, 60, 68, 249; conservative perceptions of, 29–30, 38–39, 41, 57, 67–68, 117, 125, 178–79, 189, 191, 206, 217, 229, 239, 241; in El Salvador, 69–70, 77–78, 81–83, 125; and FBI surveillance, 226–27; in Guatemala, 11, 21–24; and human rights, 3, 8–11, 35, 37, 42, 46–48, 53, 58–59, 69, 80–81, 90, 189, 229; and Iran-Contra, 199–203, 209; and liberation theology, 8, 38–39, 55, 116, 146, 148, 167–68, 172, 191, 199–200, 202, 244, 249; Reagan administration's perceptions of, 2–3, 7, 13, 61, 115–18, 120–21, 157–58, 164, 167, 170, 180–82, 223–25, 231; and Sandinistas, 66, 93, 116, 149–50, 169–71, 184–85, 230, 244 ; and the School of the Americas, 242–45; and Somoza, 2, 12, 41, 53–54, 60–61, 68, 165, 230, 250; understanding of mission, 10–11, 14–15, 18–21, 36–37, 42, 46, 80, 119–20, 230; and Vatican II, 14, 22, 44, 70, 86; views on Contras of, 11–12, 169–73, 182, 189, 206. *See also* Maryknoll associates; Maryknoll Fathers and Brothers; Maryknoll Sisters; Melville Incident; Orbis
Maryknoll, 4, 38, 55, 58, 67, 74, 116, 206. *See also* A Field Afar
Maryknoll associates, 98, 136. *See also* Donovan, Jean; Maryknoll; Survil, Bernard

Maryknoll Fathers and Brothers, 3–4, 15, 59, 70, 79, 98, 105, 124, 152, 212, 218, 231. *See also* Bourgeois, Roy; d'Escoto, Miguel; Maryknoll; Spain, John
Maryknoll Sisters, 3; conservative Catholic perceptions of, 6, 106–7, 115, 155, 163, 167–70, 173, 184–85, 188, 232; and El Salvador, 70, 74, 89–90, 93–94, 96–98; and the Ford administration, 14; and Nicaragua, 44–48, 61; protests of U.S. policies, 1, 3, 58, 63, 79–80, 93, 110, 121, 127, 144, 150–54, 233; Reagan administration's perceptions of, 2, 7, 13, 60–61, 118, 209; and Reagan, 1–2, 13, 60–61, 156, 173; and Tip O'Neill, 11, 152, 161, 163–67, 169, 173, 183–84, 186, 188, 199–200, 205–6, 209, 226, 240; and Vatican II, 18–19; World Awareness Program (WAP), 58, 66. *See also* churchwomen; Clarke, Maura; Donovan, Nancy; Dorsey, Madeline; Ford, Ita; Healy, Peggy; Jamias, Margarita; Macías, Geraldine O'Leary de; Maryknoll; Melville, Marjorie; Mulry, Annette; nuns; Petrik, Joan; Piette, Carla; Roper, Melinda
masculinity, 12, 162, 167–68, 173–74, 176, 180
la Matanza, 71
Matt, A.J., 115–16, 133
McCarthy, Colman, 193–94, 201
McCarthy, Joseph, 16–17, 39
McDonald, Larry, 51, 55, 57, 64
McFarlane, Robert C., 112, 190, 192, 195, 201, 208, 237
McGann, John, 192–95
McHugh, Matthew F., 99–100
McLaughlin, Janice, 58, 247
Medellín conference, 25–26, 31, 38, 46, 49, 52, 73, 83
Meese, Edwin, 113, 123, 191
Mein, John Gordon, 22, 28–29
Melville Incident, 21–25, 28–29, 33, 55, 117–18
Melville, Arthur, 21–25, 28, 33, 35, 41
Melville, Marjorie, 21–25, 35, 41
Melville, Thomas, 21–25, 28, 33, 35, 41
Methodists, 33, 55, 93, 222
Michaels, Ron, 69–70
Middendorf, J. William, 141, 147, 200
Mikulski, Barbara, 212, 233
Miskito (Nicaragua), 129, 138
Moakley Commission, 220, 230–31, 242–43
Moakley, Joe, 220–21, 228, 232, 239

Molina, Arturo Armando, 76–78, 80, 82–83
Mondale, Walter, 131, 158–60, 162
Moral Majority, 9, 104, 133, 147, 173–74
Morales Ehrlich, José Antonio, 78
Mother Columba, 16–17, 31
Mother Teresa, 119, 174
Mothers of Heroes and Martyrs, 138
el Mozote massacre, 126, 211
Mulry, Annette, 66, 109
Murphy, John M., 41, 51, 54–55, 60, 64–67

Narváez Murillo, Zoilamérica, 248
National Catholic Register, 9, 139, 146, 229, 241
National Catholic Reporter, 10, 22, 36, 63, 122, 245
National Guard (El Salvador), 2, 75–76, 81, 86, 96, 98, 100, 107, 126, 129, 159, 214, 218, 225–26, 237
National Literacy Crusade (Nicaragua), 132
National Review, 85, 104, 125, 151, 193, 223, 234
Navarro, Alfonso, 84
NETWORK, 59, 206, 231, 241
New Right, 104–5, 107, 147
New York Times, 23–24, 34, 64—65, 91, 96, 113, 126, 163, 190
NGIS (Nicaraguan Government Information Service), 51, 60, 64
Noriega, Manuel, 222, 243
North, Oliver, 12, 172, 189–92, 195–97, 199, 201, 204, 207–9, 226, 230, 236–37. *See also* Iran-Contra scandal
Novak, Michael, 9, 142, 154, 168–69, 173, 178, 199
Novedades, Las, 46, 49, 56, 57
nuclear weapons, 19, 114, 154, 156, 194, 196
nuns: as activists, 13, 18, 30, 85, 96–98, 110, 120; stereotypes about, 17, 118–19, 167–68, 174; Tip O'Neill's respect for, 165–66, 168, 174, 184, 186; and Vatican II, 4, 6

O'Connor, John, 158, 184
O'Hare, Joseph A., 222–23
O'Neill, Tip: conservative criticism of, 12, 161–62, 166–68, 173–76, 180–81, 184–86, 188, 199–200, 209, 232; and Maryknoll, 11, 152, 161, 163–67, 169, 173, 183–84, 186, 199–200, 205–6, 209, 226, 240; opposition to Central America policy, 163, 183, 250; retirement of, 187, 189, 231; support for Reagan's foreign policy, 128, 163
Oaker, Rosemary, 219–20

OAS (Organization of American States), 66, 67, 87, 93, 135, 141, 200
Obama, Barack, 241, 246
Obando y Bravo, Miguel, 150, 198, 229, 247–48; and U.S. government, 12, 9, 162, 179, 183–85, 192, 205, 207; and left-wing Catholics, 45, 136–37, 139, 177–80 and Somoza government, 47, 57; and Maryknoll, 61
Oberstar, James L., 169
Obey, David, 219–20
OPEN 3 (Operación Permanente de Emergencia Nacional camp), 48, 61
Operation Desert Storm, 234
Operation Just Cause, 222
Orbis Books, 38–39, 52–53, 55, 57, 67, 148, 172, 200
ORDEN, 89, 94, 96, 98
Orientación, 36, 91
Ortega, Daniel, 67, 105, 145, 173, 177–78, 181–82, 203, 205–6, 229, 247–49
OWG (Outreach Working Group on Central America), 134–36, 138, 151, 155–56
Owzarek, Rita, 230

Pahl, Marian, 22
Panama Canal, 61–62, 65, 93, 103, 133–34, 208, 242
PARA (Project for Awareness and Action), 33–34
Paraguay, 36, 93, 112
PDC (Christian Democratic Party / Partido Demócrata Cristiano) in El Salvador, 92–93, 215
PRTC (Revolutionary Party of Central American Workers / Partido Revolucionario de los Trabajadores Centroamericanos), 76
Pastora Gómez, Edén, 129
Pax Christi, 54
Peace Corps, 18
peasants. *See* campesinos
Pell, Claiborne, 118–20
Peña Arbaiza, Ricardo, 98, 106–7
Pentecostalism, 238–39
Percy, Charles H., 118, 120–21
Peru, 20, 37, 157
Petrik, Joan, 74, 89, 96, 98
Pezzullo, Lawrence, 66
Phares, Gail, 153
Philippines, 15, 32, 58, 184
Piette, Carla, 89, 97–98, 106

Pineda, Amada, 47
Pinochet, Augusto, 34
Pledge of Resistance, 145
Poindexter, John, 190–91, 195, 199, 207
Poland, 114, 120
Ponce, René Emilio, 234–35, 237
popular church, 8, 131, 136–42, 150, 152, 178, 206, 216, 231
Populorum Progressio, 22, 25
preferential option for the poor, 26, 97
Prensa, La, 46–47, 54–55, 133, 198, 229
Prensa Gráfica, La, 116, 125, 217
Price, Thomas F., 3, 15
Puebla meeting, 88, 92–93

Quest for Peace, 145, 201, 206
Quigley, Thomas, 20–21, 135, 149–50
Quixote Center, 144–45, 206

radio: CIA-funded, 32; church-operated, 48, 72, 83, 93, 178, 180; Contra-operated, 178, 198, 205; Reagan, 60, 179, 205; Salvadoran government and, 78, 94, 127, 217–18
Rambo, 175, 184
Ramírez, Sergio, 50, 67, 138
rape: of churchwomen, 2, 100–1, 107, 117–18, 127, 130, 146, 209, 219, 246; in El Salvador, 216; in Nicaragua, 47, 49–50, 201
Reagan administration, 12; 1980–81 transition team, 107–8, 151; Catholic opposition to Central America policy, 128–30, 146, 153–54, 163–64, 176–77, 202–3 226–27, 241–42; Central America policy of, 9, 11, 94, 102–3, 121, 123, 129–30, 132, 140, 144–45, 188, 205–7, 213–15; conservative Catholics and, 5, 7, 9, 11, 13, 102, 111–15, 117, 134, 141–42, 151, 157, 168, 171, 181–82, 207, 212, 224, 231, 239, 250; and El Salvador certification, 126–27, 228; gender and, 162, 167–68, 173–76, 184–85; and Maryknoll, 2–3, 7, 13, 61, 115–18, 120–21, 157–58, 164, 167, 170, 223–25, 231. *See also* Abrams, Elliott; Buchanan, Patrick; Casey, William; Haig, Alexander; Iran-Contra scandal; Kirkpatrick, Jeane; Kissinger, Henry; McFarlane, Robert C.; Meese, Edwin; North, Oliver; Regan, Donald T.; Shultz, George; Weinberger, Caspar; Whittlesey, Faith Ryan
Reagan-Wright Plan, 204
Reagan, Ronald, 221; and 1980 election, 62, 105–6, 110; and 1984 election, 131, 134, 143, 159–60, 162, 182, 224; assassination attempt against, 122; and Central America, 7, 60–61, 105–6, 111–15, 129, 132, 138, 140, 153, 179–80, 183, 205, 213, 236, 238; and conservative Catholics, 2, 5–6, 105, 131, 138–39, 162, 174; dislike of Maryknoll, 1–2, 13, 60–61, 156, 173; gender and, 162, 167–68, 173–76, 184; and Pope John Paul II, 7, 120, 131, 139–41, 151, 159, 162, 172, 185. *See also* Iran-Contra scandal
Refugee Act of 1980, 128
Regan, Donald T., 112, 182
Reilly, Robert, 151, 196
religious freedom, 19, 55, 138–40, 159, 176, 192
Religious Task Force on El Salvador/ Central America, 95reverse mission, 58, 80, 230
Rhodesia, 58
Richardson, Ronald J., 81–82, 85, 108
Ríos Montt, Efrain, 243
Rivera y Damas, Arturo, 76, 92, 97, 109, 125, 127, 214–16, 218, 231
RN (National Resistance/Resistencia Nacional), 75–76
Robelo, Alfonso, 67
Robertson, Pat, 141, 207
Rockefeller, Nelson, 30–31
Rodríguez, David, 75–76
Rogers, Mary Joseph, 4, 15
Romero, Carlos Humberto, 77–78, 81, 85–88
Romero, Óscar Arnulfo, 211, 216, 232; appeals to the U.S., 12, 70, 89, 91–92; as archbishop of San Salvador, 83–85, 87, 91–94, 99; canonization of, 245–46; conservative criticism of, 91, 116, 250; murder of, 94–98, 108, 114, 121, 127–28, 159, 193, 212, 219, 237, 243
Roper, Melinda, 109, 118–20, 150–51
Rueda, Enrique, 133, 148, 178–79, 182–83, 191, 197, 206, 231–32
Russia. *See* Soviet Union
Ryan, Paul, 240

Sagan, Catherine, 22
SALT II, 65
sanctuary movement, 128, 197, 225, 227
Sandinistas (Frente Sandinista de Liberación Nacional): and 1990 election, 214, 229–30, 236; Catholic criticism of, 137–39, 143–44, 154–55, 177–78, 181, 184–85, 198, 200, 202, 229–30, 244, 247; Catholic support for, 50, 63, 143, 149, 177, 185, 187; and the church, 105, 136–42, 191, 198; and

Contras, 129, 132–33, 138, 143–45, 153, 163, 166, 177–79, 206–7, 250; defectors, 149–50, 155, 157, 170, 248; and El Salvador, 88, 115, 143, 216; as government of Nicaragua, 66, 88, 132, 145, 149–50, 173, 177, 205–7, 214, 229; and Maryknoll, 66, 93, 116, 149–50, 169–71, 184–85, 230, 244; and Panama, 65, 222; revolutionary activity of, 47, 49–50, 56, 59–60, 63, 65, 67, 88, 165; and the Soviet Union, 173, 205; terceristas, 60; U.S. support for, 149, 164; U.S. opposition to, 66, 88–89, 105, 115–16, 129, 131–32, 136, 139–41, 147, 152, 159, 163, 170–73, 179–82, 200, 205, 229, 244. *See also* Bolanos Hunter, Miguel; d'Escoto, Miguel; Ortega, Daniel

Sandino, Augusto, 42–43, 47, 71

Santa Fe Report, 111–12, 116, 147

Sapoá accord, 206–7

Schall, James, 105, 151–52

Schlafly, Phyllis, 117–18, 133, 175, 183, 191, 194, 196, 199, 207

Scowcroft, Brent, 191, 222

Secord, Richard V., 192, 199

sexual abuse, 194, 248

Sheraton murders, 110, 126. *See also* certification

Shultz, George, 128–29, 157, 190, 196

sin, 8, 26, 69, 80, 84, 94

S/LPD (Office of Public Diplomacy for Latin America and the Caribbean), 134–36, 148–49, 155, 158

SOA (School of the Americas), 242–46

SOA Watch (School of the Americas Watch), 243–44

Sobrino, Jon, 239

Soccer War, 72

social justice. *See* justice

Somoza Debayle, Anastasio, 150; comparisons to other dictators, 88, 248–49; criticism of leftist Catholics, 49, 51–52, 57, 86; Managua earthquake, 47; opposed by Maryknollers, 2, 12, 41, 53–54, 60–61, 68, 165, 230, 250; opposition to, 45–46, 48–50, 90, 103; overthrow of, 59–68, 70, 129, 132, 136; US support for, 44, 54. *See also* Somoza Lobby

Somoza Debayle, Luis, 44

Somoza García, Anastasio, 42–44, 54

Somoza Lobby, 51, 56, 59, 62, 64–65, 70

Soviet Union: and Afghanistan, 90; and Catholicism, 104, 148; and human rights, 19, 113, 203; Iraq, 233–34; and Latin America, 62, 64, 111, 114–15, 148, 173, 205, 213–14, 221, 230; and U.S. politics, 168, 175. *See also* Communism

Spain, John, 78, 81, 125

Speaker's Special Task Force on El Salvador. *See* Moakley Commission

Specter, Arlen, 145–46, 219

Spellman, Francis, 17

Stedman, William P., Jr., 35–36

Stewart, Bill, 65–66

strikes: hunger, 45, 48, 66–67, 121; labor, 27, 56, 61, 63, 75, 86

Sullivan, John J., 110

Sumner, Gordon, 112, 116

Survil, Bernard, 69–70, 77–78, 80–82, 85

Teología de la liberación, 8, 38

TFP (Tradition, Family, and Property), 27

Theberge, James, 49–50, 123–24

Third World Priests, 36

Thomas, Cal, 174

Time, 17, 31, 104, 139, 208

Torres Restrepo, Camilo, 22, 30

Torrijos, Omar, 61–62, 65

torture: Chile, 34; El Salvador, 78–80, 83, 98, 108, 246; Guatemala, 29; Maryknoll, 3, 58, 90, 146, 181; Nicaragua, 47–50

Tower, John, 191

Trócaire, 114, 156–58

Tutela Legal, 216

UCA (University of Central America José Simeón Cañas/Universidad Centroamericana "José Simeón Cañas"), 76–77, 84, 127, 211, 216–17. *See also* Jesuit martyrs

UDHR (United Nations Declaration of Human Rights), 8, 79

UGB (White Warriors Union/Unión Guerrera Blanca), 84–86, 94, 215

U.S. aid: to Central America, 223; to Contras, 11, 129, 134, 143, 145, 171–73, 176, 180–85, 189–90, 192, 195, 199, 201, 204–8, 210, 213–14; to Costa Rica, 205; to El Salvador, 2, 71–72, 79, 82–83, 89, 92–96, 99–100, 107–11, 116, 121–22, 127–28, 146, 152–53, 159, 193, 212, 215–16, 218–20, 222, 224, 228, 231–32, 234, 236, 247; and human rights, 49, 51, 53, 59, 79, 99, 107, 110, 127–28, 134, 219–20, 222, 224, 228, 231; to Sandinistas, 88, 105, 115, 165; to Somozas, 49, 51–56, 60, 62–64. *See also* Alliance for Progress; certification; Iran-Contra; USAID

USCC (U.S. Catholic Conference of Catholic Bishops), 38, 85, 97, 103, 154, 208, 241–42
UN Commission on the Truth for El Salvador, 235, 237
United Nations, 67, 128, 140, 221, 230, 234–35, 237–38, 248
University of Notre Dame, 1, 158, 215
Ursulines, 2, 98, 101
Uruguay, 27
USAID (U.S. Agency for International Development), 35, 55, 134
USIA (United States Information Agency), 27–28, 152, 156–57

Vaky, Viron "Pete," 29
Vance, Cyrus, 62, 66, 85, 91, 93
Varelli, Frank, 225–26
Vatican II, 235; criticized by conservatives, 1, 25–27, 83, 133, 137, 141, 181, 241, 249; and divisions among Catholics, 5, 9–10, 70, 112; in Latin America, 25–27, 70, 72–73, 137; and Maryknoll, 14, 18–19, 22, 44, 70, 86; teachings of, 5, 14, 18–19, 137, 140
Vatican, the, 4, 51, 104, 177; and diplomatic relations with U.S., 1, 91, 154, 172–73; foreign policy of, 52, 81, 86; response to Communism and liberation theology of, 16–18, 36, 91–92, 120, 138, 168, 194, 245
Vega, Pablo Antonio, 46, 139–40, 198
Vekemans, Roger, 74
Via Crucis, 179–80
Vides Casanova, Eugenio, 225–26, 237–38, 246–47
Vietnam War, 75; and Catholics, 5; comparisons to Latin America, 75, 122, 170, 222–23; protests against, 24, 46, 121, 125; veterans, 147, 195, 243
Viguerie, Richard, 103, 105

Walker, William (1855), 42
Walker, William (ambassador), 215, 223, 230, 234–35
Wall Street Journal, 63, 115, 146, 153–54, 175, 185
Walsh, James A., 3–4, 15, 17, 181, 185
Walsh, Lawrence E., 191, 236
Walters, Vernon, 5, 112, 224
Wanderer, The, 9, 182, 198, 231; anticommunist views of, 39, 67, 103, 112, 115, 206; criticism of churchwomen, 117–18; criticism of liberal Catholics, 123–24, 155, 158. See also Matt, A. J.; Rueda, Enrique
Washington Post, The, 23–24, 34, 60, 108, 126, 133–35, 147, 168, 181, 185, 190, 193, 203, 241
Wattenberg, Ben, 183–84
Weinberger, Caspar, 113, 196, 204, 237
Welch, Richard, 37
Weyrich, Paul, 5, 9, 104–5, 133–35, 147–48, 154, 172, 175, 178, 183, 207
WHINSEC (Western Hemisphere Institute for Security Cooperation), 244. See also SOA
White, Robert E., 93, 106–8
Whittlesey, Faith Ryan, 112, 134–35, 142, 151
William J. Casey Fund for the Nicaraguan Freedom Fighters, 192, 195
Wilson, Charlie, 51, 55–56, 62, 64–65
Wilson, William A., 1
Wirthlin, Richard, 123
Witness for Peace, 153
WOLA (Washington Office on Latin America), 59, 164–65
women's ordination, 245–46
World Council of Churches, 59
Wright, James, 204–5, 213

Zagano, Phyllis, 194
Zamora, Rubén, 93, 217
Zepeda, Juan Orlando, 216